Women assemble

Women assemble

Women workers and the new industries in inter-war Britain

Miriam Glucksmann

ROUTLEDGE

London and New York

First published 1990
by Routledge
11 New Fetter Lane, London EC4P 4EE

Simultaneously published in the USA and Canada
by Routledge
a division of Routledge, Chapman and Hall, Inc.
29 West 35th Street, New York, NY 10001

Typeset by
NWL Editorial Services, Langport, Somerset TA10 9DG

Printed and bound in Great Britain by
Biddles Ltd, Guildford and King's Lynn

British Library Cataloguing in Publication Data
Glucksmann, Miriam
    Women assemble: women workers and the new industries in
    inter-war Britain
    1. Great Britain. Women. Employment. Historical sources
    I. Title
    331.4'0941

Library of Congress Cataloging in Publication Data
Glucksmann, Miriam.
    Women assemble: women workers and the new industries in
    inter-war Britain / Miriam Glucksmann.
        p.   cm.
    Includes bibliographical references.
    1. Women—Employment—Great Britain—History—20th
    century.   2. Assembly-line methods—History—20th
    century.   3. Great Britain—Economic conditions—
    1918–1945.   I. Title.
    HD6135.G58   1990   89–70180
    331.4'0941'09041—dc20   CIP

ISBN 0–415–03196–6
ISBN 0–415–03197–4 (pbk)

Contents

Contents

Tables

Figures

Acknowledgements

The research for this book was undertaken at the London School of Economics and Political Science over a two year period while I held the Ginsberg Fellowship in Sociology, and subsequently a Visiting Research Associateship in the Sociology Department which was funded by an award from the Leverhulme Trust. I am very grateful to the Leverhulme Trust for its financial assistance, and to the LSE for enabling me to do full-time research in this way, and in particular to Professor Percy Cohen for his support. I should also like to thank the Lipman Trust for a grant towards research expenses.

Finding women who had worked on assembly lines during the inter-war years turned out not to be as straightforward as originally anticipated, and I was helped by a number of people. Thanks are due especially to Steve Humphries and Bob Little of the Oral History Society, and to Hazel Ryder, then of Lewisham Age Concern, who set up an interviewing session for me with fourteen women. Several firms were also of great assistance: J.A. Hovell, Communications Manager at Hoover plc, supplied invaluable information and contacts, as well as his own reminiscences of the period; Mr Grahame Stephens and Mrs Connie Tull of the Nabisco Group Ltd, Production and Personnel Managers at the Peek Frean factory in Bermondsey, arranged interviews with retired employees and gave me access to internal archive material; T.P. Smith, retired Personnel Manager of Mullard Mitcham, ferreted out information on the early days of Mullard and Philips, and put me in touch with the Philips Pensioners' Club; Ruth Edge of the EMI Music Archive supplied photographs and information about the company dating from the period.

I should also like to thank those who allowed me to use their own unpublished data: Josey Castle for her transcripts of interviews with women workers in Coventry; Colleen Toomey of BBC Television for transcripts of the electronics industry programme in the series *All Our Working Lives*; Craig Littler for transcripts of Bedaux Archive microfilms on Lucas, and Tony Lawson for material on Pye. In this connection I am also endebted to Gabriele Mikoleit who worked with me on a linked project on the food processing industry, while she was employed as a researcher at South Bank Polytechnic.

Over the years I have discussed the project with many people, asked for advice about specific aspects, information about particular industries or work processes, and for comments on early drafts. Amongst others, Deidre Beddoe, Harold Benenson, Marion Kozak, Jane Lewis, the late Jill Norris, Joan Ryan, Steve Tolliday, and Stephen Wood all provided helpful information or comments. I cannot list everyone else here but should like to thank them all, especially those in the feminist history network, and trust that they will know who they are. Special thanks, for their continuing interest and constant encouragement, to Jenny Hurstfield and Liv Mjelde (who also read and commented on the draft) and to Kath and Jim Parish (for all their practical help and the many chats during breaks in the lengthy writing-up process).

My main debt however is to the retired workers whom I interviewed. They gave generously of their time and life histories, and supplied the information without which the book would have been impossible.

Abbreviations

AEU	Amalgamated Engineering Union
BSA	British Sociological Association
Cen. Pop.	Census of Population
Gen. Rep.	General Report
Ind. Tab.	Industry Tables
Gen. Tab.	General Tables
Occ. Tab.	Occupation Tables
Cen. Prod.	Census of Production
EEF	Engineering Employers' Federation
ILO	International Labour Organization
ILR	International Labour Review
Lab. Res.	Labour Research
MOLG	Ministry of Labour *Gazette*
NSOL	New Survey of London
PEP	Political and Economic Planning
TGWU	Transport and General Workers Union
TUC	Trades Union Congress

Chapter one

Introduction

My interest in women's work in the inter-war period arose not from a concern with women's history in itself but as an attempt to throw light on the origins of the present day sexual division of labour in manufacturing industry. Several years ago I had taken a job on the assembly line of a large motor components factory in London and was staggered at the rigid separation between men and women on the shopfloor (Cavendish 1982). No work on the actual assembly line was done by men and no women did any other kind of work. But men were employed in all the other jobs, from progress chasing and quality control to chargehand, supervisor, mechanical repairer and engineer. Women were narrowly restricted to work that was portrayed as less skilled than that of men, and their conditions of employment and pay rates were inferior. But from the position of the women who were tied to the line all day, men not only had the advantage of work that was physically less intense and more varied and mobile, but also they appeared to be rewarded more for doing less.

To the factory workers, both female and male, the gender segregation and subordination was a normal feature of work that they accepted almost as natural. Those who had worked there for decades said that 'it had always been like that' as long as they could remember: assembly-line work just was women's work. As it turned out, this factory was fairly typical of assembly plants not only in Britain but also throughout the western industrial world. The form of sexual division was similar in electronics factories, food processing plants and electrical components manufacture whether located in Europe, North America, or south-east Asia.

So I determined to investigate when and how that particular form of occupational segregation by gender was first established in British industry, and to explore the implications of women's place in that division of labour for their class relations and for their position in the working class in comparison with men. The search for origins soon

1

led me back to the emergence of mass production during the inter-war years as the era when assembly lines were first established on a wide scale and when large numbers of women were first drawn into such work.

In the new industries of inter-war Britain I found that women were both assemblers and assembled together. As the prime workforce in factories up and down the country women were employed for assembly-line work. There they assembled the components and final goods manufactured in radio, domestic appliance, motor components, canned food, biscuit and clothing firms. And at the same time women were themselves assembled together as a homogeneous group within such industries, occupying a position in the division of labour which was assigned to them alone. The work they were engaged on was done exclusively by women and they were subject to a common set of conditions of employment. In this way women workers were set apart from men as a distinctive section of the industrial workforce.

A major restructuring of industry was undertaken by British capital in the period between the two world wars in the attempt to recover from economic stagnation and crisis. Part of this involved the establishment of new industries using mass-production techniques, relying especially on assembly lines and conveyor belts. Such industries included electrical engineering, synthetic fibres, food processing and canning, clothing, motor vehicles, chemicals, rubber, glass and paper. They produced a new range of commodity goods, many of which were destined for household consumption – ready-made clothes, radios, irons and other domestic appliances, part-prepared food, and motor cars. All aimed for continuous flow and adopted mechanized and automated methods to achieve the high speed and volume of output required for mass production. The occupational structure and division of labour of these industries were also quite different from those of traditional heavy industry. Semi-skilled workers formed a very high proportion of the manual labour force in comparison with skilled craftworkers and labourers, and the direct work of manufacture and assembly was undertaken by semi-skilled assemblers and machine operators.

With the growth of the new industries, British capital turned to new areas of production and developed vastly enlarged new markets. Whereas it had previously concentrated on producing the means of production and heavy capital goods such as trains, ships and engineering machinery with export as their prime market, and which were often destined for further productive use, it now developed the production of domestic consumption goods for the home market, manufacturing as commodities for the first time goods which had not

previously been industrially produced. In comparison with the restricted market available for capital goods at that time, that for
consumer goods was wide open and they were produced on a mass
scale. Mass production of domestic consumer goods was predicated
on mass consumption at a national level: as the outlet for industrial
commodities switched from a limited export trade to encompass the
whole country, the market for capital's new goods extended to every
single household. To be successful this development relied on the
provision of a state-funded national infrastructure: electricity for
manufacture and domestic use, and a national road and rail network
for transporting goods to all corners of the country. All this represented a vast expansion of the field of operation of capitalist
commodity production and the extension of the wage and commodity
circuit of capital to whole new areas of life.

My contention is that with the advent of mass consumer production, women assumed a new and heightened significance within the
industrial workforce. Employers deliberately recruited them to operate the assembly lines and conveyor belts used for mass production.
Women represented the preferred source of semi-skilled labour and
were drawn into factory employment in very large numbers.[1] Consequently women became the central labour force engaged in direct
assembly work in the main wealth producing industries of the time.
Adoption of new production methods was accompanied by an alteration in the proportions of men and women employed in industrial
work. A rigid sexual division of labour was quickly established such
that women were assigned almost exclusively to assembly work and
men to everything else. In direct production, all women were engaged in assembly work, and, with the exception of car assembly,[2]
only women were assemblers. In one of the new factories making
light consumer goods, being an assembler meant being a woman and
being a woman meant being an assembler.

Thus the restructuring of industry also involved a restructuring of
the gender composition of the industrial workforce. I aim to demonstrate that women were brought to a new prominence on account of
the crucial place they occupied in the new industries. They occupied
a strategic position within the working class in relation to other
groups of wage workers, and also in relation to employers and the
process of capital accumulation.

Assembly lines epitomized the most modern and technologically
advanced production methods of the inter-war period. Automation,
mechanization, standardization, managerial control over production
and pre-planning of output reached their highest point in assembly-
line processes. Because of this women assemblers worked under
conditions that were specific to them: they were subjected to

3

machine pacing, imposed automatically by a moving conveyor belt, and had virtually no control over the work that they did. They were compelled by the automatic operation of a moving line to work at the speed laid down by management and in the manner laid down by management. Each assembler represented only one small part of a much larger collective worker, the line. She was not allowed to leave her place without permission and spent ten hours a day virtually tied to the line. Her pay was calculated not on an individual basis but on the output of the group as a whole. Men were engaged in arranging and servicing the equipment, overseeing it and ensuring smooth running of the line. But in these industries no men were subject to the same conditions of work as women assemblers. So women's position in the division of labour placed them in a distinctive relation to the process of production, to employers and to other workers. The organization of production enabled employers to exploit assemblers in a new way and to an unprecedented extent. Since the labour power of assemblers was used by capital in a specific way assembly-line work was characterized by specific relations of production.[3] Assemblers' class relations – their relation as wage labourers to capital – were distinctive to them.

The first concern of this book then is to explore how and why assembly-line work became women's work and to analyse the implications of their position as assemblers for women's class relations. My argument is that women were the pilots and pioneers of the new relation between capital and labour which was integral to mass production. They assumed a centre stage significance as workers at the very heart of the production process on which the continued survival and expansion of capital depended. The new class relations were experienced in their most acute and pure form by women. This placed women assemblers squarely in the forefront of the working class as a key section of industrial workers. They were not marginal, peripheral or secondary but central.

In what follows I use 'new industries' as a shorthand to denote those mass-production industries, conventionally termed 'light', which produced goods sold for use within the home. It is a convenient but not very precise term since not all the industries which adopted mass-production techniques were new and nor were all of the products. Similarly women were not employed in all mass-production industries, and notably not in the final assembly of motor cars. But the basic point remains that in those mass-production industries and factories where women were engaged as assemblers, they were confined to this type of work alone and excluded from all others. And, once established, the pattern of occupational segregation by gender became fixed. Jobs were constructed either as

4

masculine or as feminine in a manner which came to be accepted as normal by both men and women. As in other industries, work sex-typed as feminine was routine and repetitive. It was portrayed as clean and light, requiring no training or formal skill, but rather as depending on dexterity, concentration and the ability to tolerate monotony. All jobs that were presented as heavy and dirty or as necessitating a formal training, manual skills or technical knowledge were ipso facto 'men's work'. Since people were allocated to jobs on the basis of gender, the workforce was inevitably divided on the basis of gender.

To concentrate on restructuring in the inter-war period, as I shall, and on the new developments that were to be consolidated only many years later necessitates abstracting one aspect out of a total picture. Although the structural developments for life as we now know it originated then, at the time they coexisted with other and opposing tendencies. The late 1920s and 1930s are remembered primarily as years of economic decline and industrial decay, and for the mass unemployment which plunged millions of working people into extreme poverty and despair.[4] George Orwell, Fenner Brockway, Walter Greenwood, Allen Hutt and many other social commentators wrote about the appalling living conditions endured by masses of people that they witnessed everywhere in the older industrial areas.

Yet even at the height of the recession, there was a marked contrast between those areas where the old staple industries had been located, in the North of England, Scotland and Wales, and the much more prosperous regions of the South and the Midlands where new development and industrial reconstruction was concentrated. Inter-war Britain has sometimes been described as a country divided into 'two nations', an image forcefully put over by J.B. Priestley's *English Journey* (1934), and statistically confirmed by many industrial and social surveys undertaken at the time.[5] All attested to the very wide divergence in basic social conditions in different parts of the country as indicated by levels of unemployment, poverty, housing, life expectancy, health, nutrition and all the other criteria of living standards. So while much of the country was economically devastated and reeling under the impact of mass unemployment, new methods of production and new industries were at the same time being developed in the regions centring around London. These were to pave the way for a thoroughgoing industrial, economic and social reconstruction: the Britain of 1939 was to be very different from that of 1919. But examining the effects of new developments and of industrial restructuring undertaken by capital, in order to overcome the economic crisis, is by no means intended to negate or belittle the enormous human effects of the crisis itself.

Although my primary focus is on women employed as assemblers, paid work does not account for all work; nor does commodity production in the public formal wage economy account for all production. Unpaid domestic labour undertaken in the household also constitutes work, and the production of goods and services for direct consumption within the domestic economy also constitutes production. The reproduction of social life depends on the labour performed in both of these spheres. Historically in industrial capitalist society, responsibility for domestic production has rested on women and women have done the work necessary to reproduce labour power – to keep people up and running – both generationally and daily, mostly on the basis of unpaid domestic labour. During the inter-war years women's place was still, in terms of the dominant ideology at least, firmly in the home. Indeed this was the period when the 'ideal home' made its first appearance, run efficiently and lovingly by the 'ideal housewife' aided by domestic appliances and ready-made goods to lighten her load. Thus those very same commodities that women assembled in the electrical and food factories were bought and used by women for household consumption. Since women held responsibility for the household they were of particular significance in this development as the main purchasers of the new goods. A new circuit of production and consumption developed therefore involving women at both ends, and women acquired a centrality to capital as consumers as well as producers.

So my second concern is with the changes that began to occur within the domestic economy and the transformation of its relationship with the sphere of commodity production. These changes were to have far-reaching consequences for women and a long term impact on their work, both on unpaid domestic labour within the household and on paid employment in the wage economy. The decline in the birth rate and decreasing family size, together with a state provided infrastructure of gas, electricity and running water, reduced the proportion of their lives that women spent fully occupied in domestic labour and child rearing, and had a dramatic effect on work in the home. Gradually the reproduction of labour power came to be effected much more on the basis of factory produced goods than on domestic labour. The availability of commodities such as off-the-peg clothing, mass produced bread, canned food and electric irons which could be bought to aid or replace domestic labour, released time for alternative uses, including paid employment. Women did not work any less as a result, but they worked differently, under different conditions and for different masters.

However, the ability to buy such goods depended on having sufficient disposable cash. During the inter-war years there were large class differences in consumption and most working-class women were not able to purchase domestic commodities on a grand scale. 'Ideal' housewives were predominantly middle class and they were the main consumers of the new goods, often used to replace the work of domestic servants. On the one hand, factory work was a much more attractive form of employment to young working-class women than domestic service, and on the other, middle-class households, unable to find domestic servants, bought commodity inputs as an alternative. So the very commodities that middle-class women were buying were made by women assemblers who in previous generations could well have been employed as their domestic servants.

I shall explore the complex series of links which connected these changes occurring in and between production and consumption, domestic and commodity production, and women's domestic labour and paid employment. My aim is to show that women became incorporated into the central circuit of capital on a much larger scale than ever before and along two separate dimensions. As workers in the new industries they constituted the main source of new wage labour on which capital drew, and as the main purchasers and consumers in the domestic economy they constituted the basic market for the new manufactured commodities. A qualitatively different social relation was created between production and consumption with this link between women and capital as producers and consumers of mass consumer commodities.

Hidden from history

Yet this most significant change both at work and at home has gone unheralded and unrecognized. First, work has been generally considered worthy of the name only if carried out in the public sphere. So the massive and systematic alterations in the conditions of work and social relations of the domestic economy have occurred as if on the underside of history. Second, because labour history has focused so much on men, and especially men in trade unions, women workers have been considered for the most part only in general terms. Most studies of developments in the labour process, under the influence of Braverman (1974), have been so fixated on the fate of the skilled craftsman under the impact of mass production that his demise has been treated as the only significant result of industrial change. With so much attention being given to what was destroyed rather than what was put in its place, such studies have almost failed to recognize that direct production still carried on, let alone that women were now doing it. The overwhelming interest and importance accorded to the craft production worker has not been accorded

7

to his female successor. This basic omission of women from interpretations of twentieth-century industrial history leads inevitably to conclusions that are, at best, narrowly one-sided and, at worst, totally misleading.

Indeed, even during the inter-war years themselves little attention was devoted to the condition of women's industrial employment. At the end of the First World War women trade unionists voiced considerable anxiety about female unemployment as women were ejected from their wartime jobs. In the early 1920s government inquiries and discussions in trade union and feminist circles centred around the questions of equal pay that had surfaced in the context of women's wartime employment. The issue aroused fierce controversy and several of the official reports included minority conclusions detracting from the main recommendations.[6] Concern was also voiced about domestic service, and in particular about the large shortage of domestic servants, which was presented as an extremely serious problem.[7] So many writers suggested that improving and standardizing the conditions of domestic service work would raise its status and make it more attractive. The labour movement was aware of the increased industrial employment of women, but the main reaction of the trade unions was to object to women taking their members', that is, men's jobs, undercutting pay rates and thereby reducing men's wages. The traditional craft unions appeared not to realize that the jobs to which women were recruited were newly created ones nor that the declining numbers of skilled craftsmen required in manufacturing industry resulted directly from the development of mass-production techniques which rendered their skills obsolete, rather than because women were being taken on instead of men. In any event, the trade unions were passive, if not openly hostile, in relation to employees in the new industries. Like most other contemporary commentators, they too failed to appreciate the significance of the changes in industrial organization for women industrial workers.[8]

By the 1930s the independent women's trade unions had been incorporated into the male unions, and few demands were heard for equal pay. It was a period of high unemployment and quiescent trade unionism, and the earlier interest in promoting women's employment gave way to defensiveness about women's right to paid work in itself. Feminist discussions on the subject concerned themselves more with career opportunities for middle-class women than with factory work.[9] The university sponsored industrial and social surveys did highlight the large increase in women's factory employment in the new industries but their main concern was with poverty and living conditions. It was left to supporters of the Communist Party to document the appalling conditions of work in some of the newer areas of employment. But although Gollan (1937), Hutt (1933) and Beauchamp (1937) recognized employers' preferences for 'girl labour', they were not in a position to comprehend that young women factory workers were there to stay. Their predominant preoccupation was with the effects on workers of the very harsh conditions and unscrupulous practices that employers were able to impose in an era of staggeringly high unemployment. They interpreted employers' widespread preference for juvenile and female labour as a direct response to immediate economic circumstances. Thus no one at the time appeared to recognize the new centrality of women within the industrial workforce.

The resurgence of feminism in the late 1960s brought a renewed interest in the history of women's employment, but the attention of feminist historians has focused much more on the two world wars than on the period in between. Similar developments occurred during both wars, with women being taken on as a replacement labour force instead of men. If women had been employed on work normally done by men, then the sexual division of labour might not be quite so intransigent as it appeared. Women's employment could then be accounted for in terms of Marx's thesis of the reserve army of labour, according to which labour which is normally not engaged in waged work may be called up on to the labour market in times of labour shortage and then pushed back again into reserve to suit the economic circumstances.[10] But early enthusiasm for the applicability of this concept, based on the evidence of women's wartime employment, was short lived. The main conclusion to be drawn from the research on women's war work[11] is that jobs were usually altered or subdivided before women were allocated to them.

Despite all the talk of substitution and dilution during the war, and of men being displaced by women, very few women in fact performed exactly the same work that men had done. Definitions of which were men's and which were women's jobs changed, and the boundaries and contours of the sexual division of labour shifted, but, even during these exceptional circumstances women continued to be engaged in work which was constructed, even if only temporarily, as women's work. The clear conclusion to be drawn is that the conditions of wartime employment were exceptional, the removal of men from production in large numbers necessitating a special sexual division of labour which relied much more heavily on women, and whose implementation was facilitated partly by men not being at home and by children not being born quite so often.[12]

By contrast, the changes that I am dealing with can be fully understood only in the context of industrial restructuring during the

Introduction

inter-war years and as an effect of the fundamental changes in the organization of production that accompanied the development of mass production in 'normal' peace time conditions. The large increase in women's industrial employment between the wars can be explained neither as an extension of trends already apparent before 1914 nor as an effect of the First World War.

Moreover I shall be arguing that what happened during the inter-war years is also crucial to an understanding of developments after the Second World War. According to popular opinion, post-war changes in women's employment are to be explained as a consequence of developments that occurred during or immediately following the war itself. The present day features of women's employment tend to be traced back only as far as the war and a sharp distinction is drawn between the pre-war and post-war periods. Yet it can be clearly demonstrated that changes in women's role in the labour force during the inter-war period laid the foundation for their employment after 1945. Since many of the later developments stemmed from the industrial restructuring that had taken place before the war, the post-war situation should be viewed to a large extent as a continuation and culmination of trends already in existence before 1939. Many aspects of women's post-war pattern of employment were already apparent before the war. For example, a large shift had already occurred in the distribution and concentration of women workers between different industries and occupations; the occupational segregation by gender characteristic of post-war manufacturing industry also had originated in the inter-war period when assembly-line work was first constructed as women's work; similarly, although the pre-war norm was for women to leave work on marriage, it was quite common in the new industries for married women to stay on at work, as they were to much more widely after 1945. In other ways too the pre-war pattern prefigured many trends commonly thought to have originated only in the post-war years.

Theoretical perspectives

The large scale material changes in women's lives that began during the inter-war years inaugurated a gradual transformation which eventually affected their entire economic and social position within both household and wage economies. Precisely because they were so momentous, these developments raise many theoretical questions concerning the subordination of women at work, and the relationships between gender and class, and gender and the labour process. So they provide a good opportunity for reopening and reappraising some of the arguments and frameworks of analysis elaborated within

10

the feminist movement over recent years in relation to such questions. For example, the issue of women's class position has occasioned much debate. Feminists have been united in their criticism of the traditional and still fairly standard academic approach to class analysis that denies women a class position in their own right. Academic sociologists have conventionally taken the family as the unit for analysis, and ascribe the class of the (male) head of household to all other members of the family, regardless of whether or not they also engage in waged employment. Thus women are assigned a class position only indirectly, on the basis of their father or husband, and of his place in the occupational hierarchy. Alternatively, where women are allocated a class position on the basis of their own employment, seemingly intractable problems arise in interpreting the position of women who are temporarily or permanently out of paid employment. Empirical analysis of women's class position on the basis of their own work is also made very problematic because the standard job classifications and occupational categories used in official surveys and statistics were designed with men's work in mind and do not discriminate in any detail between the different occupations that women are engaged in. Insufficiently detailed information thus makes it extremely difficult to draw any meaningful conclusions. Damning critiques of the conventional approach made along these lines[13] go a long way towards undermining its logic, legitimacy and usefulness: if the framework can account for over half of the population only as a residual category, if at all, then its claims to general applicability must be seriously undermined.

During the 1970s, some radical feminists (for example Millett 1971; Firestone 1974; Delphy 1977) proposed an alternative feminist 'materialist' theory of class, arguing that all women as a gender constitute a class, in opposition to all men as a gender. In this conception, the genders form distinct but internally united social groupings that stand in an unequal power relationship to each other and have conflicting interests. Socialist feminists, on the other hand, devoted more attention to analysing the position of women engaged in unpaid work within the home in terms of class. A number of different theories were elaborated to explain the class relations of women's domestic labour,[14] a subject which had been completely ignored by Marxist and academic theories of class alike. But despite the fact that most women spend part of their lives in paid employment and part out of it, feminist approaches to the question of women and class have tended to focus either on women's position in paid work or in domestic labour. Consequently, no comprehensive analytical framework has been developed from a feminist perspective which could encompass both sites of women's work. Yet because the changes in women's work in the home during the inter-war years were so closely connected with changes in the conditions of their paid employment, the task of elaborating a comprehensive theory has become much more urgent. To be in any way adequate, analysis of women's class position during that historical period and of the changes that it was undergoing at that time, will be possible only on the basis of a theory capable of incorporating both spheres of women's work.

The theory of dual and segmented labour markets, originally developed in the United States to analyse the position of black workers, has been widely adopted by researchers into women's employment to account for the glaring differences between men's and women's conditions of employment.[15] The labour market, it is argued, is divided into primary and secondary sectors and 'the secondary labour market is pre-eminently female' (Barron and Norris 1976: 48). Whereas workers (primarily white men) in the more profitable and innovative primary product sector are privileged by high pay, training and promotion within the firm, secondary sector workers (primarily women or black workers) are characterized by a low level of training, low pay, absence of career opportunties, job insecurity and high turnover. The implicit assumption is that women are restricted to the more backward and labour intensive industries while the modern and growth sectors of the economy are staffed by men.

But in the case of women assemblers in the new mass-production industries of the 1930s this characterization does not really fit. It was certainly true that the market for the different types of labour required by employers was rigidly segmented on the basis of gender, and that women assemblers received lower pay and less training than men and had no career opportunties. But because the new industries were the most technologically advanced and fastest expanding of their time, they could not be classed as any other than 'primary' industries par excellence. Similarly, since women represented a central labour force in these primary industries, the association here was between women workers and the primary product sector. Would it then make sense to describe women as forming the 'secondary' labour market for the 'primary' product sector? Other problems would also arise from the attribution of secondary status to women assemblers. Not only did working-class women consider assembly-line jobs as 'plum' jobs, but the pay rates and conditions of employment of assembly work were higher than those for alternative women's work. Thus the blanket attribution of secondary status to women workers would in this case obscure important differences in the labour market situation between different groups of women workers. In the case of assemblers it is more misleading than illuminating.

The relationship between gender and class has received much attention in recent years from socialist feminists concerned to understand the origins and dynamics of gender inequality at work. Discussion of the sexual division of labour and of the antagonism between men and women at work has taken its theoretical point of departure from more general theories of women's oppression developed within the socialist feminist movement. Such theories are united in their rejection of the two opposite extreme formulations, expounded by pure radical feminism on the one hand and by an unreconstructed Marxism on the other, that would explain women's subordination as deriving either from patriarchy per se or from capitalism per se.

In place of these mutually exclusive explanations, socialist feminists have opted in favour of a framework that incorporates a system of gender domination and a system of class domination. But there is also considerable internal differentiation within this broad camp as to how the relationship between the two systems is to be conceptualized. At one end there is the position, elaborated in the work of Juliet Mitchell (1971; 1974) and Heidi Hartmann (1979b), maintaining that there are two analytically separate systems, capitalism and patriarchy, each of which has an independent effect. At the other end, the two systems are viewed, as for example by Zillah Eisenstein (1979), as being so completely fused and intertwined with each other that they form a single system of 'capitalist patriarchy' in which the two principles operate in combination and are mutually interdependent.[16] There are also a number of variations on each theme and a whole series of gradations in between them which view class and gender domination as more or less connected, and as rooted and operative variously in different institutions.

The question of the relative primacy of and form of articulation between the two principles are frequently presented as if they were purely theoretical, but in fact the problems that they address also represent basic political questions whose answers have far-reaching political implications. Conceptualization of the relationship between capitalist and patriarchal principles is necessarily linked with a particular view of the relationship between feminism and socialism. In terms of political practice, this determines the connection between feminist action and class struggle, whether one should take primacy over the other, and whether the attempt to overthrow domination based on class and gender can be undertaken jointly or autonomously. The heated controversies that have taken place over single versus dual systems theory should be interpreted in this light: whether people describe themselves as socialist feminists or feminist socialists, and where exactly they place themselves in the range of possible connections between the single and dual approaches, is an issue of fundamental political importance within the feminist and socialist movements.

These very basic questions and arguments surface again, though in a less transparent and explicit manner, in studies of gender inequality at work. For example the sexual division of labour poses the question in a particularly stark form. In industrial capitalism a sexual division of labour has systematically excluded women from certain types of work and restricted them to a limited number of low paid and low level occupations. But was women's subordinate place at work established by employers through strategies undertaken in order to reduce labour costs and divide the workforce, or should it be explained as resulting from male workers acting to secure their own privileged position? Can the prevailing pattern of occupational segregation at work be interpreted as being in the interests of capital, of men, or both?

In her study of the American automobile and electrical industries, Ruth Milkman (1987) argues that different modes of managerial control, rather than organized male workers, were fundamental in shaping the pattern of occupational segregation by gender in each industry, but that once established ideological factors played a basic role in maintaining and reproducing the pattern. Such an explanation contrasts sharply with that of Sylvia Walby (1986a), who points to the strength of patriarchal forces in determining the pattern of women's employment in Britain between 1800 and 1945. The organizations representing male workers, notably the trade unions, are singled out as playing a causal part in establishing women's subordinate position, but in addition employers and the state, through its protective legislation and unemployment policies, are also viewed as pursuing patriarchal practices.

Other writers, whilst also recognizing that the sexual division of labour cannot be derived directly from capitalism (which as a system is more concerned with lowering the costs of production and of labour, than with the gender of its workforce), view both patriarchal and capitalist principles as causal factors and so attribute the pattern of gender division to various combinations of these principles. For instance when Anne Philips and Barbara Taylor (1980) questioned the accepted definitions of skill and the traditional exclusion of women from work officially considered as 'skilled', they referred to the interests of skilled male workers as well as to employers' practices. Similarly Cynthia Cockburn's detailed history (1983) of the printing industry in Britain – a traditional male preserve from which women were virtually excluded – and her more recent study (1985) of industries adopting new technology in the 1980s both demonstrate the subtle interplay between the two factors.

Looking at gender subordination at work raises in a particularly direct way another question lying right at the very heart of the dual systems approach – whether there is a single or a primary site of women's oppression. Many of the theorists who argue for a combination of patriarchal and capitalist principles theorize each as having a different institutional base and as being located in different parts of the social structure. Thus some argue that while capitalist principles operate in the economy, patriarchal principles are operative in the sphere of reproduction and the family.[17] In this conceptualization, the family becomes the prime site not only for the construction of masculinity and femininity ('gendered subjectivity') but also for women's oppression. Gender inequality is thus theorized as originating in the sphere of reproduction. How it is then carried over from the family into other social institutions becomes a problematic question. For example how is the sexual division of labour at work to be explained, if patriarchal relations arise in the family? Either it would have to be seen as reflecting sexual divisions already created in the family, which are then 'carried over' so to speak from one sphere to the other, or it must be explained in terms of the capitalist principles operating in the sphere under consideration. But this would be no solution since we know that capitalist principles cannot in themselves account for the sexual division of labour, and that sexual division at work in any case historically predated the development of capitalism. In *Women's Oppression Today* (1980) Michèle Barrett argued that the division between men and women at work cannot provide the explanation of women's oppression at work because the logic of the capitalist division of labour does not determine the sexual division of labour. She maintains on the contrary that the gender divisions of social production in capitalism cannot be understood without reference to the organization of the household and to the ideology of familialism (1980: 181–6). On the other hand, Veronica Beechey emphasizes that the sexual division of labour at work cannot be simply 'read off' (1987: 146) from sexual division in the family. So it appears that unless some autonomy is accorded to the dynamics of the work process as a site where sexual division may also be constructed (in addition to the family), we are bound to be reduced to a functionalist account of gender inequality at work which can view relations there only as derivative of the dynamics of the family.[18]

These questions take on a rarefied air when posed in an ahistorical manner or purely in the abstract. But the static oppositions and false dichotomies can be largely avoided when the same basic questions are approached substantively and in terms of real historical circumstances. The fact that gender inequality does not derive from capitalism need not be taken to imply that there are no forms of gender inequality specific to the world of work. Nor does the evidence that gender division predated capitalism mean that at every restructuring of capital over the subsequent three hundred years, the economy was able to import forms of gender division that were already fully formed in the family or elsewhere. The bare arguments suffer badly from the absence of fleshing out with historical material which would be a necessary precondition for their explanatory validity.

When formulated in the abstract the various positions are much less convincing and have much less force than those studies that have dealt with much the same issues but in a substantive way. In *Family Fortunes* for example, Leonore Davidoff and Catherine Hall (1987) analyse in rich historical detail how gender relations were in practice built into the developing class relations of industrial capitalism. Similarly Cynthia Cockburn's work on gender relations in technological work demonstrates very clearly how certain aspects of masculinity and femininity are constructed and reproduced at work through the labour process as a consequence of the ideological sex-typing of jobs.[19] So even though the sexual division of labour at work may not be explicable in terms of the dynamics of capitalism, it occurs and is recreated in and through the labour market, the work process and workplace relations. Accordingly these merit attention in their own right: it becomes imperative to determine whether and to what extent the workplace can also be considered as a relatively autonomous site of women's oppression. In exploring the connection between gender relations and the labour process in the inter-war mass-production industries I shall therefore be asking not only whether forms of gender division and subordination existed that were specific to that labour process alone, but also how far assembly-line work could be viewed as a site for the formation of gender relations and gender inequality for a particular group of women workers.

In coming to terms with the historical transformation of women's position in inter-war Britain, it now seems to me that the problems inherent in most of these theories arise directly from the attempt to utilize two separate and heterogenous principles of explanation. However the relationship between the two principles of capitalism and patriarchy is conceived, there are bound to be problems that cannot be resolved within the analytical framework. First, what is the sphere of applicability of each principle? When is one to be called upon rather than the other and under what circumstances does it provide the explanation? Second, how are the two principles articulated with each other? Does one take priority over the other? These dilemmas are inevitable consequences of a two-headed problematic and they remain present whether or not the two principles are conceptualized as fused into one or as operating independently of each other.

A feminist and historical materialist framework

In order to explain the massive historical changes in women's lives that began during the inter-war period, any theory would have to be capable of handling developments that occurred in the public wage economy as well as in the domestic economy of the household. The changes that took place within each sphere were structurally interconnected with each other and were both implicated in the material transformation of women's lives. Because of this it would be neither legitimate nor appropriate to appeal solely to capitalism (and class) in order to explain developments in women's position in paid employment, and then to appeal to patriarchy (or male domination) to explain developments in the domestic economy. An eclectic theory which refers to one principle to explain some things, and to another to explain others would not be able to do justice to the real historical processes involved in the total reconstruction of women's labour. Rather what is required is a unified and internally coherent analytical framework capable of examining women's position both in social production and in private reproduction, in paid employment and in the household. It must be able to address the link between these two without having either to reduce one to the other or to adopt different explanatory principles for each. Just to take one example, domestic servants were subject to a particular form of patriarchal domination in the domestic economy; but during the inter-war period many were to transfer to factory work, continuing then to service only their own husbands and children in the domestic economy.

A feminist and historical materialist framework is necessary in order to understand the dynamic of changes in women's work during the inter-war period. So instead of adopting a series of explanatory principles which would each relate to one sphere alone, I intend to develop a unified theory based on analysis of relations of production. If the framework of analysis for the sexual division of labour at work is broadened out so as to encompass the much wider sexual division between the spheres of production and reproduction themselves, rather than being restricted to a consideration of sexual division within the confines of the public wage economy, then the particular conflicts between gender and class that were outlined above can be seen as effects of the articulation of that overall total sexual division.

And, as a consequence, primacy is not accorded to paid employment in the public economy as alone constitutive of class relations as such.

Since the central focus of the study is the historical transformation of the material basis of women's position, my framework is a materialist one which concentrates on the material sources of social and economic change. I shall also look at ideology and consciousness, but less discussion will be devoted to these issues. Of course ideological factors played a fundamental part in reinforcing and reproducing sexual division and subordination in the new industries, particularly through the sex-typing of work and the constructions of femininity and of women as wives, mothers and workers. Similarly, women's (and men's) understanding of their own lived experience itself constituted an important element of that experience. Their response to the situation that they found themselves in at work was deeply affected by the consciousness that they had of their place as women both in the home and at work, and this consciousness was largely responsible for determining how fully they accepted their subordinate position and the extent to which they believed it either should or could be transformed. Moreover, significant developments and alterations in the ideological representations of women, and in women's consciousness, did accompany the material changes of the inter-war period. So I shall be looking at questions of ideology and consciousness, but from this perspective. Indeed the account of women's assembly-line work that I shall present relies very heavily on such women's memory of their working lives, and therefore on *their* understanding of their position at work, and *their* consciousness of sexual division. However, from a more general theoretical viewpoint it is obvious that the changes in the material basis of women's position with which I am primarily concerned were not caused by ideology or by consciousness and that they could in no way be explained as effects of ideological change.[20]

Class 'relations'

I have said that in this feminist and historical materialist framework I shall be analysing women's class relations and their relations of production in both spheres of work. I use the term class 'relations' advisedly, in preference to class 'position', since my analysis will depart from the traditional framework which starts by defining a number of class positions and then proceeds to slot workers into these positions. The end result is a classification of class positions which can account for all kinds of wage labour. This approach is not centrally concerned with exploring the dynamics of the relation between labour and capital, or with the different dynamics which distinguish the relation between capital and different groups of wage labour. Rather it is more concerned with assigning people to pre-established categories so as to label them as occupants of a particular class position or 'location'. Poulantzas (1978), Carchedi (1977) and Wright (1978) have each formulated a classificatory approach, defining a finite number of classes on the basis of criteria such as whether workers are engaged in various forms of productive or unproductive labour, whether they work in positions of power or authority, and whether or not they have control over their work. Concrete analyses of class then consist in allocating groups of workers into classes, subclasses or class 'fractions' already predefined on the basis of such criteria, and attributing them with a class 'position' accordingly.

Such an approach suffers from the inherent problem that it provides no means of integrating sexual division into class analysis and hence of distinguishing between men and women in terms of class. Because the central interest of recent Marxist theorists of class has been with the 'middle' strata of post-war capitalist economies, the general theories that have been developed focus mainly on non manual workers and on what has been called the 'new' petty bourgeoisie. But despite the fact that women form a very large proportion of this sector as white collar and state employees, little specific attention has been devoted to dealing with the relation between gender and class.

Rather than adopting a classificatory framework, I shall focus instead on class relations and on relations of production as constitutive of class relations. The term 'relations of production' will be used to denote all the different dimensions of the conditions under which labour power is sold and the ways in which it is used once it has been exchanged for a wage. In the case of women assemblers this will involve detailed examination of the dynamics of the relation between women and capital, women and the productive process, and women and the various groups of male workers as these developed in a particular industry at a particular historical time. A similar framework could also be applied to other groups of workers and to the domestic economy where women also worked under determinate relations of production, either as paid domestic servants or on an unpaid basis in their own homes. Such a method, which explores the concrete relations of production of particular groups of workers, permits identification of differences in the class relations of different groups within the working class.

Class, in the original Marxist definition, was conceived not as a position but rather as the *relation* existing between wage labour and capital.[21] If class has to do with the relation between wage labour and capital, it follows that differences in the relation of different groups of wage labour to capital represent class differences. The premiss of

19

my analysis is that differences in relations of production constitute differences of a class nature. Thus people working under different relations of production have different class 'relations' from each other since they have a specific relation, as a particular group of labour, to capital. If the relations of production under which women work give rise to particular class relations then this means that women should be accorded those class relations in their own right.

The objective existence of class relations does not depend on the people who share those relations being fully conscious of them or organizing on their basis in order to transform them. The relations exist independently of people's consciousness or lack of consciousness about them. So although women assemblers, to take the case in point, did not actively constitute themselves into a class in E.P. Thompson's (1968) sense of 'making themselves into a class', this would by no means detract from the suggestion that they shared a set of class relations which distinguished them from other groups of workers. Indeed it is often the case that those who work under the worst conditions, and are the weakest or most exploited, are not in a position to organize around their own interests.

My hope is that analysis in terms of relations of production will elucidate the conditions underlying the consolidation of particular groups of women workers who share a common work situation and common interests. In so far as the relations of production develop into important historical contradictions they can be understood also as forming the material basis for autonomous women's struggles.

Problems with Marx

Although my analysis uses a concept originally developed by Marx, it attempts to integrate gender centrally into class analysis and feminism with historical materialism in a way which Marx did not. It departs from the traditional Marxist theory of class in other basic ways too.

To begin with, Marxist analyses of class conventionally pose a simple dichotomy between the sellers and buyers of labour power, and view the sellers as a homogeneous and undifferentiated group of wage workers, regardless of differences in gender, age, race or training. The consequent exchange between labour and capital is seen as relatively unproblematic from an analytical point of view: workers sell their labour power and capitalists pay them a wage in exchange for it. But this is far too simplistic. For one thing, history has not stood still. A number of historical developments had to occur in the first place before labour could be treated as a commodity and be bought and sold like any other commodity. And capitalism did not then stop developing over the next three centuries: new forms of production emerged, new technologies successively replaced each other and the economy was continually restructured. As an integral part of this process, the internal structure of wage labour has also been transformed as some groups of workers have disappeared and others have been formed, each with their own place in the division of labour and relations of production. Thus historical reconstruction has necessarily been accompanied by a continual transformation and restructuring of wage labour and of the class structure. Yet, despite these changes, much Marxist writing on class characterizes the exchange between wage labour and capital in the late twentieth century as identical to that in the mid-nineteenth century, so implying that the situation has remained static since the time of Marx.

Marx had argued that as a mode of production, capitalism stripped people of their own means of production so that they were unable to produce their own means of subsistence and were forced to sell their labour power for a wage. In his formulation they had 'only' their labour power to sell, and labour power was conceived as a given: the capacity to labour in itself. It was therefore seen as something which was common to all people and held in the same form by all. At a time when a wide variety of different kinds of worker was becoming subject to the same regime of wage labour in industrial capitalism, Marx was more concerned to account for the commonality of their condition and less with differences in the labour capacity they had to sell. But even during the period of which he was writing there were differences between labour power: some was more trained, more skilled or more formally educated, and thus more 'formed' than others. Marx dealt with such differences in terms of the higher or lower exchange value of skilled as opposed to unskilled labour, which resulted from the amount of labour expended in producing it (e.g. Marx 1970: 197).

However because of his focus on the homogenization of labour under the rule of capital, Marx's main concern was to develop a theory capable of accounting for structural similarities rather than the differences between different types of labour power that were apparent even before workers presented themselves on the labour market. Thus he did not devote much attention to the vital role of education either in forming or in reproducing labour power. Since Marx's time, developments in productive technology and the accompanying changes in skill requirements, together with the introduction of universal education and formation of the workforce through the education system, have resulted in wage labour being much more highly differentiated than before. So rather than selling labour power as such, people always have a particular kind of labour power to sell and basic structural differences already exist between different kinds of wage labour before they get to the labour market.

Marx's neglect of the whole process of reproduction of labour power is ultimately responsible also for the absence of the domestic economy and of women as reproducers of labour power, from Marxist analysis of class. Marx's basic theory of reproduction was pretty simplistic: his conception was restricted to the basic necessities workers had to buy in order for life to continue, that is, fuel, housing, food, and clothing. In his theory, the value of labour power was reflected in the wage which was then used to purchase those goods deemed socially necessary to live (Marx 1970: 171). So labour power was reproduced simply by exchanging (male) wages for goods. Such a conceptualization completely ignores that the reproduction of labour power, both daily and generational, rests on an enormous amount of labour being expended in domestic production. If this had been recognized, then the possibility would have been opened up of appreciating the different uses to which male and female labour power have historically been put, to the fact that women's labour has been expended in domestic labour, and that this lies at the root of the structural differences between men and women in paid employment.

Relations of production: the sale and use of labour power

The argument that I want to develop assumes that the central class relation between sellers and buyers of labour power is in fact much more complex than that of traditional Marxist theory and that it includes many more dimensions. Systematic and structural differences exist both in the actual exchange relation itself and also in the way that labour power is used once it has been sold. What is needed therefore is a detailed analysis of these two sides of the wage relation between capital and labour for particular groups of wage labour which can specify how the relations of production under which they work are distinctive to them, and how they are differentiated from those of other groups of wage labour.

Within the sphere of public production, wage labour is not all in an equal or identical relation to capital, despite the common feature of being sold for a wage. There are specific determinants of the differences between different types of wage labour outside of and prior to production so that when people look for work they already have a particular sort of labour power to sell. It may be more or less formally trained, more or less mobile, and more or less continuously available for employment. Thus in contemporary capitalism women, ethnic minority and migrant workers, and the unskilled all sell their labour power under far less favourable conditions than skilled white men.

Most women have fewer officially acknowledged 'skills' and formal training to sell than men. Similarly, because of their primary responsibility for the domestic economy and for reproducing labour power, women are not usually as continuously available for paid employment in the wage economy as men. Certain aspects of the conditions of sale of labour power are thus determined to a considerable extent by the total division of social labour between the spheres of public production and domestic reproduction such that the overall sexual division between men and women in the two spheres also has effects within the sphere of production: women's various patterns of discontinuous availability are socially structured by their dual location in the two spheres, but by the same token so too is men's pattern of continuous availability. Such differences in the conditions under which workers sell their labour power constitute a major source of different relations to capital within the working class and hence of class relations.

In addition, once it has been sold, labour power is subject to different conditions in the way that it is used. Different work processes impose different conditions of work which create value in different ways. The introduction of assembly lines, for example, provided for the exploitation of workers and the extraction of surplus value in a new way.[22] Work processes normally place different kinds of labour unequally in their technical division of labour, in positions where they are forced to work more or less intensively, under closer or looser supervision, for longer or shorter hours, and for more or less pay. A sexual division of labour also operates as a central organizing principle, alongside the technical one, systematically dividing the workforce on the basis of gender.

Such considerations are basic to the analysis of women assemblers' class relations to be developed here. This will rest on a systematic examination of their relations of production, focusing particularly on the way in which their labour power was used and on their wage exchange with capital.

Reconstructing the past

Turning now to the empirical sources on which the study is based, although I found a wealth of material on the economic and social history of inter-war Britain, little information was available about women's employment at that time and virtually none about women's work on assembly lines.[23] A search of the obvious documentary sources proved disappointing: trade union archive material drew a more or less total blank since very little attention had been devoted by the labour movement to women assemblers at the time;[24] the business histories of large firms supplied biographies of their managers and directors, and provided detailed information about profit levels and expansion, but most had precious little to say about the labour they employed or even about the production process. And although the industrial and social surveys of the late 1920s and early 1930s did make reference to the large increase in women being recruited to manufacturing industry, there was no systematic documentation of this development. Again, certain information could also be gleaned from official government statistics but this too was insufficient to form the basis for a comprehensive account.

Finding out from the people who had worked in assembly-line industries was the only way to acquire any detailed information either about women's work there or about the work process. But tracking down women who had worked as assemblers in the 1930s was no easy task. If they had been 20 years old in 1930, they would by now (in 1985 and 1986 when I was looking for them) be 75, and the age range of possible interviewees would be from 65 (14 in 1935) to about 80 (starting work at 14 in 1920). Because most women would have given up factory work when they got married, say at 25, then between forty and fifty years would have elapsed since they had worked as assemblers. Even if they had remained in the same work until the normal retirement age of 60 for women, they would still already have been retired for up to fifteen years. I was also restricted by time and financial constraints to the London area where it was undoubtedly more difficult to discover retired assemblers than in a smaller industrial town where there had been less geographical mobility. Although at first sight the Acton area of west London adjacent to the Park Royal trading estate, one of the largest in inter-war London where many new factories such as Heinz and Lyons had been set up, would have been a good place to start, in fact there had been so much migration out of and into the area that very few of those who had worked there in the 1930s were still living in the vicinity by the 1980s.

The thirty-five retired women assemblers and other workers whom I eventually managed to interview (see the Appendix) were contacted by a variety of means, through community based pensioners' organizations and sheltered accommodation for the elderly, newspaper advertisements and advice from makers of television programmes on the history of work and of London, through friends whose mother or aunt knew someone who had done assembly work, and also through the firms themselves. All the women that I came across in this way had been in paid employment before the war, but many turned out not to have worked in factories, or if they had, then not on assembly lines. So I also approached large companies that I knew had adopted mass-production techniques during the inter-war years, with a view to consulting their archives and interviewing past managers and employees. Although some were suspicious and extremely uncooperative, the personnel managers of others were interested and helpful, and put me in touch with their pensioners groups. So, for example, I was invited to attend the Philips radio company's annual pensioners' Christmas party held in the works near Mitcham in south-east London, and there I met several people whom I arranged to interview. Once a first contact had been made, it became much easier to find more.

However, there must inevitably be a question mark over the kind of information provided by people who have remained loyal to a firm for over fifty years, since they are likely to be biased in its favour. On the other hand, it would be very difficult to find, fifty years after the event, people who had been employed by a particular company and were critical of its working conditions. They would have left many years ago and no longer have any reason for contact with the firm. However, as it turned out, many of the companies' pensioners were pretty scathing about the conditions of work before the war. Through the other sources, I also managed to find a number of women who had worked on assembly lines (even in some of the same factories) but who had left because they could not stand the conditions and so had no further contact with the factory during the intervening years. Interestingly, there was no systematic difference between the two groups: both gave similar accounts of conditions and commented on them in similar fashion. However, it should be stressed that because I present their testimony in the context of other documentary material, as part of an overall picture of the assembly-line production process in a particular firm, it is quite likely that their information and interpretation of events has a significance for me which it did not have for them and of which they were unaware. This is particularly so in the case of the retired managers whom I interviewed. I have quoted them word for word but questions of central importance to me, such as the sex-typing of work and the relative pay rates of men and women, did not have any such significance for them and were answered as if quite self-evident or purely factual.

My primary data are therefore based on a variety of sources, from interviews and company archives, official statistics and surveys, to autobiographies, novels and academic journals of the period. The approach is interdisciplinary and utilizes material from social, economic, labour and business history. My aim is to deploy all the different kinds and levels of data in a complementary way so as to give an overall account both of the production process and of how it was experienced by the workforce. I have deliberately chosen quite diverse styles of presenting the material so as to reflect the very different empirical quality of the different sources. For example, what the women say about their work is interwoven with official statistics. The intention is for the reader to become acquainted with the life histories of individual women and with what it was like to work in particular factories.

Although the material covers a wide range of 'new' industries, electrical engineering and food processing were those about which the most comprehensive information was gathered. So particular attention is given to these two, which are singled out as industries for more detailed 'case study' than the others.

The theory and substantive arguments that I put forward, about the implications for women's class relations of their place in the new work process and about the structural connection between changes in the production and consumption of consumer goods, are developed directly on the basis of and in relation to the empirical material. Existing theories of sexual division at work, of gender and class, and of labour segmentation and the labour process, which were outlined above, are constantly borne in mind but they are not constantly referred to, since my concern is to develop the theory in relation to the original material that it organizes.

The trend of the book is for the argument to be developed progressively with the accumulation of evidence, with the material organized in a more and more explicitly theoretical manner in the later chapters. Thus Chapters 2 and 3 are primarily concerned with providing essential empirical background information. Chapter 2 begins with profiles of the work history of three working-class women during the inter-war years as an introduction to the main structural features of women's employment at that time. The most important developments and shifts are highlighted, and attention is drawn to the main issues and debates that were then of current interest. Statistical evidence is presented to substantiate my basic argument that women occupied a central place in the manual labour force of mass-production industries.

Chapter 3 concentrates on the restructuring of the economy and of industry that took place in the context of recovery from the economic recession of the inter-war years. It focuses on the new forms of structure and organization characterizing the emerging consumer goods industries and contrasts them with those of the older capital goods industries of the late nineteenth and early twentieth centuries. Electrical engineering, food processing and canning, synthetic fibres and motor components are explored in particular detail as these were new industries in which women were primarily employed. The social, as well as economic, impact of the new goods are examined as well as the national scale of their market.

In Chapter 4 detailed profiles are presented of work in five individual factories: Peek Frean, EMI, Lyons, Morphy Richards and Hoover, based on company histories, archive material and the testimony of retired employees. The aim is to provide a real picture of actual factories and of the people who worked in them. I try to show the effects on the production process and on the workforce of the introduction of new technology and of mass-production methods, and their implications for the sexual division of labour and for women assemblers. Similarities and differences in the regimes of the different factories should be evident from each case study and so are not interpreted or commented on in great detail. The issues introduced here by concrete example raise fundamental questions for analysis to be addressed in the three subsequent chapters which represent the theoretical core of the book.

Chapter 5 focuses on the establishment of a new form of work process with the introduction of methods of mass production. The central argument is that assembly-line work involved the emergence of class relations which were new and distinctive to it alone. I outline the relations of production specific to assembly-line work, including the new technical division of labour, the distinctive way in which labour power was used and the new payment system corresponding to that use. The analysis is of the use made of women's labour power, of the relations of production under which women worked, and of the experience and resistance of women to these new class relations. However because the production process did not assume or require in itself a particular occupational segregation by gender, an analytical distinction is made between the technical and sexual divisions of labour. In this chapter the technical division of labour and the new class relations between labour and capital are established on their own merits.

Chapter 6 looks specifically at gender and the work process. It examines how the sexual division of labour was in practice intertwined with the technical division of labour. In a new work process where many jobs were newly created, there was no pre-existing sex-typing to determine the allocation of men and women to particular jobs. Yet a strict sexual division of labour did emerge in the new industries whereby women were restricted to routine jobs on the assembly line. The reasons underlying gender segregation, division and subordination in assembly-line work, and their extent and effects, are the central themes of this chapter. In particular I explore the implications of gender division for the relationship of women workers to each other and to men. Having dealt with the material factors, issues involved in the ideological reinforcement and representation of women assembly-line workers are then considered.

Chapter 7 turns to the other end of the chain, and focuses on women's role in the domestic economy and as consumers of the goods that they were producing in factories. I outline the fundamental changes that were occurring in domestic labour within the household during the inter-war years, including the emergence of the 'ideal home' with its 'ideal housewife', the decline and changing conditions of domestic service work, and class differences in the consumption of new consumer goods. Domestic production began to be achieved less on the basis of women's direct physical labour in the home during this period and more on the basis of commodities which had not previously been industrially produced but were now newly available for purchase. Structural changes in commodity production, that were the subject of earlier chapters, can be explained adequately only by reference to the concomitant changes taking place both within the domestic economy, and between the domestic economy and commodity production. So I trace the qualitative transformation of the relation between these two spheres and its far-reaching implications.

Finally, the theory underlying the organization of material in Chapters 5, 6, and 7 is presented in an explicit form in Chapter 8. I draw together the various dimensions of class relations of women assemblers and argue that they constituted a distinctive section of the industrial workforce, who occupied a strategic position both within the working class and in relation to capital. But in a more general sense, because people have a dual location in the public wage economy and in the domestic economy, their overall class relations should be seen to result not just from their position in waged work but rather from a combination of the relations of production under which they work in both spheres. Since the division of total social labour has historically allocated the labour of men and women differently between the wage economy as opposed to domestic production and reproduction, differences in the class relations of the genders are systematically and socially produced. I return also to the questions of gender antagonism, class conflict between men and women, and the role of gender in the labour process posed earlier in this chapter.

Chapter two

The changing pattern of women's employment

Three profiles

Doris Sharland, Kath Parish and Edith Boyd were three young working-class women with very varied experiences of work in the inter-war years. The similarities and differences between them are indicative of the main structural features and changes in women's waged work which are the central theme of this chapter.

Doris Sharland

Doris Sharland comes from Kilburn in north-west London. In 1927 she was 14 and left school:

> I thought I was going to have a holiday but my mum said 'get to work'. There were a couple of girls near us already working at Imperial Dryplate and our mums used to know each other and that was how I got my first job.[1]

It was a photographic equipment factory and Doris's job was to pack glass plates in thick paper and cardboard, working completely in the dark, for 12s (shillings) a week. She cut her fingers on the glass and hated never seeing the daylight. She gave all her wages to her mother and got back 2s as pocket money.

After two and a half years Doris left and went to the new Woolworths store in Kilburn High Road as a sales assistant. The pay there was £1 a week but the hours were very long:

> This was 1929. I was there a while when I discovered I could get 27s a week – which was enormous – at the Ever Ready razor blade factory. There we used to have to count the blades in grosses and pack them in boxes. I stayed there about 18 months.

From there Doris went to the Lyons Corner House in Oxford Street as a 'nippy' or waitress but she found the conditions very bad:

I got 10s a week and you were stopped 3d [pence] for your apron and cap, so you relied on your tips. Most of the other nippies came from the North of England or Ireland and many were committing suicide because they couldn't live on the money. It wasn't so bad for me because I was living at home with my parents but it was terrible for these girls who came from the depressed areas. If you had so many rolls and somebody pinched one you had to pay for it out of that 10s. People would come in for a 6d pot of tea and sit there all afternoon listening to the orchestra and you wouldn't get any tip.

After a few months Doris got the sack: she was supposed to go in on Christmas Day to wait on all the staff but didn't go:

You got the sack for anything then.

Several jobs later, Doris went after work at the Eugene Permanent Wave factory because she had heard that the wages there were 'fantastic – over £2 a week.' It was piecework and she made sachets used for perming women's hair, attaching a peg to a stiff sheet of paper, then glueing and folding it. However, after a year or two the firm mechanized:

When they got machines in I got the sack from there. They didn't want all these girls making sachets.

Doris's final job before the war was at Kemps, a large newly built biscuit factory just across the road from Eugene's. At first she had to wrap biscuits by hand in greaseproof paper, then waxed paper, weigh and parcel them and seal the box. After a couple of years, machines were also introduced here to do the first stages of packing, but the firm was expanding and Doris was not laid off this time. She stayed at Kemps for eight years either labelling tins of biscuits for a 1/4d (a 'farthing') per tin, or transferring the packets of biscuits as they came out of the machine on to a conveyor belt into large cartons. This was also piecework, 3½d per carton that was divided between the fourteen women on the line:

You could earn up to £2 15s and it was good money but you had to sweat for it.

Like the other firms where Doris worked, Kemps employed only single women, and women were sacked when they got married:

There were two or three married but they daren't tell. They kept it quiet because they would have got the sack.

Doris left Kemps at the beginning of the Second World War in 1940 to get a job as a bus conductress, one of the best paid and most sought after jobs, previously confined to men:

> You had to be absolutely perfect to get on the buses, and I queued up for two days for my job. I earned £3 15s – and that was enormous money.

She met her husband on the buses, married in 1941 and continued working for another six years until the birth of her daughter.

Between 1927 and 1940 Doris was never out of work. It was easy to move from one job to the next and her decisions to stay or leave depended on where she could earn more money, selling herself as an experienced wrapper and packer. She continued handing her wages over to her mother until she married and left home.

It never occurred to Doris to work as a domestic servant:

> I didn't have to, but they did have a hard life. They would have half a day off a month and used to earn only about 5s a week. Mostly they came from Wales or Ireland and you used to see them walking up and down the Kilburn High Road when they were let out.

Kath Parish

Unlike Doris Sharland, Kath Parish stayed in the same job from the time she left school until she married. She comes from Coventry where there was a tradition of industrial employment for women. In 1930 she was 14:

> When you left school, you got a job. It was your natural instinct in those days. You couldn't expect your mums and dads to keep you.

Her father worked at the Rover car factory as a chargehand in the bonnet section. He arranged a job there for her in the trim and to start with she went to work with him every day. Her starting wages were £1 6s for a 47 hour week. The trim was the only shopfloor section which employed women, between sixty and eighty women out of a total workforce of two thousand. There were two forewomen who supervised the trim workers but this was the highest position in which women were employed at 'The Rover', as it was known. All the women were thus in the same grade, unlike the men who were in many different grades.

The women's work was confined to machining leather and making the car seats, door panels and carpet binding for the interior of the car. At first they all sat separately at their heavy machines but in 1933 or 1934 a conveyor system was introduced and the women were now positioned on either side of it with their sewing machines:

> Your work was put on at one end and it came to you every so often and if you didn't do it, it went to the end.

This meant that the work came faster and one could not wander off or go to the toilet until the next break:

> You weren't frantic, but you had to keep your nose to it.

Kath learnt all the different jobs and operations that had to be done and after a year she did all the work that the other women could not do in the time and that was left behind. Her wages rose to £2 10s, which was the top wage for a woman at the Rover plant.

Work in the motor industry was still seasonal in the 1930s as factories built up their stock for the annual motor show. Many people were employed for only six months out of the year, but never knew in advance whether they would be one of those to be laid off:

> You worked six months in and six months out. I was very lucky, I was never out of work.

Those who were laid off were told on a Friday evening not to come in on the following Monday morning. Despite this insecurity jobs were much sought after; people came from Birmingham and Rugby to look for jobs at 'The Rover' and in Coventry generally, as wage rates were higher than in other towns in the Midlands. Rover was one of the best local employers and 'only the cream were taken on' as conditions and wages were better than at Courtaulds, GEC or Cashes, the other local factories where women worked.

Kath's Aunt Alice worked on the sewing machines at Rover, and two of her male cousins also worked in the factory. On her father's advice she joined the Transport Workers Union when she was 15 years old:

> He said you'd better join because if there's strikes or anything you'd be the first out if you weren't in the union.

Kath met her husband Jim at the factory, on the Sports Club cycling track. When they were married in 1939 she left work because

> the men didn't like their wives working in those days. The attitude was if you were a man, you should be man enough to keep your family.

Both Kath's and Jim's mothers had been in service before they married but Kath had never thought of this as a possible line of work for herself. In fact, she did not even know of anyone amongst her friends who went into service:

They nearly all went into factories. Some tried to qualify as teachers and others went as nurses.

Edith Boyd

Edith Boyd's experience was quite different from the other two in that she had to leave home to look for work. She was born in 1911 and lived in South Shields in the North East of England, an area that was very hard hit by the economic depression. She was one of six children and her stepfather was a shipyard worker. Edith had very little option but to look for domestic service work:

> I left school at 15 and started work in a local restaurant. My aunt worked there so I was a kitchen maid. Times were bad and there was no work about – this was in 1926. They used to advertise in the newspapers for people to go into private service and you had to write to an agency in London which sent you particulars of jobs in and around London. My first one was at an inn in Buckingham-shire.

For the next ten years, Edith had a number of jobs as a residential domestic servant in London, as a 'between maid' (working between the house and the kitchen) in Highgate, as a housemaid in Hampstead, and later as parlourmaid in Bayswater and Victoria. Some of the households employed several women and Edith was one of seven in the Hampstead house in 1932:

> The wages were very small and you only got one half-day off a week and a Sunday now and again, but you couldn't afford to go far. You were paid once a month and the most I would have would be about £4 a month. Of course your food and board were all counted in.

She usually stayed in a job for a year or two and then moved on; there was no shortage of demand for maids but Edith, like many others, disliked the conditions of employment:

> I was getting really fed up with service: two half-days a week if you were lucky. You never got away before three in the afternoon and had to be back by ten. So in 1936 I left service and decided to go into factory work.

This was possible only because she was able to move in with her brother Sam and his wife Lily who had a house in Greenford and so she had somewhere to live. Her brother had also come to the South to look for work and Lily was really a friend of Edith's. Sam had gone

Figure 1 Edith Boyd in 1932, working as a maid in Hampstead, with Cook.

to visit her in one of the houses where she was working, but she was out and he met Lily.

Edith worked briefly at CAV Bosch, a German engineering factory in Acton and then went to the Hoover factory in Perivale where vacuum cleaners were manufactured:

> It was 1937 when I started work at the Hoover factory. I got more money every week and the first thing I did was to buy a bicycle on hire purchase.

She worked on an individual machine in the drilling section, but women also worked capstan, press and welding machines in the machine shop.

Edith much preferred factory work to service:

Especially after being in service so long I thought it was great, moving among people and a proper wage packet every week.

She was promoted to chargehand for her section and stayed on during the war, moving up to Cambuslang, near Glasgow when Hoover opened a large new factory there in 1944. The move was convenient because Edith had married a Scottish miner in 1941. She remained at the factory after the war until her daughter was born in 1948, by which time her husband had also started at Hoovers on the cleaning staff, having had to leave the mines owing to health trouble.

Common features

These three women's experiences of employment could be multiplied by many other examples up and down the country. Despite the different jobs they did, certain features of their experience were common to virtually all working-class girls. For a start they all expected to begin working as soon as they left school at 14. Several women told me of leaving school one day and starting work the next, having to go to work in their school gymslip because they had no other suitable clothing to wear.[2]

Parents were often eager for them to reach school-leaving age so that they would bring some money into the home. Frequently their mother arranged their first job, often in a place where other members of the family were already working. Handing over their wage packet to their mother was also a virtually universal practice which revealed the importance of their wages as a contribution to family income. This was especially so in families where the mother was a widow, the father was unemployed or, as in Doris's case, a drinker, or where there were many other children to be supported. Most young women expected to receive only a couple of shillings pocket money back from their mother every week to pay for their fares, buy a pair of stockings, and to go to the cinema or a dance. Young women's wages were lower than those of any other group (young men, adult women and men) and for this reason employers were keen to employ them. But their low wage rates were often justified on the grounds that, since they lived at home and were still partially dependent on their parents, young women did not therefore really 'need' a living wage. The fact that their earnings were so essential to the family budget was just ignored.

Like Kath Parish, the majority of women left work when they married, either as the result of a 'marriage bar' which meant that the firm they worked for did not employ married women and sacked women if they got married, or because their husbands did not want them to carry on at work (as in Kath's case), or more generally 'because married women didn't work in those days'. The usual pattern was to work in the period between leaving school and getting married, and this meant that the vast majority of women workers were young and single.

Doris, Kath and Edith and practically every other working-class woman in the country was confined to the lowest levels of the occupational hierarchy at their place of work. They were given minimal training and remained in the same low grade with a very short ladder of promotion, which in factories was usually as chargehand, forewoman or trainer supervising the work of the other women. At 18 years old they would receive adult women's wages, but from then on could expect no further increase. All of these features contrasted with the conditions of employment for men, most of whom, apart from labourers, made some advance during their working lives, received some training, and were distributed through the many different levels and grades of work.

TMA Another typical feature shared by the three women was that they were all engaged in sex-segregated work, doing jobs sex-typed as feminine. Men did not work as maids, 'nippies' at Lyons Corner Houses, biscuit packers or as machinists in the motor industry. The distinction between men's jobs and women's jobs was virtually absolute and only very rarely were both sexes employed on exactly the same work. Women did women's work, usually only with other women; they had little contact with men, and certainly none on an equal basis.

The main difference between Doris, Kath and Edith was also a basic feature of the structure of employment affecting women workers in the inter-war years, that is, the difference in job possibilities in different parts of the country. In the depressed regions of the North of England and Wales, where unemployment was high, very few jobs were available for young women locally. Edith was one of thousands who moved southwards or eastwards in the search for work to the Midlands and South East. Like her, most migrant women workers went into domestic service, which was really the only option open to them. Partly this was because the job provided them with a place to live as well as to work. Finding accommodation would otherwise have been extremely difficult to arrange, especially for a 14- or 15-year-old on her own in a large town for the first time. Equally important, domestic service was usually the only type of work advertised in local newspapers or offered by employment agencies in the depressed areas; in addition, government agencies directed young women and unemployed adult women towards this sort of work. Most women disliked working as maids and would not have chosen domestic service work if they had any other option. Once in service work, however, it was difficult to get out: most domestic servants did not save much money as they sent the bulk of their wages home to their families, and many families in the depressed areas depended on the wages of a daughter in service in London. If they wanted a different kind of job, they would need somewhere to live and would have to spend a large proportion of their wages on lodgings, and so end up having less to send home. Edith was lucky in being able to live with her brother, which gave her possibility of getting out of domestic service and into factory work. But her case is fairly unusual.

Doris was conscious of the variety of employment opportunities available to her, as a native Londoner with somewhere to live, but not to the young women from Wales whom she saw walking in Kilburn High Road when they were 'let out'. They had no option but to take some kind of living in job with little free time and very low wages, whereas she could move between shop and factory work more or less at will. There were so many maids in London that Doris could not help being aware of domestic service as an important area of work, though not one that she would ever dream of pursuing. Kath in Coventry, however, did not even know of any maids. Of course domestic service did exist in the Midlands too, but it was not an important avenue of employment for young women from the local towns as so much alternative work was available, especially in industry. Many women looked down on maids and viewed service as the worst possible form of employment, but whether or not they were able to avoid it or not depended very directly on which part of the country they came from.

Women's waged work

Recent discussion of women's employment in Britain tends to draw a sharp contrast between the years before and after the Second World War and to locate either the war itself or the years after 1945 as the main period when the foundations were laid for the features of women's present day employment. Although this characterization is accurate as far as official labour force participation is concerned, I want to show that it is not so true for occupational distribution. On the contrary, post-war changes in women's employment stem from a restructuring that was already well underway in the inter-war years.

Between 1918 and 1939 the areas of work in which women were employed underwent enormous change and it was at this time, rather than later, that the grounding was laid for the quite different pattern of employment that was to prevail after 1945.

This is not to deny the tremendous effect of the wartime employment of women. The fact that women successfully performed 'men's work' in so many industries during the war made employers fully aware of the advantages to be gained by employing women and encouraged them to allocate certain jobs to women when the labour process was modernized. However, one must not forget that millions of women were thrown out of their wartime employment, just as they had been in the aftermath of the First World War, and that very few continued in exactly the same job after the war as during it, especially if it had been a man's job.

That much of the work performed by women during the war was therefore exceptional reinforces my argument, rather than detracting from it. The enormous changes that occurred in women's employment between 1931 and 1951 were not due, or certainly not entirely due, to developments originating during and after the war. In fact, much of the post-war change represented a consolidation of trends that were already well established before the war.

Domestic service, for example, was already in steep decline before the war; the employment of women in mass-production industries was also not only already well established by the 1930s but also continually increasing in both absolute and relative terms. Factory employment taken together with clerical and retail employment, both of which had also been growing rapidly in the 1920s and 1930s, were already eclipsing the traditional sectors of women's work in the textile industry and in domestic service before the outbreak of the Second World War.

Problems in the official sources of data

However, there is a problem in presenting comprehensive figures to demonstrate the changing pattern of women's employment during the inter-war years since very little systematic analysis was undertaken at the time on an industry-by-industry, or region-by-region basis. Because of the war, no Census was taken in 1941 and this precludes the possibility of direct comparison across the two decades 1921 to 1931 and 1931 to 1941. In comparison with 1931, the 1951 Census did certainly show that marked changes had occurred in the pattern of women's employment, participation rates and industrial and occupational distribution. However, although it is evident from other sources that most of this change occurred during the course of the 1930s, rather than the 1920s or in the immediate post-war years, no sufficiently detailed figures exist which could be used to show year-by-year change during the decade.

The main sources of labour force statistics, the Census of Population, and the Ministry of Labour employment figures, both present problems and are incomparable in a number of ways. The 1931 Census, though more comprehensive, is rather early for present purposes, and the absence of a 1941 Census interrupts a neat ten yearly series of statistics. The only available figures covering the 1930s as a decade are those supplied by the Ministry of Labour.

Official labour force statistics are notorious for relying on sexist terminology and gender-blind concepts. The main terms used were 'participation', 'activity' and 'occupation': women were deemed 'economically active', 'occupied' or 'participating in the labour force' only if they were in paid employment.[3] The social and economic necessity of domestic labour was ignored and it was not recognized as work unless performed by a paid domestic servant. In this way the categories used by official administrative bodies of the state actively perpetuated the division between the public world of production and the private world of social reproduction.

The Ministry of Labour further reinforced the invisibility of women workers by counting as employed only those in insured jobs. As a result, all domestic servants were absent from their figures, that is, almost a third of all women workers, as well as women working in other uninsured jobs. They also misrepresented the extent and importance of young women's employment by collecting statistics only about those aged 16 and over, so excluding the large number of 14- to 16-year-olds who were actually at work.[4]

In spite of these drawbacks, there is no alternative but to use the official statistics and inevitably this involves relying on official classifications. It would be pointless to alter the terminology without also changing the whole method of classifying. As I am concerned here with highlighting the main features of and variations in *paid* employment some of this conventional terminology will have to be retained, but without the implication that women not in waged work were by that token not economically active or 'occupied'.

Presenting the employment statistics in terms of the organizing principles of age, marital status and region brings into clear focus the main features of women's participation in the labour force. However, these principles cannot explain the empirical data. For instance, a major reason why married women did not carry on working was the semi-official marriage bar which actively excluded them from the labour force, but this could not be guessed from the statistics. Similarly, the fact that the majority of working women were young does not explain why they were concentrated in certain occupations thought 'fit for women' only nor why work was so segregated on the basis of sex. Neither are the reasons why women from the south Wales mining valleys became domestic servants in south-east England self-evident.

Variations in women's participation rates

After the large enforced exodus of women from the workforce at the end of the First World War, the proportion of women in paid employment began to rise again from 1921. In 1931 occupied women numbered 5.6 million, and comprised 29.7 per cent of the total labour force. By 1951, these figures had risen to 6.3 million and 30.8 per cent.[5] Between 1923 and 1938 nearly 650,000 more women entered insured jobs according to Ministry of Labour figures, representing a growth of 24 per cent (MOLG December 1939: 469).[6]

Table 1 shows that, taken over the country as a whole, this growth occurred fairly steadily throughout the period apart from a temporary decline during the worst years of the recession between 1929 and 1933. Significantly the growth peaked in 1937 (falling again slightly by 1938) showing that the main period of expansion occurred in the years before the build up of war industries. So the expansion in the number of women employed during the 1930s cannot be explained as the result of war industries taking on more workers.

Women's participation rate was structured by age, marital status, and area of residence. Breaking down the statistics to examine these features separately reveals how important they were as differentiat-

Table 1 Number of women aged 16 to 64 in insured employment, 1923, 1929, and 1932–8

Date	Number	Number as % of 1923	Women as % of all insured employees
1923	2,706,600	100.0	27.4
1929	3,117,560	115.2	28.5
1932	3,021,260	111.6	30.3
1933	3,158,250	116.7	30.4
1934	3,190,040	117.9	29.4
1935	3,201,250	118.3	29.0
1936	3,324,630	122.8	28.6
1937	3,505,290	129.5	28.4
1938	3,364,764	124.0	27.9

Source: Adapted from Ministry of Labour *Gazette*, December 1938: 468

ing factors in women's overall participation in paid employment.

Age differences

The proportion of women in paid employment varied according to age and throughout the period younger women constituted the majority of the female labour force. In 1921 and 1931 69 per cent of all working women were aged under 35 (Hakim 1979: 10).[7] Within this broad figure though, changes were occurring, as can be seen from Table 2. An ever increasing proportion of women in the younger age groups went out to work so that by 1931, half of all 14- and 15-year-olds and three-quarters of all 16- and 17-year-olds were in the labour force. The 18- to 20-year age group had the highest participation rate (79 per cent) but after the age of 24 the rate fell dramatically. However, the fall was less dramatic in 1931 than in 1921 (with 36 per cent of those aged 25 to 34, and 24.5 per cent of those aged 35 to 44 remaining in the labour force), suggesting that younger married women were beginning to stay on at work until the birth of their first child rather than leaving work on marriage (Lewis 1984: 149). This important change in employment trends was to gather momentum during the 1930s, and is corroborated by my interview material.

Another significant development was that after 1931, the participation rates of older women also began to rise, so that by 1951 over 35 per cent of all women aged between 35 and 54 were in employment. Again much of this change must have occurred during the course of the 1930s but in the absence of a 1941 Census this is impossible to prove.

Table 2   Age-specific participation rates of women, England and Wales, 1911 to 1951[a]

Year	Under 14	14–15	16–17	18–20	21–24	25–34	35–44	45–54	55–64	65–74	75+
1911	356	480	693	739[b]	620[c]	338	241	230	204	138	57
1921	337	448	709	763[b]	622[c]	335	229	210	193	126	46
1931	342	509	756	790	651	363	245	211	178	102	38
1951	349	611[d]	812	848	655	373	358	350	218	70	20

Source: Lewis 1984: 147
Notes:
[a] Numbers per 1,000 in each category in the labour force
[b] 18–19 years
[c] 20–24 years
[d] 15 years

Single and married women

The most striking characteristic of the inter-war years, in comparison with the period after 1945, was that the vast majority of women in paid employment were unmarried. During the inter-war period only a small minority of married women worked full-time in situations where they were likely to be enumerated in the Census. Of working women in 1931, 77 per cent were single and 16 per cent were married. Only 10 per cent of married women worked, in comparison with 70 per cent of single women (Hakim 1979: 11–12; Gales and Marks 1974: 63).

However, it must be emphasized straightaway that such a generalization represents little more than an overall percentage, to which there were many exceptions. For instance, there were vast regional and industrial variations in the proportion of married women who worked, such that the normal pattern in many industries and areas was for married women and mothers to stay at work, so contradicting the average national trend. The best known example of this was the textile industry in parts of the North West, but the practice was also common in the expanding new industries in London and the South East.

In addition, there were large sections of the adult female population who depended entirely on their own earnings and remained in employment until retirement age. The hundreds of thousands of widows who supported themselves and their families fell into this category.[8] So too did the important minority of single women who never married: one in six women did not marry at all during the inter-war period, especially in the aftermath of the First World War when so many men were killed, and the vast majority of what was called the 'unmarried surplus' (James 1960: 284) were likely to be in continuous employment. The birth rate was also declining throughout the inter-war period and this had the effect of reducing the number of years spent on childrearing, so enabling married women to spend longer in the labour force, either before starting or after completing a family.

Apart from these structural variations, many working-class mothers regularly took on casual or temporary jobs, such as cleaning or laundry work, but this was unlikely to be included in official figures. Although part-time work in its present form did not exist in the inter-war years, it was not uncommon for factory and shop workers who had left work on marriage to be recalled by the firm where they had worked for temporary work during the summer or Christmas rush, or at other times of labour shortage. This practice was particularly common in the food processing industry, and in some sections of the motor and radio industries. Many married women might therefore work for several weeks or months each year, but not on a continuous basis.[9] Again seasonal employment of this sort did not enter the Census or Ministry of Labour statistics which therefore underestimated, on a number of different counts, the numbers of women, and especially married women, in waged employment.

The mass entry of married women to the waged labour market was strictly a post-war phenomenon, closely associated with the possibility of working on a part-time basis. During the inter-war years part-time work, in the sense of working for several hours in the day or several days in the week rather than the full working week, was unknown. The normal working week was 48 hours and there was no flexibility in the hours of work: you either worked for the full 48 hours or not at all.

In fact the introduction of part-time work goes a long way towards explaining the large difference in the employment rate of married women before and after the war. Since women had responsibility for the private reproduction of labour power, their availability for paid employment outside of the home was severely restricted once they were married and had a household to run. In the 1920s and 1930s housework, shopping, cooking and childcare were considerably more labour intensive and time consuming than they were to become in the 1950s and 1960s and so for many married women domestic labour amounted to a full-time job. Engaging in paid employment for 48 hours a week in addition was just not a viable proposition.[10]

In overall statistical terms then, married women represented a slowly growing proportion of the total female labour force between 1918 and 1939. At the same time, the proportion of all married women in paid work was also expanding, and in particular the increasing tendency of younger married women to work after 1921 was quite marked.[11] Despite these important changes to established trends, the participation rate of married women nevertheless remained significantly lower than that of either single, divorced or widowed women until 1951.

Regional variations

Variations in the level of women's participation by age and marital status were criss-crossed and sometimes contradicted by marked regional differences. For example, Table 3 shows that in areas of industrial expansion like Greater London and the South East, as well as the Midlands, the proportion of women in paid employment was relatively high (39.9 per cent and 36 per cent respectively). In rural areas, such as Wales, the proportion was much lower (21 per cent) than in the North West of England (41.9 per cent) where the textile

Table 3 Proportion of women occupied by region, 1931

Census region	Total number aged 14 and over	Total occupied aged 14+	Occupied as % of total	Out of work as % of occupied	Those occupied in region as % of national total
England and Wales	16,410,894	5,606,043	34.2	8.6	100.0
South East	5,756,538	2,079,685	36.1	5.7	37.1
Greater London included in SE	3,529,184	1,408,219	39.9	6.0	25.1
North 1[a]	830,191	191,894	23.1	9.6	3.4
North 2[b]	501,710	138,081	27.5	7.7	2.5
North 3[c]	1,402,705	496,282	35.4	9.1	8.8
North 4[d]	2,565,537	1,075,255	41.9	15.4	19.2
Midland 1[e]	1,818,582	654,625	36.0	9.2	11.7
Midland 2[f]	953,071	332,803	34.9	7.1	5.9
East	721,798	191,048	26.4	6.8	3.4
South West	877,965	240,231	27.4	5.2	4.3
Wales 1[g]	697,301	135,985	19.5	8.4	2.4
Wales 2[h]	282,493	70,154	24.8	6.1	1.3

Source: Census of Population, 1931, Occupation Tables: 154–5, and General Report: 119

Notes:

[a] Durham, Northumberland
[b] Cumberland, Westmorland, Yorkshire: East and North Ridings
[c] West Yorkshire including York
[d] Cheshire, Lancashire
[e] Gloucestershire, Herefordshire, Shropshire, Staffordshire, Warwickshire, Worcestershire
[f] Derbyshire, Leicestershire, Northamptonshire, Nottinghamshire, Peterborough
[g] Brecknockshire, Carmarthenshire, Glamorganshire, Monmouthshire
[h] Anglesey, Caernarvonshire, Cardiganshire, Denbighshire, Flintshire, Merionethshire, Montgomeryshire, Pembrokeshire, Radnorshire

Table 4 Growth in number of insured persons, male and female, by region, 1923–38

Administrative division	Estimated number of insured persons, aged 16–64, in employment				
	June 1923	June 1929	June 1932	June 1937	June 1938
			(thousands)		
London	1,856	2,235	2,192	2,695	2,677
South-eastern	628	797	798	999	1,004
South-western	633	738	719	880	892
Midlands	1,453	1,608	1,467	1,918	1,863
North-eastern	1,101	1,158	1,014	1,257	1,243
North-western	1,653	1,797	1,579	1,851	1,717
Northern	644	635	498	654	654
Wales	564	477	387	484	460
England and Wales	8,532	9,445	8,654	10,738	10,510
Scotland	1,078	1,130	981	1,203	1,197
Northern Ireland	207	222	192	230	211
Great Britain and Northern Ireland	9,817	10,797	9,827	12,171	11,918
			(index numbers)		
London	100.0	120.4	118.1	145.2	143.7
South-eastern	100.0	126.9	127.1	159.1	159.6
South-western	100.0	116.6	113.6	139.0	140.3
Midlands	100.0	110.7	101.0	132.0	127.9
North-eastern	100.0	105.2	92.1	114.2	111.8
North-western	100.0	108.7	95.5	112.0	103.5
Northern	100.0	98.6	77.3	101.6	101.2
Wales	100.0	84.6	68.6	85.8	80.9
England and Wales	100.0	107.0	101.4	125.9	123.2
Scotland	100.0	104.8	91.0	111.6	110.6
Northern Ireland	100.0	107.2	92.8	111.1	101.5
Great Britain and Northern Ireland	100.0	110.0	100.1	124.0	120.9

Source: Adapted from Ministry of Labour *Gazette*, December 1938: 469

industry, a traditional employer of women was concentrated.[12]

The dominance of London and the South East becomes even more marked if one examines the actual numbers of women in work, rather than merely comparing their activity rates. A very large proportion of all occupied women in the country as a whole lived in the South East, nearly two-fifths of the total (almost 2.1 million out of the total of 5.6 million occupied women, or 37 per cent). The North West followed with the next largest number (nearly 1.1 million or 19 per cent of the total). Taken together this means that 56 per cent of all occupied women were concentrated in these two regions.

The empirical evidence points to a tendency for higher participation rates to be increasingly concentrated as time went on in the geographical areas of industrial growth, where new jobs were created for women in manufacture and in clerical and sales work associated with business expansion. Another significant aspect of the higher rates in these areas was that they included a relatively higher proportion of married women than elsewhere. This suggests that the existence of employment opportunities as such constituted one of the main factors (as opposed to familial constraints) determining whether women continued in employment after marriage.

The absolute increase in women's employment over the course of the inter-war years was geographically concentrated in much the same way as the higher participation rate. Though women's employment grew steadily throughout the period as a whole, its greatest increase was in the areas of new industrial expansion. Table 4 shows that the number of insured persons in the South East region increased by a staggering (almost) 60 per cent between 1923 and 1938.[13] London, the Midlands and the South West also experienced a large expansion of insured persons during the same period. By contrast, growth in the North West was tiny (a 3.5 per cent increase) and Wales actually suffered a decline (due to unemployment in coal mining).

During the worst years of the recession, 1929 to 1932, employment was stationary or decreasing everywhere but after the end of the slump the fortunes of the different regions were even more divergent than before. The worst hit areas barely recovered their pre-slump situation in later years while the areas in which new industries were located experienced their greatest employment growth between 1932 and 1937.

Changing areas of women's work

A central argument of this chapter is that the foundations for women's post-war occupational distribution were laid in the inter-war period. Indeed it was in the kinds of work that women did and their distribution between different occupations and industries that the greatest change in women's employment occurred. Basically the shift was away from the traditional textile and clothing industries, and domestic service, and towards the new 'lighter' industries in manufacturing, retail and 'white-blouse' clerical work. The declining number of women in textiles, clothing and domestic service was more than offset by the increase in clerical and distributive services, in the engineering, paper and printing, chemicals, and food, drink and tobacco industries.

Table 5a Changes in numbers of women employed in selected industries,[a] England and Wales, 1921 and 1931

Census category	1921	1931	Intercensal increase	
			numbers	%
Total, all industries, including out of work	5,065,332	5,606,043	540,711	10.7
VI. Manufacture of metals, machines, etc.	244,626	293,272	48,646	19.9
4 Engineering (not machine or electrical)	32,514	35,906	3,392	10.4
5 Electrical installations, cable and apparatus	38,652	68,263	29,691	76.6
VII. Textile and textile goods	662,384	690,395	28,011	4.2
IX. Clothing (not knitted)	494,948	514,752	19,804	4.0
X. Food, drink and tobacco	199,747	224,704	24,957	12.4
XVII. Commerce and finance	741,744	886,039	144,925	19.5
600–670 Distributive trades	663,732	798,730	134,998	20.3
XXI. Personal service	1,522,879	1,737,715	214,836	14.1

Source: Census of Population 1931, Industry Tables, Table B: 714–19
Note:
[a] Based on 1931 Classification of Industries

Table 5b Changes in numbers of women employed in selected industries,[a] England and Wales, 1931 and 1951

Census category	1931	1951	Intercensal increase	
			numbers	%
V. Metal manufacture	17,423	56,868	39,445	226.4
VI. Engineering, shipbuilding and electrical goods	102,381	323,453	221,072	215.9
VII. Vehicles	49,733	116,834	67,101	134.9
VIII. Other metal goods	86,420	149,926	63,506	73.4
X. Textiles	543,257	474,657	−68,600	−12.6
XII. Clothing	488,640	448,423	−40,217	−8.2
XIII. Food, drink and tobacco	206,356	238,775	32,419	15.7
XX. Distributive trades	749,468	1,021,974	272,506	36.3
XXI. Insurance, banking and finance	73,704	138,782	65,078	88.3
XXIV. Miscellaneous services	1,683,757	1,228,967	−454,790	−27.0
Private domestic service	1,119,133	359,413	−759,720	−67.9
Total of V, VI, VII and VIII	255,957	647,081	391,124	152.8

Source: Census of Population 1951, Industry Tables, Table C: 644–8
Note:
[a] Based on 1951 Classification of Industries

Table 6 Number of insured employees[a] in selected industries. Women aged 16 to 64[b] at each mid-year, United Kingdom (in thousands)

	1923	1924	1925	1926	1927	1928	1929	1930	1931	1932	1933
Manufacturing											
Pottery, earthenware, etc.	36.4	35.7	38.6	38.3	37.8	37.6	39.0	42.8	43.4	38.8	41.1
Engineering etc.	52.8	54.5	60.7	60.6	61.0	65.3	68.1	72.0	70.3	66.5	62.9
Vehicle construction and repair	23.2	22.6	25.7	25.9	26.4	27.5	28.8	29.5	29.6	29.7	30.1
Metal industries and trades	144.5	150.0	157.6	163.5	160.1	161.7	171.6	184.1	186.9	182.3	184.2
Textiles	790.8	808.3	812.1	812.5	797.0	805.6	807.1	831.9	822.6	776.1	761.0
Clothing	376.6	374.8	378.9	380.9	382.8	384.7	385.6	394.2	411.6	408.0	415.4
Food, drink and tobacco	202.5	211.5	220.0	214.8	216.3	212.5	216.8	225.5	231.6	223.3	234.7
Total manufacturing	1,950.6										
Distributive trades	504.0	544.2	580.2	596.8	614.0	639.7	663.7	700.8	738.3	748.6	756.4
Commerce, banking, insurance and finance	79.8	76.3	73.1	71.2	72.0	72.3	74.0	74.8	75.6	78.2	78.3
All industries and services[c]	2,992.9										
Manufacturing as % of total	65.2										

Continued ...

Table 6 continued

	1934	1935	1936	1937	1938	Change 1923–37		1947	Change 1938–47	
						number	%		number	%
Manufacturing										
Pottery, earthenware, etc.	39.7	39.9	39.9	41.3	41.5	5.1	14.0	36.2	-5.3	-12.8
Engineering etc.	65.3	64.8	71.5	81.4	85.8	33.0	62.5	222.8	137.0	159.9
Vehicle construction and repair	29.8	30.8	32.6	35.7	39.3	16.0	68.7	88.8	49.5	126.0
Metal industries and trades	194.4	204.5	217.7	236.7	237.2	92.7	64.2	324.4	87.2	36.8
Textiles	739.7	714.5	709.9	711.6	688.8	-102.0	-12.9	436.6	-252.2	-36.6
Clothing	418.3	413.3	422.5	429.6	434.8	58.2	15.5	359.9	-74.9	-17.2
Food, drink and tobacco	225.8	223.2	230.3	237.8	245.8	43.3	21.4	224.0	-21.8	-8.9
Total manufacturing					2,209.7	259.1	13.3	2,224.3	14.6	0.7
Distributive trades	743.1	740.2	760.9	782.9	813.5	309.5	61.4	845.0	31.5	3.9
Commerce, banking, insurance and finance	80.8	81.4	84.0	88.1	92.8	13.0	16.3	125.6	32.8	35.3
All industries and services[c]					3,987.0	994.1	33.2	4,684.9	697.9	17.5
Manufacturing as % of total					55.4			47.5		

Source: Adapted from *British Labour Statistics, Historical Abstract 1886–1968*, Table 113: 214-15
Notes:
[a] Employed and unemployed
[b] Aged 16 and over 1923 to 1926, and 16 to 64 from 1927 onwards
[c] Including those not listed

The beginnings of this process had already been apparent before the First World War but it gathered momentum during the inter-war years. Such shifts in the distribution of women's employment can be understood only in the context of industrial restructuring undertaken in order to recover from the economic recession. Fundamental changes in the structure and organization of production, together with the development of new consumer goods industries lay at the root of women's changing occupational distribution.

Industrial distribution

By 1951, the pattern of industrial distribution had altered quite considerably in comparison with 1921, as is evident from Tables 5a and 5b.[14] Between 1921 and 1931 there had already been a large increase in the number of women employed in the manufacture of metals, machines etc, and especially in the electrical section of the industry. The food industry and the distributive trades also experienced substantial increase. In other industries the rate of expansion was lower although the actual growth in numbers was still large.

Between 1931 and 1951 these trends became much more pronounced as the pace of growth accelerated. An extra 391,124 women entered metal, engineering, electrical and vehicle manufacture. Jobs in the food industry and in clerical and retail employment also increased and at a faster rate than in the earlier period. The absolute decline in the textile and clothing industries also became apparent for the first time after 1931 (together losing 109,000 women's jobs). But the greatest change was in private domestic service, which decreased by over three-quarters of a million jobs (to nearly one-seventh of its 1931 level). Well before the war women had voted with their feet against this type of work, whenever and wherever an alternative was open to them. But the tremendous impact of this shift away from domestic work could be seen to the full only in the Census figures for 1951.

That the shift in distribution of women between industries and the changes in numbers became established during the inter-war years, and was not simply an effect of the Second World War, can be demonstrated from the year-by-year Ministry of Labour figures (Table 6).[15] The engineering, vehicles and metals industries, for example, experienced a continuous steady increase of women employees between 1923 and 1938. Even despite the temporary setback in engineering caused by the slump between 1932 and 1936, each section expanded by over 60 per cent between 1923 and 1938.[16] The same set of figures also confirms the increasing employment of women in the food industry (an extra 43,300) over the same period.

That the fate of the textile industry was sealed during the inter-war years also comes over clearly. Employment there never recovered from the severe loss suffered at the height of the recession in 1931–2, but continued to decline right up to 1938 with the loss of over 102,000 women's jobs between 1923 and 1938. By contrast, the clothing industry appeared at first sight to be unaffected by the slump. It experienced steady gradual growth throughout the fifteen years up to the war, followed by a very sharp decline, so that by 1947 it had fallen to 359,000, that is, well below its 1923 figure. However, I would suggest that part of the pre-war increase was illusory: the clothing industry had begun to mechanize before the war, with the establishment of large factories which mass-produced ready-made clothes such as women's blouses and dresses, and men's shirts, to be sold in the new department and chain stores. The new clothing factories relied on assembly lines and women workers as the main labour force, and over time they replaced many of the traditional dressmaking and tailoring parts of the industry, with consequent job loss. Men's employment was already on the decline before the war (a drop of 20,000 between 1923 and 1938), and the increased number of women followed by the sharp drop suggests that the older dressmaking and newer ready-made sections overlapped for a few years. In the long run, mechanization had the effect of both feminizing and reducing the size of the workforce.

So the share of manufacturing jobs remained high (55 per cent) as a proportion of women's total employment in insured jobs by the end of the inter-war period. Within this category however, engineering was well on the way to catching up with, if not overtaking, clothing and textiles as the major industrial employer of women. It was precisely the women-employing sections of the expanding engineering, food processing and synthetic fibres industries that were growing the most rapidly during the inter-war period. Thus industrial restructuring had the effect of drawing large numbers of women into factory employment while at the same time pushing out large numbers of men, since the older and declining industries, such as marine engineering and coal mining, were predominantly staffed by men while the newer expanding ones relied heavily on women.

In the service sector, the growth of women's jobs in the distributive trades was as staggering as anything seen in manufacturing industry. However, part at least of the 309,000 growth reflects the shift away from uninsured to insured employment which accompanied the transformation of retailing at this time, rather than any actual increase in numbers (Jefferys 1954). Women retail workers became less concentrated in the older type of small corner shops where they had been unlikely to be insured, while their numbers

Table 7a Principal occupations of women in 1921 and 1931

Occupation (1931 code numbers)	1921		1931			1921/1931
	a	b	a	b	c	d
Total occupied aged 14 +	5,036,727		5,606,043		11.3	
VII Metal workers	84,848	16	96,120	17	13.3	6.3
212 Electric welders and cutters	564		1,245		120.7	
217 Press workers and stampers	22,441		31,425		40.1	
IX Electrical apparatus makers	13,396	2	28,445	5	112.3	150
253 Coil winders	2,680		5,687		112.2	
260 Instrument makers and assemblers	1,945		8,871		356.1	
XII Textile workers	557,431	110	574,093	102	2.9	-7.3
XIII Makers of textile goods and articles of dress	533,287	105	542,809	96	1.7	-8.6
XIV Makers of foods, drinks and tobacco	69,988	13	74,888	13	7.0	0.0
XXIII Commercial, financial and insurance	504,264	100	604,833	107	19.9	7.0
XXVII Personal service	1,676,425	332	1,926,978	343	14.9	3.3
850 Indoor domestic servants	1,148,698	228	1,332,224	237	15.9	3.9
874 Charwomen, office cleaners	118,476		140,146		18.3	
XXVIII Clerks, typists and draughtswomen	429,921	85	579,945	103	34.8	21.2

Source: Census of Population 1931, Occupation Tables, Table G: 673–80
Notes:
a Numbers
b Distribution per 1,000 occupied
c Percentage increase in numbers 1921 to 1931
d Percentage change in distribution per 1,000 occupied 1921 to 1931

expanded in the new larger stores which were covered by national insurance.

In personal service employment the move was away from private domestic service and towards working in public establishments, like hotels and catering, and towards daily cleaning, waitressing, and hairdressing. Within private domestic service the trend was strongly away from residential service so that already by 1931, 40 per cent were no longer living in (PP Cmd 6650 1944–5: 25). More than a third were over 35, confirming the suggestion that where alternative industrial employment was available, younger women avoided domestic service

Table 7b   Principal occupations of women in 1931 and 1951

Occupation (1951 code numbers)	1931 a	1931 b	1951 a	1951 b	1951 c	1931/1951 d
Total occupied aged 15 +	5,483,508		6,272,876		14.4	
VI Workers in metal manufacture, engineering	142,231	25	197,906	32	39.1	28.0
VII Textile workers	581,716	104	359,129	57	–38.3	–45.2
IX Makers of textile goods and articles of dress	506,328	90	437,218	70	–13.6	–22.2
X Makers of foods, drinks and tobacco	56,243	10	83,914	13	49.2	30.0
XVIII Commercial, finance, etc.	604,951	108	757,771	121	25.3	12.0
XXII Personal service	1,934,294	347	1,464,137	234	–24.3	–32.6
876 Charwomen, office cleaners	140,146	25	215,336	34	53.7	36.0
882–5 Indoor domestic servants	1,333,222	238	723,574	115	–45.7	–51.7
XXIII Clerks, typists, etc.	197,970	35	378,437	60	91.2	71.4

Source: Census of Population 1951, General Report, Table 62: 134–5
Notes:
[a] Numbers
[b] Distribution per 1,000 occupied
[c] Percentage change in numbers 1931 to 1951
[d] Percentage change in distribution per 1,000 occupied 1931 to 1951

and those who remained were likely to be married and older.[17]

High unemployment artificially boosted the numbers of women in domestic service, partly as a result of the government policy to encourage unemployed women to train for and seek domestic work. However, this effect of the recession was in contradiction to the move away from domestic service, a development which represented one of the most dramatic changes in employment of the first half of the twentieth century. The high figure of over 1 million domestic servants in 1931 represents a hiccup in this trend. Middle-class women had bemoaned the shortage of domestic servants from the early 1920s and government commissions had already been established to investigate the matter (Chapter 1: 8). The preference of younger women like Edith Boyd for factory rather than domestic work was well recognized by contemporary commentators, though many suggested that improvements in the conditions of domestic service employment might reverse this decline in popularity.

Occupational concentration and segregation

One of the most enduring features of women's employment throughout the course of the twentieth century has been their restriction to a very limited number of occupations. But as we have seen those particular areas have changed dramatically over the decades. If we now examine the changing proportion of all employed women who were engaged in particular industries or occupations, rather than the changing size of the female workforce in each industry, the shifts already noticed come into much sharper focus.

In 1901 three-quarters of all employed women had been engaged in only three industrial groups: textiles, clothing and footwear, and miscellaneous services (Joseph 1983: 137). However, by 1951 the significance of these three industries had halved as others, such as metal manufacture and engineering, and the distributive trades, had assumed much greater importance as employers of women. The share taken by general engineering increased from only 2.2 per cent of all employed women in 1901 to 12.1 per cent by 1951, and the growth in the distributive trades occurred almost entirely between 1901 and 1931 by which time 15 per cent of all women were employed in this field. On the other hand it is also noteworthy that the declining share taken by miscellaneous services was already evident by 1931.

This fundamental transformation in the areas of concentration of women workers during the inter-war years is confirmed by looking at the principal occupations of women in 1921, 1931, and 1951 (rather than the share taken by broad industrial groups). The 150 per cent growth in the proportion of all women occupied as electrical apparatus makers between 1921 and 1931 stands out from Table 7, as does the declining proportion occupied as textile and clothing workers, trends that were both further consolidated between 1931 and 1951. During this time clerical and food occupations also increased their share of the total. The number of clerks and typists nearly doubled from just under 200,000 to 378,000, so that by 1951 60 out of every 1,000 women were so occupied in comparison with 35 in 1931. The small increase in the proportion of women employed as indoor domestic servants between 1921 and 1931 had been more than cancelled out by 1951 (a 51.7 per cent drop) and the occupations of charwoman and office cleaner accounted for much larger numbers of personal service workers.

This alteration in the industrial distribution of women was not evenly spread over the age range. As time went on, older women tended to be concentrated in the declining occupations and younger women in the new and expanding ones. The main reason for this was that as young women entered the labour market for the first time they gravitated towards the expanding occupations. The skewed age structure that resulted from these trends comes across in Table 8: of every 1,000 occupied women in age groups up to 25 a greater proportion worked in metal, electrical, food and clerical occupations than did in the over 25 age groups. The older the women the more they were concentrated in a smaller number of occupations, and particularly in personal service which accounted for over 50 per cent of those aged between 55 and 75.[18]

There were also marked geographical variations in occupational distribution. For instance while metal workers constituted a large proportion of all women in Staffordshire, Worcestershire, and Warwickshire (48 per 1,000) in 1931, textile workers were particularly concentrated in Leicestershire, the West Riding of Yorkshire, and Lancashire (138 per 1,000). Significantly, these counties also had much lower than average proportions of personal service workers.[19]

A further facet of distribution was that as the proportion of all women employed in a particular industry increased, so also did their share of total employment in that industry. For example, as the proportion of all women employed in the engineering trades doubled (from 6 per cent to 12.1 per cent) between 1931 and 1951 so also did the percentage of women as a proportion of all workers in the industry (14.7 per cent to 20.1 per cent) (Joseph 1983: 137). The opposite trend held in industries where women's employment became less concentrated. Thus in those industries in which women were concentrated, they came to comprise a greater proportion of the total workforce.[20]

The effect of industrial concentration was that women worked in highly sex-segregated conditions. In 1931 more than half were in an occupation in which over 80 per cent of the workers were women, and nearly three-quarters in an occupation in which over 50 per cent of the workers were women (Hakim 1979: 25). Even so, occupational statistics mask the true extent of sex segregation because they focus on broad occupational categories, rather than particular jobs. Very few, if any, actual jobs were done by both men and women, and it was extremely rare for them to be allocated exactly the same job within the same workplace (a circumstance that would have raised immediately the questions of equal pay and of women displacing men).

All the evidence indicates that gender segregation was fairly absolute and that jobs were classed either as masculine or feminine. Indeed a government inquiry into the distribution of women in industry conducted in 1929 found no overlap between the jobs done by men and women. The report stressed, however, that while a particular job might be done by women in one factory or town, and by men in another, it was never done by both in the same place. Metal work,

Table 8 Proportion[a] of women occupied at each age period in selected occupations, 1931

Occupation	Total over 14	Ages last birthday												
		14–	16–	18–	21–	25–	30–	35–	45–	55–	60–	65–	70–	75+
VI Metal workers (not electro plate or precious metals)	(17)	21	26	24	22	19	16	10	7	5	4	3	3	4
IX Electrical apparatus makers and fitters	(5)	6	8	8	8	6	4	2	1	0	0	0	0	0
XII Textile workers	(102)	67	77	86	101	124	145	132	101	82	70	49	33	22
XIII Makers of textile goods and articles of dress	(97)	141	107	97	97	93	99	96	83	79	79	80	76	64
XIV Makers of foods, drinks and tobacco	(13)	17	16	16	15	14	12	10	10	8	7	8	7	8
XXVII Personal service	(345)	291	314	319	306	281	301	362	444	507	551	566	547	490
850 Domestic servants	(238)	233	257	252	233	206	206	225	251	277	299	306	274	224
874 Charwomen and office cleaners	(25)	2	2	3	5	10	25	47	71	84	88	78	53	32
XXVIII Clerks, typists, etc	(103)	69	122	141	132	147	124	78	41	22	14	9	6	6
XXIX 894–9 Packers, wrappers, labellers and ticketers	(20)	49	39	30	24	19	13	8	5	3	3	2	1	1

Source: Census of Population 1931, Occupation Tables: 672
Note:
a Proportion per 1,000 total occupied at each age period

for example, was considered too heavy for women in Birmingham but was done by women in the Black Country, and whereas in a certain factory all polishing would be done by men, in the neighbouring one some or all would be done by women (Cmd 3508 1930: 13–14). Similarly, in the boot and shoe industry, women worked sole-moulding and heel-compressing machines in Northampton but not in Leicester, and in heel-making factories they often worked machines that were reserved for men in boot factories (Cmd 3508 1930: 19). The authors of the report explained such variations as the result of differences in 'local custom', so failing to realize that far from showing sex segregation to be flexible and limited, these variations in fact demonstrated how rigid it was.[21]

Women in the electrical engineering and food processing industries

It remains now to present the quantitative evidence in support of my argument that women constituted a central part of the manual labour force in many of the new mass-production industries of the inter-war period.[22] There is conclusive evidence of the emergence of a distinctive pattern of female employment in both the electrical engineering and food processing industries. This pattern can be broken down into a number of separate strands: the expansion in absolute terms of the number of women employees; the increasing proportion of women workers relative to men; the younger age structure of the female workforce; the strict occupational segregation by sex and the concentration of women in semi-skilled work.

Electrical engineering

This was one of the fastest growing industries of the inter-war period in terms of employment: in 1907 it accounted for only 5 per cent of all engineering workers, but this had grown to 15.4 per cent by 1924, and to 22.5 per cent by 1935 (Jefferys 1945: 198). Employment rose particularly fast during the 1930s, the number of insured workers increasing from 173,000 in 1924 to 367,000 in 1935 (Pollard 1983: 60). Unemployment was comparatively low, reaching 10 per cent at its highest point (Catterall 1979: 254). By 1938 electrical engineering accounted for 5 per cent of all those employed in manufacturing (double its 1920 share).

The industry contained several distinct sections and growth was particularly rapid in the 'lighter' sections producing electric lamps, batteries, telegraph, telephone and wireless apparatus, valves, electric light accessories, and heating and cooking appliances, rather than in those concerned with electrical machinery, contract and repair work or heavy cables. It was also in the 'lighter' sections that mass-production methods were adopted and that women's employment was concentrated. Employment in these sections grew by 154 per cent between 1923 and 1938, and much of this was accounted for by women.[23] Radio production, for example, expanded by 378 per cent between 1930 and 1935 alone, the work being done on assembly lines and very largely by women (Catterall 1979: 264; H.W. Richardson 1967: 88). The new work processes altered the nature of skills and required more semi-skilled workers. This catergory was wide, including in addition to machine operators and assemblers, universal millers, internal grinders and automatic feeders. All of these jobs were done by women and consequently as the proportion increased, so too did the proportion of women.

Expansion in number

In terms of absolute expansion the number of women employed in electrical engineering in England and Wales rose by 123 per cent between 1921 and 1931 (Catterall 1979: 253), representing an increase to 1.2 per cent (122 per 100,000) of women occupied (Cen.Pop. 1931 Ind.Tab.: 713). In the subsection dealing only with accumulators and batteries, telegraph and telephone apparatus, wireless and other electrical manufactures there was an even more marked increase of 212 per cent (from 13,675 to 42,724), as can be seen from Table 9. This trend was to continue over the next decade, with the number of women classed as 'manual operatives', who accounted for the largest proportion of women staff in the industry, growing by 44 per cent (from 48,300 to 69,500) between 1930 and 1935 alone. (See Table 10.) In 1937 the Ministry of Labour estimated the number of women to be 84,230 out of a total of 192,910 employees in electrical engineering (MOLG September 1938: 340). London experienced far greater increases than the country as a whole (Table 11). Here the number of women employed in electrical cables, wire and electric lamps alone rose by 64.2 per cent, from 13,950 to 22,910, in the seven years to 1930.

Increasing proportion of women

These tables also reveal the second strand in the pattern of women's employment: the increasing proportion of women relative to men. Men's employment in the industry rose by 43 per cent, in comparison with women's 123 per cent, between 1921 and 1931 (Catterall 1979: 253) and by 136 per cent in the suborders shown in Table 9, compared with women's 212 per cent. At the same time women increased their share of total employment from 26.6 per cent to 32.4 per cent.

Table 9 Women and men employed in electrical installations, cables, and apparatus (Census Industry Order VI 5), 1921 and 1931

Census order	Women		Men		Total	
	1921[a]	1931	1921[a]	1931	1921[a]	1931
173 Accumulator and batteries	–	6,908	–	7,293	–	14,201
174 Telegraph and telephone apparatus	–	7,676	–	13,987	–	21,663
175 Wireless apparatus (except valves)	–	9,243	–	14,865	–	24,108
178 Other electrical manufacturers	–	18,897	–	52,816	–	71,713
Total suborders 173, 174, 175, 178	13,675	42,724	37,697	88,961	51,372	131,685
Total Order VI 5	38,652	68,263	127,176	199,961	165,828	268,224

Source: Adapted from *Census of Population* 1931, Industry Tables: 715
Note:
[a] No separate figures available for suborders in 1921

Table 10   Average numbers employed in electrical engineering, 1930 and 1935, by age and sex (in thousands) [a]

	Operatives				Total staff			
	Men		Women		Men		Women	
	Under 18	Total	Under 18	Total	Under 18	Total	Under 18	Total
1930	16.4	103.4	13.5	48.3	18.7	131.5	15.9	60.5
1935	21.6	123.5	17.2	69.5	24.1	161.9	20.5	86.0

Source: Adapted from *Census of Production* 1935, Part II: 219, 221
Note:
[a] Excludes firms employing fewer than ten employees

Again this increase was disproportionately concentrated among manual workers, the number of male operatives increasing by 19.4 per cent between 1930 and 1935 while that of women increased by 43.9 per cent. As a consequence women's share of total employment in that grade rose from 32 per cent to 36 per cent (Table 10).

Taking Greater London alone (Table 11), the proportion of women employees rose from 36 per cent of the total in 1923 to 44 per cent in 1930. During the same period their overall numbers increased by 64.2 per cent compared with only a 17.4 per cent increase for men.

Table 11   Number of insured persons engaged in electric cables, wire, and electric lamps in Greater London, July 1923 and 1930, classified by sex and age

	1923		1930	
	Numbers	% of total	Numbers	% of total
Women	11,470	29.6	18,900	36.2
Girls	2,480	6.4	4,010	7.6
Total	13,950	36.0	22,910	43.8
Men	22,260	57.5	22,550	49.6
Boys	2,530	6.5	3,560	6.6
Total	24,790	64.0	29,110	56.2
Grand total	38,740	100.0	52,020	100.0

Source: Adapted from *New Survey of London* (1930–5), Volume II: 205

Younger age of women

All the available sources also demonstrate the different age structure of the female and male labour force in electrical engineering: while the women were predominantly young, the men were very much more evenly spread throughout the age range. This third dimension can be seen from Table 12 where 71 per cent of women workers were aged under 24, as compared with only 37 per cent of men. In 1935 under 18s accounted for 25 per cent of women operatives, but 17 per cent of men (see Table 10), and in Greater London girls actually outnumbered boys.

In his critique of youth employment, John Gollan quoted Ministry of Labour estimates that more than half of the workers in electrical engineering were under 21. This very high percentage was seen as being due to the effects of industrial 'rationalization' in increasing the demand particularly for girls because their

> suppleness of fingers makes them more suitable than boys for certain occupations.
>
> (Gollan 1937: 237)

In 1937, 64 per cent of women employees in electric cable, apparatus and other such sections of the industry were aged between 14 and 24, as against 45 per cent of men. Both figures are high but the female one is quite extreme (MOLG September 1938: 340).

The scramble for 'little fingers' was especially acute in electrical engineering. The Telephone Manufacturing Company in West Dulwich (south London) employed a loudspeaker van to scour the local streets in an attempt to recruit girl labour, and in Coventry British Thomson Houston (which merged in 1926 with Metropolitan Vickers to become Associated Electrical Industries) was similarly under pressure (Gollan 1937: 80). Many company histories confirm this preference for very young women, making it clear that as far as employers were concerned the younger the girls, the cheaper they were.

Table 12 Age of operatives in electrical manufacture, 1931, by sex[a]

	Total	Age 14–15	16–17	18–20	21–24	25–29	30–34	35–44	over 45
Women	50,049	3,764	7,698	11,628	12,382	7,326	3,334	2,636	1,281
Men	102,435	5,133	8,137	11,624	14,035	16,182	12,509	17,122	17,693

Source: Adapted from *Census of Population* 1931, Industry Tables: 587
Note:
[a] Figures refer to Orders 171–8 only: other electrical manufactures (including cables, telegraph and wireless apparatus, accumulators and batteries)

The association between low wages and young female labour was stressed also in the *New Survey of London*. Many left-wing writers in the mid-1930s (e.g. Hutt, Beauchamp, Greenwood) expressed concern at employers' practice of 'working out' young girls and then sacking them at 18, and at the 'blind alley' and 'non-progressive' conditions of employment in electrical engineering:

> Youth labour has become the basis of the industry and the practice of sacking at 18 when higher rates of wages require to be paid, with the taking on of a new younger and cheaper set of youth labour, is widespread.
>
> (Gollan 1937: 76)

Occupational segregation by gender

Turning now to the final dimension, the occupational level of women in the industry, there is convincing evidence that the overwhelming majority of women were officially classed as semi-skilled or unskilled operatives. Only 1 per cent were managers or own account workers in 1935 (calculated from Cen.Pop. 1931 Ind.Tab.: 587) but women accounted for 35 per cent of all engineering operatives (that is throughout the industry as a whole), a vast increase since 1907 when they had accounted for only 8.5 per cent (Jefferys 1945: 207). According to *Census of Production* figures for 1935, 81 per cent of women were manual operatives, as opposed to administrative, technical or clerical staff, compared with 76 per cent of men. It is safe to assume that while the remaining men were probably technicians or managers, the women were to be found in clerical work. As already shown, the number of women operatives was increasing at a much faster rate than that of men.

Such general data are really more indicative of the particular structure of the labour force in electrical engineering, with its high proportion of operatives relative to other grades, than of the difference between male and female employees. The Census gave a general idea of gender division in the kinds of work performed by women and men. Not only was the range of women's jobs far narrower, and their degree of occupational concentration consequently higher than men's, but also far fewer were officially classed as skilled workers. On the metals side of electrical engineering three occupations accounted for the majority of women workers: metal machining, pressing and stamping, and soldering and brazing. On the electrical side, women were coil winders, instrument makers and assemblers, or inspectors, viewers and testers (Cen.Pop. 1931 Ind.Tab.: 587–8). In contrast to men, very few women were electrical engineers or fitters.

However, although it is clear that the majority of women were manual workers, official statistics did not break down the numbers of men and women by occupation or skill level in any detail, and so mask the concentration of women in semi-skilled work. To locate women's position in the hierarchy of manual work requires other kinds of data that focus more directly on the sexual division of labour. Accounts of particular sections of the industry do provide a more detailed picture and the conclusion to be drawn from industrial surveys, company histories, and the oral testimonies of people who worked in factories like Philips, EMI and Morphy Richards (see Chapters 4 and 5) is that a rigid gender-based division of labour was established in electrical engineering with the adoption of methods of mass production, and that women were concentrated in semi-skilled manual work. Jobs in motor components and domestic appliances as well as in radio, gramophone and telephone manufacture were all sex-typed from the beginning.

Food processing

The pattern of women's employment in electrical engineering was mirrored in other expanding industries such as food processing. Here equivalent calculations reveal a similar absolute growth, increasing proportion relative to men, young age, and concentration in semi-skilled sex-typed work of the female labour force.

In 1931, 173,000 women and 278,000 men were employed in the food industry, representing an increase of one-fifth over the previous decade (Cen.Pop. 1931 Ind.Tab.: 716). The number of women operatives employed expanded further, from 123,000 to 132,000, between 1930 and 1935, and more than a third of them were under 18 (Table 13). The actual number of women was not much lower than that of men, but young women far exceeded young men.

In the expanding and more mechanized sections of the industry more women than men were usually employed, for instance in biscuits where women accounted for 70 per cent of operatives and girls under 18 for 23 per cent.[24] The volume of biscuit production doubled during the inter-war period and overall employment rose by 58 per cent (Rostas 1948a: 130). A handful of firms like Jacobs, Peek Frean, Huntley and Palmer, Crawford, and McVitie controlled the industry and concentrated their production in very large manufacturing units. Since over half of the total workforce was employed in just 8 firms of over 1,500 employees (Cen.Prod. 1935 Pt.III: 56), women biscuit makers became very heavily concentrated in large factories.[25]

Both Peek Frean and the Co-operative Wholesale Society (CWS) automated their biscuit plants in the early 1930s by introducing continuous production processes and conveyor belts, thereby increasing their volume of production and profits (Corley 1972: 222; Redfern 1938: 347). The declining market position of Huntley and Palmer relative to the others was directly linked with their failure to automate. However, in both instances where mechanization was undertaken and where it was not, more women were taken on: in the more modern establishments in order to cope with the enlarged scale of production, and as a cost-cutting exercise by Huntley and Palmer which attempted to replace men by women.[26]

The use of younger women became more pronounced during the 1930s: of the (nearly) 36,000 girls under 16 in food, drink and tobacco in 1936, as many as a third were employed in biscuits, bread and cake. The *South Wales Industrial Survey* noted that wherever repetition work, conveyor belts and machine minding were introduced in the baking industry, boys were replaced by girls (Ministry of Labour quoted by Gollan 1937: 100). In overall geographical terms, though, 40 per cent of employment in the biscuit industry was concentrated in London, where women also outnumbered men (NSOL 1930–5 vol.V: 48).

Traditionally the sexual division of labour in biscuit production was for men to mix dough (skilled work) and to tend ovens (unskilled) while women stamped out biscuits, took them to be baked and decorated them (NSOL 1930–5 vol.V: 48–9). However, when continuous processes were introduced men's work tended to be displaced by machine but at the same time women's increased because of the expansion of repetitive machine operating tasks. The number and proportion of women workers therefore underwent considerable growth but they remained at the same occupational level throughout, in semi-skilled and unskilled manual jobs.[27]

In certain other sections of the food processing industry where women had always outnumbered men, their traditional over-representation was reinforced as a result of technological change.

Table 13 Operatives in the food trade, 1930 and 1935, by sex and age (in thousands)[a]

| | Women | | Men | |
	Under 18	Total	Under 18	Total
1930	37.4	123.7	12.6	143.3
1935	41.8	132.0	14.8	167.1

Source: Census of Production 1935, Part III: 14
Note:
[a] Figures refer to firms employing more than ten persons

According to the 1931 Census, 13,204 women (and 12,192 men) were occupied in jam making and fruit preserving (Cen.Pop. 1931 Ind.Tab.: 716) but this was probably a large underestimate since much seasonal work was also done by temporary women workers. Robertsons jam factory in Lewisham, for example, employed 700 on a permanent basis, but took on an extra 600 temporary workers, married ex-workers in the main, during the season (J. Ryan 1981: 43). However, with the introduction of food canning, one of the most significant developments in the food industry of the inter-war period, women's employment increased. In preserved foods women were employed in a ratio to men of 5:3 and total employment grew by 7,000 to 52,000 between 1930 and 1935 (Cen. Prod. 1935 pt.III: 12), with an extra 15,000 women being taken on seasonally 'to do semi-skilled work' (Plummer 1937: 244). As elsewhere, women here too accounted for the vast majority (70 per cent) of all operatives in preserved foods, 19 per cent were under 19, and young women vastly outnumbered young men, by 7,589 to 833.[28]

Conclusion

Thus we see the same processes at work in the food processing industry as in electrical engineering. The introduction of continuous process or automatic methods of mass production led to an expansion of semi-skilled work. In both cases employers looked to women, and especially to young women, to fill these newly created jobs. The same picture was repeated in many other of the new industries such as rayon and other synthetic fibres, motor components and ready-made clothing.

Despite the patchy nature of the statistics, analysis of the empirical data does substantiate the claim that there was a connection between the introduction of mechanized production processes and the use of women as semi-skilled labour during the inter-war years. Far from being marginal to industry, women were integral to the new wealth producing industries, drawn in to fill the expanded layer of semi-skilled positions on an ever larger scale. Not only did the new division of labour place women in a central position in the manual workforce but in addition the shift to consumer goods industries as the main centres of capital accumulation made women's labour central to that accumulation. In this way the restructuring of capital and of industry made women into a numerous and prominent section of the industrial workforce which occupied a key position at the point of production. The converse is also true: the recovery of British industry from the recession of the 1920s and 1930s, and the success of the new 'primary' sector, relied on the labour of the hundreds of thousands of women who had been actively recruited into these industries. Whichever way it is approached, a new and specific relation emerged between female labour and the new sources of capital accumulation.

The validity of this argument does not require that women outnumbered men in the industries in question, but only that certain central positions in the division of labour were filled by women, and that women workers were allocated a determinate place and role in the production process. Nor does the argument require that women were employed in all of the growth industries. Rather the important point was that a close link was established between the employment of women and a particular type of production process (continuous flow or assembly line) manufacturing particular kinds of goods (primarily consumer goods intended for personal household consumption).[29]

It is impossible to calculate precisely the number of women assembly-line workers, probably around half to three-quarters of a million out of a total working population of 5.5 to 6 million. But however small the numbers, their significance resides not in their numerical size but in what they represented as a new sector of employment for women entailing quite distinctive relations of production. They were a model of new work methods in manufacturing industry, which were later emulated by employers in clerical and retail work as well. The growth of this sector was well established before the outbreak of the Second World War and in the post-war years it was consolidated with the further expansion of mass consumer industries.

Chapter three

The restructuring of industrial capitalism

Changes in the industrial distribution of women workers during the inter-war years were inextricably linked with the restructuring of the economy and the emergence of new industries. These new industries differed in such a fundamental way from the older traditional ones that the two really represented different phases of the development and organisation of capital. The aim of this chapter is to highlight the main features of industrial reorganization of the period.

Decline of nineteenth-century heavy industry

Coal mining, iron and steel, shipbuilding, textiles and mechanical engineering – the staples of the industrial revolution – were the pre-eminent industries in Britain until the First World War. Most were oriented to capital goods manufacture and all depended on export for continued success. They exported both to other industrial nations and, importantly, to the colonies. Indeed much of their wealth was predicated on British colonialism, particularly in Africa and the Indian subcontinent, either through direct sale to government agencies or firms, or by the knock-on effect at home which boosted the need for coal, as a source of power, and merchant ships as a means of transport.

What happened to these industries during the first part of the twentieth century can be understood only against the development of international capital. This process, which had been of growing importance since the late nineteenth century, had the effect of weakening the position of Britain as the dominant imperialist power. This was the basic reason underlying the demise of the staple industries: they were already well in decline by the time of the world recessions in the inter-war period, having been superseded by other national capitals as well as by international capital. That they were worse affected by the depression than other sectors of industry only reflects their prior loss of competitive position – they were much less able to withstand the cycle of slumps and booms.

The acute phase of decline affecting the staple industries during the inter-war years was precipitated by rapid contraction of the foreign markets on which their exports depended. After this they never again managed to recover their previous dominance either at home or abroad. Countries to which they had exported became self-sufficient or imposed tariffs on foreign goods. India, for example, established its own cotton goods industry and this dramatically reduced the demand for textiles from Lancashire. Moreover, as world demand was generally shifting towards consumer products, the goods on which these industries had concentrated were no longer sectors of international growth (Pollard 1983: 75).

However, even where their goods were still in demand, British firms failed to match up with their more technically advanced American, German and other rivals. British staple industries were antiquated by contrast, in many cases still using nineteenth-century plant in the 1930s, ignoring that the situation on which their early dominance was based had ceased to exist, but unable to adapt to the new circumstances. For decades they had failed to adopt new methods of production, even though other more recent British industries had taken advantage of new technology (Saul 1960).

They also lagged behind foreign competitors in organizational structure. Many companies were small and still run by the family which had originally founded them. In this they contrasted sharply with large corporations, complete with their teams of trained specialists and hierarchies of managers, which were characteristic both of other countries and of the newer industries. From the 1920s mergers were undertaken in the staple industries, but these were usually defensive (to safeguard family control) and amounted to little more than traditional arch-rivals combining in the face of a dwindling market. They were rarely accompanied by changes in organizational structure which might have enabled the company to benefit from pooling resources, economies of scale, or greater administrative efficiency. In the majority of such mergers both management practices and the organization of production remained exactly as before (Chandler 1980: 404).

The Lancashire textile industry exemplified many of these problems. It was traditionally based on many family-owned firms, each specializing in one part of the process or a particular fabric, and in competition with each other. The 'half-time system' of employing school-age girls (who spent half the day at school and half in the mill) remained in existence until the 1920s. Spinning and weaving methods were virtually unchanged since the nineteenth century and the industry had not kept up with modern technology introduced elsewhere. In the 1930s a large proportion of textile plant in America and Japan was already automatic or mechanized: mule spinning and hand looms, still dominant in Lancashire, had been replaced by the more modern ring spinning and by automatic weaving machines (Pagnamenta and Overy 1984).

Failure to re-equip was thus a basic cause of decline but the high export level of cotton goods to the colonies had given a false sense of security. The dominance of Britain in textiles was already on the wane when Indian nationalist politicians demanded a home cotton spinning industry as part of their campaign for independence from Britain. Lancashire industrialists and trades unionists, like Alice Foley,[1] tried – to no avail – to persuade Ghandi of the serious unemployment being created by this action. The emerging Indian industry even used equipment from mills in Lancashire that had gone out of business.

By the time British textile manufacturers finally realized the need for change it was too late. Eight hundred mills were closed down during the 1930s and hundreds of thousands of women lost their jobs (Beauchamp 1937: 14; Pagnamenta and Overy 1984). The extent of decay and depression in Lancashire caused by the collapse of the textile industry comes through clearly in J.B. Priestley's account of his journey there in the early 1930s:

> You cannot, in fact, keep away from it up there ... There is no escape. The whole district had been tied to prosperity, to its very existence, with threads of cotton; and you could hear them snapping all the time ... That very day a mill, a fine big building that had cost a hundred thousand pounds or so not twenty years ago, was put up for auction, with no reserve: there was not a single bid. There hardly ever is. You can have a mill rent-free up there if you are prepared to work it.
>
> (Priestley 1981: 256–7)

Since they had lost their export markets, economic recovery for the staple industries had to depend on expansion of the domestic market. Revival was slow, partial and made no independent contribution to general industrial recovery from the depression (H.W. Richardson 1967: 78–9). Extensive state involvement to shore up these industries was a very noticeable feature of their recovery. The government intervened with many legislative and financial measures intended to secure structural reorganization, since this was viewed as the essential precondition for renewed profitability. Government policy was in favour of amalgamations, mergers and cartelization, vertical integration of the various parts of the industries, their concentration into larger co-operating combines (and the closure of small or loss-making plants), and the introduction of output quotas, minimum prices and wages.

In iron and steel for example import tariffs were imposed on the understanding that reorganization would follow (Pollard 1983: 70). Large quasi-monopolies were established and many steelworks were closed during the 1930s (Mowat 1955: 425). The British Iron and Steel Federation centralized both purchasing and selling, and iron manufacturers bought up coal mines so as to control supply of their raw materials (Compton and Bott 1940: 69). Such attempts at 'rationalization' resulted in the doubling of per capita output, with consequent further loss of jobs. But even with these measures the industry remained very weak until stimulated by the rearmament boom before the Second World War (Pollard 1983: 69–70).

State intervention was greatest in the coal industry. Here too production quotas were imposed and legislation was introduced for compulsory cartelization. Neighbouring collieries were encouraged to amalgamate, sales quotas were allocated between districts, and coal royalties were nationalized. Productivity increased in this industry too and after 1925 unemployment was seldom less than 20 per cent. The coal owners, fearing complete nationalization was the next step, resisted demands for large scale mergers and increased concentration of production, and opposed labour laws which halved the hours per shift to seven and a half (Mowat 1955: 447–8).

Similar measures adopted in the cotton, heavy engineering and shipbuilding industries to rationalize and achieve larger scale units also met with limited success (Buxton and Aldcroft 1979: 21). The effects on the workforce of attempts to revive the industries were almost as disastrous as the original decline, since factory closure and redundancy were integral to state policy. In previous depressions firms had often kept running but at a reduced level of output. Now, at government insistence, a large proportion were closed down altogether in order that the rest might operate at a profit. As a result, many towns lost their only industry overnight with nothing to replace it (Branson and Heinemann 1973: 57–9).

Because the traditional industries had been so geographically concentrated, the unemployment and devastation that followed their decline was also geographically concentrated. Lancashire depended on the textile industry, and the North East on shipbuilding. The south Wales valleys were worst affected by the closure of coal mines. Heavy engineering was more widely dispersed through the Midlands and North, but many towns still suffered very high rates of unemployment as a result of factory shutdowns.

Where the economy of a whole region had relied almost entirely on a narrow range of traditional industries the situation was particularly dire. Scotland, for example, had a heavy commitment to shipbuilding and other industries that were now stagnating, and levels of unemployment there were even higher than in England or Wales. The gap widened during the 1930s as Scottish industries experienced a more rapid run-down than elsewhere. Emphasis on traditional sectors had meant a corresponding neglect of new developments, and Scotland did not manage to secure a share in the new growth industries of the 1930s, especially in those based on local consumer demand, since income levels were so low. Directly state sponsored or controlled attempts at rationalizing and streamlining capacity were nowhere more evident than in Scotland (Buxton 1980: 552).

By the inter-war period the more advanced sections of British capital had already turned away from the traditional staples and invested instead in other more profitable sectors of industry at home or abroad. A major change in the overall reorganization of British capital was its shift away from heavy industry destined for export and towards the production of consumption goods for the home market. The solution to financial crisis in the old industries was to follow suit.

Closure of shipyards, coal mines, textile mills and engineering factories, the scrapping of obsolete plant and 'shedding' of labour no longer required, were necessary components of attempts to revive capital. The creation of industrial wastelands, 'distressed areas' and mass unemployment was an inevitable by-product of 'rationalization' but the state neither acknowledged responsibility for this nor included any measures to deal with it as part of the revival strategy, until the belated Special Areas Act of 1934. In this way, state policy sided with capital in its attempt to revitalize industry, and against labour. One effect of economic development was thus to sharpen the contradiction between capital and labour: while capital was transferred elsewhere in the attempt to preserve it, those employed in the doomed industries were just discarded and provided with no alternative means of livelihood.

Many of the 'revival' measures adopted by the traditional staples – larger scale entreprises, control of prices and markets, cartelization and monopolization – were features shared with the new industries. However, it is important to recognize that such measures were imposed on the old industries from the outside and were undertaken as a last ditch stand, whereas they were characteristic of the new industries from the outset and integral to their internal structure. With their different organizational forms, the two types of industry represented earlier and later stages of the development of capital, and state intervention was necessary to impose the structures of the more advanced industries on the older ones.

The emergence of new industries

To focus on restructuring and on the new developments means isolating one aspect of a total picture from the other tendencies with which it coexisted at the time. It also involves looking at the early stages of a process which was fully consolidated only considerably later. By the end of the 1950s the reorganization of capital and industry was complete and what had been only one tendency, though of steadily increasing significance, before the Second World War, was now the dominant pattern.

Five main changes were central to the restructuring of industry: new forms of industrial organization, new range of products, new processes of production, new type of workforce, and a new form of circulation of capital. These changes were linked together and developed concomitantly. Large corporate firms, often holding a monopoly in their field of operation, used technologically advanced methods to mass produce a large range of consumer goods. The new production methods depended less on craftsmen and more on semi-skilled workers to perform repetitive assembly work in large, often purpose-built, factories. The new commodities, from cake mixes and soap flakes to electric irons, radios and motor cars, were destined for personal consumption on the domestic market, rather than for export, and were mostly intended for use in the home. The family in general and women in particular became a new and central market for capital accumulation. Indeed women, as the main purchasers of the new goods, became a prime target of advertising campaigns in magazines and on the radio, which also became much more common at this time. A sixth new feature of industrial restructuring was the geographical relocation of industry from the North of the country to the South East and Midlands, close to the most important centres of consumption.

All the new industries – electrical engineering, the motor car and aircraft industry, chemicals, synthetic fibres, food processing and canning, rubber, glass and paper – really 'took off' during the interwar years. They experienced massive growth in terms of a range of indices: volume of output, productivity, amount of labour employed, profitability. Initial investment was made during the 1920s, when one-third of gross capital formation was directed to five major growth industries (rayon, electricals, motors, chemicals and paper), but their main period of growth was in the 1930s. From then their expansion accelerated by leaps and bounds (Hannah 1983: 108, 140).[2]

The scores of the new industries on these indices were considerably higher than those of the staple industries (Compton and Bott 1940: 35–6; Glynn and Oxborrow 1976: 92–5).[3] By 1937 overall industrial production was 63 per cent above its 1913 level, with these growth sectors compensating for stagnation in the basic industries. Thus while the annual increase in output was 15.7 per cent for artificial silk, 10.2 per cent for electrical goods, and 10.1 per cent for motor cars it was only 1.9 per cent for British industry as a whole (Pollard 1983: 96–7). Electrical engineering and vehicles also both experienced what was described (Compton and Bott 1940: 208) as 'super-normal' expansion in terms of employment, along with the distributive trades, road transport, and gas, water and electricity. Profit levels in artificial silk and vehicles were the first to rise in the early 1930s, but profits were high generally throughout the decade in the aircraft, motor accessories and cycles, electric light and power industries as well.

Some of the new industries manufactured entirely new products such as rayon, aircraft and vacuum cleaners, while others applied mechanized production methods to already existing products such as ready-made clothing and processed food. Many of the new products in turn stimulated the development of others; cars, for example, required thousands of components; the use of rayon in clothing stimulated the development of soap flakes with which to wash the delicate new fabrics; the expansion of food canning vastly increased the production of tin cans.

Such developments depended on applying recent scientific and technical advances such as the internal combustion engine, ball bearings, new alloy metallurgy, welding, and precision control. Most of these had been invented but not used in Britain before the inter-war period and many of the new products were typically based on a combination of two or more of these advances (Sayers 1950). Awareness of the latest techniques being used in similar industries in other countries, especially the USA, and a concern to keep manufacturing methods fully up to date distinguished the newer from the older industries (Saul 1960). Particular attention was paid to emulating American mass-production techniques. Many firms imported American machinery or sent managers to the USA to study production methods. Peek Frean for instance sent a delegation to look at the new auto-band machines being used in biscuit manufacture in the USA (Mikoleit 1986: 56), and Austin used American consultants when the Longbridge factory was set up for the mass production of motor cars (Hannah 1983: 117). Investment in research and development was an important characteristic of all of these industries: industrial expenditure on research reached £6.5 million annually by the late 1930s (Hannah 1983: 120) and many large firms (including ICI, GEC, and British Celanese) established their own research laboratories. That applications for patents came increasingly from firms rather than from individuals was evidence of the growing importance of industrial laboratories in the invention and development of new products.[4]

Production was concentrated in a small number of very large sized plants for the purpose of achieving economies of scale from mass production. The rapid growth of large firms during the 1930s meant that their share of total output was ever increasing. Concentration of labour accompanied concentration of production, and factories in the new industries tended to employ large numbers of workers. Over 40 per cent of the workers in the electrical machinery, motor and cycle manufacturing, artificial silk, sugar and sugar confectionery industries worked in plants employing over 1,000 workers, and by 1935 nearly half the labour force were to be found in firms employing over 500 workers (Pollard 1983: 101).

Factories were distinguished from workshops by the use of power driven machinery and from the early 1920s the number of workshops declined as the proportion of factories increased. Between 1921 and 1931, 20,000 new factories were registered with the Factory Inspectorate, while 52,000 workshops closed down (Branson 1975: 150). Often factories were new and had been purpose built for continuous flow processes such as conveyor belts and assembly lines so as to enable large batch production. Many were located on the outskirts of towns or on one of the specially established trading estates where infrastructural services were already laid on. Being new the factories were able to benefit from electricity from the outset as their main source of power, for machinery as well as for lighting and heating. Electricity was in fact an essential precondition of many of the new production methods as it permitted much more efficient and flexible arrangement of machines and routing of materials than would have been possible with coal or steam (Hannah 1979: 170–4).

The structure of each industry was increasingly in the direction of monopoly or duopoly with the domination of one or two large firms, such as Unilever in soap and margarine, Courtaulds in rayon, Peek Frean and Huntley and Palmer in biscuits, and the 'big three', Austin, Ford and Morris, in motor vehicles. The largest five firms in the food industry in 1930 produced 65.9 per cent of the output of the whole industry, and the largest five in electrical engineering produced 41.7 per cent (Hannah 1983: 127). Mergers and amalgamations were an important part of the industrial organization of the new industries and many enterprises had a corporate structure. Unilever, with its many disparate interests, multidivisional structure and 50,000 employees, was the most spectacular example.

The merger wave of the 1920s was crucial in setting the future pattern for corporate structures. Indeed many of those formed during this period were successful over the long term and remain dominant to the present day.[5] Apart from benefit of economies of scale in terms of administration and production, amalgamations removed competition and enabled firms which had previously been rivals to co-operate and control both prices and markets.[6]

Trade associations, such as the British Electrical and Allied Manufacturers Association for the electrical engineering industry, were also a basic feature of many new industries. Their effect was similar to that of amalgamations in securing market control and price fixing but on an industry wide basis (Compton and Bott 1940: 47). During the 1930s firms came to rely more heavily on such formal cartels or on informal oligopolistic collusion rather than on further amalgamations for this purpose. Additional protection for the developing industries was given by government financial support, especially for technological research, by tariffs and other protectionist economic policies, including import controls.

The scale of the market for the wide range of new goods produced by such firms was also much enlarged: many aimed at a national market for their goods, encompassing the country as a whole rather than the much more localized market characteristic of earlier consumer industries, such as the food industry. This necessitated much more attention to durable packaging, distribution outlets and networks, and complex arrangements for transport by rail or road. Vertical integration was another important feature of the new industries, linked with this extension of the market. This was again particularly evident in the food industry where firms such as Unilever bought up several large grocery chains so as to extend their control over distribution. Canning companies too frequently became involved in agriculture so as to control the supply and reduce the costs of raw materials.

The establishment of corporations and of large plants was accompanied by the introduction of measures to increase the internal efficiency and running of the firm. 'Rationalization' was *the* by-word in the 1920s for a whole range of new business practices in accounting, production, and management which were seen as the modern way forward to business efficiency and success. These included the differentiation of management into separate functional hierarchies (technical development, sales, marketing, personnel), and the establishment of interconnecting departments for these functions, all responsible to a central directing department at the company Head Office.

The use of modern office machinery became standard during the inter-war period. Duplicators, typewriters, accounting machines (such as the Hollerith machine which could process accounts data very rapidly) and other equipment were introduced and used routinely to aid and speed up information processing. The wider use of telephones became normal and facilitated communication both within and between firms.[7]

More precise methods of forward budgeting and standard cost accounting were adopted with the intention of increasing financial efficiency, providing detailed assessments of the costs of alternative plans, and enabling detailed analysis of a company's pattern of expenditure to be made. Accountancy itself became a more specialized and formal profession at this time with its own training, entry qualifications and professional associations (Loft 1986).[8] Accountants generally acquired a more central role in management, often being appointed to key positions on the board of directors of large companies.

The use of 'scientific management' techniques also became common in the new industries as part of the widespread attempt to promote efficiency, eliminate waste, and generally increase management control over all aspects of production. Although their wider application was associated with developments in accountancy (Miller and O'Leary 1987)[9] the ideas on which they were based were integral to the work process of assembly-line production methods (see Chapter 5). Methods of work study, such as the notorious Bedaux system based on Taylorist principles, were widely applied on the shopfloor and, less frequently, in offices. Time and motion men and rate-fixers constituted another of the growing echelons of non-manual workers.

All of the new developments outlined here were characteristic of the new industries and were found in combination probably only in them. Economic historians differ in their definitions of the new industries, and in the weight they attribute to them as *the* source, or a source, of economic recovery. Some argue that there was a distinct group of 'new industries' and that their expansion, based on consumer demand, was the main impetus in recovery from economic recession. Others argue that the term 'new' is used synonymously with 'successful' or 'expanding', and that the definition in terms of newness is therefore tautological. Yet others emphasize that not all products of the expanding industries were new, that the 'new' industries were new in a number of different ways and that in any case, many of the old industries also exhibited some of the features held to characterize the new industries. Therefore, they argue, it is misleading to distinguish between 'old' and 'new' industries as two homogeneous and mutually exclusive groups. While acknowledging that the economic recovery of British industry rested largely on increased domestic consumption, they stress that greater production of consumption goods also stimulated the capital goods sector and because of that it is artificial to single out personal consumption as the main source of revival.[10]

However, few economic historians, whatever their position on these arguments, would deny that the restructuring of capital and of industrial organization were to be found in their most advanced form in the new consumer goods industries, nor that these experienced the largest and fastest rates of economic growth throughout the period. Business historians focus on individual companies rather than on industries as such and so avoid the debates directly. But even so the histories of many of the dominant firms of the inter-war years clearly demonstrate that their fortunes depended on the switch to corporate structure, to a pattern of products similar to that of the dominant firms in the USA and Germany and to large scale mass production (Hannah 1983; Reader 1970; 1975; Wilson 1954).

It is with the new forms and organization of capitalist production and their effects on women workers that I am concerned, rather than the new industries as such, or academic debates about them. So I use 'new industries' as a shorthand to indicate those sectors of British industry whose realization of profit rested on the adoption of mass-production methods and a new type of labour process. In the majority of cases the products of these industries were in fact new (electrical goods) or if not new (processed food) they were intended for a much wider market, and this usually resulted in fundamental changes being made to the product such that it was considerably altered from its earlier state (tinned fruit). In most cases too, mass-production industries were characterized by the organization and structure I have outlined. But my argument does not depend on these structures being specific to mass-production and women-employing industries alone and is not invalidated by the fact that other industries also shared many characteristics with the sectors that I am concentrating on.

From my point of view, the essential feature of the new industries is that they exemplified first and in the fullest form the new structures of capital accumulation which were later to be adopted by all sectors of industry. However, although the new forms of organization and methods of operating departed from previous forms of business practice and so marked an important break with the older sectors of British capital, it is significant that many of the developments were connected with fundamental changes taking place more generally in the economy at that time.

For example, the adoption of new administrative procedures reflected a more general change in the climate of opinion within British business and heightened concern to place economic and industrial organization on a more efficient footing. Faith in rationalization as a cure for the problems of industry in the 1920s was superseded in the 1930s by a commitment to planning as providing *the* route to economic progress. This developed partly out of the earlier talk of rationalization, partly out of the Labour Party's interest in nationalization and was further stimulated by the example of economic planning in the Soviet Union. It was also in harmony with Keynesian economic theory which was at its strongest in the 1930s (Samuel 1986: 25–9; Pollard 1983: 104). Even J.B. Priestley was caught up by the enthusiasm for planning:

> With her trade leaving her, her businesses going bankrupt, her mills silent and vacant, her workpeople by the thousand losing their employment, Lancashire needed a plan, a big plan. She still needs that plan.
>
> (Priestley 1981: 269)

Many public bodies confirmed this faith in planning. The research organization Political and Economic Planning (PEP) was founded in 1931 by an anonymous group of civil servants, businessmen and academics for 'the impartial study of the problems of industry'. Its journal *Planning* and the many pamphlets and reports produced by PEP during the 1930s were devoted to the discussion of how best to solve contemporary problems (Mowat 1955: 462).[11] In addition, government appointed commissions such as the Board of Trade Committee on Trade and Industry (the Balfour Committee),[12] the Management Research Group (an association of managers and directors of some of the most important firms in the country which met regularly to discuss questions of mutual interest),[13] as well as trade associations established for various product groupings (such as BEAMA and the biscuit industry association) all expressed a belief in science, technology, efficiency and modern methods of administration as the means of economic progress.

The tendency to market monopoly which was a characteristic of the new industries was also a more general feature of the inter-war British economy. Restrictive market practices, in the form of price controls and output quotas, introduced by trade associations became normal throughout the economy and free competition more or less disappeared with the approval of the three main political parties, Conservative, Labour and Liberal, and even of the very traditional weekly journal *The Economist* (Pollard 1983: 105–6). The Balfour Committee Report reflected the contemporary belief that rationalization could lead to economic growth only if it enabled firms to switch their resources to high productivity areas of the economy. It expressed the view that this could be better achieved by large consolidated enterprises with a deliberate management strategy, than by long term competition between small firms with capitalists and workers gradually transferring to growth industries as in the traditional free market model (Hannah 1983: 105–7).

Active state intervention in the cartelization of industry during the 1930s was not confined to shoring up the declining heavy industries. In agriculture the government created marketing boards for milk, bacon, potatoes and hops to standardize and control prices and output, and to stimulate production with the aid of subsidies to farmers. The largest scheme was the Milk Marketing Board (established in 1933) which covered the whole country and acted as the intermediary between farmers and milk companies in all contracts for the sale of milk (Mowat 1955: 438).

Official government encouragement was also given to the formation of the giant chemical company ICI in 1926 (Reader 1970; 1975; Hannah 1983: 109) with its interests in drugs, explosives and poison gas. Britain lagged behind Europe in the production of chemicals and the merger of the four firms which came together to form ICI (Nobel Industries, Brunner Mond, British Dyestuffs Corporation and United Alkali Company) was proposed by the government as a solution to the problem and to prevent German penetration of the British market. ICI developed along monopolistic lines. It was the largest manufacturing enterprise in the UK in the 1920s and 1930s and from its formation employed 47,000 people in the UK alone. It owned many foreign factories, sometimes jointly with American firms, both in the British colonies and in other industrial countries. In addition to heavy chemicals and its products of obvious military and strategic importance to the government, ICI's large range of products also included paint, metals, leathercloth, plastics, solvents, dyestuffs, fertilizers and high pressure engineering. Through successful integration into the international cartel system of the 1930s, ICI became synonymous with the British chemical industry as a whole.

Government-sponsored schemes to secure monopoly conditions across a range of industries were only one aspect of the shift from a laissez-faire economic policy to much more thoroughgoing state intervention in the economy that occurred during the inter-war years. This included the nationalization of civil aviation and of London Transport, and the establishment of public corporations to cope with the problems of the administration of large nationally important industries or public utilities which depended on large capital sums and secure market control. The BBC, the Forestry Commission and the Central Electricity Board (CEB) were among the public corporations formed between the wars. They were independent of direct government control but were run by publicly appointed boards and were intended to operate like joint stock companies but with public interest substituting for the profit motive (Pollard 1983: 106).

The CEB had the most far-reaching consequences of all the public corporations. The establishment of a national grid to provide an integrated nationwide supply of electricity for both industrial and domestic use was of momentous significance. The supply of electricity in Britain had been technically backward, particularly in comparison with Germany, and consumption per head was way below other industrial countries in the mid-1920s leading to government concern that the absence of cheap electricity would be an important factor in delaying industrial revival. The CEB was set up in 1926, businessmen were engaged to carry out government policy in this field and the Board was given the right to monopolize all the wholesaling of electricity which had previously been divided amongst hundreds of small, separate and independent undertakings.

The CEB began establishing a national network for electricity supply in the late 1920s, the whole system being connected by means of a national grid of high-tension transmission cables. Small power stations were closed down and 144 large super-stations were built by 1935. The building of the grid provided a significant proportion of the few jobs available for men in the most depressed industrial areas (100,000 at the bottom of the slump) (Pollard 1983: 60). In 1934 the grid was operating in most of the country[14] and by the late 1930s the amount of electricity generated had increased dramatically (from 6,600 million units in 1925 to 26,400 in 1939) (Pollard 1983: 59), its price had dropped, and Britain had caught up both technically and in per capita consumption with Germany (Battersea power station in south London being larger than any German station) (Hannah 1977: 217–19).

In many ways electricity symbolized the new industries and its contribution to industrial infrastructure cannot be overestimated: not only was it the basis of their production methods, but also it freed them from having to be located close to the coalfields of the north and west, as the traditional industries had been. Increasing numbers of houses were wired up each year, in the late 1930s 700,000 to 800,000 a year. Overall the number of houses connected rose from half a million in 1919 to 8 million in 1938, representing just under two-thirds of the total housing stock. Electric light was the main incentive for the mass of domestic consumers to install electricity initially, but once electrified, household consumption of electricity increased with the wider use of electric cookers, radios, refrigerators, electric irons, vacuum cleaners and other consumer durables (Hannah 1979: 187–9). Throughout the 1930s consumption of electricity by both domestic and industrial users continued to increase and the conversion from gas to electric street lighting, and of some railway traction added further sources of demand.

With the public supply of electricity and the creation of conditions favourable to the operation of large monopolistic firms, state economic intervention in Britain during the 1920s and 1930s effectively provided the industrial infrastructure necessary for renewed capital accumulation along the lines of the other more advanced capitalist countries. By the end of the inter-war period many firms in the new industries were emulating forms of organization, production methods, and product lines that had already been standard in American companies for several decades.

The American influence was strong in another way too: many British plants were under direct American ownership, including Fords, Boots, Associated Electrical Industries and International Nickel, four of the largest fifty companies in 1930 (Hannah 1983: 116). By 1936, 224 American companies were operating in Britain, General Motors had acquired Vauxhall, and Proctor and Gamble had acquired Hedley. American canning firms established subsidiaries in Britain, the most notable being Heinz which had a huge purpose-built factory in west London for the mass production of canned food. Hoover was Canadian owned.

Large British firms dominant in their field of the new industries also expanded overseas and established subsidiaries in Europe and North America, rather than just within the confines of the British Empire as had been the case with the old staple industries. The Gramophone Company, for instance, owned fifty factories in nineteen countries (G. Jones 1985; Catterall 1979). Overseas acquisitions and operations were of crucial financial importance and integral to the overall corporate strategy of Unilever, ICI, Courtaulds, Cadbury and EMI (Hannah 1983: 118–20). Internationalization of capital investment and accumulation was thus another important feature of the dominant firms in the new industries, and demonstrates the increasing similarity between the more advanced sections of British capital and their American counterparts.

Electrical engineering

Electrical engineering was one of the most important sources of growth in the economy and together with the motor, cycle and aircraft section, it was the fastest growing field in engineering throughout the inter-war period, especially in the 1930s. For the most part it was a genuinely new industry, manufacturing a wide range of new products (including telephones, electricity meters, radios, irons, cookers, radiant fires, water heaters, magnetos) as well as mass producing for the first time other electrical goods that were already in use (batteries, valves, cable, lamps and light bulbs).

In the years immediately following the First World War, the British electrical engineering industry was like a branch factory for American and German companies such as Westinghouse and Siemens. However, with the building of the national grid and the rising use of electricity, the market increased first for the heavy equipment and cable used in installation and large contract work, and later for appliances and consumer durables. British companies established themselves in both fields, those in the heavy part of the industry being much stronger in the 1920s while those in the lighter sections came into their own in the 1930s.

Output fell after the General Strike in 1926, but after this electrical engineering experienced uninterrupted expansion and was hardly affected by the slump of 1929 to 1932. In 1934 output increased by 23 per cent in comparison with 10 per cent for all manufacturing industries, and over the period 1920 to 1938 output increased at an annual rate of 4.7 per cent (Catterall 1979: 241, 252).[15]

As in the new industries generally, large companies such as AEI, GEC, EMI, Lucas and STC dominated. Many of these were formed as a result of mergers.[16] Already by the early 1930s 30 per cent of capital invested in the industry was controlled by four giant concerns (Plummer 1937: 47). Although the high degree of specialization permitted many small companies to survive, the industry was dominated by the large corporations and by a small number of very large manufacturing units with much higher productivity. Thus, fifteen companies were responsible for 90 per cent of the output of cables, and six for telephone equipment (Plummer 1937: 47–8). In 1930 AEI and GEC were among the top thirty companies in terms of market value (Hannah 1983: 102) and in 1935 they were two of the largest fifteen employers in the country, with workforces of 30,000 and 24,000 respectively (Johnman 1986).

The demand for electric equipment remained high throughout the depression. 'The speed of radio development has been remarkable, even for modern times', wrote Plummer in 1937 (p. 42). From small beginnings, radios and valves were big business by the 1930s. The breakthrough came in the late 1920s when home constructed sets gave way to factory produced models, manufactured by the latest flow assembly methods. Demand was high, both for first time buyers and replacement sets, so that by 1935 1.7 million were being mass produced a year. The number of licences issued rose from 2.4 million in 1927 to 6 million in 1933 and 9 million by 1939, and the value of radio output increased from £8.4 million to £15.5 million between 1930 and 1935 (Catterall 1979: 262–4). Radios, unlike cars, were taken up faster by the poor than the rich. Consumer expenditure more than trebled from £6 million to £20 million between 1930 and 1938 and at the same time employment doubled from 30,000 to 60,000 (H.W. Richardson 1967: 88).

Domestic appliance manufacture was also a phenomenon of the 1930s, when electricity became the nationwide source of domestic power. Expansion was closely linked to the number of homes wired up for electricity: by 1939 77 per cent of those with electricity owned irons, 27 per cent vacuum cleaners, and 18 per cent electric cookers. Hair dryers, washing machines, refrigerators, and water heaters were less common. With the emphasis on large kitchens in the late 1930s, 'pleasant and roomy' enough to allow space for the family and 'a host of appliances' (Corley 1966: 21–2), local councils arranged demonstrations of the benefits of domestic electric equipment and associations, such as the Electrical Association for Women, were set up to instruct 'housewives' in the use of electricity. Electricity showrooms appeared on many high streets and small electrical goods shops sprang up on the new housing estates, many offering hire purchase agreements for the most costly items. Hoover however still relied on its team of door-to-door salesmen and their advertising songs (Weightman and Humphries 1984: 66), but vacuum cleaners were mainly a middle-class purchase since most working-class homes did not yet have carpets.

Foreign firms had dominated until domestic manufacture expanded in the early 1930s. In the 1920s 80 per cent of vacuum cleaners, for example, were imported but by 1935 97 per cent were domestically made (Aldcroft 1970: 198). Growth of the market assisted moves to mass production and concentration, and several existing electrical firms, including EMI, Pressed Steel and English Electric, went into appliance manufacture. Specialist middle-sized firms like Morphy Richards, Belling and Creda led the way in adopting the latest technology to produce electric fires, irons, toasters and hair dryers. Morphy Richards, though formed only in 1936, had gained 20 per cent of the market in irons within three years, relying on bought-out components to produce its 5,000 per week by assembly-line methods (Corley 1966: 35).

The new products of the electrical engineering industry were many and varied, some intended for industrial use or as components for other new products like the motor car, while others were for use in the home. Practically every household owned a radio by the mid-1930s and people were able to be in touch with what was going on in the world at large or the latest popular music, at the turn of a switch in their own front room. Radio was the first real mass media and brought with it an enormous change in people's lives, including the beginnings of private entertainment, consumed individually and separately by each family in its own home – a quite different experience from going out to the cinema and other social entertainment.

The vast majority of houses were wired up with electricity by 1939, giving the benefit of brighter lighting and doing away with gas fumes in working-class homes. Until after the war the purchase of domestic appliances was largely confined to the better off where increasing use went hand in hand with 'the servant problem'. By the mid-1930s maids expected their employers to provide Hoovers, irons, and even washing machines. Adverts for domestic servants often mentioned ownership of electric appliances as an enticement to a position involving only 'light' work. But instead of employing others to do their housework, the tendency now was for middle-class women to purchase the new 'labour-saving' commodities and do the work themselves or with the help of a 'daily' cleaning woman.

The chain linking production and consumption in the domestic economy underwent radical structural change during the inter-war period with, on the one hand, the introduction of housework machinery, growing commoditization of the means of cooking, cleaning, and washing, and, on the other, the widespread employment of women in factories manufacturing these commodities – many of whom might have been domestic servants had factory work not been available.

Food processing

Many sections of this industry were well established long before the inter-war years: grain milling, bread and flour confectionery, sugar and sugar confectionery, biscuits, cocoa and chocolate, jam making and fruit preserving amongst others. Many production units were already large and there was a tradition of employing women in biscuit and chocolate manufacture. Nevertheless the industry was transformed in structure and organization during the inter-war years. Its scale of production expanded with mechanization and mass production and it became structurally integrated with both raw materials production and with retail distribution. The mass consumption of factory produced food was a new feature of the period which depended on mass production of processed food and an associated revolution in food retailing. As technical problems of perishability and transport were solved, a continually wider range of goods was produced. Automatic machinery was introduced into the making of biscuits, preserves and jam. Flour milling and the production of ready-made mixes expanded, and canning emerged as an important and entirely new section of the industry.

The main product change was the appearance of far more ready-made, processed and convenience foods needing minimal preparation at home. Tinned vegetables, soup and fruit are an obvious example. But packets of powdered custard, jelly, blancmange and cake mixes which required only the addition of milk, water or an egg also came to be widely used. Quick Quaker Oats took only two minutes to prepare and, along with puffed wheat, shredded wheat and cornflakes which needed no cooking, supplanted the traditional Scotch oats as the conventional middle-class breakfast. Snack foods also came into their own with the help of considerable advertising: over a million packets of potato crisps were sold in 1928 and the variety of chocolate bars was wide and continually changing (Burnett 1979: 292). Bread and biscuits were increasingly factory rather than home made.

A second new development was that most of these factory processed foods were branded goods each with their own name, design and distinctive packaging – the idea being that consumers would become loyal to particular brands (and to the companies which manufactured them), again with the help of advertising, free gift schemes and other gimmicks. A third concomitant change was that factory produced food was now ready for purchase and use without the need for additional preparation on the part of the retailer. Branded foods left the factory in consumer-size packages, already weighed, standardized, labelled, and often priced. This change was of enormous significance for retailing, removing many functions of the traditional small shopkeeper who had previously bought in bulk and done the weighing and packing of staple foods like tea, butter, salt and flour for each customer individually. Pre-packaged food was especially suitable for selling in the new multiple chain groceries and other large food stores that emerged at this time, where the customer received less individual attention, shopping was quicker, and the turnover of goods much greater.

Mass production of food required a change in the system of distribution, a need answered by the emergence of multiple shops. Prices were often lower in these mass market operations than in the small corner shop, since they were able to have lower profit margins by relying on much faster turnover. Many multiples too were structurally integrated with food manufacturers by direct ownership.[17] An increasing proportion of food sales was through such stores and the Co-operative Wholesale Society, as opposed to the small corner shop.[18] Most employees in the new retail outlets were women and, as shown in Chapter 2, shop work expanded enormously as a form of employment for women during the inter-war years. But the new 'women's' jobs were less skilled, in terms of formal training or apprenticeship, than those of the traditional shopkeeper or sales assistant had been.

The food industry was probably less geographically concentrated in the Midlands and South East than other new industries, although most factories were to be found in the large conurbations of London, Birmingham, Manchester and Liverpool. In other respects, however, its structure conformed to that of the new industries. A process of mergers and 'rationalization' resulted in much greater concentration and in the consolidation of a small number of very large companies which dominated their market.[19] Their manufacture was concentrated in a small number of large plants so that employment in the expanding sectors of the industry became much more highly concentrated. Indeed five food companies were among the largest manufacturing employers in 1935: Unilever employed 60,000, CWS 36,381, Imperial Tobacco 30,000, Cadbury-Fry 11,685, and Scottish CWS 8,000 (Johnman 1986).

Direct American influence was probably greater in food processing than in any other new industry. Moves towards mechanization deliberately copied the American model: Peek Frean used American machinery, and the expansion of Lyons' vast Cadby Hall site in Hammersmith drew heavily on American ideas for continuous flow production of cakes and ice-cream (H.W. Richardson 1976: 170). Heinz was not the only American company to set up a manufacturing plant in Britain: Quaker, Shredded Wheat and Kelloggs all built factories and gained virtual control of the new breakfast cereals market (Collins 1976: 33–6).

Canning was *the* major new industry in food production of the inter-war period. Its success rested on large resources being invested in research into the perishability in foodstuffs, the selection of suitable crops for canning and the correct stage for harvesting. It 'took off' in the late 1920s, and expanded rapidly. Even between 1924 and 1930 there was a ten-fold increase in the volume of production (Plummer 1937: 243). The number of canning factories rose quickly, fruit and vegetable ones alone increasing from twenty-seven to seventy-four between 1927 and 1933 (Johnston 1976: 174).

Canneries 'were planned and equipped on the most up to date American lines' (Plummer 1937: 233) and the industry was mechanized from the outset. Efficient organization was vital as canning had to be done at exactly the right time and temperature, and the season for most crops was short. (Milk for example was delivered, canned and sealed within a day.) The need for bulk supplies of standarized size and quality encouraged canning companies to purchase from large farms (on whom they could impose standards) rather than small growers. Contract growing by farms for canneries became common and was a further boost to large scale commercial farming. Indeed, many of the larger canning firms, like Chivers near Cambridge, bought up farms to secure complete control over their supply of crops (Plummer 1937: 228–37).

Clearly the food industry was quite transformed during the inter-war years. Not only did the scale of manufacture mushroom, with the creation of a mass market, but also the industry became much more structurally integrated both with agriculture and retail. Manufacturers produced for mass consumption and a national market, and attempted to secure control over their distribution outlets. Wholesalers were knocked out as manufacturers moved directly into retail themselves.

At the same time, commercial catering expanded with Lyons Corner Houses, and milk and bun shops springing up in town centres. Most branches of Woolworths and Marks and Spencer introduced self-service canteens for customers. It was no longer the custom for workers to go home at lunch-time: often they lived too far away and would have spent the whole hour in travel. Instead they ate at one of these local catering establishments. Factories and offices also started to provide canteens for their staff, and the school meals service was also expanded in the wake of concern about children's inadequate diet. They too tended no longer to go home at midday. Such developments in catering relied on mass produced food and acted as a further stimulus to the food processing industry. As eating out became increasingly common, with the opening of 'popular' and municipal restaurants and milk bars, commercial catering constituted an important new and large outlet for the food processing industry in addition to private households (Mikoleit 1986: 25–6).

Towards the end of the period the price of food had gone down and the national diet had changed. People generally ate more food, more varied food and more processed food. The amount of time spent on food preparation within the home was reduced and shopping was transformed. Unlike other products of the new industries, processed food was within the reach of better-off working-class families, although the class variation in food consumption patterns was still enormous.[20] Tinned milk and jam became standard purchases even for the poor, tinned milk being cheaper than fresh, and jam being used to make bread, still their staple food, more palatable (Burnett 1979: 312). In her autobiography of childhood in an extremely poor miner's family in the Forest of Dean in Gloucestershire, Winifred Foley (1974) vividly recalls her pleasure at licking out the last drops from her great-aunt's tin of milk. This was one of the few luxuries for the old lady, and a treat for Polly (as Winifred was known) and her little brothers and sisters to be looked forward to eagerly every week! Jam was an even greater and rarer treat for the Foley family.

These changes in the food industry were of tremendous significance for women and for the household economy. Quite apart from the enormous expansion of employment for women in retail and catering as well as in production, the preparation of food within the home was transformed. The mass production of processed food meant that much of this task was removed from the home and done at an earlier stage in the chain of production and consumption, with the result that a greater proportion of bought food was already almost table ready. The availability of ready-made food was of particular importance for those middle-class households that had previously depended on domestic servants to make their food and cook their meals, and the development of the industry as a whole should be viewed in the context of the expansion of the managerial and professional sections of the middle class that could not get or afford servants.

In broader structural terms, the emergence of commercial factory-made mass produced food represents the commoditization of one of the most important aspects of the reproduction of labour power and its partial removal from the domestic economy. It also represents the socialization of what had previously been done individually in each househould, as, for example, when it became the norm for women to buy bread made on a mass scale under factory conditions rather than each baking it separately themselves either in their own homes or in households where they worked as domestic servants.

Rayon

Rayon or 'artificial silk' was another totally new industry which experienced phenomenal growth in the inter-war period in terms of output, productivity and employment. It was the first synthetic fibre to be commercially produced and led to what many historians have described as a revolution in both fashion and the clothing industry. Between 1919 and 1939 the output of rayon yarn rose from 5.5 to 111.0 million pounds (weight) plus 59 million pounds of staple fibre. Fixed capital formation in the industry in 1939 was 213 per cent of the 1920 level (Harrop 1979: 290) and employment (including manufacture and weaving) had risen to 100,000 of whom the majority were women.[21] Between 1921 and 1931 the number of artificial silk spinners alone increased by 418 per cent, by far the largest increase for any industry (Cen. Pop. 1931 Ind.Tab.: 613,716). And as demand for rayon continued to rise the scope for intensive production led to the introduction of a three-shift 24-hour continuous process system.

Rayon was 'essentially an industry of large units and extensive combines' (Plummer 1937: 219). Courtaulds, the old established Essex silk throwing firm, and British Celanese were the dominant firms, with issued capital of £32 million and £13.5 million respectively in 1939 (Pollard 1983: 62). Both were vertically integrated, backwards to chemical production, and forwards to making cloth in their own weaving and knitting factories.

The average size of manufacturing plants was 1,800 operatives (Rostas 1948b: 154), and nearly half the work force was employed in eleven firms with over 1,500 workers each (Cen.Prod. 1935 Pt I: 101). Factories were also newly built. Courtaulds deliberately chose Coventry as the site for one of its new factories: the traditional silk industry there had declined and unemployed women who had been silk workers would be available. British Celanese chose a site near Derby for similar reasons (Harrop 1979: 291–2).

The introduction of rayon was said to have revealed an insatiable demand for clothing by women who 'consumed' 77 per cent of all rayon (Plummer 1937: 208; Harrop 1979: 284). As the adverts said, the material was soft, lustrous and smooth with good 'draping qualities', much cheaper than silk, cotton or wool but not as strong. Stockings were the big breakthrough for rayon – they were cheaper than silk and lighter than cotton or wool – worn with the short skirts of the late 1920s. Rayon fitted well with the general fashion trend to lighter, less formal clothes. Underwear became thinner and briefer as slips replaced heavy petticoats, and the two-way stretch elastic suspender belt replaced the corset.

A growing proportion of women's dresses and blouses in the 1930s were made of rayon and in factories, and sold in chain and department stores. The lower price of mass produced clothing put rayon underwear and dresses within the reach of many working-class women. It was popular also because it was easier to wash than heavier natural fibres. Only soap flakes and water were needed rather than the heavy labour of boiling and mangling traditionally associated with clothes laundering.

Mass produced clothing boosted manufacture and retail, and the employment of women in both, in a manner similar to the food industry. It also took another task out of the domestic economy and turned it into a commodity to be bought and sold. Middle-class women no longer relied so much on dressmakers for their clothes (the number of skilled dressmakers declined with the rise of the factory based clothing industry) and ready-made, easily washed clothes made it easier for them to look after their own clothes without domestic servants to do their mending, sewing and washing. Better off and younger working-class women on the other hand became much less likely to make their own clothes than their mothers, relying instead on the chain stores for ready-made dresses, skirts and blouses.

Motor components

The motor industry in many ways typified the structure and organization of the new industries. It experienced rapid growth in terms of output, productivity and employment, became concentrated in a small number of large concerns (such as Austin, Morris, and Ford, and later Rootes, Standard, and Vauxhall) which shared the market between them, and introduced mass-production methods.

However, one significant feature of the British motor industry was the tendency of firms to manufacture very few of the components themselves, but to rely instead on specialist component manufacturers. A PEP survey in 1938 found that 'bought-out' components accounted for as much as between 63 per cent and 74 per cent of the production costs of a number of motor firms (Church and Miller 1977: 181). This meant that the car plants themselves were basically massive assembly operations (since around 7,000 components went into the final assembly of a vehicle) and represented the final stage in a chain that went back to steel, safety glass, rubber tyres, electrical equipment and a host of other products from a large number of industries.

The structure of the motor component industries was also typical of the new industries with a small number of large firms dominating the market. Lucas, based in Birmingham, produced most of the lighting, charging and starting apparatus, and took over its competitors Rotax and CAV during this period. Triplex was the dominant firm in glass, Dunlop in tyres, Smiths in instruments and clocks, and Lockheed and Girling in brakes (Harrop 1966). Half of the plate glass produced in Britain and two-thirds of the rubber went to car assembly plants (Aldcroft 1970: 187).

Indeed the components industries were often further ahead than the assembly firms, both technically, in their use of mass-production methods, and structurally, in their size and organization. As a result their productivity was also higher: in 1935 output per operative in components manufacture was almost half of the American level, compared with about one-fifth in assembly (PEP *Engineering Reports* ii, Motor Vehicles, 1950: 133). The moving conveyor belt was standard at both Lucas and Smiths long before the use of a moving track became widespread in final assembly. Dunlop employed 28,000 and Lucas 20,000 in 1935 while the largest assembly firm, Austin, employed 19,000 in the same year (Johnman 1986).

Although final assembly was largely 'men's work', apart from the trim where women were employed, many of the components and accessories manufacturers, particularly on the electrical side, relied on women as the bulk of their manual workforce. In this way, women constituted a significant portion of the motor vehicle production industry taken as a whole, and were concentrated in its most advanced sections – despite the fact that most discussion of the industry and of the new working conditions that it pioneered assumes or implies that the workforce was totally male. This predominance of women in components manufacture is a very important point to which I shall return.

During the inter-war years the retail price of a new car halved from £259 in 1924 to £130 in 1935 (Aldcroft 1970: 183–4), and the proportion of people who owned a car increased from one in forty-four to one in twenty-four, about one family out of six; 1.8 million cars were registered by 1937 (Mowat 1955: 454; Branson and Heinemann 1973: 262–8). Paradoxically, car sales rose rather than fell during the Depression, indicating the relative prosperity of the sort of people who bought cars.

Conclusion

In this account of the new industries, I have focused on those of particular significance for women both as producers and consumers. In addition to those singled out, the aircraft, rubber, chemicals, aluminium, glass, paper and printing industries all underwent technical development and expansion in the inter-war period. Women were employed in some sections of all these too.

All of these new industries depended on the home rather than export market. Most were sheltered from foreign competition by tariffs, and depended on state support and a high degree of scientific research. In structure they tended to be dominated by a small number of large firms, with international connections, operating as a cartel, whose production units were very large and brought together thousands of workers in one workplace. Most were located close to their main markets, to the north and west of London, the South East and the Midlands. Geographical concentration and the wholesale relocation of industry from the North and West to the South and East, and to the largest conurbations, was a fundamental feature of the new industries, causing enormous regional variations in employment and prosperity.

Use of the different products had different effects and it is important to recognize the structural impact of each. Although most were purchased for household use they affected the domestic economy and women's work within it in a number of different ways, as I have tried to indicate. For example, mass produced ready-made food and clothing did away with a certain amount of domestic labour for those who could afford them, and brought a new range of commercial commodities into the domestic economy for the first time. When women had prepared food or made clothes on an unpaid basis in their own home or on a paid basis as domestic servants, neither their labour nor the products of it had impinged at all on the sphere of commodity production. By contrast the production of these goods on a capitalist commodity basis did impinge on the domestic economy: their purchase by women for consumption in the home inaugurated a new, much closer and highly structured relation between these two spheres.

The installation of electricity also affected the home but not in the same way: radios brought the outside world into each individual house and electric lighting was more convenient and easier to use than gas. The electrical industries relied on the domestic economy as a major market for their goods but their use was not a substitute for women's labour in the same way as factory made clothing or food. Domestic appliances were a partial exception to this: they aided housework but did not replace it.

Motor cars were bought and used more by men than women. Unlike ready-made food and clothing they had no impact on the reproduction of labour power. Rather they represented the beginnings of mass private and individual ownership of the means of transport. Expansion of the motor industry went hand in hand with the development of road as the major form of transport for both goods and people and the associated shift away from rail and water. Nevertheless the purchase of private cars depended on a high level of wages and on a new connection being established between wages and the purchase of consumer goods. In the long run the desire to own luxury goods such as cars or refrigerators may have operated as a stimulus for married women to enter paid employment, especially in the post-war period.

Road transport also had another significance. Along with radio broadcasting and electricity, roads were provided on a national scale by the state or state-run public bodies, to be used by industry and the population as a whole (or whoever could afford to use them). As such they represented a form of social infrastructure available uniformly throughout the country which everyone could plug into. So there was a further consolidation of the country as a single geographical and economic unit with standardized infrastructural provision.

Chapter four

Five factories

This chapter presents profiles of several factories in the 'new industries' with the intention of giving an idea of their labour process and how it was experienced by women workers in the factory. Peek Frean, EMI, Lyons, Morphy Richard and Hoover were large and well known companies in the electrical engineering or processed foods industries, all engaged in mass producing ready-made branded foods or domestic electric appliances for the mass market. With the partial exception of Hoover, all employed mechanized methods of production and a high proportion of women as factory operatives.

I have selected these particular firms precisely because their names and products are familiar to everyone in Britain but these five examples could be multiplied by many others, equally or less well known. The information is based on a number of sources: interviews with retired women who worked in each factory, also with a few men who worked on the shopfloor, company histories and internal documents, and in the case of Lyons and Morphy Richards (where it was not possible to contact women with experience of the factory) interviews with retired managers. Needless to say, the nature of women's work, the conditions of their employment, and changes in work organization had a quite different meaning and significance for the women who worked on the shopfloor than for the managers, and I have drawn attention to this difference.

Employers' policies in these particular companies, as in others, shared certain common features: deliberate location in a 'green fields' site or where there would be a plentiful supply of female labour with no previous industrial experience, the attempt to keep out trade unions either by making conditions of employment insecure and harsh (Lyons and EMI) or by more paternalistic methods (Peek Frean and Morphy Richards), the adoption of continuous flow methods of production wherever possible and the transition from partial to complete mechanization.

In Peek Frean, EMI, Lyons and Morphy Richards the adoption of continuous flow production was clearly linked with the increasing employment of women. Hoover, however, was in some ways 'the exception that proves the rule' and has been included for that reason. Although vacuum cleaners were a new product and were manufactured in large quantities, there was not a genuine mass market for them until after the Second World War. Production and work methods were in many ways more similar to the traditional metal and engineering industries than to the new electrical industries. The production process was not highly mechanized, its different stages were not integrated or continuous and there was no assembly line. Significantly more men than women were engaged in the production and assembly of Hoovers.

The rigid division of jobs into either 'men's' or 'women's' work in all five cases goes almost without saying, but what happened when new processes were introduced or production methods became more mechanized? One of the main aims of presenting the material in the form of a profile is to be able to outline the actual changes that were introduced into a particular labour process, in a particular factory, and to examine their effects on the division between 'men's' and 'women's' work, the sex-typing of newly created jobs and on the proportion of men and women workers employed. This method also provides a means of focusing on women workers' experience of mechanization and for this reason a certain number of the specific jobs that were done by women have been outlined in some detail. Attention has also been given to the introduction of assembly lines, the moving conveyor belt, the Bedaux system of work study and the effects of these on women workers.

For women, what it was like working in one of these factories included many features apart from the actual work: how you got the job, how much training you received, the pay, what the other women were like, whether they were younger or older, married or single, how strict the discipline was, whether you could work at your own pace or were on a moving conveyor and so on.

On the management side, notions of cheap labour and women's fingers, men's work and women's work, whether married women were more suitable employees or alternatively whether younger women were faster and more malleable, all underlay a firm's recruitment policy. They also affected the way it organized production and allocated jobs between different sections of the workforce, and the technical and sexual divisions of labour it built into the work process. However, management was not much concerned with women's experience of and response to the material outcome of these ideas and policies embodied in the conditions of work encountered by the women in every aspect of their work, every day of their working lives. Managers were even less concerned with what the women thought about the changes in the organization of work.

The questions and issues arising from this examination of individual factories constitute fundamental themes for this study. Here they are introduced in the context of particular cases only, intended to provide a background for the following two chapters where the issues they raise and their implications for the analysis of gender and work will be further discussed.

Peek Frean

The Peek Frean biscuit factory in Bermondsey, south London, was built in a market garden in the 1870s and is still on the same, but now much more built up, site. The original Peek and Frean who founded the firm in 1857 were soon joined by John Carr and the company was basically in the hands of the Carr family from the late nineteenth century until recently.[1] There probably never was a Mrs Peek though the firm produced Christmas puddings named after her.

The firm was one of six quality makers of biscuits and flourished in the early twentieth century with a nationwide distribution of biscuits in its own vans, the introduction of many new product lines, the addition of new buildings and more employees. A film made of the factory in 1906 gives the impression of a massive and carefully co-ordinated operation devoted to biscuit making: from the daily early morning arrival of sacks of flour and sugar and churns of milk, through the various stages of production, to the dispatch of thousands of boxes and crates of biscuit in vans drawn by horses from the factory's own stables, also kept on the site. Nearly 3,000 people worked on the site and more than half were women.

Peek Frean prided itself on being modern and 'the first' to introduce many developments: it was the first factory to introduce electric light, to install telephones, to employ women as clerks and during the inter-war period it was the first to develop an automatic biscuit-making machine when 'ideas of automaticity were in the air' (*Condensed History*: 36). The aim was to make biscuit production as automatic as possible and ultimately to combine all the operations in biscuit making into a single continuous process. The firm kept up with American developments in biscuit technology, sending engineers to the Mid-West to study and order the latest cutting and panning machines.

By 1930 Peek Frean was technically the most advanced biscuit manufacturer, way ahead of its competitors, particularly Huntley and Palmer, and, unlike them, it encountered few problems during the

Depression (Corley 1972). It had the benefit of mechanized production, the Bedaux time and motion system and a disciplined and un-unionized workforce of 4,000. Production was more or less completely mechanized apart from creaming, jamming and packing. A new building 'of modern cantilevered construction' was purpose built in 1937 for the new layout appropriate to continuous production (*Condensed History*: 50–1). A new 'Meltis' factory for chocolate and confectionery was built in Bedford and many more were established in British colonies including Canada, Australia and three in India (*1857–1957*: 13).

Many new lines of biscuits were introduced during the inter-war years from Lemon Puff Cream, Araby Sandwich, Blackcurrant Waffle, and Barmouth Cream to the more sophisticated but less exotic sounding Cheeselets, Savourettes and Twiglets 'for the cocktail age' as well as Vita-Wheat, promoted as a health biscuit. Indeed 350 lines were being produced in 1939 and the company had managed to survive competition from the 'cheap' biscuit manufacturers by introducing some cheaper lines of its own (*1857–1957*: 10). However the emphasis still remained on the more expensive 'quality' biscuit made with real butter, milk and chocolate in hygienic surroundings. The company also kept up with latest developments in office technology and accounting methods, introducing a new accounts system in 1927, a mechanized ledger in 1931 and reorganizing all its offices in 1938 (*Historical Survey*: 13, 57, 98).

At the same time it prided itself on its welfare provisions for employees also introduced during the 1920s and 1930s: a doctor, dentist and optician were available on the site, a week's paid holiday for all employees was introduced in 1919 and a pension scheme in 1929. There was a large sports ground and games room, dances and socials were organized, and the house journal, *The Biscuit Box* was distributed to all workers with the idea of keeping them in touch with all developments in the factory as well as social events. (It also gave handy tips, such as how to remove egg stain from spoons!) In 1937 Peek Frean was one of the first factories to introduce 'Music While You Work' (piped record music) on the shopfloor. Rates of pay were kept above the legal minimum for the biscuit industry and in 1936 the working week was cut from forty-eight to forty-six and a half hours. Some of these facilities were quite unusual at the time, particularly the paid holiday and the shorter working week, though the reason for the dentist will become apparent. The company boasted of the many employees with a long service record and thousands of visitors were shown round the shopfloor every year to show off the model conditions.

Possibly as a result of these provisions there was little trade union activity in Peek Frean during the inter-war years, management nego-

tiating instead with the Works Committee it had established express-
ly for this purpose at the end of the First World War. According to a
company document the policy of 'discussion and compromise' was
highly successful, since only one partial stoppage of two days occurred in its first hundred years of operation (*1857–1957*: 43). The
labour policy underlying the provision of welfare and relatively favourable   conditions   of   employment,   ahead   of   statutory
requirements, appears to have been aimed at ensuring that the workforce was aware of the benefits of working for this particular
company, and would therefore be loyal to the firm and remain for
many years. The policy could be interpreted as a rather far-sighted
pre-emptive measure against the emergence of a strong trade union
within the factory, based on the assumption that workers who had at
least something to be grateful for in comparison with workers in
other nearby factories would be less likely to take part in union activity. The introduction of 'Music While You Work', for example, was
not motivated solely by altruism, in spite of the fact that it was
presented as a concession to the women's demands:

> This industrial innovation led to investigations by the Medical Re-
> search Council; different kinds of music were tried and the results
> given were that with light music the results were lowest, marches
> slightly improved on this, waltzes provided a further lifting of re-
> sults and fox-trots and one-steps were easy winners.... There was a
> relief from boredom and it diverted the mind from monotonous
> conditions of work, etc.
>
> (*Historical Survey*: 93)

Presumably only fox-trot and one-step records were played as a result
of this research. Mechanization and welfare seemed to go hand in
hand here and it was probably this association that enabled Peek
Frean to introduce the Bedaux system with little opposition from the
Works Committee and workforce.[2]

During the inter-war years, Peek Frean had its pick of school leavers. It was quite a performance to get a job there. When Winnie
Young started work in 1926:

> You used to have to put your name down and really you had to
> have someone, a relation, already working there and they'd ask if
> there were any jobs going. The manager gave them a little green
> card for you. So my uncle put in for me and when there was a vac-
> ancy I came for the job with my green card. I was working at
> Lipton's for the first six months after I left school and I didn't like
> it. At that time if you left school and you could get to Peek Freans
> then you were highly honoured because it was a better job.

Winnie was probably in a particularly good position to secure her green card: her grandfather had worked at Peek Frean as a hostler, and her aunt and brother also worked there as well as the uncle. Later on one of her sisters left domestic service and joined her there. Chrissie Minett, who started work in her school gymslip, had a brother working as a trucker at Peek Frean who spoke for her, and Nell Williams's sister and husband-to-be were already there.

Then there was the hurdle of the medical before they accepted you for a job, an event that seems to have stuck in the minds of retired employees for sixty years:

> My sister got me a pass to get in, and when the job came through this woman would start off with your head, take a pencil and run it right through your head and then you'd go to the doctor to be examined. The doctor looked at your feet and weighed you. He even used to examine your toenails and your fingers. You had to be very clean.
>
> (Nell Williams)

The 14-year-olds were not put on the main production jobs until they reached 16. They 'waited on' older women, carrying trays around or sorting dried fruit or were used as messengers. Nell Williams started in 1919 as a messenger in the wafer room and earned 7s 9d a week. By the time Winnie started 'helping' in the stores the wages had risen to 9s 3d but the discipline was just as strict:

> I helped prepare the fruit for the Christmas puddings. This lady put raisins through a mincer and we used to have a little box and she would weigh you so many and you had to sit with a basin and a wet rag and go through them to see if there were any stones left. Then she'd weigh them again after we'd done them to see we hadn't eaten any. Or you'd cut up cherries for the top or walnuts. That's how I got me day suspension and I thought I was going to be sacked because they were ever so strict. They'd done walnuts that day and I was standing with all the girls chatting waiting to go home and I said 'Oh look, a little walnut' and as I went to pick it up and put it in my mouth I felt a hand on my shoulder. I nearly froze – it was the man who used to walk around to make sure we didn't eat anything cos you weren't allowed to eat a biscuit or anything. He took my name and number and when I came in the next morning I had to go and see the manager. He said 'I don't know what to do with you, whether to sack you or what.' I said 'Oh please don't sack me'. I was crying because you couldn't get a job. Well evidently they gave me a day's suspension – all that for a shrivelled up walnut I never even had the pleasure of tasting. They

sent a letter to my mother saying if I never did anything else wrong in a year they would expunge it off me record card.

(Winnie Young)

No talking was allowed, no eating, especially not of Peek Frean's biscuits, and no larking about. The forewomen were very strict with the young girls and told them off for every little misdemeanour. Winnie was told off for wearing too much lipstick and had to remove it. Chrissie Minett and her partner on the creaming machine talked a lot and were not very fast workers; the forewoman frequently shouted at them across the room to stop talking.

The hours were 8 am to 6 pm (and 8 am to 12 pm on Saturday mornings) with no tea breaks at all, the only break in the day being at lunch-time. If you arrived late, an hour was docked off your pay. Nell was always hungry in the morning:

You couldn't eat a bit of lunch. We never used to get nothing to eat of a morning because my mother couldn't afford it. Of course when you'd come in here you'd eat a biscuit – well, he [the police-man] had you. They were very strict but you had to obey.

There were frequent body searches on the premises as well as at the gate for tools and food that might surreptitiously be taken home. The forewomen often told them off and sent them to the manager's office if the misdemeanour was serious. They went round in constant fear of managers asking them what they were doing while they were on an errand around the factory and of the nasty policeman who snooped around to check up on them. He was particularly bad at Christmas time, hiding to catch out anyone drinking the rum that went into the puddings. While on one of these prowls he pounced on two elderly widows having a quiet feast of rolls and fish with some of Peek Frean's butter laid out on an upturned biscuit tin in the Christmas pudding section and got them suspended:

He was a horrible man, this policeman. You'd be walking down the stairs and he'd come up to you and say 'What have you got in your pockets?'

(Winnie Young)

They all agreed that the discipline at Peek Frean was worse than at school but even so

If you got in here it was something. It was an honour because it was strict and you knew you were sure of a job.

(Nell Williams)

This very strict discipline remained in force until the Second World

War when Peek Frean had to compete for women workers with munitions factories where discipline was not so stringent.

Although most of the women were young there were also many older unmarried women who spent their whole working life at Peek Frean:

> During the First World War a lot of the ladies had lost their husbands or young men and so they carried on working. I worked with eight or ten of these elderly women – well to me they were elderly though I suppose they were in their 30s – and they would be there until they retired because they didn't get married and they couldn't afford to leave. They were the ones who used to earn the money because they were so quick.
>
> (Chrissie Minett)

Years of experience had made these older women very quick at the work, so they earned more than the younger ones. All three of the women who spoke to me emphasized the hostility of the older single women towards the others and how they cheated and were spiteful:

> We used to have a lot of broken or split biscuits that would break as easy as anything and you couldn't put those under a stencil because they would break. These elderly women would push in front and get a tray and sort out the biscuits with a crack and take the best ones for themselves and you'd be left with a tray full of biscuits that would break as soon as you touched them.
>
> (Chrissie Minett)

No love was lost between the two groups, the younger ones viewing the older ones as cliquey and greedy sourpusses, matey with the foreladies and disdainful of their youth, whose whole lives revolved around the factory and how much money they could get. They were the supervisors' favourites, got all the good jobs where it was easier to earn money and could pick the week they wanted for their holidays. The older ones no doubt were impatient with the more casual attitude of the younger ones and envious that most would get married and have the option of not having to go out to work for their living.

As soon as they reached 18, all the boys who had been taken on at 14 to work in the bake-house were sacked:

> The day they was 18, on the Friday they'd get their cards.
>
> (Winnie Young)

The girls on the other hand were transferred to adult work when they reached 16. Chrissie was put on 'creaming' as soon as she was 16 and

Nell and Winnie were both put on assorted packing, as were most of the other young women.

Creaming and jamming were not mechanized until the late 1930s and Chrissie Minett worked with her partner Rose in the creaming department from 1929 until she left to marry in 1936:

> We had a steel stencil fixed on to the bench, a bowl of cream and a sort of scraper. You had to take the cream out, put the biscuit under the stencil, scrape over and pull it out. Then my friend would top it with another biscuit. It was a sandwich biscuit. There was a machine for creaming but it nearly always used to be hand creaming because there were so many different kinds of biscuits.

Because Chrissie and Rose talked such a lot, they only earned about 26s when others were getting over £2 a week. The work was hard on their fingers and teeth:

> They were very particular: they wouldn't let any cream show on the sides of the biscuit. Some of the biscuits were so hard with the sugar grains attached you had no finger left. We used to have thumbstools but you couldn't work so quick with them on. If your fingers got so bad they bled, you'd have to go down to the surgery. There was a dentist too cos everybody used to lick their fingers – well you couldn't help it. You would have a damp cloth at the side of you to wipe the stencil down so that you kept your biscuits very clean. I used to lick for the simple reason that I was a messy worker! You'd lose time if you had to keep going and washing your cloth out. It was easier to lick but I lost a lot of teeth that way.

On hot summer days when the cream melted, they were sent home and lost pay and sometimes they were switched to jamming, which also had its problems:

> My goodness, hot jam is one of the worst things there is. I was lucky I never really had a severe burn.

The Bedaux system was introduced soon after Chrissie started in the creaming department:

> The time and motion – what they called the Bedaux system – came in and they marked down how many trays you'd done. We were always on the slow side, Rose and me, but they timed the ones who were ever so quick. They even timed you when you had to go to the ladies room. Say you had 20 minutes for a tray, they'd alter it so you got to do that tray in 15 minutes. You just had to work faster. They all had a moan 'Don't they think we work hard enough' but I don't remember a strike over it.

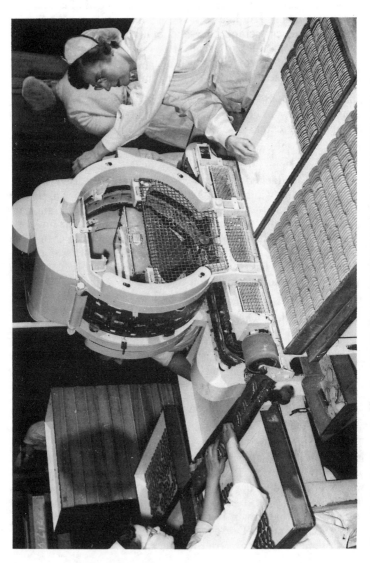

Figure 2   Peek Frean: ornamenting biscuits. Reproduced by permission of the Nabisco Group.

Later on creaming was done by machine and put on a moving conveyor belt like packing, except for the fancy biscuits like Barmouth and Bakewells that had layers of jam and cream and still had to be done by hand.

In the packing department Nell and Winnie were given a few weeks training in how to line a biscuit tin with corrugated paper and lifters and how to fill it correctly so that there was the right number of biscuits, and they were the right way up and in the proper place. In the days before mechanization each woman filled a whole tin. They fetched their own empty tins and men waited on them pushing around large trolleys with trays of biscuits to be packed. The women had to lift the trays themselves and place them above their work bench ready for packing – the trays were heavy and the cause of many sprained wrists. There were 4-pound and 9-pound tins and lots of different assortments, each of which had to be packed differently. When they had been taught the principles of packing, each particular arrangement was shown only once and then they were expected to copy it correctly. They put the completed tins on the floor to be checked and then taken away by the truckers.

It was a piecework system with a halfpenny or penny for each tin packed, and the forewoman noted down the number of tins packed on each woman's 'check'. The wage rate was 28s for pieceworkers but if they did not manage to reach that wage, that is, the number of tins needed to reach 28s on the piecework rate, then they were sacked. Once they had been trained they were considered qualified and were expected to achieve the necessary number. Some tins were harder to pack than others; some kinds of biscuit like Bourbons were very sharp and hurt their fingers but this was just too bad. No allowance was made for some biscuits being more awkward to handle than others, nor for a 'bad baking':

> If you got a bad baking – that's all the work breaking as you picked it up – you couldn't earn your money if you were piecework. If you couldn't do the work they'd put a penny in your wage packet and a note 'We have made your money up by 1d but should it occur again you will have to have your cards.'
>
> (Nell Williams)

Often their tins were checked to make sure they had not put the biscuits in back to front or in the wrong place:

> Once you packed a tin it was like a picture really. Everything had to be perfect. The checker would take a tin from you and she'd be nearly quarter of an hour sorting your tin out and perhaps you only had two minutes to pack that one. If it was a round biscuit like

103

Figure 3 Peek Freen: packing assorted biscuits on an assembly line. Reproduced by permission of the Nabisco Group.

Marie, it was four rows and then you had a space and put a lifter in, then two more layers and lifters and then your tin paper. If it was a dry biscuit you had to put a bit of shavings each end so they never moved, and if it was shortcake or patacake you had to have tier paper and then you'd pack it right up to the top, and fold the paper over and put your lid on. If she came to check your tin and there was the wrong number in it or the lining was half an inch too low, you'd have to repack it. She looked at every biscuit and then gave it to the forelady. If you had packed many bad biscuits that day then they had you in front of the manager and it went on your record. If it was on your record so many times, then you were suspended.

(Winnie Young)

At the time the pay seemed 'marvellous'. They received more than the men who waited on them, a fact which they found rather disturbing as 'girls' did not usually earn more than older men, and many had older male relatives working as truckers.

In the early 1930s moving mechanical tables were introduced and packing was reorganized on an assembly-line principle. By this time, the packers' wages had gone up to £2 15s, still 5s more than the men who waited on them. Eight to twelve women stood by the U-shaped belt (see Figure 3). Each had trays on a ledge above her with just the one or two kinds of biscuits which she had to pack. The tins moved automatically along the table and as they passed by each woman had to put 'her' biscuits in. The job was thus fragmented with each woman now filling only part of a tin instead of the whole tin as before. The jobs near the end of the line were much more awkward than those at the beginning:

The first girl took the full tin off and put the empty one on and lined it. Her parts were easy to get in but as it went round there was only a little bit of room left for you to get yours in.

(Winnie Young)

From the management's point of view this system had certain obvious advantages: productivity could be speeded up and precisely determined in advance since the pace of work was externally imposed by the speed of the moving table, which was controlled by the supervisors. The pay was geared to a group bonus for the whole line rather than an individual piecework system: under the Bedaux system a basic rate had to be achieved and all work in excess was paid at a premium rate. This meant that the faster the belt moved and the more tins that were packed, the more the group earned as a whole, since they each received the same bonus. The indirect staff of forewomen and supervisors received part of the bonus and so it was in their interest to keep the women working as fast and continuously as possible and the speed of the belt as high as possible.The group bonus system automatically imposed collective self-discipline on the women by making those who were slow or could not keep up unpopular with the rest who would 'lose money' through no fault of their own:

> You'd just about earn your money on the mechanical table but you all had to pull together. If they never pulled together, well you never earned your money. Once they put that motor on you had to keep it going. If you had a girl in front of you who was slow well, you'd had it. You all had to put so many biscuits in and if she wasn't quick enough to get hers in, you couldn't get yours in either. If you stopped to help her out then you had trouble with the next girl. If you had to have the machine stopped because you couldn't get your work in there was trouble. One day the Bedaux man was watching us and the girl in front of me couldn't keep up so of course I couldn't get mine in, and he came over and said to her 'See you get that work in. She can't get hers in until you put yours in'. But she couldn't do it.
>
> (Nell Williams)

The Bedaux engineer timed the jobs to see if they were quick enough and 'he knew how much you had to do to earn your money' (Winnie Young). They had to do five or six rounds each of about twenty-six tins in a morning, depending on how long the particular arrangement took to pack. Once the belt was switched on, they could not stop working at all until lunch-time, not even to go to the toilet, as there was no spare girl to take over.[3] Later a ten minute tea break was introduced, first in the morning only and then in the afternoon as well. The supervisors attempted to foster a competitive spirit between the women working on different mechanical tables, no doubt on the assumption that competition would be an added incentive to work faster: the groups were organized as teams and the number of B points (Bedaux points on the bonus scheme) achieved by each was written up on a board at the back of the room.

One of the few benefits of the Bedaux system from Chrissie's point of view was that the work was graded and jobs that were difficult were allocated more time per tray or more B points. The older single women now had no need to push in front and grab all the easier jobs and unbroken biscuits:

> You had to work harder to keep up but it seemed as if you were all on an equal footing. Under the Bedaux system it evened itself out.

You weren't allowed to push or anything like that. We used to do Cerise biscuits – you had to squeeze marshmallow stuff on to them the same as you would do piping on a cake. Before Bedaux you were lucky if you got one of those jobs because they were easier. All biscuits were different – Bourbon were sharp and much harder to cream. When the Bedaux system came in they timed all the jobs and instead of giving you twenty minutes for a tray, you had different times for different biscuits. Bourbon got more B's because they were more difficult. Say for one tray you got 20 B's; when you'd finished you'd book it and try for another tray and that would be a different B. That stopped the elderly ladies rushing for all the good work.

It is surprising that the firm waited until the adoption of the Bedaux system to introduce this sort of job grading and timing since it would have been quite straightforward to integrate it into the old piecework system.

Although the Bedaux system had the effect of 'evening things out', in the creaming department where there was still no conveyor and women operated individual machines and earned an individual bonus, one would imagine that the conflict it encouraged between faster and slower workers on the mechanical tables would only have reinforced the hostility already felt by the older single women who were such quick workers towards those slower than themselves. By the time the moving conveyor came in Winnie and Nell were both experienced and fast but, unlike some, they were sympathetic to those who could not keep up, and tried to help them by inserting their biscuits as well as their own or by making up an extra tin and crediting it to the slow woman.

Peek Frean operated a strict marriage bar:

> When you got married you had to leave. You had to go: you had no option. They'd say 'you, you and you, you're finished.' They'd give you a bread saw, and a wedding cake if you had been there three years. A lot of girls kept their wedding rings round their necks, but if they found out you'd have to see the supervisor.
>
> (Nell Williams)

From 1933 however, the firm adopted the policy of inviting back women who had been forced to leave when they married for seasonal work during the rush periods at Easter and from August until Christmas. They worked full-time on a temporary basis and did not receive any holiday pay. All three of the women I spoke to were asked to return. Winnie Young married the same year this married women's work was introduced:

At Christmas time they wrote and said packing was starting and would I like to come back. Then I came back again at Easter to do walnut creams. Things were so bad [i.e. experienced women were in short supply] that they would have had to pay the girls to work their holidays. They started with married women so they never lost any work and didn't have to train anyone new. We thought we'd get a week's holiday for the length of time we'd been there but they just put us off on the Monday with nothing.

Taking back married women was clearly a cheap and convenient method of overcoming the problem of labour shortages, but it was a very unusual practice at the time, especially given their own rigid marriage bar, and was probably pioneered by Peek Frean.[4] For the women it could be very tiring: a nine hour day as well as running a home. Some found it too much: when Chrissie returned after she was married the bus and train journey from Peckham Rye to Bermondsey and the long hours made it a twelve hour day and very tiring. She was only 24 but she started falling asleep in the cinema:

My husband said 'You're not going back to that place anymore. You're working too much'. We needed the money really because my husband was doing shift work and didn't earn a lot. But I went to the office and told the man 'It's too much for me and my husband says there's going to be another war, and he'd rather we spent the time together'.

Supervisors were just as strict with the returned married women as they had been with the single women but the question now uppermost in their minds was not whether they were married but whether they were pregnant – a sackable offence for married women, as getting married was for single women. Nell was one of the first to come back:

They asked whether I was pregnant. You had to swear you wasn't pregnant. They even wanted a certificate off the doctor. One girl was pregnant and they came round and gave her her cards. Another time a girl sued them: she'd had a bad life at home and her father was a beast. When he left she gradually put on weight and the forelady sent her up to the surgery to be examined. Every year when you came back they asked if you was pregnant but when people refused to get a certificate from the doctor they had to cut it out.

This obsession with pregnancy was somewhat inconsistent since management apparently did not object to employing women once the child was born. Winnie returned regularly before the war to work on a seasonal basis from the time her daughter was 3, leaving her with her own mother while she was at the factory.

The returning married women also had problems with the older unmarried women who had worked for years at Peek Frean. They seemed to be even more hostile to them than to the younger women and tried to make life difficult for them:

> Oh the old maids didn't like it. When I first came back when I was married, they haunted me. If you tried to get on with your work, they used to snatch the tray away from you so you couldn't get any biscuits. They watched out for when you needed more work and they'd take the only full tray before they needed one, and tip an empty one on to the trolley for you – just to be mean. One of them said to me 'You don't need to work. You've got a man to keep you.' It was so awful I started to cry one day and old Carr, the Managing Director, saw me. He had me up in the office and I told him 'I think the trouble is that I sleep with a man and they don't'. Well he soon asked for the Works Committee girl and I don't know what he said to her but it was all different when she came back. They kept saying to each other 'Don't do that or you'll get the sack', and if the men refused to give you a tray, they would warn them too 'Don't do it 'cos you're going to be sacked'.

> (Nell Williams)

The film of Peek Frean in 1906 shows a strict sexual division of labour in the production process with men mixing the dough and other ingredients by hand in stalls that looked like the divisions in a cowshed, and feeding the mixture into a dough-making machine. Women stamped out the biscuits on trays with various cutting machines and men then put the trays in the ovens and took them out when ready. Boys of about 12 helped to move the hot trays out of the way to be stacked up, a job known as 'chucking under', which was later done by girls of 14 to 16. Women were responsible for all the stages of packing, into packets, cartons, boxes, and tins and did all the weighing, labelling, and soldering. The only packing done by men was of large crates and packing cases for export. The jobs were sex-typed along the conventional lines of skilled or heavy work for men (mixing dough was considered skilled, and crate packing was heavy) and work which was light or required little training being reserved for women.

By the time in the late 1920s and early 1930s that Nell, Winnie and Chrissie were talking about, production had been mechanized with the dough making and biscuit stamping being done automatically by machine and the trays of biscuits travelling mechanically on belts from the dough machine to and through the oven and to packing. This meant that the jobs of the skilled men, some of the labourers

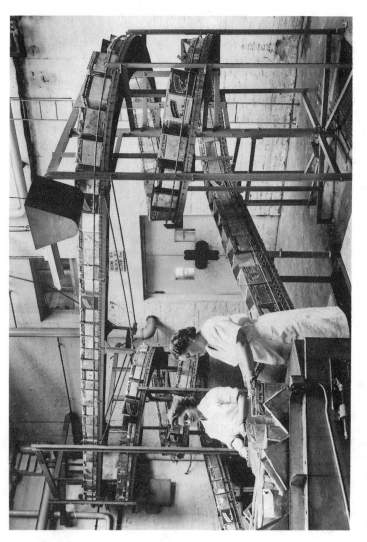

Figure 4 Peek Frean: fitting new technology into old buildings. Reproduced by permission of the Nabisco Group.

and the women biscuit cutters had been replaced by machine. Packing was the main manual task that remained and since this was still considered 'women's work' the effect of mechanization was to increase the proportion of women workers in comparison with men. Virtually all the male manual workers were labourers and truckers, apart from those who worked at night earning more for doing the same packing work that women did during the day. The women did not however seem to resent the men's higher rate of pay.

In the supervisory scale all positions above that of forewoman were held by men, as were all technical posts. The vast majority of women were packers, and once they reached 16, and were trained and qualified, there was only one grade. The only other shopfloor jobs held by women were that of trainer, checker, and supervisor which gave a certain amount of authority over other women and the men who waited on them.

Many single women gave a lifetime's unbroken service to Peek Frean, working there continuously from the age of 14 to 65 and beyond, and many widows and married women also clocked up long service records. However, only a small number of these were made into supervisors, all the others remaining in the same grade from the age of 16 until they retired. Apart from the women supervisors, all those with authority over the juniors, from the Bedaux man to the managers, were older men. Older women were thus subservient to men with decades less experience than themselves and decades younger. In this context the common argument that the short period of women's working life was the reason for not training or promoting them to higher technical or supervisory positions did not have much credibility.

Electrical and Musical Instruments Limited

The Gramophone Company was an early British multinational firm with strong American links. It was founded in 1898 and specialized in manufacturing gramophones and records under the famous His Master's Voice (HMV) trademark symbolized by a fox terrier dog listening to a gramophone. It owned plants in many countries including India, Spain and Tsarist Russia but gradually the bulk of its operations became more oriented towards Britain as production was concentrated in its huge factory complex at Hayes in Middlesex, to the west of London. In 1907 the company bought a tract of land in open country, surrounded by farms, cherry orchards and brick fields as the location for a new recording and manufacturing unit purpose built on the lines of the most up to date industrial design, together with an administrative headquarters. Production began at Hayes in

1913 (*A Voice to Remember*). In 1921 the American Victor Company acquired the majority of Gramophone Company equity, and it was technically an American subsidiary for the following decade until in 1931 it amalgamated with the British owned Columbia Company and was renamed Electrical and Musical Instruments Ltd (EMI) (G. Jones 1985). Many plants were closed down in the process of rationalization that followed the formation of EMI with further concentration at Hayes, research and development received a boost, and the product line was diversified to include radios, and later electric irons, washing machines and fridges.

Nowadays the firm is Thorn EMI, having been taken over twice, by Ferguson and Thorn in the post-war period. The Hayes factory still manufactures records but its main concerns now are radar, missile components and other military equipment supplied under a Ministry of Defence contract. It is hard to believe that the site was in agricultural land when some of the present employees started work there in the mid-1930s:

> I remember coming up Cherry Lane going to work in the mornings and seeing about 40 women hoeing between rows of lettuces, with sacks on their backs to keep them from the weather.
>
> (Doug Witt)

Now it is just off the M4 motorway in the continuous built up area between London and Heathrow airport. The factory complex is still large (but with fewer buildings than in the old days) but it is surrounded by many other large plants, mainly electrical engineering and food, and the surrounding area of Hayes gives the impression of being one huge industrial estate.

When Doris Edwards and Eileen Jones started work at 'The Gram' in the 1930s they reckoned that 25,000 people were employed at the site. It appeared to them like a completely self-contained village: it had timber yards, sawmills and a carpentry and varnishing shop to make the wooden cabinets for radios and gramophones, as well as the machine, record and cabinet factories and research building all in separate five storey buildings, the recording studios, administrative block, canteen, and the factory's own railway sidings alongside the buildings for goods inwards and outwards. It had its own artesian wells and power station (that produced so much electricity that the surplus could be fed into the national grid). The site was more or less a self-sufficient production unit, manufacturing virtually all the components needed for radios, apart from valves, from nuts and bolts to transformers.

Jobs were scarce and people came from many miles away to work at such a large employer as the Gram, from Southall, Staines, and Slough and some travelled there every day from as far away as Dagenham, right on the opposite side of London. Three trains were parked all day in the sidings at Hayes railway station waiting for the thousands of passengers that would suddenly rush out of the factory at 5.30 pm, and there was a large hoarding at the station advertising EMI as *the* local factory. Even so most people cycled to work and the surrounding roads were a sea of bicycles in the early morning and late afternoon. The factory had enormous bike sheds, but not enough, and women living in nearby houses made a living by minding as many as 150 bikes a day in their gardens, charging 6d a week.

Doris met her husband Reg at work and they moved to a house on a new estate in Hayes where most of the other inhabitants also worked at The Gram:

> I remember opening the front door to come to work at quarter past seven in the morning and everybody else was opening their doors, all down the road. It was just like a mining village going on shift, only much vaster because nearly all of Hayes worked at The Gramophone Company.

The factory power station's hooter was sounded every morning:

> At five and twenty past seven that hooter went and I don't know how far away you could hear it. You could hear it comfortably at West Drayton and they told me you could even hear it at Windsor. Everybody knew they had five minutes to get to work, and that hooter went again at 7.30 precisely. You could set your clocks by it. At 7.33 the gates were shut and if you were late you were out. The foreman would send a message down to say that if she wants to keep her job, tell her to come back at lunchtime. So if you travelled any distance you just kicked your heels until lunchtime.
>
> (Doug Witt)

Doris has always lived locally and started work at the Gram in 1936 when she was only 13. Her mother had worked in the machine factory there before she was married. Now she was a widow and went cleaning but this did not bring in enough to feed the family so Doris was sent out to work as soon as possible. Youths under 16 were not employed on assembly work: the boys were mostly employed as apprentices but the girls were used as messengers for fetching, carrying and general skivvying work for the office staff:

> Line work was not considered what they called 'children's work', between 14 and 16 years old.
>
> (Doug Witt)

So Doris's job was first as the Chief Inspector's office girl, and then in the stores in goods inwards. In the winter it was so cold there that she and the other girls had to put their feet in cardboard boxes. When she started her pay was 3d an hour, rising in tiny annual increments of a farthing while all other places seemed to rise in halfpenny steps.

Reg also had to support a large family with an unemployed father and had had several jobs in radio factories before he was taken on at EMI to check coils and transformers for 6d an hour. He cycled ten miles there and back each day from Sunbury and had to arrive by 7.30 am even when the roads were covered in ice and snow. After a few months he was moved to the calibration department for the enormous rate of 9d an hour, earning three times as much as Doris.

Eileen also met her husband at work. She started at 16 on the condensor line, painting on a metal blob after they had been soldered. When the company bought up the bicycle firm Rudge Whitworth and transferred its production from the Midlands to a new site in Dawley, Eileen was given a job painting lines on bicycle frames. The frames were suspended from a moving conveyor and the women had to take one off, paint it with the aid of a stencil, replace it, and then take off the next frame for the same operation. Sometimes they hit their heads on the conveyor. With practice Eileen could line up to one hundred frames a day.

Barry Jones was shaping handlebars in the next shop when they met. He was an unemployed miner from the Rhondda valley who had started work at 14 as a blacksmith in the colliery after his father had died of lung disease. He had to keep his mother, who had been in debt ever since borrowing money during the 1926 strike, and four older sisters, only one of whom had succeeded in finding a job locally, serving in a sweet shop. Gradually the sisters all answered adverts placed in the local paper for maids in Slough and London, and one after another they left to go into service. He and his mother decided to join them in England. The sisters eventually left service for factory work – all four worked at EMI. The whole family settled in the Hayes area as did many others from their community in south Wales. Other men from the same pit were already working at EMI when Barry arrived, and people who had lived in the same street in Porth ended up living on the same private housing estate where he and Eileen bought a house. They are still friendly with people 'from home' who moved up at the same time as them sixty years ago.

Employment at EMI was always insecure. There was short time working and you could be laid off with no warning in the middle of the day or at the end of the week and told to come back the following day, week or not at all. Significantly though it was very rare for the 14- to 16-year-olds, the cheapest workers, to be laid off. Every Monday morning there would be a queue of eighty to ninety people lined up outside the Personnel Manager's office in the hope of getting work even if there was only one vacancy. When Doug Witt was taken on as a clerk at 14 years old in 1935 he was told to look out of the window and count the number of people waiting to take his job if he did not do it properly. Soon he was given the unpleasant task of preparing the insurance cards of those about to be laid off and on one occasion the whole family of his neighbour and friend who had got him the job were sacked:

> I came home at 5.00 and I said to my mum 'Cor, they haven't half sacked some today.' She said 'Yes, I know.' I said 'How do you know?' She said all the Hempsteads had got the sack, barring Jock who worked in the wages the same as me. The whole lot got the sack – that's the mother, father, three sons and four daughters. That split the family up. They all spread out looking for work.

Complaints about low pay or working conditions were always met by the threat from management of the thousands of unemployed who would be only too willing to accept them. In such circumstances there was very little scope for trade unionists to organize and workers who were viewed as potential 'troublemakers' were sacked at the first sign of rumblings of discontent. In the early 1920s the unions had won agreement to a closed shop: all shopfloor workers had to be union members (*Management Minute* October 1920). After the Second World War the same agreement existed and most of the women were in the Electrical Trades Union. During the 1930s, though, no one remembers any organized union activity.

Until 1936 employment was even less secure: in common with the rest of the record and radio industry, work at The Gram was seasonal. Manual workers were taken on in March and worked through until November while stocks were built up for the radio show and Christmas. When the stocks ran down again in the new year, production was started up again, letters would go out and 11,000 to 12,000 would start work again. But in the mean time the vast majority of production workers were laid off, except for a skeleton maintenance staff. However, most clerical workers were employed permanently since sales continued throughout the year.

The radio season coincided with the agricultural season, both reaching a peak in the summer and a trough in the winter, and this meant that local unemployment was particularly severe from November to March. The only secure employment seemed to be on the railways. In November 1935, a few months after Doug Witt started work, he was sent over to the fourth floor of the assembly

Figure 5 EMI: early use of conveyor belts in portable gramophone production. Reproduced by permission of EMI Music Archive.

factory where hundreds of women worked:

> One of the managers was saying: 'We'll have that line of universals [a type of machine] out. We'll have this row out, that bench out, we'll clear those three bays out, we'll have this group of benches out. We'll clear the annexe floor in the other building out entirely.' I thought, what's he talking about? Anyway I saw a couple of little girls I knew and one was crying. The other said 'That old sod's just sacked us'. When I got back to our office there was a great big pile of papers on the table and I had to put them each in an envelope with an insurance card, with the right surname on it, and stick it together with the wages packet. I was doing that all day and when I came out at 5.00 there was a queue opposite our door, three deep, nearly down to the railway station, all waiting for their cards. It was heartbreaking.

All those I spoke to who had worked at EMI before the war reckoned that women outnumbered men by ten to one on the production side. Most were young and single, but women did span the entire age range since many stayed on after marriage. They would take a week's holiday when they got married, then return to work until they were pregnant and 'practically dropping'. The firm did not operate a marriage bar; on the contrary it viewed those married women with large families of five or six children to support, and perhaps no husband or an unemployed husband, as 'bread and butter' workers.[5]

> They kept married women on and they took married women on, what's called 'bread and butter' workers. They came because they needed the money, so they weren't going to jeopardize their situation by getting involved with people that were talking about strikes.
>
> (Doug Witt)

Women worked in all parts of the plant, making cabinets, working drills and presses in the machine factory, coil winding, soldering condensors, subassembling components, and assembling radios, gramophones, and irons. The older married women were concentrated in the machine factory doing the heaviest work, while the younger ones were concentrated in assembly. The 'leading hand' in charge of a group of women was usually a woman, but women were not employed any higher than this in the supervisory scale. The formal training period for most jobs was one week, though it took much longer to be proficient at it, particularly to be able to reach the speed needed to earn bonus. Women's wages were fairly uniform at

Figure 6 Mullard valve production: operating an individual machine. Reproduced by permission of EMI Music Archive.

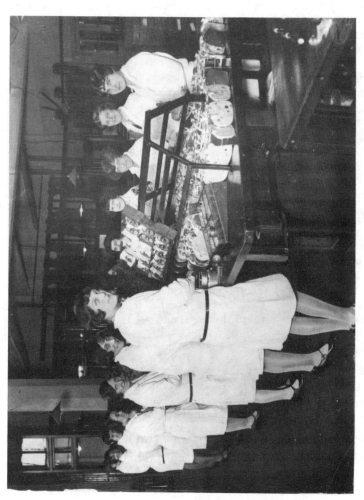

Figure 7 Mullard valve production: a 'static' assembly line. Reproduced by permission of EMI Music Archive.

around £2 a week despite the different work they were doing, and this indicates that from the firm's point of view they constituted an undifferentiated grade of labour, probably 'unskilled'. The company had a policy of incentive work for all women operatives, based on a piece-work target for those on individual machines or on a group bonus for those on assembly-line work, and the bonus element amounted to between 25 per cent and 35 per cent of their wages.

Around 2,000 women worked on the final assembly floor of the radio factory alone. Each shop had six lines with over one hundred women to a line, sitting on either side of it.[6] Production was organized on an assembly-line principle from the 1920s and most of the lines had a moving conveyor belt which dictated the speed at which they had to work. The longest ones went right down the side of the shop, turned the corner, and came back up the other side again. The lines without a moving conveyor still worked on a flow principle and the work was timed in the same way as on the moving lines, but instead of having to pick up and replace the set on to the conveyor belt, each woman would pass the set on to the woman sitting behind her for the next operation as soon as she had completed her own job on it.[7]

There was a large clock at the front of the lines with a dial that went round at a certain speed. Every time it reached the 12 o'clock position a bell rung that meant you should have finished your operation and passed the set on

> If you were slow, you automatically placed yourself in the position of being 'up the wall' [with a pile-up of work to be done that you had not been able to do in the time]. You took your jobs off the line and stacked them on the bench behind you, and those women sitting behind you weren't getting any work to do because you were 'up the wall'. Then the foreman came and would tear you off a strip. Someone would have to be called to help you out, get your work done, push them through, and get them 'down the wall' again.
>
> (Phil Hardy)

The radios were assembled in parts. For example, the chassis would come along the line and the first woman would put a valve holder on to it and put it back on the line. The next one might screw it down and attach a pin holder to it, a round plastic disc with little pins underneath. Then it would go on to the next woman who would turn it over and solder three wires on to the disc. Then the next one would solder another three on, and so on to the end of the line until the radio was complete except for the valve. This was inserted by the men who conducted the check-test on the set at the end of the line, because 'valves had a market value and were the one commodity that went missing' (Doug Witt). Most of the work consisted of using an electrically heated pot of solder for soldering joints or a screwdriver to attach subcomponents to the set.

The time allotted for the completion of each job was set by the rate-fixers who went round timing the jobs, and this timing was used as the basis of the bonus system. A certain number of sets had to be completed each hour to reach the basic wage rate, but since between a quarter and a third of the actual wage earned consisted of the bonus element, the women had to achieve not 100 per cent performance but between 125 per cent and 135 per cent in order to earn their average wage. The earnings discrepancy between the faster and slower workers probably amounted only to this 10 per cent variation and this would lead to a difference of not more than a few pence in the pay packet. The work was not dirty but it was monotonous and hard and the foreman could speed up the belt to make them work faster:

> The foreman would turn that belt up a bit, make it go a bit faster to try and get more out. Some of the women couldn't cope and they'd be 'up the wall' and the foreman would be down to them. I've seen women in tears, being told off by the foreman for not keeping up. Very often the women complained about the speed but of course in those days you never knew whether you'd be working next week or doing a full week this week.
>
> (Phil Hardy)

The insecurity of employment clearly prevented the women from resisting speed-ups in any effective way: if they complained too loud or could not work fast enough they would be thrown out, so they had to try to keep up with the speed.

Men also worked on the line, a few dotted amongst the women, but the majority at the end of the line. They were inspecting the women's work and looking for dry joints:

> The man was always in what they called a strategic position, doing the awkward bit and making sure the line was running all day. He was called a line watcher or a machine steward. He had more training than the women and was paid more.
>
> (Phil Hardy)

After inspection, the chassis would go on to another line for finishing work. The chassis was put into case, lined up and screwed down. The knobs were put on and all the dials and knobs checked to see that they turned and moved as they should and were tuned in to the right wavelength. This was often done by men on the night shift.

In the supervisory scale, women 'leading hands' were lower than male foremen and women were not employed on any checking and inspecting work that required technical knowledge. Women who were very fast workers and knew all the hundreds of different jobs on the line were employed as floating workers, popularly known as 'piddle breakers' (presumably because they took over when others went to the toilet). When other women were absent, 'up the wall', or went to the toilet, the piddle breaker would take over to ensure there was no interruption to the work as the line was kept running all day. The 'piddle breaker' seemed to have the highest level of technical expertise that it was permissible for women to attain, and more security of pay: she received a flat rate set at 5 shillings more than the average bonus.

In the cabinet factory women assembled cabinets. They were employed also winding wire on to coils for electric current to be passed through; some were small but others were huge. Women subassembled the pick-up arms and horns for gramophones as well as assembling the turntables as a whole. They assembled electric irons, a job involving exposure to asbestos. In the machine factory women worked heavy presses of up to 20 tons, stamping out condensors of various sizes, often with the safety guard up. This made it easier for them to work more quickly and so reach their target; the chargehands turned a blind eye as it was the only way to earn their average wage on piecework. This work was heavier and noisier than assembly and relied on physical strength rather than 'nimble fingers'. However, it was still considered to be 'women's work' and had been ever since they first did it during the First World War.

Although many women worked on individual machines, most were concentrated together in assembly where they worked in mass conditions. Here each woman was only one out of 100 on her line, one out of 600 in her shop, and one out of 2,000 on the assembly floor as a whole. The men who worked there described the assembly floors as 'a seething mass of women':

> You wouldn't have to get in their way at lunch time or going home at night. You couldn't go up the stairs at all. It was a solid phalanx of women, four or five abreast coming down all the stairways. They were in a hurry to get out and you just had to wait until the endless stream of life had gone. It was one mass of moving women.
>
> (Reg Edwards)

Most women were hourly paid manual workers and their conditions of employment were those of operatives, rather than the much more favourable ones of 'staff'. Staff included supervisors upwards on the direct production side, all those engaged on technical and inspection work, and all white collar workers. The majority of those with staff status were men, apart from a small minority of women clerical workers. While men were more evenly distributed between the two categories of worker, women were overwhelmingly concentrated on one side of the divide.

Operatives had to clock on four times a day, lower staff twice and the higher-ups not at all. Operatives worked a 48-hour week from 7.30 am until 5 pm on Monday to Friday with a half-hour break for lunch, and 7.30 am to 12 pm on Saturday, and could also do overtime. Office workers did a 40-hour week, 9 am to 5 pm during the week and 9 am to 12.30 pm on Saturdays, with no overtime. Staff had a regular income that did not depend on targets being achieved, and they were not laid off for parts of a day or week. Operatives could be sacked without notice whereas the staff had to have at least a week's notice. There were separate canteens, the works' self-service with wooden tables and benches, the staff with small tables and waitress service. No one received sick-pay but staff had one week's paid holiday a year while operatives had none. There were also variations in conditions (and different canteens) between different grades within the staff hierarchy but the basic divide was between works and staff. The different categories of worker wore different coloured overalls, or no overalls, so their grade and status was immediately visible. Inspectors wore brown overalls with blue collars and cuffs, while the women wore plain white. Safety was lax and many women in the machine factory did not have a complete set of fingers as a result of accidents, with no industrial compensation. Discipline on the other hand was strict and included random body searches at the gate.

J. Lyons and Co. Ltd

Lyons catering and food manufacturing company grew out of the nineteenth century family tobacco business of Montague Gluckstein and his cousin Alfred Salmon in the East End of London. In 1894 they bought a large site in Hammersmith, in west London, later known as Cadby Hall, from which they manufactured the meals and snacks to be served in the chain of tea shops and restaurants they had opened under the name of Joe Lyons.[8] The business expanded continuously up to the First World War and after, with tea shops and corner houses being opened throughout the country and food production expanding to meet the increased demand.

During the inter-war years, though, the company's expansion came to depend much more on the wholesaling of prepared and packaged foods, especially cakes, bread, and ice-cream, than on the tea shops. New buildings were erected at Cadby Hall for the mass production of many different types of baked goods, and American machinery, mixings and methods were emulated. Continuous line production was adopted as far as possible and a nationwide network of outlets and agents was established as well as a rail system for national transport and distribution. Profits rose rapidly in the 1920s and stabilized in the 1930s, increasing by 300 per cent during the inter-war years as a whole (D.J. Richardson 1970–1: 273).

The manufacture of cakes and ice-cream was concentrated at Cadby Hall, and tea, cocoa and chocolate and other products previously also manufactured there were moved out to a new green fields factory site in Greenford, Middlesex where

> in the remarkably short space of twenty years, what had been a rural area had become a centre of industy, due in considerable measure, to the coming of Lyons to the vicinity.
>
> (*Fifty Years*: 24)

The company soon had its own research, accounting and statistics departments, its own printing works and it also made its own cardboard boxes and stationery.

However, unlike many other large industrial food concerns, such as Unilever, Lyons depended on buying in raw materials from independent sources such as millers for flour and Covent Garden market for fruit; nor did it gain control of its retail outlets, apart from the tea shops, and these represented only a 'drop in the ocean' of total sales by the 1930s (interview with manager David Taylor).

By 1939 the company had 35,000 employees of whom at least 8,000 were based at Cadby Hall. A large proportion of this total were women: 90 per cent of those in catering (D.J. Richardson 1970–1: 386), and an ever increasing proportion in manufacturing as a result of the company's deliberate policy of mechanizing and employing women to operate the new production processes. The company became aware of the benefits of employing 'feminine labour' during the First World War, when male waiters, clerks and van drivers were replaced by women and by the 1920s

> the employment of women in positions formerly occupied by men had become an accomplished fact. The waitress had come to replace the waiter: the clerk had for the most part changed sex, and if the women who ... had driven the horse vans were replaced by the demobilised men, it was an exception to what has been the rule.
>
> (*Fifty Years*: 23)

On the production side, however, there was no *direct* replacement of men by women: men were sacked as their jobs were mechanized and women were taken on to fill newly created unskilled positions as operatives, jobs that had not existed before and had therefore never been done by men. The number and proportion of women manual workers increased as new work processes were adopted. Automatic machinery was introduced progressively from 1924 with the effect (and intention) of lowering labour costs and increasing productivity per operative. With increasing mechanization the same number of women operated a larger amount of plant and as production expanded, more were taken on. In this way, the proportion of women to men operatives continuously increased as a result of automation and volume production.

For example, both men and women had been employed making sponge cakes prior to complete mechanization, though with a strict division between men's work and women's work. Men mixed batter in a Hobart machine, and the eggs and sugar in another machine. Two men then lifted the bowls off the machine, emptied the contents into another bowl, and hand stirred it into the batter. At the same time the tins in which the sponges were baked were hand greased by women, put on to wires and passed through a depositing machine which deposited the correct amount of batter into the frame. These were placed on trays, passed into the oven, taken out again when cooked and put on to racks for cooling – all manually. When cool, women banged the cakes out of their tins by hand, put the tins into a washing machine and when they came out hand greased them again ready for the next load. The cakes were transferred on to wooden trays and trolleys and taken to the side of the packing belt where women were standing ready to pack them. Box-forming machines formed the cartons and dropped them on to the travelling band, and as this passed by the women packed the cakes into the boxes, four cakes to a packet, and two packets to a carton. The carton was then closed by an automatic closer and overwrapped by an overwrapping packaging machine. Women operated the depositing machines, greased the tins and did all the packing of the finished product while men did the stirring and mixing of the ingredients, and the heavy work of transferring the trays to and from the ovens.

In 1931, the sponge cake department was mechanized completely so that all the remaining operations not yet done by machine were now all done automatically. Production was now achieved by means of one continuous movement along a single travelling band on which all the different stages of operations were integrated and carried out mechanically. Compressed air machines blew air into the batter, reducing the time taken to whip the mixture from twenty minutes to five minutes, blew the mixture into a bowl and stirred in flour. The batter then passed automatically into a hopper without any handling and was automatically deposited by machine across the sponge tins which were now on a continuous band travelling towards the oven. They passed through the oven, into a cooler and on to a cooling pad where the frames tilted so that the women could pick the cakes out of the frames and place them straight into the cartons which were travelling alongside on another belt. On their return along the band, the tins were washed and automatically greased.

Clearly, this new system eliminated many of the jobs previously done by hand. All the manual washing and greasing of tins and loading and transferring of trays were cut out and with them most of the jobs which men had done. Women were retained on packing – virtually the only remaining manual operation – but each dealt with a far greater volume of sponges than previously. Men were discharged but as additional bands were built to increase the volume of sponge production, more women were taken on. This same automatic sponge cake plant first used in 1931 was still in use in 1958 and was considered to be Lyons' most economical and labour saving plant (*Lyons Bakery Memo*: 2).

The first automatic band had been introduced a year earlier in 1930 for Swiss roll and had been specially built for the firm to an American design. Prior to mechanization, a certain amount of automatic machinery had already been used in the Swiss roll department as in sponges. Up to the stage of emerging from the ovens, the process for Swiss roll was the same as for sponge cakes except that the trays were paper lined and the batter was wider and not so deep. The sponge then travelled along a moving band to automatic spreaders which covered the top with jam. Then women pushed a roller to cut the sponge into individual Swiss roll lengths by hand and also hand rolled the cakes. The Swiss rolls carried on to the cartonning machine and were picked off by hand, boxed and wrapped in the same way as sponges. Later when the continuous line was set up the cutting and rolling were also automated.

From about 1924 and the development of production for wholesale, the policy was for a single product to be produced in such volume that it constituted a whole production unit on its own and was organized as a separate department. In the 1930s in addition to the sponge cake and Swiss roll departments, there were separate departments also for layer cake, snow cake, pies, French pastry, and the English and Vienna bakeries as well as ice-cream and bread. The trend was towards mechanization in all these departments, but it was more advanced and developed more rapidly in some areas than others. Jam tarts and pie production were only partially automated by the outbreak of war but ice-cream was rapidly transformed in the early 1930s from a more or less totally manual process to a completely automatic one, apart from final wrapping.

The factory buildings had been purpose built for production but not really for automation. Straight line production required floors of 300 to 400 yards in length: the Cadby Hall buildings were several storeys high, but each floor was not really long enough as a single production unit. This led to problems in layout and placed constraints on the mechanization of the entire product range. For some, different stages in the production process had to be carried out on different floors of the same building and connected by conveyors up and down: the mixing floor would be at the top; the next floor would be the oven floor; the one below would be the finishing floor and the lowest would be for packing.

Production was truly on a mass scale: twenty-six miles of Swiss roll were manufactured every day, 850,000 'Kup Cakes' a week and 53 tons (1 million) of buns, scones, crumpets and muffins. At Christmas and in the summer there were special seasonal lines, produced in massive quantities over a short period of time: mince pie production started up five weeks before Christmas with one band doing 5,000 an hour but within two weeks this was increased to 40,000 an hour on five lines so as to churn out a quarter of a million every day. In the summer of 1939, 5 million gallons of ice-cream were manufactured.

Consumption of bread (as a cheap staple food) increased during the depression and Lyons entered plant bread baking on a grand scale in the mid-1920s. Rapid progress was made in mechanizing this area of production too and within a few years 350 tons of bread were being made each week and Lyons was one of the first plants to produce a sliced loaf ('Reddy Kutt') and a wrapped loaf ('Purity Loaf'). As the company acknowledged, plant baking 'reshaped the trade from a craft into an industry' (*The Baking Industry: A Profile*: 1) and the bulk of bread production shifted from numerous small bakeries to mass production in large industrial plants. Labour costs were much lower in the large plants and the imposition of minimum wages for bakery workers further undermined the position of the craft bakers so that by the end of the inter-war period many ceased producing themselves and became retail outlets for bread bought wholesale from Lyons or ABC (*The Baking Industry: A Profile*: 4).

The *New Survey of London*'s account of mechanization in the baking trade could well be based on Lyons. The connection between the introduction of machines and the use of unskilled and female labour is emphasized

When [flour confectionery] processes are completely mechanized the departments are generally arranged on successive floors with the mixers at the top, so that the dough descends the building during manufacture to the despatching department on the ground floor. In such a factory it is possible to work without any of the employees, save the foreman in the mixing department and the foreman in charge of the plant itself, knowing anything about baking, and though all employees call themselves bakers they are for the most part skilled machine minders. For bread baking men only are employed, but in larger concerns where flour confectionery is made girls are largely employed.

(NSOL 1930–5 Vol II: 27, 36–7)

Certainly in Cadby Hall, wherever the process was more mechanized, there were women working. Cake decorating was done by hand and this was the only skilled work done by women. There were forewomen, but none in the more senior supervisory posts nor in any position requiring technical knowledge or formal training that lasted more than a few days. Most were engaged on packing or other repetitive jobs at the side of the band where their pace of work was set by the speed of the conveyor.

Bedaux time study engineers were brought into Lyons in 1928 and introduced a time and motion bonus system which imposed a standard of 80 B points to be achieved in 60 minutes, that is, 33 per cent higher than basic performance per hour. Some very experienced workers on individual machines could reach up to 120 B points an hour but workers on the line were very unlikely to. The bonus was an extra 25 per cent of wages paid for producing the extra 33 per cent but there was no choice for the women to decide whether or not to aim for 133 per cent since the bands were fixed at this speed. The system was unpopular with the women subjected to it:

> It caused a lot of trouble. It wasn't popular because they thought they were being taken for a ride. Its name had to be changed because the Bedaux system became a dirty word.
>
> (Ray Dickens)[9]

Although the name was altered to 'Time and Motion' the same basic system remained in operation for many years.

Management attitudes towards women workers were quite contradictory: women were regarded with some contempt as completely unskilled workers performing what were basically labouring jobs. In fact, most assembly-line work depends on considerable practical experience and manual dexterity at the particular combination of tasks, which take time to learn, especially when they have to be done at speed. Lyons was no exception to this: when men were employed on the night shift in the Swiss roll plant, they had difficulty performing these 'unskilled labouring' tasks that 'anyone' could do and they had to be trained. Until then there was the problem of Swiss roll uncontrollably emerging from the ovens and buckling on the band because the men couldn't cope with the rolling machines. Drastic steps had to be taken to prevent Swiss roll running all over the shopfloor and complete chaos:

> I can well remember being in charge of the night staff and we had to train them from the raw. It sounds funny but once you are in continuous production, if you can't check down the other end, you are in one hell of a mess. We were cutting Swiss rolls off the sheets because men weren't coping with the rolling of them at all. We had to take it off the band and put it on trays, hang it out of the window and so on and get it out of the way until we could shut the plant down. Once you were in production there was a run of about 12 to 15 minutes before you could do anything about it and you got this pumped stuff coming out all the time.
>
> (David Taylor)

The men took some time to train but in the end they got used to the work. However, the manager in charge did not draw the obvious conclusion from this event about women workers' unacknowledged expertise!

Lyons was generally known among the local women I have spoken to as a bad employer and several, apart from Doris Sharland, mentioned avoiding taking a job there. The firm recruited women workers from the local Labour Exchanges in Fulham and Hammersmith. This was odd at a time when people were queuing up for jobs outside factories (as indeed men were for the night shift at Lyons) and the usual pattern was for women to hear about vacancies through an informal network of friends and relatives. It confirms the impression of bad conditions of work.

Certainly conditions of employment on the catering side of the firm were quite ruthless and included instant dismissal for contravening any of the many rules, very low pay, and an intricate system of checking up on all bills made out by the waitresses. (It was estimated that the availability of cheap clerical labour made this control system economical.) This labour policy was explicitly based on the assumption that women workers were cheap and plentiful since supply so greatly exceeded demand and that insecurity and fear of being sacked was a good deterrent against breaking the rules as well as trade union activity. The company successfully overcame a lightning strike by catering staff in 1920 after a 'nippy' was dismissed for wearing a union badge. Blacklegs were rapidly recruited and transported to the tea shops in company cars, and all strikers who did not return to work by 9 am the following morning were sacked (D.J. Richardson 1970–1: 401–2). Unlike many other employers of the time, there was no tradition of paternalism to counterbalance such harsh conditions (D.J. Richardson 1970–1: 410–14).

Even if employment conditions in the factory were not as bad as in the tea shops, similar assumptions no doubt underlay labour policy on both sides of the business. There was no trade union representation at all in Cadby Hall and although operatives complained, there was no serious unrest since:

> we had a very loyal staff and most people were only too happy to have a job.

> (Ray Dickens)

However, the production would have come to a standstill during the General Strike of 1926 without the

> loyalty of the company's employees [managers] ... who readily exchanged their black coats for overalls.

> (*Fifty Years*: 25)

Labour turnover among women workers appears to have been fairly high and I could not find any women who had worked in the factory during the inter-war years either through the firm or independently. These facts, combined with management's low opinion of women operatives, suggest that there was not a very collective spirit in the factory, to say the least, and that women were unlikely to develop any long term commitment to the firm or to stay if they found better conditions elsewhere.

Loyalty was a common theme in the company's publications and internal documents in terms of both its desirability and its importance to a smooth and high level of production. The frequency and emphasis of such discussions suggests that loyalty was notable for its absence rather than its presence, which is hardly surprising given the company's overall labour policy. An introductory lecture to bakery management trainees for example stresses that the

> spirit of working together amongst supervision and the operators ... must start at the head. We try to inspire the operators with confidence in their supervision ... both as technician and as leader of his staff. Then we try to encourage a sense of craftsmanship and pride so that they can take a real interest in whatever they happen to be making. This is easier in some departments than in others; the wedding cake decorator has more scope here than, say, the

operator in the sponge cake department.... Other factors contributing to good morale are Loyalty, the importance of maintaining production.... If we have lost time either through mistakes or the breakdown of machinery, then somehow or another, by improvisation or by overtime or by 'pulling out the stops' by the supervision, however it is managed the goods must get to the customer on time.

(Lyons Bakery Memo: 15)[10]

Taking the conditions of work and Lyons' overall labour policy into consideration, this 'loyalty' was evidently conceived as a one-way process, from the operators to the company, and was no doubt perceived as such by the women at the time. High morale was of concern only in so far as it boosted production and this, rather than any genuine consideration for the conditions of employees separate from what they produced, was hardly masked in the discussions of loyalty. There was no mention of welfare, or any of the other trappings of paternalism normally associated with the expression of such a management ideology, operating in the opposite direction as a means of securing this loyalty.

Morphy Richards

Morphy Richards (MR) electrical engineering factory was established in Kent in 1936 to manufacture radiant fires. Gramophone pick-ups and irons were soon added, electric irons becoming the source of the company's great success. At first production was seasonal and one hundred irons were produced each day. Within a year this had increased to 1,000 daily and 5,000 a week, production was continuous throughout the year, and the workforce had grown to 500. At first the factory was housed in a disused oast house, known as 'the Barn', until a brand new purpose-built building was opened in 1938.

Morphy and Richards were both originally radio engineers. When they set up business together Richards concentrated on sales and advertising, while Morphy did all the production engineering for the electric irons himself. The idea was to buy in as many components as possible and operate primarily as a volume production assembly operation on a continuous flow principle. Morphy's idea was that while the pioneer of a product usually encountered many teething problems, the producer of the second edition, such as himself, was more likely to be successful. HMV already had an iron on the market but it was heavy and expensive. Morphy Richards' aim was to market a mass product within the price range of 'the average housewife not

131

on an enormous income' (Fred Douglas, retired manager) with design features that would distinguish it from its competitors. The MR iron was lighter and cheaper than HMV's (22s 6d instead of £7), with a distinctive shape and green pilot light in the handle indicating whether or not the heat was rising. The success of the product ('we couldn't make enough of them') revealed the enormous size of the potential market and led to very fast expansion in the early years of the firm before the war.

Location in the north Kent outer suburbs of London was deliberate: it was just beside a main road with easy transport for its component suppliers and close to its main market in London and the South East. However, the main reason was the large supply of female labour available locally, 'raw' in the sense of having no previous industrial experience and looking for employment. To begin with the firm recruited women who had been seasonal agricultural workers picking fruit and hops, but soon began recruiting from a source that turned out to be large and highly suitable: a very large housing estate was being built in St Mary Cray by the London County Council, mainly to rehouse victims of TB and other diseases from London to the fresh air of the Kent countryside. Most of the men travelled to London daily to work, but many were ill. In both cases, many wives and daughters were looking for work. Although the original location decision was not motivated by this convenient labour source, the decision to stay in that particular area and invest in new plant and buildings there probably was.

It was common for several women from the same family to work in the factory, and the firm relied on informal word-of-mouth recruitment, rather than the Labour Exchange. When a new assembly line was about to come on stream, they would let the women know that twenty-five or fifty jobs were be going, and there was no problem in finding the additional workers from amongst the relatives and friends of existing workers. Many of the new waves of recruits also lived on the same housing estate and this meant that most of the women who worked at MR knew each other. The company did not operate a marriage bar but took on women aged between 15 and 40 regardless of whether or not they were married. Before the war however the proportion of older married women with children was low: most were young and single, or married but childless.

At least three-quarters of the workers were women. From his previous experience, Morphy had the idea that iron assembly was similar to radio assembly and since 'putting little electrical components together was women's work', all the jobs were designed 'with women's fingers in mind' (Fred Douglas). Women formed the vast majority of the 'direct' workers and all started as operators although a few rose to the lower levels of supervision and inspection. There were twenty-four women on each iron assembly line, and therefore twenty-four separate stages of assembly. A new recruit was trained on the more simple jobs and then sat with another woman to gain practical experience. The firm reckoned that it took six months to be proficient at any one job and fast enough to keep up with the speed of production. Most women learned more than just their own job: this involved no technical training but competence in using different kinds of machines. Management, interestingly, viewed this ability as 'skill rather than dexterity', despite the 'nimble fingers' argument, because 'operating some of the machines would just seem impossible to somebody coming to it new' (Fred Douglas).

The first operator took out an already chromium plated and polished sole plate (cast for Morphy Richards by Qualcast) and fixed it on to a carpet-lined wooden pad and clipped the bi-metal (which measured the temperature) into the little trough at the bottom with an L-shaped clamp. Then she slid it along the line to the next woman, who inserted the heating element. These had already been wound in a separate subassembly section of the factory and the second woman would have a tray of such elements in front of her. She also attached an asbestos (!) pad on top of the element to keep the heat in and clamped this down into place. The third woman threaded a cable into the handle and screwed the handle on to the plate. The fourth put the thermostat control knob and bridge across the top of the bi-metal. This was a graded disc that put pressure on the bi-metal as the knob was turned to give high or low heat and it had to be fixed on to the front of the bridge that went over the bi-metal. Another twenty similar operations were carried out until finally the iron was tested and the cover put over the whole lot. Each job was timed to take about one minute so each line would produce sixty irons an hour. Most jobs involved using a screwdriver and these hung from a bar on a spring in front of each woman so that they could be easily reached. It was mostly wrist work and there were a lot of wrist problems until pneumatic powered air tools were introduced some time after the war.

There were three grades of operator: the basic operator who concentrated on one job, the operator who was competent at three jobs, and the 'utility' operator who knew all the jobs and could be moved up and down the line as required. The higher grades were paid a higher basic hourly rate, though this only amounted to an extra farthing or halfpenny, and also a higher bonus since this was calculated as a percentage of the basic money. The women who did inspection either on the line or before the cover was attached to the iron were given a basic knowledge of electrics, like Ohm's Law, so that they could understand what the machine was reading and why. They were also paid a little more. Above the operators was the leading hand: she was still an hourly paid worker whose rate was a penny or so above the highest rate on the line and her job was to co-ordinate the line, to train people, to step in on the line if no one else was available, and to sort out small queries for the women.

The forewoman was the first line of supervision. From the earliest days women were employed in this position and the only route to it was up through the line. Forewomen were above the leading hand, in charge of all iron assembly, weekly, rather than hourly, paid workers, and on the staff which gave certain privileges. It was MR policy to have forewomen supervising women operatives. From management's point of view they had certain valuable assets, mainly because women 'were good with people' and knew how to get them to work: they encouraged operators to get on with their work and keep up a steady speed, partly by introducing competition between the different lines and marking up their rate of production every hour:

> We always thought that the rhythm and general run of a line was very much linked to the supervisor, encouraging people to do the job properly and speedily. The girls didn't just work for the bonus – that didn't give them the speed. Forewomen instilled the rhythm – made it like a football team sort of effort. They had come up the line and knew the duds or the difficult girls and how to handle them.
>
> (Fred Douglas)

In fact many women were reluctant to become leading hands, inspectors or supervisors, perhaps not surprisingly because this would mean inspecting the work of or being in authority over their own close friends or relatives.

The next rung in the supervisory ladder were superintendent, foremen(!), and factory manager but no women were employed in these positions:

> They didn't get to be superintendent or anything like that because that had to be somebody with basic engineering who could talk to the engineers and the women didn't have the engineering knowledge for that. It would probably have been a chap with a basic engineering training.
>
> (Fred Douglas)

All the men were indirect workers: either the labourers who humped the components and finished product around, the various grades of supervisor, or the engineers and time-study men. The policy was to keep wage rates for the unskilled men 25 per cent above women's earnings (contrasting with the situation at Peek Frean) but this could not be adhered to exactly since all the direct women workers were on a low basic hourly rate with a variable incentive bonus, while the indirects were paid a standard time-rate.

There were six lines assembling irons each with twenty-four women. In the early days there was no moving conveyor belt and the women sat elbow to elbow facing the line. Each picked her work up off the line as the woman in front slid it to her and when she had finished her job, she replaced it on the line closer to the woman doing the next job. Often there were two lines of women, one on either side of the line, doing different assemblies. After a year or two, a roller system was introduced so that the work could be rolled on little trolleys along the line from one woman to the next so as to speed up the passing on. This system, however, still left the operators in control over when to pass on the work and hence ultimately over the speed of work. The first operator would put the next plate on the line as soon as she had finished clamping the one before but the frequency would basically depend on her speed and gauging when the minute was up by the clock. Similarly, although the jobs were timed and there was no question of choosing their own pace of work, each successive woman also had to gauge the time and there was nothing to stop them doing a whole load of irons very quickly and then having a rest.

The importance to management of rhythm and of the forewomen's ability to instil rhythm and a fast pace of work becomes clear in a static continuous flow operation like this where assemblers had responsibility for the movement of the work. The pace of work had to be personally imposed by those in authority, whereas under a full-blown moving belt system the pace is automatically imposed and does not have to depend to nearly the same degree on external goading or the 'football team' mentality. After the war, moving conveyors were introduced and the seating was reorganized into the more conventional arrangement where women sat back to back, sideways to the line.

On the static system if a delay occurred because one woman missed out an iron, then the others could immediately see what was happening. The woman at the front of the line could wait to put out the next plate until the delayed one had caught up, and the women behind her just waited for the next completed one to come along. It did not cause any great problem, except that they would lose one iron's bonus points. Being able to regulate the pace of work and adapt to hold-ups meant that such problems could be coped with and overcome informally without the whole system snarling up. Once the moving conveyor was introduced, however, such delays could send

135

the system 'haywire' (Fred Douglas): the plates would continue to be put on to the belt at regular timed intervals without interruption and if one operator was delayed or missed out one iron, this would automatically create a pile-up behind her and the women in front would have a space. In bad cases this could be sorted out only by putting the utility operator on to the line to clear the backlog and smooth out the uneven flow of work or, more drastically, by switching off the belt so that no more plates would travel down until the blockage was cleared.

The Bedaux system of work study was in operation from the outset but was worked out by the company's own engineers. The jobs were organized in such a way that each should take the same length of time to complete and the hourly target and incentive bonus were supposed to encourage speed. The bonus element was fixed at a high proportion of the women's wages (i.e. the hourly rate was low), no doubt to encourage speedy production. Even so, without a mechanically moving conveyor, the actual speed of work could not be guaranteed. There was a large variation between lines which worked faster and slower: some women managed to earn an extra 80 per cent on their basic rate while others only reached 40 per cent. Until such wide variations were evened out by mechanical means which imposed the same speed of work on all, 'good' supervisors were all important to the production system.[11]

Discipline in the factory was fairly lax in comparison with some others. Women were allowed to talk and smoke while they worked but not to eat, for fear of greasy fingers marking the work. Clocking in was cut down from four times to twice a day and they were 'put on their honour' not to leave before the right time. It was a 47-hour working week originally from 8 am to 6 pm, but soon cut to 5.30 pm, and 8 am to 12 pm on Saturday. Pay was not docked for lateness, but a warning was issued if it occurred more than twice in a short space of time. The firm's policy was to let 'group reaction' of the others on the line do the disciplining: if someone else was late they could not start work (or earn money) and so would have a go at her for putting them out. There were ten-minute tea breaks (fairly unusual for pre-war factories) when the women went line by line to the canteen and stopped work completely. After moving conveyors were introduced, production did not stop for the break but a tea-trolley was rolled round and each woman was replaced by the utility operator while she took her ten minutes.

The firm was not a member of the Engineering Employers Federation (EEF) and there were no unions in the factory before the war. Management philosophy was to keep pay and conditions above the EEF minimum, so preventing open discontent or the emergence of trade unions, and retaining their independence from 'outside inter-ference' by the EEF including the recognition of trade unions that such membership would involve. The new building had piped music and an air ventilation system on the shopfloor. A nurse and doctor were available (and dealt with many sprained wrists) and all em-ployees ate in the same canteen, though manual workers bought self-service meals and did not sit at the more expensive waitress-ser-vice tables, which were open to them, but which were in fact used only by the managers. The firm's industrial relations policy aimed to se-cure efficient and continuous production by acquiring the goodwill and co-operation of the workforce through 'firm but fair' manage-ment and the creation of a personal atmosphere where most people knew each other.

After 1945 Morphy Richards expanded rapidly, built several new factories, and increased the workforce to 4,000, in one instance tak-ing over a pickle factory together with the whole of its workforce. Hair dryers, pop toasters, electric kettles and other small electric domestic appliances were manufactured as well as irons. The success of the company was due to the growing mass market for such goods which really took off in the 1950s. Much of their advertising material emphasized the role of their products in easing the burden of the housewife so that she could be more glamorous when her husband returned from work in the evening. The factories experienced a severe labour shortage and much higher turnover than before the war and resorted to introducing their own fleet of double-decker buses to bring in women from the surrounding villages and towns. The Personnel Department deliberately set out to recruit married women with children by starting up three shifts (morning, afternoon, or early evening) for women to work part-time. Everything went well until Morphy sold out to EMI and Morphy Richards then had to compete much more directly with AEI and GEC. In 1970 the Kent factories were closed down and all their production was transferred to the Manchester area. Electrical goods are still produced under the Morphy Richards name but now they are part of the same Thorn EMI empire which also owns HMV, Morphy Richards' original competitor.

Hoover

Hoover was a Canadian owned company that started business in Bri-tain in 1919 as an assembly and sales operation, using parts manufactured in its Canadian factory. Import tariffs led it to shift total production of Hoovers destined for the British market to Eng-land and a modern purpose-built factory was opened in Perivale, on the western outskirts of London. It was a famous art deco building with an Egyptian style façade which won several architectural awards; since production there ceased in the early 1980s, it has been the subject of a preservation order. In the early 1930s there were fields around the site but soon other factories, mostly light engineering and food (including Smiths crisps, Macleans toothpaste, Gillette razor blades, Trico windscreens and Michelin tyres), joined Hoover on the Western Avenue, which linked London with other towns, like Slough, where new industries were also locating.

The factory employed about 1,500 production workers, 500 office staff and a large sales force. The sales staff were all men trained in aggressive American-style techniques which they plied door-to-door. At their frequent meetings in Perivale they were taught answers to all housewives' possible objections to purchasing a Hoover, and often finished by a rousing rendition of one of the songs out of the Hoover songbook, including the well-known

> All the dirt, all the grit,
> Hoover gets it every bit,
> For it beats as it sweeps as it cleans.
> It deserves all its fame, for it backs up every claim,
> For it beats as it sweeps as it cleans.
>
> (Quoted in Weightman and Humphries 1984: 66)

It was a model factory in the sense of using the most up to date American machinery and in being clean, modern and providing all the facilities of an employer that wanted to secure a stable, reliable, and fairly contented workforce. The top floor of the building housed the canteen, the firm had its own fire brigade and resident doctor, overalls were provided free for all (brown for the shopfloor, white for the managers) and were also laundered weekly free of charge. The shopfloor and work benches had to be kept scrupulously clean and tidy, and every week the Works Manager went round to inspect. The superintendent (foreman) would make a preliminary inspection first as not one piece of paper was to be showing or one tin out of place and he was the one who would be in trouble if the shop did not come up to scratch. No smoking was allowed anywhere in the building except the canteen and foremen stood looking down the spiral stairs that led to it to make sure that no one lit up before they reached the canteen. Smoking in the factory was an instantly dismissible offence.

The hours were long, 7 am till 5.30 pm, but no Saturday working. Most workers came from the Southall area, though many came from as far away as East London, and travelled to work by bicycle. Edith Boyd was delighted to be able to buy a brand new bike soon after she started at Hoover and received a much larger pay packet than she had as a maid. By then she lived relatively close to the factory at Greenford and did not have a very long journey. Les White travelled all the way from Bow (over 20 miles, from north-east to south-west London, right through the centre of town) by bicycle leaving home at 5 am to get to Hoover by 7 am. He didn't get home in the evening till 8 pm! There were enormous bike sheds but you had to cross a large courtyard to reach them and no cycling or even scooting were permitted inside the factory gates. This could be very frustrating if you were in a hurry: you had to clock in on the floor where you worked, and at 7.02 the foreman removed the clock cards from the machine. There was a great temptation to cycle across the yard because otherwise the foreman would want to know why you were late and quarter of an hour's pay would be docked from your wages. If you were consistently late two weeks running you would be sacked.

The wages were high for the time (£3 10s for men per week and £2 15s for women) and to get a job at Hoover was considered quite a catch. You had to be personally recommended and then prove that you could do the work. You had to achieve the required speed to reach 150 per cent of the basic hourly rate. This was 9d for women and 1s for men, but the work was organized on a piecework system where each job was timed and allocated a price. The rule was that women had to be able to make about 4d an hour bonus and men 6d so as to make an average hourly rate of 1s 1d or 1s 6d including the bonus. Although these were high wages for both sexes, it is clear that men won out both on the basic and on the bonus. The rate-fixers gave a lower price to women's bonus points.

There were arguments with the rate-fixers about the time they allocated for the completion of particular jobs, but the main conflict over this was between the superintendents and the rate-fixers rather than the workers. This was because

> the superintendent was pledged to get out a certain number of machines and if the rate-fixer made the rate too hard, then the operators were going to beef. You see the superintendent was responsible for seeing that everyone earned time and a half. If they couldn't do it, then the superintendent's in trouble, and if he didn't like the rate he wouldn't sign the form. The form had to be signed by the person who did the rate and by his superintendent, and if they didn't like it they wouldn't sign the form. There were occasional blow-ups – which made life interesting.
>
> (Les White)

This conflict between supervisors (rather than operators) and the rate-fixers occurred elsewhere, for example at the Wolsey hosiery factory in Leicester when the Bedaux system was introduced.[12]

Four models of Hoover were manufactured in the 1930s, all upright: the Junior, the Senior, the Dustette and a larger industrial cleaner. Each stage of production was done separately in a different section of the shopfloor. There was no continuous flow principle in operation. Each person worked their own machine or machines for their own time-rate and had two trolleys by the side of them, one with components to be worked on and the other for their finished work. These were wheeled between the different stages of the process by labourers though the work was arranged in such a way that each person was standing close to the person doing the next job in the sequence.

The layout of the building was designed so that different stages of the production process were housed on the different floors. On the ground floor was the machine shop including the foundry and press shop where there were automatic and capstan lathes, drills, heat processing equipment and plastic and bakelite moulding. This was mainly the preserve of the skilled men, the only section of the workforce to be 100 per cent unionized, in the Amalgamated Engineering Union. Above were the various assembly floors including one for handles and bags (where most workers were women) and the canteen was on the top floor.

About three or four hundred women worked as semi-skilled and unskilled manual workers at Hoover. They were mostly in their 20s. Hoover did not take on school leavers but looked for 'more mature' women. They did not operate a marriage bar but most women left on marriage, and this reduced their average age in comparison with the men. Unlike the other factories I have described women were considerably outnumbered by men. This was partly because all the metal components for Hoovers were manufactured on the site by skilled men and partly because much of the actual assembly work was also done by men. The skilled men die-cast the metal for the casing and the motor in the machine room and men also monopolized work in the paint spray shop. The question of employing women in these jobs probably never arose, but even if it did, the skilled men in the engineering union would have been in a strong position to exclude them. In those days the Hoover was a much heavier object than today, entirely made of metal rather than plastic, and parts of its construction and assembly were more similar to motor car manufacture than to the type of smaller domestic electrical appliances like radios and irons manufactured by other electrical and light engineering plants. The casting, burnishing, polishing, plating and painting, the rivetting together of the parts and the heavier assembly operations were all done by men, the motor and case assembly in particular being considered 'too robust' for women. There was a strict demarcation between women's jobs and men's jobs with no overlap between them.

Women did work in the machine shop and Edith Boyd maintained that women could work most of the machines there except the die-casting. However, they did repetition work only and no machine setting or maintenance. They were restricted to operating machines that were set up by men:

> At first when I started [in 1937] in Hoover I was doing drilling for the smaller parts. Each operator worked on her own. There were men called setters who saw to the machines when they went wrong. The work was brought to us by labourers and a new job always had to be set right before an operator could start and a rate-fixer timed how long it should take. Each day, near finishing time, you took your work to the store, where it was all weighed and counted, and noted against your clock card number. After it left the drilling section, it would go on to another section for further work on it.
>
> (Edith Boyd)

Women's other jobs in the factory were also strictly demarcated from men's. They sewed the bags in which the dust was collected, sitting in long rows at their sewing machines. This was intricate work and required quite a bit of training. They assembled the brushes which swept the carpet and attached them to the agitator. They also assembled the Hoover handles from lengths of metal tubing, glued on a rubber grip and inserted the electric wiring and switch into the handle. Armature winding was a specialist job and this too was women's work. It involved winding many yards of wire round a copper core – the basic part of the motor – covered with insulating material. They sat in straight lines at benches operating a foot pedal machine and each armature could take thirteen minutes to wind. This job also necessitated training and two sisters who had worked in the armature department for many years initiated newcomers. Armature winding must have been similar to coil winding, though possibly more fiddly, and coil winding was defined as women's work throughout the electrical industries at that time. To the male workers armature winding appeared to be 'skilled' because of its intricacy and the training required, while bag sewing was 'semi-skilled' 'because sewing is a woman's know how' (Les White). After winding, the armatures were soldered but this again was 'men's work'. The last job on which women were employed was inspection, including inspection of the plating and painting done by men of the part finished article, as well as final inspection. Women inspectors were indirect workers and paid a higher hourly rate than the other women since they did not work for a bonus.

Women were thus restricted to five main areas of work in the Hoover factory. The decision as to what was women's and what was men's work appears somewhat idiosyncratic. In other factories it was unusual to have women so much in charge of inspection, especially of work done by men, but on the other hand some of the assembly operations done by men in Hoover may well have been done by women elsewhere. There is no way of discovering the rationale that lay behind Hoover's particular sex-typing of jobs. The important point however was that there was complete gender segregation: all work was sex-typed and divided up on the principle that jobs were either women's or men's. None was to be done by both men and women.

The arrangement of each person working their own machine and putting their completed work in a trolley applied throughout the assembly section even where a group bonus was paid to the section as a whole. It was called an assembly line but this was really a misnomer. It certainly bore no resemblance to assembly lines in the other factories I have described, where the work was organized on a continuous flow principle along a mechanical conveyor belt. Whether or not the belt moved, under the normal assembly-line system each person passed on each piece of work to the next person as soon as they had done their bit to it, and so did the following person. At Hoover however, although the work travelled from one person to the next, there was nothing mechanical about it. It went trolley full by trolley full (and each trolley might take several hours to fill), there was no conveyor, no belt, and no direct passing of the completed work to the next person on a one-by-one basis.

Even more unusual for an assembly operation was the arrangement of the rivetting machines: ten different machines had to be used one after another and one man walked along the row of machines doing all the ten rivets to one piece of casing or motor. In a more 'Fordist' arrangement there would have been ten men, one standing by each of the rivetting machines and the work would have passed along the line of them, probably on a moving conveyor. The men would not have moved. The way the work was organized at Hoover meant that the pressure was determined much more by each person's own target than by a mechanical line or by what the section as a whole had to produce. In this sense it was like a modified piecework system.[13]

Chapter five

Women assembling: work, wages and assembly-line production

Assembly-line production represented not only a distinctive form of production and a new stage in the development of capitalism, but also gave rise to new relations of production and thereby to new class relations. The pivotal argument of this chapter is that mass-production methods entailed the emergence of new class relations for assembly-line workers, based on a new technical division of labour, new forms of exploitation, and a corresponding change in the wage form.

For Marx the main characteristic of the proletariat was that it sold its labour power to capital in exchange for a wage. This feature was the basis for the formation and consolidation of the working class. It bound together all those who worked under conditions of wage labour and distinguished them as a class from the 'working' classes of earlier or other modes of production as well as from other classes in the capitalist mode of production. The main body of twentieth-century western Marxist thought has followed Marx in focusing primarily only on this one central but very general characteristic, as defining the working class and forming the material basis for its unity. Only rarely and recently has the possibility of internal divisions and differences within the class of wage labour been admitted, and, more often than not, such recognition has resulted in a wholesale abandonment of the basic theory rather than an attempt to develop its conceptual framework in order to integrate these insights.

Yet there is no reason why the concept of relations of production could not be used to demonstrate what differentiates the class as well as what unites it. If, as Marx proposed, it is precisely the relationship between capital and labour that gives rise to class relations, then it should also be the case that structural differences in the nature of that relationship between different groups of wage labour and capital would entail structurally different class relations for the people concerned. Neither Marx himself nor later Marxists appear to have recognized this implication of his basic explanatory framework or its significance for the theory of class. However, I would suggest that grasping this point fully and in all of its ramifications does provide the potential for developing Marx's original theory in a fundamental way, rendering it capable not only of analysing the historical development of specific types and groups of wage labour as they have existed from the late nineteenth century to the present day but also of introducing into the theory the possibility of divisions within the class. Elaborating such an approach would inevitably involve a transformation, rather than just an uncritical development, of the basic theory since it undermines some of the central tenets of Marx's political economy.

While selling labour power for a wage may be the basic criterion for the constitution of the working class as such, there are other dimensions of the relation between capital and wage labour in addition to that basic exchange. These too represent part of the material basis and are constitutive of class relations, giving them their specific shape and particularity. The detailed content of these dimensions will depend on the actual circumstances and cannot be specified in advance of analysis of the particular group of wage labour. I am proposing that in addition to the basic exchange of labour power for a wage, relations of production may differ along two central axes: the conditions under which labour power is sold and the way it is used once it has been sold.

This chapter will be devoted to the second of these, analysing the relations of production of women assembly-line workers and examining what was new, what was distinctive and what was specific about the way that their labour power was used in the mass-production industries of inter-war Britain. I shall be dealing here with one central structural determinant of class relations, namely the relation between labour and capital in waged employment within the sphere of production (but without making the assumption that this could provide the total explanation of the overall determination of class relations).

My contention is that there was indeed something distinctive about the exchange between women assembly-line workers and capital and that, viewed historically, their labour power was used in a new and different way. In theoretical terms this implies that the class relations of women assembly-line workers were specific ones, distinct from those of other types of workers in assembly-line industries and from women working under very different conditions in other occupations or industries. Although I am concentrating only on this one group of workers, in principle the method of analysis could equally well be applied also to the other new types of worker that emerged with the introduction of mass production (and of course more generally to all of the main groups of wage worker during the history of capitalism).

Analysing the class relations of assembly-line workers in this way presupposes in the first place that assembly-line production was a distinctive form of production. This basic point, underlying my entire argument, is one that has to be demonstrated rather than taken as given. Just what was so special about assembly-line methods to warrant this privileged position? In the same way that capitalists had to find new commodities to produce, new forms of industrial structure, and new markets to exploit if they were to survive the economic crisis of the inter-war years, so too the viability of production for mass consumption, which was the overall response of capital to that crisis, depended on developing a technology and ways of arranging the organization of manufacture which would ensure the fast and steady production of goods in large quantities. It is impossible to envisage production in the vast quantities necessary for mass consumption without a major change in the methods of production. Continuous flow production was the essential principle on which methods of mass production were based and the feature that distinguished production methods of the new industries from those of the traditional staple industries. Continuous flow production relied on automatic manufacture by machine and integration of the various stages of production into a single uninterrupted process and at its heart lay the assembly line.

Assembly lines were the productive hub of the factory, the centre and culminating point of all other production. In industries where manufacture consisted of assembling components on a conveyor belt, such as electrical goods production, all other operations in the rest of the factory and all the earlier stages in the production process were geared towards their ultimate destination on the assembly line. Every component had to be produced and ready in sufficient quantities to be transported to the line and all work done in the toolroom, machine or press shop, was oriented towards the final process of assembly. In other types of industry, such as food processing, where no actual assembly of components took place, 'assembly' lines in the literal sense did not exist. Production was nevertheless based on exactly the same principle with moving conveyor belts serving an identical function to assembly lines. The continuous flow of production was achieved in both cases by the same principle of a moving belt.

'Assembly-line methods' is therefore a term to designate all continuous flow production processes based on this principle in the food processing, ready-made clothing, domestic appliances, motor components and other electrical engineering industries, whether they relied on a band, a belt or an actual assembly line. In the inter-war period assembly-line methods embodied capitalist production methods at their most advanced, in terms of technology and workshop organization. The principles on which they were based represented the very essence of mass-production methods, the high point of existing techniques and the model for other forms of production process. But in addition assembly-line methods also had a wider and symbolic significance as a model for other types of work process to emulate. Their intrinsic principles were gradually applied to other manufacturing processes, and later also to shops and offices as well as factories.

It is self-evident that the creation of the assembly-line worker resulted directly from the introduction of assembly-line methods. The new technology had involved a wholesale reorganization of the shop-floor from the period of craft manufacture, including the development of new work methods, new jobs, new grades and types of worker and new relations between workers and management and between different groups of workers. However the actual assembly-line worker stands out from all of the other new workers as the one who experienced the new production methods in their purest and most acute form and who alone was subjected to direct control and domination by the line. This gave her a very special position in relation to the production process itself, to all other groups of worker, to their employers and to the process of profit maximization and capital accumulation.

Since assembly-line workers in the new industries were more or less exclusively female, looking at the relations of production of assembly-line work will therefore imply looking at the relations of production of *women* workers. All the illustrations and examples given of assembly-line workers will be of women. From a technical point of view all methods of production, including mass production, are in fact gender neutral and do not presuppose the participation of either gender. In practice though, the work process associated with the new methods of production was gendered in a very strict and definite way right from the outset, as are most work processes. Alongside their new technical division of labour, the new industries quickly developed a sexual division of labour which allocated men and women to different functions, positions and levels in that technical division of labour.

Assembly-line work was one area that became almost exclusively 'women's work' as was shown in Chapter 4. All the factories described there employed women as the majority of their manual labour force and relied on them to operate the assembly lines. At EMI women constituted nine-tenths of the workforce, at Morphy Richards three-quarters, and at Peek Frean and Lyons well over half. Hoover was the exception that proved the rule: production was not organized on assembly lines and women accounted for under one-third of the workforce. This association of women with assembly-line work was a characteristic common to virtually all factories in the newly developing or expanding consumer goods industries which adopted methods of mass production.[1] The main exception was final assembly of vehicles in the motor industry, but the moving track was not in such common use here and women were excluded for other reasons as well. In motor components manufacture on the other hand, the usual association obtained and at Lucas in Birmingham four-fifths of the workers were women.

In most instances the sexual division of labour is inextricably intertwined with and inseparable in practice from the technical division of labour. However, it is important to distinguish analytically between these two elements and to examine them separately and on their own merits. The development of mass production as a system did not require the equation of women with assembly-line work even though this was what happened historically as the practical effect of the sexual division of labour. In principle though the technical division of labour and the occupational structure which developed out of the new methods of production were independent of the gender of the workforce. The rest of this chapter will be concerned with analysing the development and characteristics of assembly-line production, the distinctive technical division of labour and skill structure associated with it, and the relations of production of assembly-line workers. The discussion will be based on the assumption that assembly-line workers were women but since the new class relations between labour and capital need to be established on their own merits, the focus will be on the technical division of labour and its effects on the workforce. Questions about the gendering of the work process, the sexual division of labour and why and how assembly-line work became women's work will be addressed in Chapter 6.

The assembly-line production process

Mass production depended on the development of manufacturing technology that could turn out products continuously and in volume, and from the 1920s the efforts of industrial engineers were geared towards perfecting and refining such techniques. The basic objective was the same for any manufacturing process: break it down into its constituent elements, simplify these into subdivided stages and then reintegrate them on a continuous flow principle with as many tasks as possible being mechanized. All impediments to the smooth and uninterrupted through-flow of work from beginning to end of the production process were to be eliminated along with all possible sources of waste (time, labour, physical effort).

Electrical engineering provides one of the clearest examples of the new methods of production. The components of the particular product to be manufactured, whether a radio set or a pop-toaster, were reduced to small simple parts that could be automatically produced by machine. Once the machine was set, the task of stamping out was repetitive and routine and could be undertaken by relatively untrained workers. The next stage was to subassemble the components from the parts, and finally to assemble these into the finished product. The logic of the system was to extend this method progressively to its furthest possible limits and so the quest was always for further technical development to make the parts ever simpler and more easily amenable to mechanical production. Once the various stages in the production process had been differentiated they were allocated as distinct tasks to workers responsible only for a single stage in the total process and placed sequentially at different work stations in the order of the work to be done.

The most rudimentary type of assembly 'line' consisted merely of the operators sitting in a row to attach components and passing on their completed work by hand to the next person. This arrangement was superseded first by the introduction of a stationary table, band or belt that ran the length of the operators and along which they pushed the product, still by hand. The later adoption of rollers represented an intermediate stage, permitting the work to be moved along mechanically and more quickly, until the moving conveyor belt was finally perfected. In the EMI radio and gramophone factory for example, components were physically handed on between operators until a moving belt was introduced in the 1930s. Morphy Richards also started with a static line but soon introduced a roller system before eventually building a moving conveyor but at Philips, by contrast, there was a moving belt right from the outset.

Similar principles of production were also evident in food processing. At Lyons and Peek Frean hand-mixing of ingredients for dough or cake mixture was replaced by machine-mixing, and the various stages of production were linked to each other in a single continuous operation. Moving belts carried the mixture through ovens, coolers and cutting machines and thus eliminated the need for any manual transfer of part-prepared product from one stage in the process to the next. Cartons and wrappers for packaging were also machine prepared, but on a separate belt, ready for hand-packing of the finished product. It was essential that these two continuous flow operations were co-ordinated and synchronized in such a way that both product and cartons were produced in the right quantities and at the correct intervals for each other.

Historical development

Since technical innovations in machinery and methods of work had been introduced from the late nineteenth century, some assembly-line methods were not completely new. None the less, the adoption of methods of mass production in the 1920s and 1930s was on such an extensive scale in comparison with anything that had existed before that it really represented a wholesale leap to a new technological level. The speed with which the new methods were adopted during this period and their widespread use marked the consolidation of a more technologically advanced form of manufacture, and one that might legitimately be viewed as a new phase in the history of mechanization of production.

First there had been production by hand, transcended by production by machine (what Marx called machinofacture). Here machines, such as lathes, were manufactured as the means of production and the parts they produced were, with some hand-finishing, the finished goods. Assembly-line methods introduced an extra stage into this process whereby the means of production were now used to produce an intermediary product, components as opposed to final goods. To be finished the output of lathes and other automatic machines now had to undergo an additional stage in the production process involving assembly of the final product from the components.[2]

The gradual and hesitant transition from manual craft to machine manufacture had already been evident in, for example, the Coventry cycle, ribbon and watch industries where assembly-line-type methods had been in use from the 1890s and 1900s (Castle 1984: 17). In the engineering industry too the general trend from the turn of the century had been to develop specialist machines which could turn out part-finished goods. Capstan and turret lathes, milling machines, grinders, borers and radial drills were the new machines of the turn of the century, whose subsequent refinement was also accompanied by changes in workshop organization:

> to bench fitting and erecting was added assembling. On large jobs belt-assembly or another form of regular progress of work with each worker fitting a part took the place of the gang erecting one job at a time.
>
> (Jefferys 1945: 202–3)

Later the exigencies of production during the First World War, especially in munitions, stimulated further development and application of automatic machines for repetition work. The tendency to subdivide and fragment existing industrial processes was greatly accelerated, even when there was no actual change in the technology. Complex processes, previously carried out by a single craft worker, were broken down into their constituent operations and each was redefined as a separate job capable of being performed by workers who needed training in this one part of the process alone. In the production of tools and gauges, for example, 'roughing out' was separated from 'finishing', and the setting up of capstan lathes and other automatic machines was separated from operating them (Kozak 1976: 99). Since this occurred in the context of women being employed on work normally done by men, the process of job fragmentation went hand in hand with feminization of the workforce. In one machine-shed, skilled jobs were split into as many as twenty-two separate operations, each more repetitive and specialized but less skilled, to be performed by twenty-two women, who naturally required far less training than the craftsmen they replaced (Drake 1919: 45).

Despite this creeping tendency to mechanization, the full development of assembly-line methods was achieved only in the particular economic circumstances of the inter-war years and as a direct consequence of the industrial transition towards the mass production of consumer goods. In the same way that craft manufacture had represented a distinct stage in the historical development of manufacture, with its corresponding relations of production and particular types of wage labour, so now did assembly-line production, and it also brought into being its own characteristic class relations. These held sway in Britain throughout the heyday of mass production from the 1930s until the 1970s. Since then, assembly-line methods have been progressively superseded by computer-aided and more highly automated manufacturing systems, whose introduction has again been accompanied by an alteration of the structure of the workforce and of the relations of production.

But although assembly-line production systems were in wide use throughout the consumer goods industries by the mid-1930s, it is important to appreciate that adopting such methods was not an overnight or once-for-all business. Their implementation by particular firms frequently depended on overcoming severe problems of capital investment, arising from the large cost of outlay on retooling and re-equipping, and also of developing a range of products that was both sellable in mass quantities and technically capable of being mass produced. The material constraint of developing appropriate equipment and techniques was also considerable, and the level of

150

mechanization in all the new industries was in fact patchy and uneven, reflecting clearly the conditions under which technological development was made. Full mechanization even of one process might occur over many years since a total production system of specialist machinery could not be designed in its entirety in one go. Most were developed in parts and only gradually integrated with each other. Nor was there any final stage of technical perfection to be reached since the system was always amenable to further refinements.

Moreover the material problems associated with implementing assembly-production systems also formed an essential background to women's work in particular factories. The type of job they performed, the nature of their tasks, whether on individual machines or on static or moving belts, were directly affected by the degree to which such problems had been solved. In food processing especially, old and new processes coexisted with each other for several years so that workers in the same factory might be working at quite different levels of technology.

And just as production systems could not be introduced overnight, neither did the relations of production associated with them appear in one fell swoop. These also developed gradually and were subject to adjustment and refinement. In instances where craft and assembly manufacturing systems coexisted with each other or where different stages in a production process were based on both old and new methods, different forms of relations of production also coexisted and overlapped, affecting different sections of the labour force in different ways.

Control over the work process

Continuous flow process systems had a profound effect on the arrangement of work on the shop floor, placing the accent firmly on rational calculability, mechanization, standardization and efficiency so as to achieve their purpose of fast production by means of a single smooth process. From the employers' point of view, continuous production methods ensured a fast and large output which they could plan in advance. Precise control over production permitted them to make detailed projections of output schedules with confidence. Conversely, the success of the whole operation also depended on efficient pre-planning so that the right components were available in the right numbers in the right place at the right time. Production in the component manufacturing workshops had to be co-ordinated with the assembly section; sufficient stores had to be available and capable of being transported easily around the factory; the assembly lines had to be fed at all times but not flooded with too many components. There also had to be a constant means of removing the completed product from the line either to stores or directly for distribution. Without well planned and efficient organization the whole process could rapidly beome snarled up with backlogs or shortages that could bring final assembly to a halt. In turn this would then reverberate back on the other processes leading up to it.

It was only with the moving belt that the system reached its full potential from the employers' standpoint.[3] Controlling the speed of the belt and hence the operatives' work gave total control over production and permitted planned output schedules to be automatically achieved. The numbers of product to come off the line in any one day or part of a day could be decided in advance and kept to in practice, provided there were no hold-ups with components, machine breakdowns or stoppages. The moving conveyor thus marked a significant refinement over the static conveyor and was the ultimate goal to which employers in mass-production industries aspired.

Time was of the essence in the rational calculability of the assembly line: all stages in the process were calculable in terms of time as well as money, and all time wasted could be converted into lost output and profits. Since the basic aim of capitalist enterprises was to produce as much as possible as quickly as possible, managers were made responsible for arranging the most intensive use of time and for eliminating any potential source of lost seconds or minutes. The recently developed methods of production planning, cost accounting, internal communication and the various other appurtenances of 'rational' business administration, referred to in Chapter 3 as part of the new form of industrial organization, provided the underpinning necessary for a fast and continuous flow of finished goods. The very organization of assembly lines embodied many basic principles of scientific management: the division between conception and execution of tasks, the divorce of direct from indirect labour, job analysis and fragmentation, continual subdivision of labour, the reduction of skill levels and so forth.

It is indubitable that, as a consequence of adopting assembly lines, employers acquired much more effective control not only over the whole production process but also over the workforce than had ever been the case under craft manufacture. The material to be presented later in this chapter provides clear evidence that the relations of production of assembly-line workers were characterized by unprecedented domination through machine pacing and subordination to managerial control. But the thrust of my argument is that although employers took all the advantages that this control offered them and exploited it to the limit, for their own benefit and to the detriment of assembly-line workers, their acquisition of such absolute control over the workforce was an *effect* that resulted from their increased control of the process of production, rather than a motivating reason for the adoption of those methods in the first place.

This point needs emphasis since much post-Braverman writing on deskilling and the labour process implies that employers introduced new machinery precisely in order to wrest control over production from workers. In this interpretation, the conscious class aims of the ruling class become the motor of historical change and history is a history of conscious intentionality. As a result, the adoption of new methods of production becomes a mere strategy of employers in their struggle with the working class: capitalists attempt to promote new methods and workers attempt to stop them. In this way, what I present as the effect of the adoption of new technology is turned upside-down into its main intention.

My contention was that capitalists were forced first by financial crisis and then by competition to adopt mass-production methods. Theirs was a reactive response to changed economic circumstances which they only partially understood. To continue in business they had to alter the way they made profit and those who were able to introduce mechanized production methods and to produce goods for the domestic mass market were the ones who survived. In this way, they were forced by circumstance to produce commodities and realize profits in a different way. It is not realistic to imagine them sitting in the company board-room consciously deciding to build conveyor belts with the aim of weakening the position of their workforce. So although this was a practical effect of that adoption, they did not adopt new production methods in order to gain power or to acquire control over the labour process. Changes in the production process cannot be reduced to the class-conscious motivations of the ruling class and so discussions which view deskilling of the workforce as an end in itself and the production process merely as the means to that end are starting from the wrong premise.

Within the new system of production there was of course room for manoeuvre both by employers and workers. Employers could adopt a number of different strategies in relation to their employees and, as the examples of Chapter 4 showed, factory regimes did vary considerably from each other. Workers also challenged the new arrangements and the intensification of work they implied. But these actions were undertaken *within* the confines of the new structure of production: employers' strategies in themselves and workers' reactions to them neither brought into being or into question the new system of production itself.

Recognition of this point carries the implication that the labour process cannot be conceived as an area capable of being explained internally, solely in its own terms. Any particular labour process is in fact embedded in a particular circuit of production and circulation (in this case the wage and commodity circuit of mass production and mass consumption), the level of technological development and the social relations of production which together form the overall structure of a particular form of production. This is not to deny that employers could and did tinker with and alter particular work processes, but to become wholly intelligible, the labour process has to be located within the context of overall structure of the production system of which it too is a part. It cannot be understood sui generis. During the inter-war period the new structure of mass production and mass consumption formed the necessary background against which all capitalist firms were operating and which forced them, by imposing particular demands and constraints, to conform to the new standards or go to the wall.[4]

Technical division of labour and skill structure

Mass-production methods entailed a quite distinct technical division of labour from craft manufacture, including the development of new forms of work, a distinctive range of skills and occupational structure. The creation of new types of worker, each in a different relation to production, which resulted from these developments, was basic to the process of restructuring class relations.

Direct and indirect work

One fundamental feature of the new organization of work was the strict division between direct and indirect parts of the production process, and hence between workers engaged in direct and indirect work. Although other direct workers were to be found elsewhere in the factory (e.g. manufacturing the parts to be assembled), assemblers comprised virtually the whole of the direct workforce in final assembly shops since it was they who did the actual work of directly producing the final product. Most other workers were concerned with servicing this assembly process: theirs was the indirect work of arranging for the supply of components, setting and servicing machinery, organizing the jobs on the line, inspecting the final product and so forth. Although their work was of course integral to the whole operation, they did not themselves engage in direct production: they were involved in the process of production but did not themselves undertake the direct work of actually making the goods.[5]

Conveyor belt production was arranged in such a way that assemblers did nothing but assemble. If the direct assembly worker devoted her entire time and energy to that single task alone, management would be able to increase the speed of the line, a situation which encouraged continuous attempts to refine the division between assembly and non-assembly work and between direct and indirect work. Any part of the job that could possibly be considered extraneous would be removed and allocated to other workers. For example, before the introduction of the continuous flow principle, machine operators would probably have fetched the raw materials they needed from wherever stocks were kept and carried them several times a day to their machine. They would also have taken their completed work to be counted and costed at intervals throughout the day. Under the new arrangement however, the operator would remain stationary, devoting all work-time to operating the machine rather than spending some of it around the shop fetching and carrying. The parts would instead be brought to her by another worker, the progress chaser, who spent all day supplying operators with components. When completed, the work would be taken away by a labourer who transported the product of all operators to inspectors or bonus clerks. Because all the 'extra' work was removed, machine operators now concentrated on operating to the total exclusion of everything else, while a new type of specialized worker emerged in the form of the progress chaser, also responsible for one job alone.

As intended, the concerted application of this principle at all levels on the shopfloor introduced an extremely rigid demarcation between the direct workers who operated assembly lines or individual machines and the indirect workers who serviced them. The effect of this division, and one of utmost significance for the analysis of the relations of production of assembly-line workers, was to place direct and indirect workers in a very different relation to the actual process of production and hence to the creation of value, since the labour of assemblers was very directly connected up with the output of products in a way that the labour of others was not. The mode of extraction of surplus value differed in the two cases and this contributed to a difference in relations of production between direct and indirect workers, arising particularly out of the distinctive form of machine pacing to which direct workers were now subject.

Because the basic principles of job analysis and fragmentation which underlay the division between direct and indirect work were also applied within each category, the tendency was for the division of labour to be made increasingly detailed and minute and for jobs to be made ever more specialized and repetitive. Tasks were differentiated from each other as far as organizationally possible and allocated to workers employed to undertake one task alone. For example, if final assembly jobs included a certain amount of subassembly of components, management often deemed it more efficient to remove these and set up a second line, devoted solely to subassembly. The tasks of the workers on the two lines would now be more repetitive than previously since they were more fragmented.

New jobs

Inevitably, this very detailed division of labour gave rise to the proliferation of many types and grades of worker each trained only to the level required by her or his particular tasks and paid accordingly. Indeed, the emergence of new jobs, direct assembly as well as the indirect jobs, represented another important dimension of the technical division of labour characteristic of assembly-line methods of production. Conveyor belts were serviced by machine setters, repairers, electricians, and maintenance men responsible for seeing that the machinery worked properly; progress chasers kept assemblers constantly supplied with sufficient numbers of the right components; inspectors or quality controllers checked the finished product before it was dispatched; labourers transported the goods from the end of the line to the stores.

In addition to such workers who acted as adjuncts to the actual assembly process, other groups of indirect worker emerged or were newly consolidated as single-function groups. These included rate-fixers, work-study staff and bonus clerks who undertook the various lower level managerial functions of administering the new systems of job evaluation and payment schemes. The supervisory grade too was usually extended into a more complex hierarchy of chargehands, foremen or women and supervisors, often with several intervening steps between them. The new skilled trade of electrician was directly created by the dependence of the new industries on electricity as the main source of power. Skilled engineers were required to oversee machinery and

> they also went further afield ... large drawing offices, planning, progress, rate-fixing and costing departments needed men with a sound knowledge of production techniques and problems.
>
> (Jefferys 1945: 207)

But quite apart from these, conveyor belt production also relied on the participation of many highly educated and professionally qualified engineers and technicians, such as the various types of production engineers, each with their own range of skills, who designed and organized the detailed workings of the line. Installation and operation of the new technology presupposed the involvement of such professional 'cadres' on a scale quite unknown in craft manufacture.

In this way a number of distinct and separate processes, all arising out of the change in the production process, lay behind the enormous proliferation of new grades and types of worker: the fragmentation, particularly of manual and lower managerial jobs; the actual creation of new jobs linked with the new techniques in use and the new source of power; greater elaboration of the hierarchy of levels within particular grades of work such as supervision or inspection; the increasing number and type of highly trained technical personnel on whom the system relied. So the popular impression that adoption of mechanized production methods produced a homogeneous mass of deskilled labour on the shopfloor is oversimplistic. In fact the same logic that attempted to divide jobs into ever simpler and more repetitive parts simultaneously also produced new specialisms and technical competencies.[6]

Skill profiles

In the food processing industry, for example, the proportion of workers who were skilled, in terms of Census categories, remained unchanged over the whole of the inter-war period at around 36 per cent. However, after 1931 there was a marked decline in the numbers engaged in particular skilled occupations: bakers and pastry cooks, sugar and sweet boilers, and confectionery makers, moulderers and coverers were particularly badly affected; significantly these worked in sections of the industry most subject to mechanization (Mikoleit 1986: 110–12). But clearly, the fact that the overall proportion of skilled workers did not decline indicates that some new skilled occupations must also have been created at the same time, though probably not in direct production.[7]

In engineering the situation was somewhat different. The proportion of skilled craftsmen fell from 50 per cent to 32 per cent of all engineering workers between 1921 and 1933 while that of semi-skilled workers increased from 30 per cent to 57 per cent (Jefferys 1945: 207). These proportions were more marked in electrical engineering and other mass-production sections of the industry. Craft skills had been based on general apprenticeships which gave an all-round training, enabling the tradesman to set and operate a wide variety of machines including those with which he might not be familiar. By contrast semi-skilled work was much narrower, more specialized and tied to the use of particular machines, such as internal grinding, universal milling machines, or automatic feeders. Again electrical engineering represented this development at its most extreme. Increasingly workers with no direct engineering experience were able to undertake work in the new trades, and the numbers of new apprentices declined sharply.[8]

The work of the remaining skilled engineers within mass-production industries was concentrated on setting and maintaining machines but they did not themselves operate the machines. Gone were the days of the skilled craftsman and his labourer who together manufactured an entire product from start to finish and who undertook all of the different mechanical and manual operations. In the past, each craftsman possessed all the necessary manual skills and technical knowledge to set and operate whatever machinery was necessary to execute his task. But traditional craftwork was just not appropriate to continuous flow production.

Consequently, the division between direct and indirect work and the emergence of new types of work resulted in mass-production industry possessing a distinctive occupational structure, quite different from that of craft manufacture in the old staple industries. Its central feature was the predominance on the shopfloor of semi-skilled workers. The vast majority of direct production workers were officially classified in this way and their proportion was very high in comparison with that of both craftsmen and labourers. No longer could the all-round tradesman of craft manufacture be such a central stage character. Semi-skilled workers had to be proficient in the use of a small number of machines which they learned to operate on the job rather than through formal craft training. A large part of their expertise lay, not in knowing how to set or repair their machines or understanding their internal workings, but in the rapidity with which they could operate them, a dexterity that could sometimes take months or years to perfect.

Relations of production of assembly-line workers

The next part of this chapter focuses on what has been referred to as 'relations of production' and the effects for the direct workforce of the new forms of work organization embodied in mass-production methods. The aim is to show what was specific about the relations of production of assembly-line workers as distinct from those of other groups of workers.

I suggested earlier that the exploitation of workers, or the extraction of surplus value, has frequently been treated as if it occurred in one general or invariant form, common to all types of capitalist production. The inevitable result of such an assumption is to make impossible the articulation of different experiences of exploitation.

A similar point could also be made about the collectivization of workers under the impact of the division of labour, again often presented as taking only one general form. What I am trying to develop is an approach that could overcome this problem by means of a method capable of differentiating structurally between different forms of exploitation or collectivization, and of a theory able to acknowledge that different groups of workers working under the same method of production or workers involved in different processes of production might be exploited or collectivized in different ways. Analysing the conditions of assembly-line work represents a test case for this approach that will attempt to demonstrate that the form of exploitation, and hence the relations of production and class relations, were specific to assembly-line work.

Two main elements comprise the relations of production of assembly-line workers: the way in which their labour power was used and the payment form which corresponded to that use. These will be explored in turn, using the accounts of Doris Hanslow and Jessie Evans to illustrate the argument. Developing an approach such as this necessarily relies on detailed historical substantiation, and their testimonies are presented with this in mind. Doris worked in clothing, an industry not examined in detail so far in this study, but one where the assembly-line principle was also introduced. Jessie worked at Philips, probably the most modern and highly mechanized radio factory of the inter-war years. Although the primary focus is on assemblers, brief comparison will also be made with other types of direct worker (loom operators in the nineteenth- and early twentieth-century weaving industry, or individual machine operators in mass production) as well as with indirect workers in assembly-line industries, in order to highlight what was specific to assemblers.

Attention has already been drawn to one fundamental feature of the use of labour power in assembly work, namely that assemblers constituted the direct workforce in a regime based on the rigid distinction between direct and indirect work. Assemblers produced products under conditions which did not permit them to regulate either their own labour or the product. Their conditions of work, including this lack of control, differed in important respects from those of indirect workers. Indeed the division created between the indirect and direct aspects of the production process contributed directly to the very tight external regulation of direct work.

Two additional features, which I shall now examine, were also characteristic of the use of labour power in assembly-line work. The first consisted in managerial control over labour by means of machine pacing and the second in the emergence of a new form of collective worker, where the unit of labour was considered to be the assembly line as a whole rather than the individual assembler. The main reason for singling out these two features is that they stood out very strongly from the factory case studies as more or less 'defining' assembly-line work, and they were also of the greatest significance in the memory of assemblers.

However, neither machine regulation of labour nor collectivization of the worker were in themselves unique to mass production: machine pacing had been widespread in a number of industries for several decades, and it could also be said that wherever there is a division of labour, the unit of labour is bound to be collective. Nevertheless, what I intend to show is that the *type* of machine pacing and the *form* of the collective worker that developed under the conditions of mass production were distinctive, and specific to the use of labour power in assembly-line work alone. Moreover these two features were so closely linked together that each reinforced the operation of the other, with the result that their combined effect was greater than either the sum or the parts. The basic division between indirect and direct work underlay both machine pacing and the emergence of the collective worker, given that both presupposed that assemblers were direct workers. So the essence of the argument to be developed about the use of assembly-line labour power is that their relations of production were characterized by their use as direct labour, by machine pacing and by the collective worker. Together these amounted to a new form of domination over the worker by capital.

The use of labour power

Doris Hanslow

Doris Hanslow worked at Rogers shirt and collar factory near Bermondsey in south London from 1924 to 1934. It was a large factory employing about 500 people and the finished shirts bore the 'Rocola' trademark, a make still in existence today. When she started, the work had already been fragmented and a detailed division of labour introduced. There were separate workshops for sewing the different parts of shirt (sleeves, collars and so on) and Doris worked in the collar shop. Collar making itself had also been subdivided into fourteen separate jobs. Each woman was trained in several but would normally spend her entire time on one task only, completing one-fourteenth of the work. Doris's speciality was attaching the little tab that went over the collar stud. The separate machines were not placed in the sequence of the tasks and each woman worked on her own. Their completed work was put in large bundles and only transferred from one stage to the next, that is, from one worker to the next, several times during the day with long intervals in between. Each woman was paid a piece-rate according to the number of times she did her own particular part of the collar. The women could talk to each other and could regulate their own pace of work, speeding up and slowing down as it suited them and they could leave their machines to go to the toilet if necessary.

All of this changed in 1928 when a conveyor belt was introduced and the work reorganized on continuous flow lines. The women continued to do the same jobs on their old machines but these were now grouped in a single line along a moving belt in the order of the work to be done. Eight to twelve sat on each side of the line and the collars were now made up one by one, one after another so that they were complete by the time they arrived at the end of the line:

> The first job was the little tab. Then the collars were cut out and you'd get a piece of tape and stick the tab in. The next woman on the belt was what we called the 'patent turner': she had a tin in the shape of a collar and folded it all the way round. Then it would go on again to the stitcher who stitched on the top of the collar. The next job was to trim up the bits to get it level. Then it went on to the inserter and that was a really long job because you had to stitch all the way round the neck band and get the collar to fit just so. Then it went on again to the buttonholer who had to work the large buttonhole machine. There were usually two inserters and two patent turners with the irons because those were longer jobs.[9]

The belt was covered in white canvas, divided into sections by blue lines which showed the women where they were to put their completed work:

> the line would go for two or three spaces and then the forelady would put a new pile of work out and there were two young girls standing at the top of the line picking up each piece of work and laying it on the belt ready to go.

Doris certainly noticed the difference: everything went much faster now and there was no time for getting behind or catching up in the one minute that was allowed for each job:

> On the individual machines you'd get your work coming down in grosses all tied up with a band and you'd sit and just work your way through it in your own time. If something went wrong and you got behind, you would carry on working to catch up as you were on piecework. You'd say to yourself 'I'm not talking to anybody, I'm going to hurry and catch up.' But when this conveyor came in, the girl at your side was getting your next bit ready and it was slowly

Figure 8 Doris Hanslow.

moving up the belt towards you while you were doing your job, so you had to get on and get yours done and put back on to the belt as quick as you could so that you were ready to pick up the next piece of work.

The women's work was frequently inspected for mistakes and they felt under constant scrutiny. Checkers walked around all day pointing out their mistakes. One forelady was in charge: she switched the belt on and off and set its speed. Managers came round once a day to see that production was running smoothly.

It was obvious to all concerned that after the introduction of the belt the women no longer had control over their own pace of work since it was externally imposed by the speed at which management set the belt. The work had to be done much faster, at an even speed throughout the day and with no interruptions. Each woman's work was linked in a chain with all the others, dependent on all those in front for her work, and all those behind in turn dependent on her. All had to work at exactly the same speed, but because they were compelled to by the belt rather than by mutual agreement. Under the old system where they worked separately, so long as they all produced approximately the same amount over the same time-span there had been no problem of hold-up or backlog because they did not have to wait on each individual piece of work as was now the case.

Under the new regime talking was banned and they had to ask permission to go to the toilet. If they got behind with the work, the only time they could catch up (or relieve themselves) was the five minutes every hour when the machines were turned off:

> If a machine was faulty or a drop of oil was getting on to the material your work would pile up while the machine was being seen to and all the other girls were carrying on working. So in that five minutes when the machines were turned off you'd have to hurry and try to catch up with your work because you're putting everyone else out. In any case there usually wasn't time to get to the toilet: everybody would want to go and so you'd all be queuing and sometimes the bell would go and you'd have to go back to work and you've missed out.

Doris experienced the new system as putting her under much greater pressure than the old. She could no longer decide how best to organize the work for herself or how to pace herself. She often got hot and flustered and was desperate for the belt to be turned off:

> When you worked on your own machine you were more composed because you were doing it in your own way. On the conveyor you

were always het up and girls were getting upset. That forelady was a terrible woman but she had to do her job I suppose. It was her discretion when to switch off the belt and we used to sit there watching the clock just thinking 'oh God hurry up and turn that thing off, so's we can sit quiet, just for a minute or two'. You used to get like that some days with all the machines going. And if she was busy or talking to someone she wasn't looking at the clock and didn't realize there was all us girls just longing for it to stop. Before the belt came in, you could regulate your own work and go out to the toilet when you wanted, not all tear out together at the same time and stand there and wait for someone to come out, which I thought was horrible. You couldn't leave your machine when you were on the conveyor because people would be getting behind and in a lather.

In Doris's view the new system also increased the power of the forelady because it was she who now controlled when the women started and stopped working. In the morning she could not switch on the belt until all operators were present so if someone arrived late and delayed her switching it on she was very angry and gave them a severe telling off:

> The foreladies felt so important when the conveyor came in. They liked being in charge. They must have been told that they must get so much work out of us and they were hurrying up and down and watching you all the time to see you were working fast enough but to be quite honest they used to get on your nerves. They wanted to see that work come off the belt so much. They got so much bonus out of it so it did them a bit of good to keep us at it. I hated our forelady – she was the type that everyone feared her, yet in them days we never said boo to a goose. I used to wish she would just go and leave or drop dead.

The reason for the introduction of the belt was quite clear to the women: 'to get out more work for less money'. They had to work harder for much the same wages as before while the firm was getting more collars, more quickly and more cheaply. But although the women were well aware of their employers' tactics, they were in no position to resist the new conditions or even to complain about speed-ups. If they could not keep up the pace they were sacked. There was no trade union. Many of the women were single, widows or had unemployed husbands and so were desperate for the work. They just had to endure the new conditions or leave:

> When they used to speed up the belt no one could keep up at first.

You'd have incidents where a girl was reduced to tears and working so hard to keep up but circumstances were so bad, especially for the widows, that they couldn't let anything get in their way. No one complained aloud when they speeded up the belt; they were all too afraid to stand together.

Conditions seemed to Doris to becoming more and more like a sweatshop. It was a very long day, from 7.30 in the morning sometimes until 6 in the evening, and then she had a long journey home to the Downham Estate in the suburbs. At night she fell into bed shattered but had to get up early again the following morning to catch the workmen's (*sic*) bus at 6.30 am. This bus was not very reliable and so she tended to arrive at work either very early and then had to hang around, or else just a little late and then she was shut out of the factory for the whole morning and lost half a day's pay.

Once inside, they started work on the machines straight away. There was no time to calm down after the journey, or to have anything to eat or drink until the belt was turned off at ten past ten:

Sometimes you'd just get there by a hair's breadth and tear up the stairs because that lever would be dead on 7.30 for you to start work. There was no time to put a little powder on or comb your hair. The forelady shouted at you to hurry up and you'd be getting all worked up.

One day it was all too much and Doris walked out:

This particular morning I'd just got there in time and I was sweating, I was hot. I thought I'll just put me bag on the floor underneath the machine and start. But as I sat down she started to shout 'Hang on, you were late' but I wasn't late, not really, and I thought if she only knew the rush I'd had to get there and I hadn't been able to stop for breakfast or anything. I'd just about had enough of her and I was so hot. I said to her 'I can't take any more of this or of you, I just can't' and I walked out and came home.

Doris went to a tribunal and was given dole money after complaining about the sweatshop conditions but some months later she returned to Rogers and her old job.

Although some of the women could stand the intensity of work on the belt better than others, they felt sorry for those who had difficulty coping; yet they could do little to help:

When I walked out and said to them 'I'm fed up and going home' they were all on my side but they were too afraid to say 'well, let's stop work and see what's the matter'. If anything went wrong and a girl fainted or got her finger stuck under the machine they'd have a spare girl who knew all the jobs to take over straightaway so they never lost any work. You were all feeling for that girl who'd fainted or cut her finger and all watching what was going on but you couldn't stop to help her because the work had to go on.

Since the introduction of conveyor belts was fairly widespread in the clothing industry during the 1920s and 1930s, the example of Rogers was only one amongst many. Mechanization was at first confined to the cheaper ready-made end of the market which manufactured women's clothes and men's shirts and underwear for chain stores like Marks and Spencer, C & A, or the CWS. Both of the latter two had their own factories where production was also based on assembly lines. 'High class' tailoring of suits and coats continued to be carried out on traditional lines for some years until they too could be mass produced. The fact that the clothing industry, especially in London, had traditionally been a sweated trade, may account for the particularly harsh conditions that Rogers were able to impose.[10]

Doris Hanslow's testimony is particularly valuable since she was in a good position to make a direct comparison of how the same work was organized before and after the arrival of the belt, and to pinpoint the effects on the workforce of the actual introduction of continuous flow methods. Her experience of Rogers illustrates well the characteristic uses of labour power in assembly-line production that I want to emphasize: control of both work and worker by machine pacing and the emergence of a new type of collective worker.

Machine pacing

Working on an assembly line was quite different from operating an individual machine as well as from other positions in the division of labour typical of the new industries. Most of these permitted the worker some element of control over the work process. But on a moving belt the assembler had no control whatsoever: she could decide neither how to accomplish her tasks, nor how many pieces to complete, nor what bonus or level of wages to aim at; nor could she alter her pace of work throughout the day. All these were determined by management and laid down in advance through their control over 'speeds and feeds'. Assemblers were subject to external regulation, imposed automatically by the mechanical operation of the belt.

Because the work travelled along the line at frequent and equal intervals and since each piece or set had to be completed as a whole before being replaced on the belt, it was not possible for assemblers to slow down and speed up again at will so as to create periods of relative rest for themselves; nor could they reorganize the job or arrange it in the way they found simplest or most convenient, for instance by subdividing it or completing two whole pieces in one go. Even such minimal control as this was physically impossible because the operation of the line required the work to be completed constantly and at a predetermined speed.

It was the same with the total amount of work: assemblers were not in a position to decide their own target for output or earnings since management preset the belt speed which determined the level of production to be achieved within any particular time-span (minute, hour, day or week). This also automatically preset the level of wages as well. If bonus points were tied to the amount of production, the speed at which belts were set usually represented the maximum level of bonus that could be earned. So assemblers were forced, again by mechanical means, to work at top speed to reach top bonus whether they wanted to or not.

As speed was the essence of assembly-line methods, the work was invariably fast and intense. Women applying for such work were accepted only if they could reach the required speed. If, after a trial period, they could not make the grade, they were sacked. Permanent workers too had to be able to achieve the speed without fail all day and every day; if they slowed down they too would be sacked. Many could not stand the speed and fainted or 'were carried out screaming' (as Jessie Evans describes). Others, like Doris Hanslow, tolerated the intensity for just so long and then snapped. In many ways it was a survival of the fittest and the most experienced, though the high wages of assembly work relative to other forms of employment (as well as widespread unemployment) were an incentive to thousands of women to try assembly work. Workers either reached the speed and accepted the conditions or they left. They were not in a position to challenge them even when they were unionized since the organization of work was a prerogative of management and not a negotiable issue.

Assemblers' control over their own work was thus extremely circumscribed and was nonexistent over the work process as a whole. Accomplishing the tasks in the given time depended on possessing certain dexterities and expertise but not on choosing how fast or how best to do the work. Their evident manual skills were exercised within a framework which they had no say in determining and which they were unable to alter. They were externally compelled by the very organization of the production process to work in a certain way and at a certain speed. Virtually every physical movement they made was predetermined by management since very little time was left over in the job schedule for movements that did not directly contribute to output.

From the employers' standpoint continuous flow processes possessed tremendous advantages over earlier systems of production. For the first time they really acquired the ability to predetermine production totally, both in terms of the volume of output and the time it would take to complete. But perhaps even more significantly, and in marked contrast with other production systems, control over the process of production also included control over the workers engaged in direct production since these could now also be mechanically regulated by the conveyor belt. Production quotas were translated by managers into hours per assembly line at a particular belt speed and this automatically guaranteed that assemblers worked at the level of intensity demanded by employers. As a consequence of adopting assembly-line methods, employers thus gained very much tighter control over all aspects of the process of production, including an essential section of the labour force. They acquired the capacity not only to impose the level of intensity but also to increase it through speed-ups, thus cutting labour costs by making the work even harder and faster. The system also encouraged constant attempts at refinement to increase output, for example by the application of scientific management techniques.

Although assemblers were indispensable to the operation of the line, it was the line that ran them, rather than them running the machines. They were subjected to a more extreme form of machine domination than existed in other or earlier forms of work organization, with the result that assemblers were machine dominated in a way that individual machine operators were not.

Individual machine operators in the textile, weaving and hosiery industry had already been subject to machine pacing from the late nineteenth century. The speed of looms or other machines had been preset and was outside of the control of the worker. However, operators still retained limited scope for variation in how they achieved the task and, even though their hourly output rate was laid down, they were often still able to pace themselves within the hour and so decide to work extra fast for a few minutes and then take it easy for the next few. So although machine pacing in itself was by no means peculiar to assembly-line methods, it was transformed, as we shall see, by being so closely integrated with the collective work unit. Collective machine pacing imposed on the collective assembly-line worker a more total form of subordination to managerially controlled technology than could ever be the case for machine-paced individual workers.

Machine pacing also placed assemblers in a quite different relation to the process of production from all the different kinds of indirect labour, none of whose work was machine paced. Mechanics, electricians, progress chasers, chargehands and supervisors were all essential to the production process but their output was neither regulated by machine, automatically imposed, nor externally controlled.

Indeed, it was machine pacing that brought about the fundamental division between assemblers and their immediate superiors, chargehands and supervisors. Basically, supervisors controlled the line and assemblers were controlled by it. Supervisors acted as the finger that pressed the button: they were in charge of starting and stopping the belt, adjusting its speed and deciding what degree of problems or hold-ups was sufficient to switch it off.

But the fact that the line automatically compelled operators to work at the required speed meant that one of the traditional functions of supervisors – ensuring that operators kept 'at it' all the time – was also mechanized to a certain extent. Where there was no moving belt, supervisors imposed work conditions by means of their own personal authority. Management relied on them to 'inspire' workers to do what was required, whether by creating a 'happy family' atmosphere, a competitive 'football team' mentality (as at Morphy Richards), or by harsh discipline backed up with the sanction of threats, fines and ultimately the sack (as at EMI or Peek Frean). Although the imposition of work discipline by mechanical means divested supervisors of some of their authority on the shopfloor, in practice they tended to retain power over assemblers but because their function had changed it now had a different source.

Supervisors now acted as the human appendage that controlled the belt and so they no longer had personal authority. However, since it was general practice for supervisors to receive higher wages when assemblers produced more, the organization of the new system actively encouraged them to demand ever higher levels of effort from line workers. Bonus schemes normally allocated to supervisors a proportion of the bonus points (sometimes as much as one-third) earned by line workers. So it was now in the direct financial interest of supervisors to increase work intensity and to speed up the belt. Certainly it appeared to Doris Hanslow that the forelady had more power after the conveyor was introduced than before because under the new arrangements the women could not stop working until she got around to switching off the belt. It was clear to Doris that the forelady was getting a rake-off and, as she saw it, that was the reason for the forelady's anger when latecomers delayed her switching on the belt and for her attempting to keep it going as long as possible.

Such arrangements meant that although the undermining of supervisors' authority could have resulted in their resistance to the new work methods,[11] in practice this was successfully averted by a new type of divide-and-rule policy whereby they benefited directly from their more limited function of maintaining and increasing the level of work intensity for direct assemblers. Supervisors retained their basic managerial function for getting out as much work as possible under the conditions of continuous flow processes, albeit in a different manner. Supervisors and assemblers were thus in a quite distinct and different relation to the production process from each other and the conflict and hostility between them, which was only too evident on many shopfloors, arose from an objective material base.

Machine pacing in assembly-line work did not operate separately on its own or in isolation from other aspects of the work process. On the contrary it was totally integrated with the collectivization of the work unit and it was really only in the context of the collective worker that the full potential of machine pacing was realized. The combination of the two greatly increased the effect of machine domination by imposing additional constraints on operators, and, by the same token, also conferred further gains on employers.

The collective worker

The assembly line represented the ultimate extension of the collectivization of the worker, through which the physical production process imposed an almost physical collectivity. The individual assembler was fully integrated only as one small part of a very much larger collective worker – the line – and her pay and bonus were dependent on the output of that line as a whole.

Of course it is true that any division of labour, regardless of the production process in which it occurs, necessarily creates a collective production unit or collective worker of which each individual worker represents the *n*th part. In conventional terminology, 'collective worker' refers to the sum total of all those, working at different levels of skill and training, who contribute to the overall process of production. This would include draughtsmen, engineers, manual workers and all the other grades of work, who occupy a variety of positions in the division of labour and who stand in a number of different relations to the production process. Naturally the collective worker in this general sense also existed in mass production processes where it included rate-fixers, engineers, progress chasers and many others in addition to assemblers. However, the point about assembly-line methods was that they also created an additional and highly specific form of collective worker, as a result of their extremely detailed technical division of labour. The labour unit characteristic of assembly-line production was made up of a very large number of individual workers, all performing similar tasks at the same skill level, each in an identical relation to the production process. This 'collective worker,' which took the form of all those who comprised the assembly line, was distinctive to and created by assembly-line methods. It complemented and coexisted with the more general form of collective worker inherent in the overall division of labour in mass production.

Since assembly-line work was so highly fragmented, the tasks to be performed by each individual worker amounted to only a fraction of the total necessary to produce the completed product. Consequently each woman represented only a fractional part of the total collective worker. What precise numerical fraction she represented depended on the length of the particular assembly line. At Rogers she represented about a twentieth of the collective worker, at Philips a forty-fifth but at EMI only a sixtieth. Each operator soldered only her five joints out of the hundreds that had to be soldered on a radio assembly line, or packed her two biscuits out of the tens that went into a tin of assorted biscuits. The longer the line, the greater the division of labour and the more highly fragmented the work. Each individual job had little significance in itself: its meaning was acquired only in the context of all the others. Similarly there was no independence for any individual within the collective: each woman was of importance only as the operator doing the job at her particular position in the line. She was trained in her fraction of the work alone and usually had no knowledge of other jobs on the line, let alone of the process as a whole.

But a very long line could have contradictory effects: although tasks were even more fragmented and each worker came to represent an even smaller fraction of the total collective worker, yet by the same token, the chain also became more interdependent. With a longer chain it was even more crucial that no links were missing since one gap or one link out of balance could put out the whole lot. The result of one woman getting 'up the wall' could have a dramatic effect on the work of fifty-nine others. So an inevitable result of a more detailed technical division of labour was to make the larger collective worker, and all the women who comprised it, even more interlinked. Although each woman might have felt that she was only a very small cog in a very large wheel, in fact all of the other nineteen, forty-four or fifty-nine cogs relied directly on her performing her tasks exactly as she was supposed, so that they could complete their own successfully. At the end of the week, they also all depended directly on each other for their wages since the volume of production determined the level of payment.

Being assembled together on the same line did not immediately entail any real social collectivity between the women. Rather the form of collectivity was primarily mechanical: the workers who comprised the line were linked mechanically through the arrangement of tasks and their position on the line, rather than through any form of social interaction. On the contrary, not only did the line not depend on social interaction between the links in the chain, but also in most cases assembly lines were so organized, by staggered spacing between seats or no talking rules, as to deliberately discourage contact and prevent communication between workers. In reality of course, there always was social contact between assembly-line workers and lines did become social as well as mechanical collectivities, but this was not required or imposed by the operation of the line.

The collectivity imposed by the assembly line had a second aspect: as well as being mechanical it was also serial, a feature resulting from the importance of the positioning of the links in the chain. Since tasks had to be carried out one after another in a pre-ordained sequence, the physical ordering of the work positions was crucial. Continuous production relied on all operators being continuously present at 'their' place and they were not permitted to leave the belt without special permission from the chargehand or forelady. So the line physically tied assemblers, as a particular fraction of the larger collective worker, not only to their own individual machine but also to their particular location in the line. The form of interdependence of the collective assembly-line worker reflected the serial nature of this link between all of the elements of the chain.

I have already suggested that machine pacing took on distinctive characteristics in the context of the collective worker. Whereas machine-paced individual operators did not affect any of the other machine-paced individual operators even when they were doing the same work, the opposite was the case for machine-paced assembly-line workers since they all depended on all the others all of the time. If an individual machine operator stopped work or her machine broke down only she was affected, but on an assembly line the same stoppage would have an immediate effect on everyone else on the line. Moreover, while machine-paced individual workers might have limited scope for variation in skill or speed, this was effectively eliminated in the case of the collective assembly-line worker; here there was no room at all for any individual variation in speed or in performance of the task. The moving belt forced all assemblers to work at exactly the same speed while individual machine operators working on their own might have some room for varying their pace.

For management the labour unit consisted of the collective worker and the line as such rather than the individuals who comprised it. It was this unit as a whole that produced the goods and it was accordingly paid as one unit, the basic wage rate and bonus being calculated on the basis of completed whole products made by the line as a whole rather than part-products made by individuals. It was paid to the whole line collectively, and then subdivided into however many operators were on the line. Similarly incentives too were aimed at the collective rather than individual worker: the bonus was a group bonus and everyone received the same amount. Indeed it was common for management to encourage different lines to compete against each other to achieve the highest level of output, and hence bonus. A league table of the various teams' positions was prominently displayed at the front of the main assembly area at GEC in Coventry (Castle 1984: 99), Philips and many other factories. Such competition invoked 'team spirit' rather than individual competitiveness, though chargehands were at pains to stress that team spirit was not incompatible with individual gain: if the whole line worked faster then the collective would earn more bonus and each individual woman would automatically benefit.

Collective machine pacing and collective payment introduced an element of collective self-disciplining into assembly-line work. The system exerted enormous pressure on each woman to keep working all the time and at the required speed. If she left her position or her machine broke down or she could not reach the speed, all the others would 'lose' work, and hence money, solely on account of her. Because of this, mutual pressure by the women on each other was at least partly responsible for the smooth running of the line. Since getting 'up the wall' put out all the other women they were likely to complain if someone did not 'pull her weight'. Pressure from the others was usually sufficient to make people try to speed up or buckle under and so it was often not necessary for supervisors to tell them off. In this way, collective self-disciplining was virtually built into this form of work organization and so replaced another of the functions of supervision. No doubt it was also more effective! From management's standpoint it had the added benefit of preventing individuals from objecting to harsh working conditions and so making collective resistance very unlikely to occur. It took much more for a whole line to get together and object than for an individual, and as individual complaints were usually snuffed out by collective pressure before they were publicly expressed, collective objections or actions were even less on the cards than individual ones.

Managers were well aware of the existence of collective self-discipline and built on it to their own advantage. At Rogers some of the older women with many years' experience of their machines could work extremely fast, this being the only way to earn reasonable wages on a piecework system. When the conveyor belt was introduced and the bonus system altered, these women found themselves 'out of pocket', taking home less than under the previous system. Because the only way of making up their money was by working faster, not only did they not resist when the forelady speeded up the belt but also on the contrary they actually encouraged the other women to keep up with the new speed rather than complain about it. At Peek Frean too when women could not keep up others either helped out or moaned at them. In both instances the response was engendered by the system itself rather than by the women's personalities: their negative reaction when one person disrupted the flow of work arose naturally from the circumstances since every other person who also comprised the larger collective worker did actually suffer. Assembly-line workers did not need to have mean, individualistic or money-grabbing personalities in order to discipline each other; it just happened automatically as a result of collective machine pacing.

However, the pressure to keep going at all times could also have effects that were counter-productive to output, management or established job demarcations. For example, if machines were not working properly it was sometimes quicker for assemblers to mend them themselves rather than calling for a mechanic as they were supposed to. Going by the book would have involved stopping work, losing money (if the line was not paid 'waiting time' for breakdowns), and affecting all the others in the chain. Doing the repair oneself did not have such dramatic effects even though it might end up with the finished product being faulty. However, the do-it-yourself approach could only be a short-term solution because inspectors would pin the fault on the particular worker sooner or later. At Rogers, where the women were not paid when machine breakdowns stopped the line from working, Doris Hanslow became quite adept at mending her own machine. But at Philips breakdown time was paid at the basic rate and the women could enjoy a paid rest while machines were being mended. This even stimulated some minor acts of sabotage at times when the pace of work was particularly fast so that they could enjoy a few minutes' respite.

Being one small part of a large collective worker thus had a number of contradictory effects. Since any one person could sabotage the system or send it haywire each assembler possessed the potential power to resist or disrupt the line as a whole (although this was very rarely used). At the same time each person depended on all the others for her work and her earnings. Similarly the day-to-day solidarity that developed among assembly workers was also contradictory: they helped each other out but they also disciplined each other. The very organization of the work process placed extremely narrow limits on collective action. Yet despite this, resistance did occur and there were strikes against changes in work conditions and speed-ups. While the assembly line automatically imposed a mechanical and serial collectivity on the women, the kind of collective social grouping that they could form was thus much more open-ended.

Jessie Evans

Jessie Evans's account of her experience at the Philips radio factory illustrates well the links between the different aspects of the use of labour power characteristic of continuous flow production. The Dutch firm, originally based in Eindhoven, bought up the Mullard valve factory in Mitcham in 1927 and built a new factory on the same site to manufacture radio sets. Since production was mechanized and on a moving belt from the outset, Miss Evans could not provide information about the effects of mechanization on a pre-existing workforce. However, her experience gives a clear account both of the relationship of assembly-line workers to the production process and of the new form of collective worker. The later introduction of the Bedaux system of 'scientific management' reinforced both of these features by greatly increasing the intensity of work.

There were seven very long lines in the main assembly shop, each over a quarter of a mile in length, and with forty-five work positions. As well as the forty-five operators, there were four 'spare girls', two for each side of the line, and also inspectors, repairers and casers (all men) who sat at the end of the line, as well as the chargehand. To cross from one side of the line to the other involved walking all the way to the end of the line because climbing over the belt was not allowed.

The seating was staggered so that operators did not sit directly side by side across the line, and their sets therefore did not collide as they replaced them on the belt. Most of the jobs involved soldering joints and electrical wiring, and each operator had a reel of solder and a soldering iron on her bench or a three tier rack of wires, resistors, condensers and other components which she attached with pliers. Each line had its own belt-feeder who filled up the boxes and replenished the solder from the stores department as often as twice a day.

The speed of the line was timed so that sets reached operators at three-minute intervals and this position was marked on the belt by a paint spot. Every time a paint spot came along there was another set on it waiting to be assembled and the one that had just been worked on had to be replaced on the same paint spot to travel on to the next operator. The job of any one assembler might consist of as many as forty-five joints each, all to be soldered in the three minutes allowed

Figure 9 Jessie Evans.

for each set. Needless to say it was some time before a newcomer could take over the whole job herself and many months before she was proficient at it. Each woman had a sample set by her bench with 'her' joints marked in red paint; this enabled the inspectors to pin dry joints or other faults on the particular woman responsible for them and helped the spare girls take over the job with the minimum of delay.

Since assembly work was paid at the adult wage rate only those aged 18 and over were allowed to work on the belt. Younger women worked on individual machines in the subassembly shop above the main assembly or on small presses in the machine shop. New recruits to assembly were assessed for dexterity, allocated to a particular job and given basic instruction in soldering or wiring in the training school. Then they would sit at an extra bench placed alongside an existing worker to learn the job from her.

Jessie Evans had already been working for eleven years in a variety of jobs by the time she started at Philips in 1936. She stayed there until she retired in 1974, having been promoted from operator to spare girl before the war, to 'spare spare' (who could do all the jobs of all the lines) during the war and to chargehand in the 1950s when women were first employed in this position. In her opinion the firm was a good employer and paid well, but only at the cost of very hard work and harsh conditions.

> Forty-five joints in three minutes was hard work. You had no time to look up even and there was no time to talk. The whole belt was timed to do so many sets an hour and you had to keep up with the belt. If you didn't then you were no good and you were put out – sacked. It was awful really – some women used to be carried out screaming hysterics. Really sweated labour it was until the war broke out.

Everything depended on all forty-five keeping to the same high speed all the time:

> Women who were slow would hold you up. If you what they called 'dropped a set' and it didn't get to the end of the line, then the bonus was less because the full number of sets for the hour hadn't been done. If you had one bad worker on the belt, it stopped everybody. If you were a bit slow you saw that paint spot coming towards you and it was awful.

Miss Evans could keep up with the pace pretty well. She took some pride in being a fast worker; sometimes she even had a little time to spare before the inevitable next paint spot arrived. But those who found the work much harder than she did still tried their best to keep up because they needed the money. However, she thought that many women would not have been able to stand the work at all:

> People didn't leave on account of the speed because they couldn't afford to. In those days you were fighting for your job. If you had a job you did your best to keep it because there were always others who wanted it. Most of my friends went into shop work. It was a lot easier than the factory but the pay wasn't so good. But many of them couldn't have stood the pace. It was hectic all right.

It was a very long day from 7.30 am to 5 pm, Monday to Friday, with no proper break apart from lunch:

> They allowed you five minutes at the end of the day but that was for washing your hands and then there was a mad rush to get out to the cloakroom. You weren't given a tea-break in the day at all. There was a ten-minute break but it wasn't paid and you had to make up the time by working even faster. The chargehand increased the speed of the belt so you made up the ten minutes in your working hour and of course that meant you were working still faster. The belt didn't actually go faster but he used a different set of paint spots on the line that were closer together and so they came round sooner than the usual three minutes. The time-study people worked out the time it had to take to do a set making up for the tea-break time. The ten minutes included going to the trolley to fetch your tea and walking back with it.

Other than this they were stuck to the line for nine and a half hours a day and discipline was strict: no one could leave without permission and the foremen were quite intimidating:

> You had to tell the spare girl if you wanted to go to the toilet and she wrote your name on the blackboard and then crossed it off when you came back. There was no talking allowed and no larking about. The supervisors had to be very very strict to keep their jobs. One chargehand, Mr Collins, was injured in the First World War and had a steel plate in his chest. If he wanted to upset anybody he'd walk down the belt and bang on this tin plate with his screwdriver. The foremen were always worried about things going missing and of course we had a drawer in our bench to keep tools in. Mr Bennett, one of the supervisors, was a funny old man. On a Friday he would come up the line and shout 'Drawers, drawers, I want to see your drawers, girls!' And we all had to open the drawers in our bench and show we hadn't hidden any components in there to take home.

In Jessie Evans's view, working on the line was much harder than working individual machines in subassembly or the machine shop because it permitted less control over the work and no choice over speed:

> In subassembly you worked individually and the jobs had different timings. On one you'd get five minutes to do a hundred pieces and on another an hour to do a hundred pieces. It varied depending on the job and it was the same in the machine shop. I would say that work was easier because it was *your* speed as to how much money you earned but on the belt you had to keep up otherwise other people lost their money.

When the Bedaux system was introduced rate-fixers and time-study men reorganized the work. The belt was speeded up and the pace became even more intense:

> There was a department called the 'set fathers'. These were the time-study men who originally built the set and split the job into three minute pieces. You would start a new set and a rate-fixer would stand by the side of you with a stopwatch timing your hand movements and assessing how much could be fitted into the three minutes. The set fathers came and showed you what your job was and the best way to do it – supposedly – but you would sort your own way round really. Once they'd timed the set you would start at what they called a 60M hour which is a minute's work in a minute but it didn't stay like that. To get your bonus you had to do a 75M hour which is a minute's work in three-quarters of a minute so they speeded up the line till it reached that speed. Once they started speeding up nearly everyone got behind. The Bedaux system was very unpopular. You'd do one speed for a week and then they'd put it up again until it got to the 75M hour and it stopped at that. You had to do that to earn your money.

When a new type of set was to be produced the Bedaux engineers chalked temporary spots on the belt. As the speed of the line was gradually increased this first set of spots would be rubbed out and others chalked on at closer intervals. When the assemblers eventually reached the top speed of 75M after about a month, the spots were painted on in their permanent position and the line speed was set at the top bonus rate. (The bonus points were called M for Mitcham, rather than B for Bedaux.)

The Bedaux system was intended to work as an incentive scheme for assemblers. At the top bonus rate the line earned 1s 3d a day. But at a maximum weekly wage of £2 10s, this top bonus rate (earned only when there had been no faults or hold-ups all week) amounted to not much more than 6 shillings, or one-eighth of the total wage. Often it was considerably less. Everyone found the new pace much harder and at the faster speed even very experienced assemblers made mistakes. But the bonus system was arranged so that they paid for the mistakes they made because of the increased speed:

> At the end of the line there was a big blackboard and if you got one dry joint your name would go up on that board and that meant you'd lost a third of your bonus – just for one dry joint. Three dry joints in a day and you lost the whole lot.

In a situation where they were soldering forty-five joints every three minutes for nine and a half hours it was quite easy to lose the whole bonus on a regular basis. So although the bonus was earned as a group and depended on the total output of all forty-five operators, each operator could lose her own individual portion of it even when the line achieved the top bonus rate and when her dry joints did not affect the total output. The line as a whole could also lose the bonus through no fault of their own:

> Equipment not working properly was one of the trials and tribulations. The reel of solder would break or the iron go cold or burn out and then everyone was waiting behind you and losing their bonus.

The first two jobs on the line were reserved for boys on the grounds that they were too mechanical for women since they involved using a hammer and punch to insert components into the empty case. However, Miss Evans encountered no problem in doing the jobs when she was 'spare girl'. Whereas women stayed permanently on the line, boys worked as assemblers only until they were old enough to earn the adult men's rate and then they were put on 'proper men's' work.

Occasionally one of the boys indulged in minor sabotage to the benefit of the rest of the line:

> If it got too hectic he would cause a fuse so that we could have a rest while the electrics were repaired. The break would go against the electricians for however long it took them to repair it, so we didn't lose much money. Everyone was pleased when that happened.

No one criticized the boys' attempts to liven things up:

> One bit of excitement was when the two boys saw a rat under the belt and they chased the rat with the hammers they used to bang the rivets in with. They chased it all round the shopfloor and everybody was standing up on their chairs until they caught it!

Sabotage was in fact one of the very few ways of relieving the intensity of work. Although there was a stoppage one afternoon, when the whole line downed tools over a dispute with the chargehand about their bonus being docked, they returned to work when it was restored. Miss Evans could not recall any other stoppages in the period before the Second World War: the women complained about the speed but not so loud that they jeopardized their jobs, being only too well aware that other women were waiting outside the factory gate ready to take their place.

The wage exchange

A key premiss of the argument about relations of production being made in this chapter is that the use of labour power can be organized according to different structural arrangements, for example collectively or individually, machine paced or not. And just as there has been no single way in which labour power has been used common throughout the history of capitalism, so too there is no single wage form. Different payment systems are closely associated with the particular way in which labour power is used. The wage form encapsulates the relationship between employer, worker and output and is thus indicative of the nature of the exchange between labour and capital. Different wage forms reflect variations in this exchange between different methods of production, different positions in the division of labour and different types of worker.

Looking at the wage exchange in this way again involves a critique of received Marxist theory. In his analysis of machinofacture in Volume 1 of *Capital*, Marx drew attention to how the development of factory based production and the introduction of machinery altered the relationship between worker and capitalist. But these insights were never fully integrated into his interpretation of the exchange between wage labour and capital. The salient characteristic of wage labour that Marx was concerned to demonstrate was the homogenization of the conditions under which workers sold their labour power: in nineteenth-century Britain more and more workers were drawn into factory employment where they sold their labour power under similar conditions. The only feature Marx analysed in any depth, apart from the exchange of labour for a wage, was that of the intensity, and varying degrees of intensity, of exploitation.

Although Marx focused – necessarily – on what was the most significant feature of his time, the tendency among later Marxists has been to present the particular form of exchange of labour power with capital that was characteristic of factory work in nineteenth-century Britain as the single and only possible form. The mere fact of exchange is taken to mean that all exchanges between capital and labour are identical. While homogenization may well have been the most important characteristic of the exchange in the late nineteenth century, historical developments in the mode of production during the intervening period have meant that differentiation, rather than homogenization, of the conditions under which different groups of workers sell their labour power, has become of much greater significance. The argument being developed here presupposes that the exchange between capital and labour does not exist in a single, constant or unchanging form, pure and transhistorical. On the contrary, it always takes a specific form which changes with historical development of the mode of production and varies for different groups of workers, occupying different positions in the division of labour, and working under different processes of production. Although the actual exchange of labour power for a wage is certainly basic and common to all instances of wage labour, this exchange always occurs under particular circumstances and in a specific form.

The unitary approach can comprehend neither the variation and specificity between different forms of wage exchange, nor their important theoretical implications for the analysis of class relations. If the exchange between capital and labour is constitutive of class relations, it follows that variations in the form of exchange will engender variations also in the class relations that arise from the exchange. However, because the unitary approach ignores that there can be important differences in the form of exchange, the inevitable corollary is to present a unitary conception of the working class as comprising a single undifferentiated group, and by implication, also a unitary conception of the conflict between wage labour and capital. Nor is it in a position to recognize the significance of differences between systems of payment as indicators of the nature of the exchange.

These considerations are of direct relevance to the analysis of the wage exchange of assembly-line work since assemblers were subject not only to a distinctive use of their labour power but also to a distinctive payment system. This was developed by employers as that most appropriate to the organization of assembly-line work and as such it reflected the specific form of exchange between capital and assembly-line workers. Employers' capacity to impose the speed and intensity of work gave them a high measure of control over the production process and relatively unrestricted use of labour power. They had power to predetermine the volume of output, the level of work intensity and ultimately the size of the wage. The wage form of assemblers corresponded to and reflected this high degree of control. In other systems of production, by contrast, where employers could not determine output so closely, different types of payment systems were in operation.

In essence the payment system of assembly-line work was based on a pre-fixed rate of production per hour and paid to a group of workers as a single production unit. For the hourly rate, the direct assembly-line worker sold a particular intensity of labour power, the level of which was determined by the employer, through effort norms built into the time-rate and imposed by the speed of the line. The combination of these elements characterized the payment system of direct assemblers and distinguished it from that both of the other direct workers and of indirect workers. Although inseparable in practice the elements merit individual attention.

Group payment

The first point to note about the new payment system is that it was a collective one. Since the line as a whole constituted the basic productive unit, all the women who comprised it were paid on a group basis. Collective machine pacing eliminated variations in output between individual workers that might have existed when individuals operated machines independently of each other, and the collective payment system reflected this characteristic of the new production relations. Although each woman was employed as an individual, the real contractual relationship of output to wage was between the collective worker, or all the women on the line, and the employer rather than with each as an individual. The wage rate was set as a collective rate independently of individuals.

The examples of Rogers and Peek Frean demonstrate how the introduction of a group payment system accompanied the reorganization of work on assembly lines. Previously Doris Hanslow had been paid on a piecework basis for however many collar tabs she attached during the course of the week. To a certain extent it was up to her how hard she worked and how much she earned. Women who worked faster than her earned more and those who were slower earned less. Under the new system, where the speed of work was externally set, everyone earned exactly the same. Doris no longer had any control over how hard she had to work to earn her wage nor over the actual amount she received in her weekly pay packet. The collective rate was there for her to take or leave but not to negotiate over. If she wanted to be employed at Rogers she was compelled to accept the pre-set collective wage and the pace of work on which it was based.

It was similar for Winnie Young and Nell Williams at Peek Frean when biscuit packing was 'rationalized'. Several major changes occurred simultaneously: their jobs were fragmented, a moving conveyor was introduced and, for the first time, their wages were calculated for the whole line as a single unit. Under the old system they had received one halfpenny for each tin they packed and weekly earnings equalled the total number of tins packed by each woman multiplied by the rate per tin. Under the new system they were paid a collective time-rate and all received the same amount.

Group payment thus marked a first important break between the payment system of assemblers and individual machine operators whose wages depended solely on their own work: with the introduction of assembly lines, individual piecework was replaced by group payment.

Rate-of-production wage

The second feature of the new payment system is that it was essentially based on a production as opposed to piece-rate, measured in terms of products per hour. Rather than being paid a rate for each piece they produced, assemblers were paid a basic hourly rate of so many pence per hour for a given rate of production. The weekly wage amounted to forty-four, forty-eight or however many hours they worked multiplied by the hourly rate.

Payment systems based on pre-fixed production rates contrasted in significant ways with piece-rate systems. Under a pure piecework system, earnings depended only on the number of pieces produced, with no day-rate, fall-back rate or time element affecting the wage. Workers were paid for the number of products rather than for the length of time they worked, and so their wages depended on counting pieces rather than measuring time. In its original historical form, pieceworkers contracted with the employer to produce the object at a given price. It could therefore appear that the product, rather than labour power, was being sold and bought. In the pre-factory outwork system, where independent workers owned their tools, they did indeed sell their products rather than their labour power to the capitalist at the agreed price. However, under the factory system they were in reality selling their labour power and not the product, but their labour was converted into a price per piece, set by the factory owner. Certain aspects of the earlier outwork system thus survived in factory production, and continued to exist in a modified form in many industries right up until the introduction of methods of mass production.[12]

By the beginning of the twentieth century most piecework systems included a time-based element in the form of production targets, imposed by management so that the worker had to produce a minimum number of pieces in the day to earn at all, but all of these were paid at the normal piece-rate price. The immediate predecessor to the time/effort rate characteristic of assembly-line payment systems was usually an individual piecework system such as this with an in-built time/target element. A target would be set for individual machine operators, stipulating the minimum amount to be produced in an hour. This was to ensure that they were capable of operating the machine efficiently but it was a lower limit which all workers were expected to surpass. There was no upper limit and the piece-rate payment system was intended to act as an incentive to the worker to produce as many pieces above the minimum as possible and earn as large a wage as she could. Normally only a small portion of the actual wage accrued to the minimum target part of the work, while most was payment for the additional work. There could be large variations between the earnings of people doing exactly the same work when they worked individually and at their own pace. Under such arrangements, where employers could not impose a particular intensity of work, they could not determine in advance either the precise volume of output or their total wages bill.

The situation at the Lucas motor components factory for example contrasted sharply with that at Rogers or Peek Frean. Machine operators there continued to be paid on an individual piecework system until the early 1930s when management brought in Bedaux engineers to undertake a complete overhaul of the organization of production and of the payment system. Up until then foremen had authority to set piecework prices and negotiated individually with pieceworkers over the price they set as well as their general level of earnings (Tolliday 1983: 49).

The form of assembly-line payment differed markedly from this, however, since here management held absolute control over the level of output and work intensity. With the introduction of continuous flow production methods, many factories switched from a piece to a time/effort system based on a rate of product over time. Wage rates were so calculated that the new earnings level approximated that of the faster workers under the old piecework system. Moving conveyors were generally set at the speed of the fastest, rather than average worker, and all had to reach that standard. As a result, those who had previously worked at average speed now had to work harder but, because of the greater intensity, they would take home a bit more money. This change helped to give the new system the appearance of including an incentive. On the other hand, very fast individual workers could also lose out under a collective time-based system. There was no variation in earnings and workers were sacked if they could not keep up with the maximum rather than minimum speed.

The moving conveyor belt was the key to this standardization: it had to be set at a certain speed, which automatically determined the volume of output, the intensity of work per hour, and the size of the wage. For example, at Morphy Richards during the period of the static belt, wide variations existed between different lines in both output and wages. Supervisors played an essential role in keeping up the pace of work, but 'encouragement' and bonus incentives were insufficient to remove the variations, effectively eliminated only by the introduction of the conveyor. Only with the benefit of a moving belt could employers pre-plan with any certainty. At the same time supervisors also lost their role in determining pay rates and negotiating over individual wages.

However, workers employed in different parts of the total assembly operation were paid according to different principles. Indirect workers alone were paid a pure time-rate in the form of a guaranteed flat-rate unrelated to any measure of their own output and which did not require a particular level of work intensity. Their earnings were based solely on the rate per hour or per day in a similar way to most non-manual jobs today: they had to perform satisfactorily in order to receive the time-rate but no explicit efforts norms were laid down. In sharp contrast to assemblers, the output of supervisors, electricians, and progress chasers was not mechanically regulated and could not be quantified. Correspondingly they received a flat-rate payment of so much per hour multiplied by the number of hours they worked.

But in addition to the flat-rate, most also received a bonus but this was based on the output of the direct assemblers. Supervisors' bonus 'earnings' were thus linked not to their own effort but to that of others. By contrast, direct assemblers were paid on the basis of a time-rate which included an in-built effort norm. Whatever bonus they earned was based solely on their own volume of output and effort. So calling both types of 'extra' earnings by the same term is quite misleading since they were entirely different.

To add to this confusion in referring to all the different so-called extras as 'bonuses', the inclusion of effort norms and bonus payments in the time-based system often led to assemblers being described, incorrectly, as pieceworkers. It also made the payment systems of pieceworkers and assemblers appear more similar than they in fact were. Employers emphasized the similarities between the two by focusing on the earnings level and obscuring the new effort principle underlying the rate-of-production wage form. This served to mask the fundamental difference between the two. While machine-paced direct workers were paid on the basis of a time-rate with an in-built effort norm, individual operators were usually paid a modified time/target piece-rate similar to that outlined earlier where an effort norm might be required but could not be imposed. Individual machine operators could determine their level of earnings to a certain limited extent and the payment system to which they were subject did include more of a genuine incentive than could ever be the case on a moving belt. Here, both effort norm and bonus earnings were built into the time-rate, determined by management and beyond the control of direct assemblers. There was certainly no incentive in the accepted sense of the word.

Bonus

The payment system for direct assemblers in virtually all the factories I have come across included in-built effort norms, in the form of group bonus points, masquerading as an incentive bonus.[13] When Jessie Evans started at Philips the hourly rate was 8½d, 2d above the rate in her previous job, but this included an in-built effort norm. The number of biscuit tins Winnie Young and Nell Williams had to pack in an hour, the number of collars Doris Hanslow had to make up, and the number of radio sets the workers at Philips and EMI had to assemble was laid down in advance and they had to make up that number to earn the time-rate.

The supposed underlying principle of bonus schemes was that workers were to be paid a bonus for whatever they produced in excess of the amount that had to be done in an hour to earn the hourly rate. A worker who performed an hour's work in fifty-five minutes therefore 'saved' five minutes in every hour, and would be able to earn somewhat over the nine hours earnings within a day. However, only a proportion of the 'saved' time counted for earnings under this system, customarily a half in engineering establishments covered by the Engineering Employers Federation rates (NSOL 1930–5 Vol. II: 141–2). Under a genuine piecework system, by contrast, the worker received the whole of the proportionate extra value of each additional piece produced.

Although setting the level of effort was presented as a purely neutral and technical matter, in fact it was a management prerogative. It is only too obvious that where management set the effort norm with a moving belt, the amount 'saved' and hence the incentive was more illusion than reality. Management could establish the hourly effort norm at sixty pieces to be done in an hour, and set the belt speed so that seventy-five would in fact be produced. Bonus earnings would then accrue to the extra fifteen. Workers would be extolled to reach that level of production so as to earn all the bonus they possibly could although in fact they had no choice but to reach that level. However, because they *lost* points if someone got 'up the wall' or 'dropped a set', it also appeared to them that they earned extra bonus by working harder. Of course they did gain part of the value of the additional output between sixty and seventy-five, but this could amount only to a tiny portion of their eventual weekly earnings. That it was commonly presented by supervisors, and appeared to workers, as a genuine bonus was very useful to management since it could be used as the proverbial carrot and stick. Collective self-disciplining of the line also relied to some extent on the women's belief that the bonus was worth striving for.

The bonus was also useful to management as a penalty system. At Philips workers were docked bonus points for dry joints even if the faults were due to mechanical breakdown. Bonus points were subtracted from their wage on an individual basis. The penalty system was thus used by management as a form of quality control, built into the payment system and paid for by the workers. In this way employers got the best of both worlds by treating assemblers as individuals or as a collective unit according to what best suited their own financial interest. Bonus was paid only for collective output but at the same time it could also be subtracted from individuals.

Implications

This discussion implies that payment systems should not be taken at face value. Although they appear merely technical, they in fact encapsulate the degree of domination exerted by capital over labour. If one follows the basic argument of Marxist economics, wages are exchanged for the use of labour power, rather than for a particular amount of labour power or level of output. What employers buy is the right to use the labour power for a given time period and, within reason, in the way that they determine. The various wage forms operate as mechanisms for imposing levels of work intensity and at the same time reflect the degree of control of capital over the use of labour power. Different wage forms or systems of payment are therefore good indicators of differences in the exchange between labour and capital. That different forms of exchange exist implies that workers can be in different structural relations to the production process and to capital and, conversely, the existence of different structural relations gives rise to different wage forms.

In assembly-line industries the different basis on which indirect and direct workers, and individual machine operators and collectively machine-paced assemblers, were paid was quite apparent. For pieceworkers, each piece had a price and their wage was based on the number of pieces multiplied by the price. Assemblers' wages were based on a rate of products per hour, while indirect workers received a pure time-rate.

It should be clear by now how closely the wage form of direct assembly work was connected to the specific exchange between assemblers and their employers and how it formed an integral part of their relations of production. The emergence of this new rate-of-production wage form accompanied the introduction of collective machine pacing and should be viewed as another dimension of the overall rationalization and standardization of work made possible by continuous flow methods of production. Collective rates were paid to collective workers: the collective element in the payment system corresponded to the fact that the basic work unit was a collective one. Similarly the time-rate with its in-built effort norm mirrored the manner in which machine pacing guaranteed a pre-set volume of output over any given time span. The assembler sold her labour power for a certain number of hours a week but had no control over the pace at which she would work or her level of output. The organization of mass production gave employers relatively unrestricted use of her labour power through their control over all aspects of production and they determined the level of intensity.

Before moving on it is important to make a clear distinction between the *form* and the *level* of wages and to note that the foregoing discussion refers to the form of the payment system only and not to the actual level of wages. Although the wage form was determined by the production process to which it corresponded and can be explained internally from within that system, the same does not hold for the level of wages. The actual wage level that women could command was closely connected to their position in the labour market, and the relative weakness of that position in comparison with men, which was in turn affected by their role in the domestic economy.

So a full explanation of the level, rather than the form, of wages earned by women assemblers would have to refer to factors, to be explored in Chapters 6 and 7, which lay outside of the sphere of paid employment but impinged on their place within it. While the wage form of male assembly-line workers at the Ford plant in Michigan approximated to that of women assemblers in the new industries in Britain, their wage rates were considerably higher. In both cases wage rates exceeded those for similar work, but different factors entered into the determination of the actual level of wages. At Ford the $5 day represented a managerial attempt to undermine organized resistance to machine pacing. In the British factories, although assemblers' wage rates were set somewhat higher than those generally prevailing for manual female labour so as to attract women into this type of employment, they still remained within the normal range of 'women's wages' as determined by women's position in the labour market, and that meant lower than men's wages.

Resistance to assembly-line relations of production

If the form of wage exchange characteristic of assembly-line production was a specific one, so also were the conflicts between labour and capital arising from it. Just as the basic exchange of labour power for a wage never exists in a pure form but always within given relations of production, so the nature of the contradictions varies according to the form of exchange. Most industrial struggles have been specific ones: workers have not challenged the central wage relation of capitalism itself but rather the particular form in which they encountered it. Most have also been defensive attempts to protect existing conditions and prevent employers introducing changes to alter the exchange between capital and labour even further in their favour. New ways of organizing production are bound to produce new conflicts and assembly-line methods were no exception to this.

Significantly, resistance to assembly-line relations of production focused on speed-ups and the adoption of the Bedaux system. It was strongest not in new factories where workers were recruited to a work process organized from the outset on continuous flow principles, but rather in older ones where these principles were brought in to replace existing work methods.

In the former case, the Bedaux system was icing on the cake, merely perfecting the existing form of work organization (for example at Philips and Peek Frean) and systematizing the group payment system. Workers in such plants were very rarely, if ever, in a position to challenge the organization of production. At Philips and other factories already organized on a continuous flow principle, women were recruited precisely to undertake assembly-line work; their wages were higher than in alternative local employment; only those who could keep up with the pace were retained; management vehemently opposed the entry of trade unions and union members were victimized. Thus management already had effective control over the whole production process and took on labour on the basis of the particular form of wage exchange associated with it. Under such circumstances it would be unrealistic to imagine assemblers opposing what they encountered as a basic condition of their employment. They might, and did, resist changes in the bonus arrangements and their resultant increases in work intensity and deteriorating conditions, but they did not challenge the assembly-line system as such. That many of the women who could not stand the conditions left the job rather than organizing against them, could be interpreted as a passive form of protest. Indeed, one authoritative study of industrial conflict in Britain during the first half of the twentieth century acknowledged high turnover, along with strikes, as an important index of industrial unrest (Knowles 1952: 210).

On the other hand, where the Bedaux system was adopted as a means of reorganizing or speeding-up existing work methods on the lines of continuous flow, loss of control, intensification, and deteriorating conditions of work and pay were experienced by all subjected to them as being directly due to the Bedaux system. Under these circumstances it is not surprising that the system became a focus of active opposition in itself. Thus the most fiercely fought strikes against assembly-line relations of production consisted in attempts by workers to prevent the erosion of existing working conditions by means of the Bedaux system. The same survey of industrial conflict singled out the Bedaux system as a major factor in the upsurge of industrial militancy during the 1930s: systems of work measurement became one of the main causes of strikes, in contrast to the years following the First World War, when they had been largely for trade union recognition (Knowles 1952: 53, 231).

One of the best known and protracted struggles occurred at the Lucas motor components factory in Birmingham where Bedaux engineers planned a total reorganization of production methods. However, implementation was sabotaged from the outset. Groups of workers collectively refused rate-fixing and threatened to throw the rate-fixers out of the windows. Jessie McCullough was filing shock absorbers when the Bedaux engineers tried to use her speed of work as the norm for all the other women in the shop:

> One day I turned round and saw someone standing behind me while I was working. I asked them what they were doing and they said they were timing me. Why me and not her, I said, pointing to another woman. The fact was I've always worked quickly ... they obviously wanted to set the time by me and the others would have to keep up with it. Well, I had a talk with the girls about it and in the end ... we all refused.
>
> (Quoted in Leeson 1973: 130–1)

Jessie went to the TGWU to collect application forms for all the women in her shop, after the AEU had refused to take them in. She was instrumental in unionizing a large proportion of the workforce and active in the strike, but afterwards she was sacked and blacklisted in factories throughout Birmingham.

The Bedaux system already had a bad reputation in the Midlands and the women's worst fears were confirmed as soon as the engineers arrived at Lucas. Thousands refused to work and held mass meetings in the street outside the factory, supported by the Communist party. The action, involving more than ten thousand women, has been described (Tolliday 1983: 51) as a spontaneous eruption rather than an organized strike: there were fights with the police, arrests, and a great sense of solidarity.

After only a few days the firm backed down: managers realized, even before the strike began, that their handling of the situation was inept. As soon as the women walked out, they rapidly withdrew the Bedaux engineers, in order to save the situation in the long run and pre-empt having to recognize the TGWU to which many workers now belonged. The women were elated and held a victory meeting, but in fact they had been outflanked and their cause for celebration was short lived. Lucas's appeared to back down so completely now with the intention of reintroducing the plan more gradually at a later date and under a different name. They reckoned that the workforce would accept it more readily if it was presented as a homegrown plan, and had no connotations with the detested Bedaux system. During the later part of 1932 and 1933 a Time Study department was established and the Lucas Point Plan introduced. It was exactly the same as the Bedaux scheme and was implemented by Bedaux engineers but:

> Great care was taken to ensure that the Bedaux men that were brought in concealed their true identity. Lucas paid a third of their salary, so they could be said to be 'on the staff', but they were wholly responsible to Bedaux.
>
> (Nockolds 1976: 288)

Although the women were not taken in by this subterfuge they had effectively lost the initative and, despite several more stoppages, were eventually defeated. In the summer of 1934 the Bedaux system was fully implemented throughout the company.

Women were in the forefront of opposition to the Bedaux system not only at Lucas but also in factories throughout the country, and sometimes with greater long term success. In the clothing industry, active resistance resulted in at least two firms (Horne Brothers and Hector Powe) (Lab.Res. Vol. XXII June 1933: 258) dropping the scheme, and concessions were also won at the Wolsey hosiery factory in Leicester after a lengthy strike (Littler 1982: 119–28). Women also organized (unsuccessful) strikes against the Bedaux system at the Venesta Plywood Company and at Elliotts Engineering Works, both in London (Lab.Res. Vol. XXIII Jan. 1934: 20). At the Rover car plant in Coventry women were used as guinea-pigs: management intended to apply the system in the first instance only to women working in the trim and when it had been accepted there, extend it to the rest of the male workforce. The women were not in a trade union and would be less able to resist than organized craftsmen. However, events did not proceed as smoothly as planned. The women downed tools, were supported by men in the National Union of Vehicle Builders who joined the strike, and eventually the scheme was withdrawn, in this case permanently (Tolliday 1982: 6–15; Carr 1979: 474–8).

Such strikes were most likely to be successful when they involved the entire workforce (as at Lucas) or at least several sections of it (Wolsey and Rover). In some cases supervisors were affected by the work reorganization imposed by the Bedaux system and united with operators against it. In others, where women were used as guinea-pigs, male workers supported the women's actions against Bedaux so as to prevent it being applied to them later on. However, in plants where the Bedaux system merely perfected already existing assembly-line methods, supervisors were already divided from operators and often benefited further from implementing the system. Under such circumstances, united action by the two sections was unthinkable. Lack of unity stacked the cards firmly against the outbreak of active opposition, and absence of support from lower supervision made any that did occur unlikely to be effective.

Another crucial factor militating against successful resistance was the lack of support by the organized labour movement. Most women who took part in protests were not trade union members, had little experience of organization and often found it difficult to interest local union officials in the issues that concerned them. Many strikes were spontaneous and not backed by trade unions. Often, as at Lucas and Rover, it was the women who wanted to join a union and who made the first approach – either to be rebuffed or, once admitted, remain peripheral to the union's main objective of male recruitment.

The new industries were very poorly unionized in general and only a small proportion of women were members. Although employers actively prevented the formation of union branches, the trade unions themselves did not represent much of a threat since they were extremely slow to recruit women assemblers.[14] TUC conferences and union journals railed against speed-ups and the Bedaux system, but they were reluctant to support those worst affected by them. Most craft unions, including the Amalgamated Engineering Union and the Electrical Trades Union, were in any case opposed to women entering hitherto male preserves of industry and excluded them from membership. Many general unions also viewed women as a threat to their overwhelmingly male membership and undertook female recruitment campaigns not with the primary aim of representing women but in order to prevent them undercutting men's wages. A number of unions even operated marriage bars; some appealed to women only indirectly through husbands and fathers; others approached women on totally inappropriate grounds, promising 'health and beauty' through improved working conditions (Boston 1980: 162). The attitude of most trade unions towards women workers appeared to differ little from that of employers: women were temporary, uncommitted and unreliable workers and unionists. The tendency of the unions was to dismiss workers in the new industries as 'green' labour, young or casual, and not worth the effort of recruiting.

The violent opposition provoked by the Bedaux system is to be understood as resistance to the newly emerging relations of production of mass production and to increased control of employers over the process of production. The conflict between assembly-line workers and rate-fixers and supervisors, common in so many factories in the late 1920s and early 1930s, also arose directly from the new way capital used direct labour and the role it gave to indirect workers in this process.

Conclusion: the class relations of women assemblers

The relations of production of women assemblers were thus distinctive in terms of the use of their labour power and in the wage exchange corresponding to that use. As direct production workers, they occupied a place in the division of labour in which they were used as a collective work unit and subjected to a particularly intense form of machine pacing. Managerial control over the total production process included control over assembly-line workers. These characteristics were fundamental to the way that assembly-line labour power was used in mass-production industries. The payment system, based on a time-rate with an in-built effort norm equivalent to the speed of the line (which I have called a 'rate-of-production' payment system), reflected the real degree of control exerted by employers over the production process and their power to predetermine the volume of output and level of work intensity. The wage exchange too was integral to the relations of production and to class relations. As a consequence, women assembly-line workers were in a specific relation to production and to capital which gave them distinctive class relations. Neither individual machine operators nor the various kinds of indirect worker were subject to the same use of labour power or wage exchange as assemblers and their relations of production differed accordingly.

In general the ability of capitalist employers to extract surplus value and to exploit their workforce depends on the extent to which they can determine the use of labour power. The capacity to determine precisely the quantity of output of labour for each hour of use of labour power constitutes the core essential of the extraction of surplus value: the greater the control they enjoy, the better position they are in to intensify the use of labour power and so increase the extraction of surplus value.[15] In the case of assemblers, the very high degree of control exerted by employers over the use of their labour power resulted in assembly-line workers being subjected to an enhanced and distinctively predetermined form of exploitation. This particular form of exploitation was the distinguishing characteristic of the relations of production or class relations of assemblers as opposed to those of other groups of workers employed in mass production.

These comments refer to the class relations of women assemblers engendered from within the sphere of production and to those alone. As such they are capable of providing only a partial explanation of the totality of class relations of women assemblers, that is, those that arose from this particular form of paid employment. I have tried to demonstrate that the organization of assembly-line production did indeed create a new kind of worker, with a corresponding wage form and distinctive relations of production. But it would be quite wrong to take this as a complete explanation of all aspects of the class relations of women assemblers. Since the availability of women for such employment and the conditions under which they sold their labour power were determined by factors outside of the sphere of production, a comprehensive theory would need to include analysis of these other factors as well, and notably the relations of production in the domestic economy. The existence of particular class relations in one sphere was linked with specific relations of production existing also in the other. Chapters 7 and especially 8 will be concerned with the wider determination of the emergence of the new relations of production since they are explicable only within a broader context of the overall structure of the mode of production as a whole.

This chapter has attempted to undertake a structural analysis of the relations of production of women assemblers and of the specific exchange that they made with capital. Looking at the class relations of different groups of wage labour in this way, as being structurally distinctive goes right to the heart of the Marxist theory of class by calling into question the existence of a material basis for the unity of all wage workers. It implies that the mere fact of selling labour power for a wage does not make all workers working class in the same way since the exchange they make with capital is a historically specific one. On the other hand it does make possible a materialist analysis of the class relations of women, as distinct from men. Although the argument here has been about a particular group of women workers, the method could in principle be extended to analyse the class relations of any group of workers, of either sex.

By its lack of structural differentiation, received Marxist theory not only masks differences between particular forms of exchange but also more fundamentally suppresses the basic division between men and women in the production and reproduction of capitalist social relations. So although the structurally differentiated approach undermines certain basic tenets, it in fact strengthens the theory of class analysis by giving it far greater capacity to examine new and varying historical forms.

Chapter six

Women assembled: gender and the division of labour

In this chapter I shall look in greater detail at the relation between gender and the work process in the new industries and concentrate on several issues arising from the position of women as the central productive labour force. The division of labour will be the major focus of attention. I shall examine first the specific form taken by the sexual division of labour in assembly-line production and analyse the way it interlocked with the technical division of labour. Another area of concern is whether the work process can be considered as a site for the active creation of gender inequality and subordination. It has long been accepted that the sexual division of labour at work reinforces and complements gender inequality created elsewhere (family, education and other social institutions). But to what extent did the sexual division of labour and the way that women's labour was used at work actually contribute themselves to the production of gender division? A further area for exploration is the sex-typing of jobs in the new industries and the construction of assembly-line work as a feminine occupation. Here my objective is to examine how ideological and material factors combined to produce the unequivocal sex-typing of new jobs and to allocate them exclusively to one sex or the other on the basis of gender.

Relationship between technical and sexual divisions of labour

In general terms it could be argued that during the history of industrial capitalism job allocation on the basis of gender has been characterized by two fundamental features: segregation between the sexes and the subordinate position of women. Both have been of enduring significance and were basic to the sexual division of labour long before the invention of assembly lines.

Segregation – the more or less total separation between men's work and women's work – has held sway over time and through many different occupations and industries. Whatever differences existed between the actual content and type of work in different industries, they shared the common characteristic of gender segregation. Women and men performed different work (or work that was presented as being different). That there has been so little overlap in the work allocated to men and to women is evidence of the immense force of gender segregation in employment.[1]

But the horizontal division created by occupational segregation has been overlaid by a vertical division which placed women as a gender at the bottom of the occupational hierarchy below men, in terms of pay, skill and authority. In the majority of occupations women have been effectively excluded from all forms of extended training and hence from formally acknowledged skills.[2] They have consistently commanded lower wage rates than men, and the authority to which they were subject was always held by men. Historically this subordinate position of women at work has been as fundamental as segregation.

Taken together gender segregation and the subordination of women constitute what might be called basic principles by which the sexual division of labour and the gender allocation of work have in general been organized. As enduring principles they have been closely connected to women's position in the domestic economy (responsibility for the household, domestic labour, and the reproduction of labour power) which was also persistent through historical change, and which affected the position of women in the labour market.

However, these principles never had an existence above or beyond particular historical circumstances and were not found in a pure form or in the abstract. They enmeshed with changing technical divisions of labour to produce different sexual divisions of labour whose detailed structure varied according to each concrete case. Just as the adoption of new methods of production can give rise to the transformation of the technical division of labour, so too the emergence of a new technical division of labour may be accompanied by an alteration in the sexual division of labour. In practice the sexual division of labour is always embedded in and interlocked with the prevailing technical division of labour. Its characteristics are peculiar to particular methods of production since they are shaped by and acquire their detailed form from the occupational structure in which they are found.

So what were the distinctive characteristics of the sexual division of labour associated with assembly-line work and to what extent did they follow traditional patterns of allocating work on the basis of gender? How in practice did the technical division of labour distinctive to mass production (and outlined in Chapter 5) interlock with the sexual division of labour? Newly created jobs represent a special test case in this connection since the work they involved had not previously been performed by either women or men.

In general terms the sexual division of labour in assembly-line work unquestionably conformed to the established pattern: work was allocated on the basis of gender, segregation was fairly absolute and women were in a subordinate position. Routine and repetitive work requiring manual dexterity and speed, but little formal training, was allocated to women. Heavy and dirty labouring work, jobs that required extended or formal training, and all positions of authority were allocated to men. In electrical engineering for example this principle operated throughout the industry and in every factory, in machine shops and in assembly, even when the work position or actual job content was new. In machine shops women manufactured components, operating a wide range of stamping, pressing, milling and grinding machines and lathes. In assembly shops they combined the subcomponents and assembled the final product with solder, screwdrivers or by hand. Most package-making and packing of completed goods was also allocated to women.

To a large extent work of this type had always been 'women's work' even in the period before mass production. Because women had always performed it, it was not surprising that they were now seen as the appropriate labour force for semi-skilled manual work in mass-production industries. Traditional descriptions of women's jobs as 'light' and 'clean', relying on the 'nimble fingers' of the operators, were soon also applied to the new jobs women did on the assembly line. And in turn such feminine qualities confirmed the undisputed status of such jobs as 'women's work'.

But the broad features of the sexual division of labour took on a specific form in the new industries. Its particular structure was an effect of the way in which traditional principles of work allocation by gender enmeshed with the new technical division of labour of mass production. These now combined to give women a central role at the point of production as a result of the enormous increase in the numbers of semi-skilled workers required by mass-production methods, and of the crucial position of the semi-skilled at the heart of the whole process of production. The new industries were distinct precisely in this expansion of the type of semi-skilled work traditionally done by women. Since direct production in assembly industries depended overwhelmingly on semi-skilled workers, women came to occupy the central position in production. Thus women were brought to the forefront of the work process and industrial workforce, both numerically and strategically. Their overall position in the technical division of labour was altered and so too was their relation to men. Men and women were each placed in a definite, but different, position in the new work process which in turn affected the relationship between them.

One consequence of this process was that assembly-line industries developed a definite structure in their sexual division of labour which was typical of them. Thus the sexual composition of the workforce was similar in many mass-production industries, and the adoption of mass-production methods had the effect of imposing a similar pattern of sexual composition on the workforce in different industries even when it had been very different before. This can be demonstrated by examining several traditional industries whose workforces originally had a divergent gender composition and seeing what happened when methods of mass production were introduced. Whatever the starting point, the outcome appears to have been the same – a high proportion of women working as semi-skilled operatives. But the nature of the pre-existing gender division determined whether the number of women employed or the overall ratio of women to men actually increased, decreased or remained constant to produce the common pattern. Different changes were to be expected in different industries depending on whether it was an entirely new industry, an established one where the workforce was traditionally female, or an established one with a mixed labour force.

Electrical engineering is an example of the first category. Here assembly-line methods were in operation from the outset, and by 1935 35 per cent of all manual operatives were women (Jefferys 1945: 206) (with a much higher proportion in certain subsections and occupations). The consolidation of electrical engineering as a new industry, combined with the introduction of mass-production techniques into other parts of engineering, altered the ratio of women to men in the engineering industry as a whole in favour of women. In the first decade of the century engineering had been the exclusive preserve of men (they accounted for 97 per cent of operatives) but after the introduction of mass production the proportion of women began to rise dramatically so that they accounted for over 13 per cent of operatives taken even over the engineering industry as a whole by 1935.[3]

By contrast clothing had been a traditional women's industry, employing approximately twice as many women as men. Men had worked as skilled tailors and boot and shoe makers while women were concentrated as sewing machinists for lighter clothing. The effect of mass production here was to increase further the ratio of women to men. The decline of the bespoke and dressmaking trades led to a reduction in the numbers of skilled women as well as men, but at the same time the enormous expansion of factory-based and newly mechanized ready-made sections of the industry led to a large increase in women sewing machinists. This process was already quite pronounced by 1931: there were 7,000 fewer male tailors than in 1921 but 8,000 more women.[4]

The use of power-driven machinery had a similar effect throughout the clothing industry: women entered cutting – previously a male preserve – when electrically propelled knives were introduced, and with the advent of steam presses and machines to make shoe uppers they also entered pressing and shoe making (PP Cmd 3508 1930: 12, 18). In this way technological development in this second type of industry resulted in an absolute increase both in the numbers of women employed and in their overall proportion to men. Most of the remaining skilled manual jobs were retained by men (NSOL 1930–5 Vol. II: Ch.V).

In industries where both sexes had been employed traditionally, such as food processing, mechanization had the effect of automating much of the labour intensive 'women's work'. It could therefore reduce the demand for women workers and actually displace them from their jobs. However, the scale of production usually expanded to such an extent following the adoption of mass-production methods that those made redundant were absorbed on alternative work, and often many additional women were recruited in the longer term.

The cocoa and chocolate industry provides an illustration. At Cadbury hundreds of women were made redundant as a direct result of mechanization undertaken in the late 1920s. But by the mid-1930s the scale of production had increased dramatically and women were taken on again (Cadbury Brothers 1945: 17, 28–9, 60). At Lyons and Peek Frean technical innovation was introduced more gradually and consequently the effect on women's employment was less extreme. None was actually dismissed: their original jobs disappeared but they themselves were redeployed on new semi-skilled jobs or automated versions of their old jobs. Winnie Young and Nell Williams continued as biscuit packers at Peek Frean but on a mechanized conveyor rather than individually. Similarly the mechanization of sponge cake and Swiss roll production at Lyons did away with certain women's jobs but created others. In both factories more women were taken on as the scale of production grew. On the other hand traditional men's jobs in pastry and biscuit making did disappear permanently and many men were sacked as a direct result of the adoption of assembly-line methods: dough-mixing machines replaced skilled men, and conveyor belts and continuous process production replaced labourers who had previously transferred goods between one stage of the manufacturing process and the next.

In this third type of industry mass-production methods had a complex effect on the sex ratio: the original fairly high ratio of women to men on the shopfloor became even higher. However, because men took all of the newly created indirect jobs (electricians, rate-fixers, production engineers and so on), it is possible that the overall ratio of women to men in the industry as a whole did not change very much (if the numbers of men taken on in these new jobs equalled the extra numbers of women recruited as direct production workers).[5]

This survey reveals that the introduction of methods of mass production into three industries increased the ratio of women to men and imposed a convergent sexual composition common to the labour force of all, regardless of their different starting points. The rise in the proportion of women, both absolute and relative, was systematically linked with the alteration in the technical division of labour. The growth of the semi-skilled layer resulted directly from the adoption of mass-production techniques, and it was because women were so closely associated with such work that their employment expanded so dramatically.

As a technical method, assembly-line production did not require the participation of either gender in any predetermined way. But in practice the technical division of labour incorporated a rigid gender structure right from the start. In general terms the basic distribution of work by gender operated to allocate direct assembly-line work exclusively to women and virtually everything else to men, including all the new work positions. Thus women were recruited as assemblers but not as bonus clerks, progress chasers or quality controllers even though these new positions were, in theory at least, gender indeterminate and wide open for sex-typing. But in the event assembling was more or less the sole new occupation to be sex-typed as 'women's work' while all the others were constructed as 'men's work' and joined the remaining traditional jobs as masculine occupations.

As a result of this allocation a rigid segregation obtained between men and women on the shopfloor: they were never engaged on the same work; they were never in the same grade and they never earned the same wages. Similarly, all women were in a lower position in the hierarchy of the division of labour than men (except labourers); they had no control over the performance of their work and no technical know-how. Apart from the few women chargehands and supervisors, women had no authority over others and no women, including forewomen, ever had authority over a man. Men on the other hand controlled the technology and held all positions of effective authority.

In some respects this gender division was only to be expected. What occurred with the advent of mass production could be viewed as a continuation of trends already in existence. In engineering women had been recruited to routine and repetitive work operating small, light or relatively simple machines from the end of the nineteenth century. The exclusion of women from work involving extended training or technical competence can be understood in the same way as continuing an established situation. It would have been more surprising to find women suddenly being trained and employed as machine setters, electricians, or maintenance men *(sic)* when this had never happened before. Similarly women had rarely been found in the hierarchy of supervision higher than chargehand or forewomen in charge of other women, and there would be no particular reason to expect the traditional equation between men and authority to be disrupted under the new conditions of mass production.

A more detailed examination of the sexual division of labour in assembly-line industries, however, reveals that it possessed specific characteristics produced as an effect of the combination of the general enduring gender-based principles of work allocation with the technical division of labour of mass production. Three such characteristics can be distinguished which constituted distinctive properties of the sexual division of labour of assembly-line industries.

Women and men: direct and indirect producers

The first of these was that the division between direct and indirect producers was reproduced as a division between the sexes. The separation of direct production workers on the assembly line from all the indirect workers who serviced them was a basic division of the new technical division of labour of mass production. Since all women were allocated to semi-skilled production work and men to everything else, including all servicing, the division between direct and indirect producers was effectively constituted as a division between women and men. Women were the productive hub of the factory around whose activity all the indirect workers, the men, were organized. Assemblers were serviced by machine setters, electricians, belt feeders, labourers and many other grades of indirect worker.

This double division between women and men as direct and indirect workers was immediately visible to anyone entering the assembly shop in any factory, whether it was Siemens telephone factory in south London, GEC in Coventry or HMV. The physical layout was everywhere the same: on the one hand scores of women seated in parallel lines along conveyor belts, heads down over components they were assembling, seemingly attached to the belt themselves as they did not move away from it; on the other hand, a much smaller number of men standing up and walking around the shopfloor bringing or taking components, adjusting the machinery or inspecting the product as the women completed their work.

The segregation between women and men as direct and indirect workers was pretty absolute. No men worked as assemblers and in the few instances where they did work at the belt, they were not engaged on the same assembly work as women. At EMI a few men were thinly interspersed among the hundreds of women but these were inspectors conducting check tests and quality control. At Philips the first couple of jobs on the line were done by youths but they did this work on a temporary basis only before going on to higher things – the jobs were defined, significantly, as mechanical and therefore appropriate only to men. The fact that a few other men were also direct production workers hardly detracts from the overall equation. These would most likely be skilled tradesmen who had undergone a craft training. They probably manufactured specialist components or tools and worked on their own rather than in a group. They certainly did not do assembly work on the line. This segregation between women's and men's work was complemented and reinforced by other differences in the conditions of work between the sexes which marked off women as a separate category: lower pay, strict disciplining of their every move, no acknowledgement of their expertise, and absence of control over the work process.

In this way women's place in the division of labour concentrated them in a group at the point of production as the main direct productive workforce. As assembly-line workers they were the ones who were subjected to the new ways in which labour was used that were specific to methods of mass production. It was women who were machine dominated, whose work was machine paced, who had no control over the speed of their work. It was women who, because of the subdivision of tasks and the length of the assembly line, formed the large collective worker. It was also women who occupied the lowest position in the hierarchy of the division of labour, yet at the same time the success of the whole production process depended on each and every woman performing her allotted task in the right way and at the right speed. Thus by their very numbers and the reliance of the system of production on their co-operation, women's position was also a strategic one in which they had the potential to make or break the whole system.

I argued in Chapter 5 that the assembly-line worker was a new kind of worker, subject to new relations of production. Because assembly-line workers were women, women were therefore the first to experience these new relations. As the key direct production workers they represented the section of the labour force that was the most directly and intensely subject to the relation between capital and worker which characterized mass production. The fact that the most technologically advanced methods of capitalist production relied on women as their direct production workers marks a fundamental break between the new industries and earlier forms of craft manufacture.[6] There men had occupied the central position as direct production workers and although women had also worked as machine operators they did not in any sense or to the same extent occupy the key position that they now acquired. This alteration in the gender composition of direct production workers which accompanied the change in the form and method of production has been one of the most significant developments in the history of British (and other) industry in the twentieth century.

Women assembled

A second effect of the technical division of labour on the sexual division was that the sexes confronted each other as groups with a very different internal composition and also a very different place in the overall workforce. Women formed a large homogeneous group who were all in the same grade, with the same level of skill, all performing similar tasks and all receiving the same level of wages. Men, in sharp contrast, were in a much more heterogeneous position, spread throughout all the occupations and all the levels in the division of labour, possessing varying degrees of skill, engaged in many different kinds of work, and being paid accordingly more or less.

As assembly-line workers women performed basically only one type of work and all women did this work. Because of the segregation and exclusive allocation of women to the assembly line, women were located in one and only one position in the division of labour, and this position contained only women. For women, gender relations were therefore coterminous with their position in the division of labour: gender was the fundamental division which separated them from the rest of the labour force. A crucial effect of this was to make the sexual division of labour of great salience for women since it was one of the main forms of their subordination. They were thrown together as a sex on the shopfloor and uniting in order to pursue the interests that arose out of their position in the technical division of labour would also automatically and simultaneously involve uniting as a sex. Gender division inherent in the division of labour was thus absolutely central to women's relation both to men, to the process of production and to capital. It represented an essential determining component in the constitution of women's class relations.

For men the situation was entirely different: the division of labour effectively separated them as a gender not only from women as a gender but it also separated men from each other because they were divided up amongst all of the many levels of the occupational structure, both horizontal and vertical (with the exception of assembly). Although 'men's work' was as rigidly defined as 'women's work' it was a much wider and more inclusive category, encompassing very many different skills and kinds of work whereas for women the definition was extremely restrictive and exclusive. Women were restricted to a very narrow band of work – assembly and machine operating – and the whole residual category of all other work was 'men's work'.

The result of this difference was that while women were united by their place in the division of labour, men on the contrary were divided by it. The position of men in the division of labour did not depend directly on gender. In determining their class position therefore, in the sense of their relation to production and to capital, men's place in the technical division of labour would be determining but, unlike women, their gender would not. Men might organize together as supervisors and unite as a grade, for example in reaction to the Bedaux system, but in this case they would be acting on the basis of their particular place in the division of labour, and not simultaneously as men, or on the basis of gender which would be the case for women assemblers. It is virtually impossible to conceive of any circumstances under which men would unite as a gender in defence of their interests in the same way as women. For men therefore the salient divisions in terms of class were only those pertaining to their relation to production as workers, while for women the sexual division of labour was at the same time also the most immediate class division.

So women were 'assembled together' as a collective worker. They were also assembled together by virtue of their unique place in the division of labour. The homogeneity of their position in the technical division of labour placed all of them in one and the same identical situation to each other in relation to the work process and to the incumbents of all other positions in the division of labour. The effect of this was to assemble women together as a gender and to divide them as a gender from all men.

Subordination to managerial control

There are two senses in which women could be subordinate to men: they could be in a subordinate position relative to men in the hierarchy of the division of labour and they could be directly subject to male authority. Although women were in the lowest position on the shopfloor in mass-production industries, the exact nature of this subordination and of male authority over women was specific to the division of labour of this production process.

In traditional manufacturing industry women machine operators had worked directly under the supervision of a male setter who held individual authority over her. Where women and men were both involved in direct production in engineering, textiles or potteries, women usually worked under the direct supervision of a particular man (who could well have been an older male relative) who set her machine, determined her output target and imposed discipline. In such circumstances the relation between women workers and management was indirect and mediated by men: women were more immediately subject to the man in charge of their machine, spindle, or loom and to his personal face-to-face authority. As workers, both women and men were subordinate to capital but the system of production was organized in such a way that gave men a dominant position and placed them in a relation of direct authority over women. The relationship between women and men at work was analogous to that within the household since in both situations the inequality with men and the power and authority of individual men over individual women were all tied up in a single relationship.

Such a situation no longer existed in assembly-line industries. Women were still in a subordinate position but the form of their domination had changed. The structural and functional differentiation of the various layers and grades of worker meant that men and women were never in the same work group but always in separate ones which had little direct contact with each other. Men were no longer at the centre of production as direct workers; rather they worked in separate but parallel grades. Women worked only with other women on the line and not on a one-to-one basis with men. Male production workers were therefore no longer in the position of having direct authority over women. Often the frontline supervisory position of chargehand or supervisor over the line was taken by a woman. In factories where skilled craftsmen were still employed they were unlikely to have direct contact with women through their work and would have no authority over them by virtue of their position in the division of labour.

In this way, the nature of the power structure between men and women was altered by the technical division of labour. Progress chasers, quality controllers and all the other grades of men were in a higher position in the occupational hierarchy than women. But their superior position did not give them direct personal authority over women assemblers. They serviced and inspected women's work but any complaints they had about it had to be passed on to the chargehand or supervisor who alone possessed the formal right of authority and discipline over the line.

As direct production workers, women were now subject to the

exigencies of the assembly line. They were much more directly subordinate to technological control than had been the case in earlier or other systems of production. Machine pacing subjected assembly-line workers to a new form of domination by technology: they were subject to the operation of the belt and this was directly under managerial control. The less direct relation between women and men in the division of labour meant that men were no longer put in the position of mediating the domination of capital over women. Women were not subordinate to other production workers but more directly to the line and this imposed its discipline in a mechanical and automatic way.

This is not to deny that the power structure on the shopfloor was patriarchal, but rather to say that the form of patriarchy was transformed. Although both men and women were subordinate to capital and to the system of production, men were nevertheless in a superior position relative to all women. Some men had authority over women but no woman held authority over any man, although a few women were put in charge of other women. The relative inferiority of women in the division of labour became a social inequality now differentiated from subordination to male authority. Women were now transparently subordinate primarily to capital rather than to men: machine pacing represented the patent form of their subordination. Rate-fixers, quality controllers and other men acted as agents of that subordination and women were subject to the authority vested in them in that capacity. Inequality, power and authority were more differentiated from each other and no longer coexisted in a single relationship between individual men and women as had been the case in traditional manufacturing industry. In this sense the structure of the shopfloor, its authority relations and its forms of female subordination, while undoubtedly patriarchal, took on a specific form in assembly-line industries.[7]

Conclusion: the creation of gender subordination at work

One conclusion to be drawn from this discussion is that the creation of women's subordination at work occurred in and through the work process: women's position at work actively produced gender inequality rather than simply reflecting it. In this sense it is legitimate to view the work process as a distinctive site for the construction of both gender itself (through the creation of 'feminine' occupations) and of gender inequality (through the sexual division of labour) as well as of women's subordination. Women's position in the work process was not just carried over from other social institutions and did not simply reflect or reinforce an already fully formed subordination created outside of paid employment and prior to it. Any explanation in terms of reflection or reinforcement would be incapable of accounting for the specific forms of subordination that characterize particular work processes, including those distinctive to assembly-line work. And if the specific forms of subordination are properties of the workplace, then this should be acknowledged in its own right as a site for the creation of gender and gender division. Moreover inequalities created at work contribute to the overall pattern of relations between the sexes and may have important implications for other areas of life.

The traditional exclusion of women from control of technology, technical knowledge and skill, effected in the past by exclusion from craft apprenticeships, was perpetuated in assembly-line industries as a consequence of the combination of the technical and sexual divisions of labour. The skills that women brought to assembly work or learned on the job (dexterity, attention to detail, speed) went unrecognized and were discounted as innate sexual characteristics. A long term form of gender inequality involving male power and female subordination in relation to machinery was thus created anew in new circumstances.

Material basis of segregation

The reasons underlying the segregation between women's and men's jobs in the new industries become apparent only against the wider context of the differing work responsibilities of the two sexes in the waged public and unwaged domestic economy. The duality of women's position as workers in both spheres had a determining effect on their position in the labour market: for the majority participation in paid employment was not usually continuous or uninterrupted, and when they left it was to work in the unwaged domestic economy. Women always worked in this unpaid sector, whether or not they were also employed in waged work. Men on the other hand worked only in the one sphere; they were responsible for bringing income into the household but not for working there.

In a general sense – and the following remarks are not limited to assembly-line work – the divergent conditions of waged employment offered to the sexes were directly connected to their different structural position in the two spheres of work, and this applies also to the question of occupational segregation. Women's subordinate position in the waged sector was materially based in the duality of their structural insertion in the domestic and the wage economy. Although for working-class women work proceeded through a series of stages, inside and outside the home, which varied over the life-cycle, it should be emphasized that paid work was not an incidental but rather a fundamental feature of their situation. If they had remained permanently in the home or had been excluded from waged employment as such, the whole system of connections between commodity production and the domestic economy would have broken down.

I want to suggest that the public and domestic economy were linked with each other as two end-poles of a closed circuit which operated together to produce the particular conditions of women's employment. In the domestic economy women had primary responsibilty for both the daily reproduction of labour power and for childbearing and rearing. These acted as a filter on their availability for engaging in paid work outside of the home and so placed women in a weaker labour market position than men. Since women's work in the home produced goods and services for use and for direct consumption, rather than for exchange, it did not generate any income. The purchase of commodities to be consumed in the domestic economy relied on income being brought in from the waged sector of work. Male wages were the primary source of this income and this meant that both the domestic economy and the women who worked in it were to a large extent financially dependent on men.

Once the circuit of work and wages in the two sectors was established,[8] it recreated itself constantly as a system in equilibrium encompassing both sexes in both spheres. As a closed circuit there was effectively no point at which it could be broken into without disturbing the whole balance between the sexes in both spheres. So even when women did not in practice conform to the discontinuous pattern and remained permanently in waged work this had no effect in altering the system: they were still treated like all other women on the understanding that women as a sex were supported financially by men as a sex.

Male wages represented a 'family wage' in that men were supposed to support unwaged dependants. Whether the level of male wages was actually sufficient for this purpose is a moot point, especially in the case of lower paid manual workers. But whatever the level of male wages, women's wages were always lower and never amounted to a 'family wage'. In the conventional model women were expected to provide a certain proportion of household income at different periods in their life, but not the major or stable part. When viewed in this context it becomes clear that there were men's wages and women's wages, and that while women were paid as women, men were paid, in ideology if not in reality, a family wage.

Differential wages for the sexes as such applied as much in the new industries as elsewhere. Men earned more than women and all women earned approximately the same amount with little variation between them, unlike men between whom there was a significant differential. So just like their position in the division of labour, women's wages were also homogeneous: determined by considerations of gender while men's pay was determined by class as well since the differentials between them reflected their different positions in the division of labour. The general rule was for the lowest man's wage to be above all women's wages. At Peek Frean where the wages of women packers earning the highest bonus rate exceeded those of male labourers the women felt uncomfortable because the situation was so unusual. But at Morphy Richards the labourers earned 25 per cent more than the best paid women. If in a few cases the highest female wage was larger than the lowest male wage, the general rule was for the highest male wage to be well above the highest female wage, and usually the lowest also was as well. Despite all the arguments about the rate for the job and assurances that assembly-line wage rates reflected the skill and effort (or lack of it) required by the work, in fact it was a rate paid for the sex that undertook the work rather than a rate for the job.

All this may seem obvious, but to break into the system would have been tantamount to a social cataclysm. Imagine how different the relation between men and women would have been if women had been paid the same as men. If men were no longer the breadwinners, would it have been possible to maintain domestic labour as an exclusively female responsibility? Why should women do unpaid work in the home and depend on a man when they could support themselves and be financially independent? But if both men and women remained continuously in the waged sector how would the reproduction of labour power be achieved? It is only too obvious that, had women in fact earned the same as men, then the domestic economy would have been disrupted, the structural connection between the waged and unwaged sectors of work would also have changed, as well as the established relations between the sexes to both spheres.

Women's wartime employment can be seen as a case in point. The experience was exceptional not only in breaching the traditional gender allocation of jobs. The reason why so many more married women were available for paid employment was precisely because their husbands were not at home: there was therefore less domestic labour to be done, and fewer children were being born and needing to be cared for. An abnormal situation in the domestic economy therefore released more women for full-time employment outside of the domestic sphere. After the return of men from the war, women were ejected from their wartime jobs and these were returned to men. It was not a question of whether women had the ability to continue doing men's work; since they had already done it neither they nor employers needed proof of the fact. The question was the much more basic one of whether it was economically possible for them to remain in the same jobs. There would have been profound implications for the running of the domestic economy if women had retained their wartime jobs, and serious consequences for men's employment at a time when unemployment was already high. However, the question never really arose since domestic labour returned to its normal level after the war and again imposed constraints on women's availability for waged work.

The material reasons behind the strict segregation in assembly-line work become intelligible when examined against this background. One might ask why, on the one hand, were no men allocated to actual assembly work and why, on the other, were no women allocated to any of the other new jobs in mass production? Alternatively, what would have been the implications of mixed-sex allocation to the same work?

The first question is one that was not asked at the time but that has become relevant since and that I have been asked many times. At first sight it might seem probable that when millions of men were unemployed some at least would enter assembly work: even though the wages were low, they would be earning more than if they were not working at all. But as it happened not only did men not apply for this sort of work, but also employers did not actively recruit them. A series of interrelated reasons can be suggested to account for this. First, unemployment rates varied enormously by region and in the areas where the new industries were concentrated male unemployment was not so high as in many others. It was therefore likely that jobs would also be available for men as well as for women in these regions either in the new industries themselves, or in related 'infrastructural' employment in electricity installation, road-building or in the construction industry. Second, the wages paid for assembly-line work were not men's wages and were widely recognized as such. If some men accepted such rates of pay this could have the effect of lowering men's wages for other work more generally. The inability to earn a 'family wage' or support dependants would have operated as a severe deterrent, and the trade unions too were strongly opposed to men accepting women's wages. Third, by the time assembly-line industries were established assembly was already sex-typed as 'women's work', with all the representations of special female characteristics and aptitudes necessary for its performance, and was generally accepted as such by employers, unions, men and women. Men just did not put themselves forward for women's work and employers just did not employ them for it. On the contrary they went out of their way actively to recruit women. All this was unplanned and occurred auto-matically as if by a natural process. At the time there was no suggestion that men should have done assembly-line work; everyone would have found it most peculiar. It has become a relevant question only later when gender division and the sex-typing of work have been challenged and opened up as important issues.

The exclusion of women from all non-assembly jobs really takes more explaining than the exclusion of men from assembly lines. As I have stressed the content of many of these new jobs contained noth-ing that could have been conventionally conceived as inherently masculine or more appropriate to men than to women, in terms of strength or formal qualifications required. Nor were the trade unions in a position to exclude women from these types of work: if em-ployers had tried to allocate such work to women it is unlikely that unions would have had the strength to stop them.

But what did differentiate these jobs from the assembly line was that all required some training (in work-study, electrical inspection, or stock-keeping) and most incorporated a career structure in which those who started at the bottom proceeded some way up the ladder during their working life, gaining higher earnings on the way. To have placed women in any of these jobs would by the same token have meant giving them this training, the possibility of promotion and what amounted to a man's wage. Such a situation would immediately have broken the equation between women, semi-skilled work, low pay and homogeneous position. If women were employed as progress chasers or rate-fixers they would have had to be paid the same rate for the job as men doing the same work, that is, more than assembly workers since these jobs occupied a higher position in the division of labour. The principle of a woman's wage, for working-class women, would have been undermined.

The alternative possibility, in order to maintain the exclusiveness of male and female job categories and the nexus of conditions associ-ated with it, would have been to reclassify rate-fixing and progress chasing as women's work, exclude men and thereby feminize them to-tally, remunerating them at the same level as, or slightly above, other women's work on the assembly line. But what then would have hap-pened to the internal career structure and its rising level of wages? No other area of women's work included a career structure and this would have been a strong reason against feminizing the whole area of work. Being higher up in the occupational ladder would have put some women on a par with men in equivalent positions in parallel career ladders and placed them above men lower down in these lad-ders, a situation which was unknown in British industry. Had such a possibility been seriously considered the argument that women would not stay long enough and that there would not be enough of them to fill the higher reaches of the ladder would also have been heard. In fact it never came to that. The odds were firmly stacked right from the start against women ever being considered an appropriate workforce for such types of employment because of the training and remuneration they involved, regardless of the fact that the actual work content had no masculine connotations. The differential pay rates to men and women were so inextricably linked with the segregation between men's and women's work and with the homogeneous position of women in the division of labour that altering one of these would automatically have broken into the others.[9]

Although none of the new jobs in mass production was captured by women, feminization did occur in other areas of employment during the inter-war period, especially in clerical and retail work. Women typists and clerks replaced men with the mechanization of typing and filing but at the same time the status of the job declined as it was deskilled, expanded and allocated to women. The routine and repetitive tasks undertaken by women office workers differed considerably in content and nature from the type of work done earlier by the male clerk. Those parts of the earlier job involving more formal training or giving effective authority in the office were separated out from the routine and lower level tasks and these were allocated to men and women respectively. The result of the process was again that there was no overlap and no mixed-sex allocation of tasks. The feminization of clerical work was accompanied, needless to say, by the development of two scales of pay, one for women and the other for men.[10] A similar process occurred with the expansion of the retail trade and the growth of chain, multiple and department stores where women were employed as shop assistants doing routine work while men assumed the administrative and managerial positions.[11]

A consideration of the possible alternatives thus helps to clarify the reasons underlying the segregation between men and women in the new industries. The exclusion of each from jobs allocated to the other was integral to the maintenance of the whole nexus of different conditions of employment. Their positions in the division of labour permitted them to receive divergent wage levels but with the appearance that they were being paid the rate for the job rather than for their sex. However, if any mixed-sex job allocation had occurred the whole system would have been disrupted and differential pay rates brought into question, unless men and women were paid unequally for exactly the same work. If men had been employed on assembly lines and women in the many other jobs an impossible situation would have arisen because it would have brought into question this whole division.

Interestingly, the pattern of segregation and sex-typing of work that emerged in assembly-line industries in the inter-war years remained virtually unchanged for decades. In the 1970s exactly the same sexual division of labour was still evident in light engineering and food processing industries as in the 1930s (Cavendish 1982). In some factories women were just being allowed to enter progress chasing and quality control, but significantly men moved out of the work at the same time as women moved in. The lowest levels were effectively feminized but an informal bar prevented women from rising in the relevant career ladder. The homogeneity of women's wages was maintained since women progress chasers and quality controllers were paid rates equivalent to that of reject operator on the line, below that of chargehand and commensurate with women's assembly-line wages. In this way a 'solution' was found to the 'problem' of maintaining gender division and women's common position on the shopfloor while at the same time opening up a new area of work for them. Feminizing a restricted number of low grades of work effectively reproduced and replicated gender segregation and division, and demonstrated once again the tenacity of sex-typing of jobs.

That the sexual division of labour in the domestic economy and in assembly-line industries were connected in a complex and highly structured way should now be evident. But the relation between the two was not one of reflection, where women's position in the one sphere determined their position in the other. Nor was it a functional one in which the function or *raison d'être* of women's position in one sphere was to maintain their place in the other. But equally neither should the two be conceived as a totally independent series whose internal structure could be explained solely in its own terms. I would suggest rather that the two sexual divisions of labour continually and mutually created and re-created each other, both materially and ideologically. Women's subordinate position in the two spheres was fundamental to the balance between them and to the circuit as a whole. An imbalance in one would have produced disequilibrium in both, in the overall relation between the sexes, and in the structural manner in which those relations were produced and reproduced from one generation to the next. At a larger structural level then, strict segregation between the sexes at work becomes intelligible and this general explanation also applied to the new industries. New types of work not previously done by men could not be given to women without challenging the equilibrium. For the same reason there could be no work allocated irrespective of gender. Nor could women's work be remunerated at the same level as men's. In the given circuit between the two sectors of work and the relation of men and women to each, these represented structural impossibilities.

Ideological construction of women's work: sex-typing and the marriage bar

Although gender segregation and subordination in assembly-line work had a real material basis, nobody understood or explained the situation in those terms. There were received notions as to what sort of work was women's work, and what was a suitable wage for a man. People's understanding of their own place as men or women in the occupational structure also played an important part in producing and maintaining the divisions. The particular ideological construction and representation of women as wage workers in that period reflected material factors but at the same time also contributed to producing the outcome. The ideological construction of women's work, to which I now turn, thus had a material weight of its own. Having allocated women to a particular type of employment and to particular jobs, a host of reasons was put forward as a rationale for that allocation. Such reasons explained and legitimized what was in effect the result of material factors by reference to women's personality, attitudes, aptitudes and physical attributes.

Factories in the new industries were generally presented as modern, light and airy places and the work as clean and light. Such work required clean, neat and tidy workers and the factory workers were portrayed in similar terms to the work they performed. Publicity material from Heinz and Peek Frean drew a pleasant picture of women operators, spic and span in their freshly ironed overalls and caps, doing light and clean work in attractive and hygienic surroundings. Curiously enough, the women had acquired the same characteristics as the work they undertook. Descriptions of the older traditional industries stood in marked contrast: there the work was heavy and dirty by comparison with the new industries and, coincidentally, the women who worked there were rough and uncouth! Even at EMI the women who operated heavy presses in the machine shop were described as large, strong, untidy, and bawdy in contrast to those neat and tidy assembly-line workers in the adjacent shop! Somehow workers took on attributes of the work, and whether or not they were viewed as respectable or genteel appeared to rest directly on the nature of their work.

In a similar fashion, fiddliness and monotony, the two basic features of assembly-line work, were ascribed to assembly-line workers who 'became' both dextrous and boring themselves. The fiddly and repetitive nature of assembly-line work was characterized as particularly suited to women precisely because of their 'nimble fingers' and tolerance of monotony. Women were thought to be naturally good at sewing and many tasks described as having an affinity with sewing. It

216

was true that the coils used in coil winding did look like cotton reels in so much as both had long strands wound round them, but that was about the extent of the similarity. Many coils were very large and most required several types of wire of different thicknesses to be wound round them. None of the other components, implements or tasks bore any resemblance to sewing or bore any affinity with domestic labour. Other work in electrical engineering involved soldering, rivetting and using nuts and screwdrivers to attach components. Biscuit making involved operating a variety of automatic machines, making boxes, and packing with great speed. Considerable dexterity was required for all of these jobs and somehow sewing became a shorthand for this.

The sewing analogy figured prominently at the second Mullard valve factory built in Blackburn in 1938. Many of the new women recruits had previously worked in mills and

> they could work on wire and valves without any trouble. Their fingers were like knitting needles.

In the words of the plant manager:

> The people from the mills were a great advantage to the assembly of the valve components. Great dexterity was needed and good eyesight and the ladies who had been working in cotton fell into the job quite quickly and were quite adaptable to our product.
> (Both managers quoted in the BBC TV programme
> *All Our Working Lives*)

Yet as Ethel Tillotson's description of the actual work made clear it was dexterity rather than sewing skills as such that were required:

> You had trays at either side of you and you had to pick up a grid and cathodes, heaters and all these things and put them on top of each other and they were so fragile. It was really surprising how we didn't damage them but it was a skill that came naturally to you and they [the managers] said they never had any others adapt to this kind of work so quickly.

The preference for young workers in many factories demonstrated employers' search for those who commanded the lowest wage rates, and who might submit more willingly to the harsh discipline. But this preference was frequently rationalized by the argument that the younger the hands, the more nimble the fingers. In the rayon factories in Macclesfield girls of fourteen were immediately started on adult work. Managers in this industry took the argument about youth and nimble fingers to quite ridiculous extremes, suggesting that only the very youngest had sufficiently pliable fingers and that any woman over 17 was too old to learn. Juvenile labour was considerably cheaper but one employer avoided referring to this when giving evidence against a proposed reduction in the hours for young workers. 'Throwing' work was dependent on juveniles, he argued, because

> if the children were to reach 17 years before entering the factories they would have lost the necessary pliability of fingers.
> (William Wadworth, managing director of
> William Frost and Sons, giving evidence
> on behalf of the Rayon and Silk Association
> at the Industrial Court in Westminster.
> Quoted in Norris 1985: 56)

That only a proportion of women in fact possessed sufficiently pliable fingers to learn the fiddly work somehow got lost in this general attribution of nimble fingers to women as a sex. One rayon worker explained how she was subjected to a rigorous aptitude test before being accepted and made it clear that not all of those tested reached the grade:

> The works manager showed us the sort of knot we had to do. Then he gave us little pieces of silk to see if our fingers were nimble enough to tie the knots. When I went there were about ten of us, but out of that ten, there was only four of us that got jobs.
> (Quoted in Norris 1985: 57)

The 'training' offered for most jobs in the new industries was hardly worthy of the name. Usually it amounted to little more than a test of dexterity whose main purpose was to weed out those with potential for doing the work. Jessie Evans's description of her dexterity test at Philips was not much different from the rayon factory and not everyone passed at Philips either.

Inconsistencies and contradictions in employers' ideas about who constituted the 'best' workers spilled over into the nimble fingers issue, so that whichever group of women, younger or older, married or unmarried, in fact constituted the preferred labour force, were automatically attributed with the most nimble fingers. This, rather than any other reason, was used to legitimize the recruitment of the particular section of women.

The second requirement of the job was the ability to withstand monotony and to tolerate repetition work. Women alone and as a gender were believed to possess this quality, and again they acquired the characteristics of the work. Really it was the work that was inherently monotonous and routine, but analogous personality characteristics were attributed to those who performed it. The managers from Morphy Richards and Lyons, for instance, were adamant that women had no problem in doing boring repetitive work: they had no curiosity and were not interested in any more than their own tiny section of the work. The fact that women never asked about the final product or the production process as a whole was evidence enough. One Lyons manager had started work as an apprentice and gradually worked his way up, but the glaring difference between his training and the work meted out to women on the shopfloor had not given him any understanding of the position in which women were put or any empathy for their response to that position. On the contrary, he found their ability to tolerate repetition work quite perplexing:

> We [that is, the men] were really taught our trade but one thing that worried me as a young apprentice was how these girls could work at the same place doing one individual job day in and day out, whether it was working on a finishing band picking up a sandwich, spreading the jam on it and the cream, or putting a top on it and putting it back on the band and I thought 'My God, this must be terrible'.

> (Ray Dickens)

It probably was terrible but those were the conditions that went with the job and the women had no other choice than to take it as it was or leave it. The same manager was 'horrified' at Christmas time when mince pie production reached its peak:

> The production line was so long that it went through walls in the building and you couldn't see what was happening at the other end of the line. I went along one day and asked a woman if she knew what happened to the mince pie after it passed her and she said 'No'. I said 'Well aren't you interested?' 'No, not really.' All they were interested in was the little part they did.

This manager could therefore be content in the belief that Lyons had given women the type of work that really suited them, as demonstrated by their lack of interest in the production process as a whole. From his point of view the work was pretty boring but so too were the women who did it! One wonders what would have happened if the women had actually protested against the repetition, shown some interest in how the line was designed or demanded a technical training. No doubt the short answer would have been that these were not necessary for the performance of their work and if they were dissatisfied there were plenty of others waiting at the factory gates.

Women's perceived tolerance of repetition work was, in addition, viewed as reflecting their passivity and obedience to authority – two further sexual characteristics which distinguished women from men but which were also basic demands of the job. Employers interpreted such traits as innate personality characteristics rather than responses to lack of control over the work. If women were dominated by the line and their every movement physically controlled by it, they had no alternative than to be passive and obedient in relation to its demands. Any other behaviour would have cost them their job. Being restricted to the repeated performance all day of a minute task, with no time to sneeze or look up, was unlikely to stimulate a great interest in the process of production as a whole.

Since women were actively excluded from work that contained any intrinsic meaning or that could ever be considered inherently satisfying, a realistic reaction would be to develop an interest in the speed with which they could do the work and the money they could earn from it, in other words, those aspects of the work over which they did have some very limited control. Their work was by nature restricted to a tiny part of the total process and their place in the division of labour excluded them from all aspects of the design, organization and maintenance of the work process. Criticizing them for lacking interest in the process as a whole therefore only added insult to injury. However, at the same time such criticism helped to reinforce employers' convictions that they had allocated to women work which they were especially suited to: by fortunate coincidence, the requirements of their jobs somehow 'matched' women's perceived innate lack of curiosity or technical ability.

As might be expected many women did find assembly-line work exceedingly boring. They were not as impervious to monotony as employers imagined. No doubt many gave it up because they could not stand it, but even those who carried on for decades complained of monotony. On the other hand, since this was a condition of the work they did not expect it to be interesting. The fact they did not challenge repetition work as such did not mean that they did not experience it as boring. Edie Bedding, for example, found working on the baked bean line at the Heinz factory quite soporific:

When these beans came along the conveyor belt, they were coming along ever so thick, you just had to turn them ever so lightly with your hand, just to make sure there were no black ones in there, and there was a small container where you dropped the black beans. And I was doing this for eight hours a day, sitting by the belt watching these beans go past, and it used to almost send me to sleep staring at them, because we weren't allowed to talk at all, we had to get on with our work.

(Quoted in Weightman and Humphries 1984: 64)

Eileen Jones's interpretation of why boring jobs were given to women did not stop her working at EMI but at the same time she resented managers treating her as mindless because of it:

> When they invented jobs that were boring and repetitive they said 'Women can do that' and that was the reason they put them on. Then afterwards they gave nimble fingers as an excuse for having given that job to a woman. It was insulting, you know, when people said 'Well, you can think about what you're going to cook for dinner while you're doing that job.'

At the Pearce Duff food factory in Bermondsey the policy was to throw new starters in at the deep end by giving them the most repetitive and monotonous job first. If they could stand packing custard powder for six months they graduated to preparing jellies or spices or cutting up the glacé cherries and angelica to go in packets of sponge cake mix. The custard job was like an initiation test and if they could tolerate it then they were likely to be 'good' workers and remain in the firm's employ for many years. Eliza Hawkins worked at Pearce Duff from 1924 to 1935 and reached the position of forelady. She too found the custard job pretty tough-going but the friendly atmosphere of the place made up for the boredom of the work:

> I found the custard boring when I first started but after a while I got used to it. A few of my friends and myself all left school together and went there and got jobs. It was a friendly place. Some left 'cos they thought it was boring but if you stuck to it and really tried, then you'd get rid of that boring feeling, especially when you got to go on different jobs. Girls who could cope with the custard powder bit would often stay then till they got married.

Assembly lines were not developed to give work to women but as an efficient method of mass production. Women were recruited because of the type of employment offered by such work. Yet some of the comments made about the affinity between the content of assembly-line work and the qualities demanded to perform it on the one hand, and women's natural attributes on the other, almost turned reality on its head by suggesting that assembly lines were developed in order to give work to women. Once such work was constructed as women's work, no doubt the detailed division of jobs and the design of jigs and tools were made with the gender of the workforce in mind. But while such considerations may have been a factor in the practical organization and implementation of the work, they were not relevant to the emergence of the production process in itself.[12]

The lack of training offered to women was explained in terms of their eventual domestic status, even when most remained in employment for over ten years. Although it was a financial necessity for working-class women to engage in waged work and most married women did so, although often on a casual, temporary or part-time basis, the ideology was that, once married, women did not need to earn a wage. Furthermore, orientation to their future place in the home was also used to explain women's perceived lack of interest in gaining skills and contentment with their lowly position. That these were obviously connected in the sense that women were given no opportunity and therefore did not have the possibility of improving their lot did not seem to enter the minds of those who pronounced on the matter. In giving evidence to the Committee on Women in Industry at the end of the First World War, Sir Alfred Herbert, representing the Machine Tool and Engineering Federation, explained the difference between men and women in this respect:

> A woman is quick to learn any particular job. She is intelligent, obedient and generally a good worker ... Moreover, she is by disposition more adapted to continue a repetition job without getting weary of it. A boy is anxious to learn, to improve his position and for this very reason he becomes impatient of continuing to perform any repetition job when once he has mastered it. He is keen (and very properly so) to go on with something else, and thus have a chance of development. A woman looks on her work merely as an incident in her career. She is content to go on working on the same job so long as the conditions are favourable, and her earnings reasonable, with the knowledge that the work is not her life.
>
> (Edited from Cmd 167 1919, Vol. XXXI, Appendix I: 54)

A later government inquiry into women's industrial work posed the question of why women were concentrated in repetition work when they had successfully carried out skilled work during the war. Again the answer lay in their 'attitude towards industrial work', determined by the marriage factor, which in turn affected employers' attitude towards them:

> Work in the factory is looked upon by most as a temporary career, which fills in the time and enables them to earn a living between school and marriage, and for this reason they tend to seek the easily learned repetition work and are apt to lack the enterprise and ambition which would make such processes seem irksome ... naturally the firm would not consider it worth while to spend the time

teaching a woman, when the chance of her remaining in their service is so small.

(PP Cmd 3508 1930: 29)

In this interpretation, women were blamed for the sort of work they did: it was they who chose easily learned and boring work and employers had little to answer for. No one ever suggested that it was 'not worth' training women as nurses or as teachers even though they were formally sacked on marriage and would not be likely to spend longer in paid employment than a factory worker. Looking at the question in practical terms, even if it had taken two years to train them, employers would have reaped the benefits for another eight years on average, but this probability was also never raised.

Despite the prevalence of the view that it was women themselves who were not committed to a career or to long-term employment, employers took active steps to ensure that this was the case by sacking them on marriage if they did not leave voluntarily. When working-class women married and took on responsibility for running a household they were, for all practical purposes, taking on full-time work and one that was incompatible with a 48-hour week factory job. In many factories there was therefore no need for a formal marriage bar in order to exclude married women since most left on marriage. Some factories did operate one, usually the old established paternalistic firms like Peek Frean or Courtaulds who aimed to control the local labour market by paying well but also by imposing harsh discipline, thereby earning a reputation as a 'good employer' and ensuring its pick of women workers. To avoid being sacked in these factories women hid their wedding rings and kept quiet about marriage plans just as women did in offices and schools where there was a formal marriage bar.

The legally enforced marriage bar covered all local government and civil service employment, including teaching, and most other office work. In professional and non-manual occupations work was not so physically arduous as in a factory, and women were likely to be better off financially and in a better position to afford labour-saving domestic appliances and convenience foods, or to employ other women as domestic helps. In their situation then, waged or salaried employment was potentially more compatible with domestic responsibility. Hence the need for a formal marriage bar: if married women were to be removed, forcible means were necessary to achieve the end.[13]

By whatever means the exclusion was effected during the inter-war period, either voluntary or forced, those women who contravened the ban became objects of fierce hostility from men, other women, and the trade unions. Many working-class husbands did not think it was right for their wives to work. Maybe some, like Chrissie Minett's, recognized that it was too much to do both jobs. But for many it indicated their own inability to support a family. A working wife was therefore a reflection on their own inadequacy as a man. In terms of the earlier discussion of the nature of men's insertion in the waged economy and the domestic economy, there was some basis to the prescription that wives should not have to work since the male wage was supposedly a 'family wage'. But this was overlaid with concerns about respectability and masculinity. The main consideration for some husbands was that it was degrading for him if his wife worked, rather than that she was exhausted by doing two full-time jobs.

In an era of high unemployment married women who worked were vilified in the media as greedy and selfish, taking a job away from a single woman who was in greater need of the money. At the same time, employers portrayed married women as too independent and unreliable because they were not so dependent on earning their own living as a single woman. Thus, whichever way they turned, there was an argument against married women and from every quarter. Newspapers, magazines, and even trade union journals echoed the general opposition, frequently going so far as to state that married women were taking jobs from men and that by making their own families richer they were making others poorer. Since the first proposition was completely without base, the inference was also incorrect but knowledge of the truth of the matter was no protection against the popular force of the argument.

Trade unions reflected much of the ideology about married women working, and more generally about women workers being a threat to men by undercutting wages. In some ways this could be understood as a defence of skilled workers and of men's jobs as such at a time when unemployment was high and the labour movement had its back against the wall. It was true that at the level of industrial employment as a whole the number of women was increasing and that of men was declining, but to argue that there was competition over any particular jobs was ludicrous. Trade union leaders must have been aware that the labour market was completely segmented on a sexual basis and that there was no actual substitution of men by women. However, rather than taking on board the new circumstances and attempting to recruit more women, most unions dismissed them as potential trade unionists or demonstrated only a token interest in them. Instead they echoed the general refrain about the scourge of the 'married woman' worker and reiterated the traditional concerns of the skilled male worker for whom having a working wife appeared to be almost as degrading as being unemployed.[14]

The violent reactions aroused by the whole question of married women working and the vehemence with which they were voiced could only indicate the existence of contradictions and tensions. Changes were occurring in both waged and unwaged work which had the potential to enable women to be financially independent of men and to question their traditional place in the home. Such developments raised the possibility of opening up and redefining the traditional economic and social position of women and this would have momentous implications for the domestic economy and the reproduction of labour power. In this light, the opposition to married women working represented a rearguard attempt to turn back the tide and firmly retrench married women in the home.

I have tried to distinguish, somewhat schematically, between the material and ideological factors that determined the allocation of women to assembly-line work and exclusion from everything else. The ideological sex-typing of jobs on the one hand and the attribution of certain qualities both to the work and to women had a material force of their own in producing and reproducing gender division and subordination. They were not just reflections which justified and legitimized an already existing situation, but rather they contributed to its creation and continual recreation. Without such ideological representation the whole process would never have developed in such an unplanned way in the first place nor perpetuated itself so automatically over the years without need for deliberate intervention. On the other hand, however powerful these representations they did not cause women to do assembly-line work. The real explanation lay in the dual structural location of women's work in the domestic and the public economy, and on the conditions under which they sold their labour power which arose out of this particular position.

Chapter seven

Homeward bound: changes in domestic production and consumption

I have concentrated so far on one side of what was in fact a dual process that necessarily included the consumption of commodities as well as their production. Since the full cycle of capital involves distribution and exchange as well as production, the mass production of consumer commodities also implied mass consumption. Production of consumer goods could represent a viable solution to the economic crisis of the 1920s and 1930s only if there was a market for those commodities. This chapter now turns to the other side of the process. I shall explore first the role of women as purchasers and users of the new commodities they had produced or assembled in factories. I hope to show that women were as centrally involved as consumers as they were as producers, and that the two sides of the circuit were inextricably linked. My second focus is the great exodus from domestic service which heralded a major change in the role of working-class women in the domestic economy.

Circuits of domestic production and consumption

Although my main concern has been with the production of commodities in the formal economy it is important to remember that the domestic economy also constituted a centre for production in its own right. However, these two centres of production operated on a quite different basis and each had its own separate circuit of production and consumption. In the domestic economy labour power was produced and reproduced, and goods and services were made that were necessary for this function. The products of domestic labour were intended for direct use and they were consumed within the household. They were not produced as commodities in order to be exchanged for money outside of the household and their consumption did not realize any profit. The circuit of domestic production and consumption therefore occurred almost entirely within the domestic economy.

Commodity consumer products on the other hand were made for the very purpose of being sold and making a profit. Their circuit of production and consumption was not confined to the one sector in which they were produced. On the contrary they were destined for personal and domestic consumption in the domestic economy rather than in the commodity sector itself.

During the period between the industrial revolution and until the advent of mass production these two circuits had remained fairly insulated from each other. However, I would contend that developments within each sphere during the inter-war years had the effect of bringing their circuits into closer contact with each other and of establishing many more connections between them. Part of the reason for this was that the domestic economy became a prime site for the consumption of commodity products. So I aim to highlight the links between the developments in the two spheres and to demonstrate the new ways in which they became connected, concentrating on the changes that occurred within the household, especially those concerning domestic labour.

Many products of the new industries were intended, as I have already stressed, for consumption in the household, from radios and electric irons to cake mixes, canned food and off-the-peg clothes. The domestic economy therefore became of heightened significance to the main wealth accumulating industries as the central market for their goods. Women's responsibility for managing the household economy normally extended to control over spending the family income and purchasing the commodities to be used in the home. Since women rather than men held the purse strings, industry geared its marketing, sales promotion and advertising campaigns towards them. Many of the new mass-produced commodities which could now be bought replaced goods previously made within the home or, in the case of domestic appliances, made less arduous the labour that had to be expended on housework. In this way women began to buy more things rather than to make them themselves. The production and reproduction of labour power within the domestic economy continued to be done on a non-commodity basis for direct use rather than exchange, but some of the labour involved in domestic production could now be removed or replaced by the purchase of commodities. Although this process was particularly evident in middle-class households where it was closely connected with the decline of domestic service, certain of the new commodities were also within the reach of better-off sections of the working class living in areas of industrial expansion in the South East and Midlands.

A series of linked developments thus served to bring about a new and much closer relation between women and capital along a number of different dimensions all of which individually integrated women more fully into the central circuit of production and consumption of capital and into the wage economy. On the one hand, as women moved out of domestic service work and into employment in factories, shops and offices in ever increasing numbers they entered the formal economy on a scale unknown before. On the other hand, as the central direct labour force in the new consumer industries they were incorporated into commodity production on a new basis. And, at the same time, capital depended on women also as consumers, as the essential market for the new commodities. Because women both produced and consumed the new goods, were wage earners as well as spenders, they became indispensable to the extension both of commodity production and of the wage economy.

Although these changes in women's position as producers and consumers of commodities were linked as two complementary chains in a circuit, the end result was achieved only after a long, gradual and uneven process. It was not pre-planned and it did not happen in one fell swoop or as a result of a single chain of events which followed each other in a neat fashion. Although the process began in the inter-war years it would have been impossible at that time to predict how the trends would proceed in the future and what their end-point would have been. Historically the process was fully consolidated only much later, in the post-war period of the late 1950s and early 1960s, culminating in the mass production of a whole host of consumer perishables and durables, a much greater level of commoditization of the reproduction of labour power, and the waged employment of the vast majority of women outside of the domestic economy. These three developments were in fact intimately interconnected but they occurred as the result of processes that were, in empirical and historical terms, partly independent of each other. For this reason it is much easier to grasp the link between them when looking back at them from the end-point rather than from the beginning.

Domestic labour

During the inter-war years different groups of women were differently affected by and involved in these processes of commodity production and consumption and there were enormous class and regional variations. Putting it crudely, working-class women were the producers and middle-class women the main consumers of most of the new goods. But even these empirical facts were connected in a complex spiral of links: one of the reasons why middle-class women became the main consumers was because they could not find domestic servants and so bought domestic appliances and processed food instead of paying servants to do the work involved; domestic servants were not available precisely because young working-class women much preferred working in factories to being domestic servants and avoided such work whenever they could. Consequently, those very women who might have gone into service in an earlier period now worked in assembly industries making the goods which middle-class women bought to aid domestic labour because they could no longer get servants. And quite apart from this chain of connected developments and in addition to it, the higher wages which working-class women earned in factory work enabled them too to ease the burden of their domestic labour in the home by purchasing some of the new labour saving goods. Domestic labour was thus undergoing enormous changes in both middle- and working-class households.

Consumer commodities

Buying factory or bakery-made bread for example rather than baking it oneself or engaging a cook to do the work may have cost more in money but it cost less in labour. It was no longer necessary to buy the ingredients, to mix the dough, to prepare the oven (which would probably have involved lighting a fire in the kitchen range), or to wash up the utensils after baking. Purchasing bread as a commodity good thus replaced both time and energy previously expended in making home-made bread, labour which could now be put to alternative uses. The same considerations applied to other ready-made or part-prepared food, such as tinned soup and baked beans or custard powder, blancmange or jelly mixes. Similarly buying clothes off-the-peg in chain stores such as Marks and Spencer or the Co-op which had been mass produced in factories took less time and involved considerably less work than buying the material to make blouses, skirts and dresses oneself. The clothes may not have lasted as long as home-made ones but as most of them were made of the new lightweight synthetic materials they were much easier to launder and so had the added advantage of saving time also on washing, drying and ironing which was one of the heaviest, time-consuming, arduous and hated of household tasks.

Domestic appliances on the other hand, unlike ready-made clothing or food, aided rather than substituted for women's labour. Possessing a gas or electric cooker to replace the old kitchen range made power for cooking immediately available at the turn of a switch. It also did away with the need for actually lighting a fire in the kitchen and so saved on cleaning up all the dirt and dust produced by the fire. Gas geysers or electric water heaters had a similar effect in replacing the old coppers that had been used to heat water. These

Figure 10 Hot water on tap. Reproduced by permission of the Electricity Council.

also had required a coal fire to be lit underneath them. Having running hot water on tap not only removed the need to keep coal in the kitchen (and the cleaning associated with the copper), but also made it unnecessary to carry hot water to different rooms around the house in heavy containers for bathing and washing, and made much easier one of the arduous and time-consuming activities involved in the weekly wash. Being in a position to buy commodities such as these would undoubtedly have a profound impact on the nature of domestic labour and would release a certain proportion of domestic labour time to be used in other ways.[1] For many middle-class women this meant managing their home without employing servants and doing their housework themselves; for working-class women it would give the possibility of engaging in paid employment on a more continuous basis or for longer periods of time. On the other hand for them to ease their domestic burden by such means would have been possible only on the basis of a high enough family wage to buy the goods in the first place. It was estimated that by 1938 9 million women 'performed their basic housework unaided' (PEP 1945: 26).

Family size

However, the availability of consumer commodities was not the only factor affecting the amount of work to be undertaken in the domestic economy by the inter-war period. Two other independent developments were also responsible. The first was the reduction in family size. This had been declining since the 1870s and by the 1930s had spread to all but the very wealthiest and very poorest sections of the population. The fertility rate fell steadily from 1870 when there were 295 legitimate live births for every 1,000 married women aged between 15 and 44, to 222 in 1901 and 111 in 1931. At the same time average family size dropped from five in 1900 to two in the 1930s. In the first decade of the century 55 per cent of women had more than three children, and 25 per cent more than five, but by the 1940s the percentages had fallen to 30 per cent and 9 per cent respectively (Lewis 1984: 5–6; Gittins 1982: 35–6). The middle classes had been the first to limit the number of children during the late nineteenth century but they were followed fairly rapidly by the working class. However because of the time gap, the class differential actually widened between 1910 and 1924 and did not contract until the inter-war years. Since childbearing and rearing was one of the main activities involved in domestic labour, this decline had a dramatic effect not only on women's health and energy but also on the amount of time and work they spent on childcare.

A large proportion of the women I interviewed who had worked in the new industries were born into families of six, seven or eight children but they themselves followed the statistical trend in having far fewer children than their mothers. Doris Hanslow was born in 1910 and was one of eight children; she had two herself. Winnie Young was one of seven and had two children herself. Eliza Hawkins's mother had five surviving children and several who had died, whereas she herself bore three. Ann Leadbitter was one of five and had one, and Jessie Evans was one of seven but, like her colleague Wynne Cleverley from Mullards, did not have any children herself.

It had been a necessity for most of these mothers to work outside of the home in order to support the family either because they were on their own or because of their husband's low income. However, their domestic responsibilities restricted them to taking casual or temporary jobs which permitted them also to look after the children. Eliza Hawkins's mother worked as a wood chopper and she remembered having to bundle up the sticks when she came home from work. Winnie Young's mother worked as a cook and went into other people's houses on a daily basis to do their washing. Ann Leadbitter's mother was widowed at 30 during the First World War and was left with five small children to look after. She did two jobs, tailoring and night cleaning in offices, and the children had to wait on the doorstep until she came home from work. Nell Williams's mother was also a widow and she had seven children to support apart from herself:

> She had to work but she couldn't get a job in a factory. She did confinements and also cleaning out big houses over in Blackheath Hill. She used to get half a crown for that for a day's work. Then when Mum came home she'd get a bit of shopping and bring it home in her apron, but she wouldn't touch a bit of that bread 'cos she had seven of us and she had to feed the lot of us. Because Mum was a midwife there they called our street 'Incubator Street'. She did everything for them and I was the probationer. I used to have to go round to their houses after school and wash the dirty napkins out.

As if this was not enough, she also took in washing to do in her own home:

> My mother used to bring the washing in at night, put 1d in the gas and hang all the clothes out in the living room, which was the only room. They would be dry by the next morning and she'd get up and iron them and we used to have to take them back and collect the money on them.

Clearly conditions were markedly different for the two generations. With their large numbers of children to support the mothers were only able to seek work that could be done part-time or on an irregular basis. They were all very poor and the money they earned was essential to make ends meet and to provide basic necessities such as food and clothing for the children. While the daughters still lived at home the wages they brought into the parental home were still needed to keep the family from the extremes of poverty. But when they later set up their own households on marriage, they often moved into new houses with laid-on electricity and gas. They all had fewer offspring than their mothers and neither their domestic nor their waged work were affected for so long or so much by childcare. Most could afford to buy consumer goods and appliances that would have been out of their mothers' reach.

Infrastructural facilities

The other development affecting domestic labour was the provision of the infrastructure for the modern home: running water on tap, sewage disposal, houses wired for electricity and a laid-on supply of gas. Most better-off homes already benefited from all of these fa-cilities soon after the turn of the century, but the provision for working-class homes varied widely. In the depressed areas of the North, Scotland and Wales taps in the street and 'middens' (collec-tive outside toilets for the whole street which had to be emptied by horse and cart) were commonplace until the Second World War and meant that many houses had no running water, private toilet, or place to wash. The situation was better in the areas of economic ex-pansion. Most of the new municipal houses built during the inter-war period were provided with inside toilets and running water and were wired for electricity; the majority also had bathrooms with water hea-ters. Quite apart from the higher standards of hygiene and sanitation made possible by these facilities, the labour involved in keeping the family, its clothes and the house clean was obviously a totally differ-ent proposition where these facilities were laid on and where they were not.

Again most of the women I interviewed contrasted the absence of such infrastructure in their parental home with its presence in their own home. Many were married in the early 1930s and usually moved to a different house on marriage. It was clear that it was when they set up their own household that most acquired these new facilities for the first time. When they were children lighting had been by gas mantle, the toilet was outside, there was no bathroom and no run-ning hot water, and no possibility of electric appliances since there was no electricity in the home. As Nell Williams said:

There were no loos, no electric light, no inside toilet.

Ann Leadbitter's mother also had to manage without any laid-on facilities apart from gas:

There were three floors and we lived at the top and it was all the way downstairs to the water and the toilet. We didn't have any running water and we had a gas stove on the landing. There was a gas mantle but you had to burn it first. We didn't have a bathroom and Friday night Mum used to get the old tin bath and put a kettle of water in it. The last one in had the dirty water! There was a boiler but the landlady wouldn't let us use it. So we used to take all our clothes off and Mum would go to Brickwall Street baths and have them washed, mangled and ironed and then we'd put them on clean again.

However, some women whose parents were not in such dire straits as these two remembered their parents' house being wired up for electricity before they left home. But in all cases this was for electric light only, rather than sockets for plugging in appliances. Doris Sharland's father was an electrician and wired up his own home in 1924 but others like Jessie Evans and Kath Parish paid to have it installed. In the mid-1920s Doris Hanslow moved with her parents from Bermondsey to a new house on the Downham Estate built by the London County Council. There they had a bathroom for the first time:

When we first moved out to Downham, we used to invite all our old friends from Bermondsey down for the weekend to stay.. .. It was a big attraction then, our friends would be thrilled to bits with our lovely new house, and so were we. We'd give them a guided tour, first they wanted to go upstairs and look at the bathroom and toilet, because nobody had got one you see, and they couldn't get over how lovely it was.

(Quoted in Weightman and Humphries 1984: 142)

In this first new house there was no electricity but by the time Doris married in 1936 and moved to a nearby house on the same estate it had been laid on:

I remember looking at the switch and I was afraid to touch it for a while.

(Interview with M.G.)

However, the majority benefited from these infrastructural facilities only after they had left their parental home. Winnie Young first got electric light when she married in 1933. Eliza Hawkins had not known electricity at home but it was laid on in the house she and her husband moved to on a new council estate in Surrey Docks when they married in 1935. It was also laid on in Les White's new house on an estate in Perivale in 1939. Wynne Cleverley was married in 1935 and she and her husband bought a house in Mitcham that was nearly new in 1937:

We were both earning about £3 12s 6d and our repayments were £3 11s 5d a week and that took some finding. So you see our combined wages were important. We'd had gas lighting at home before I was married but we never had gas lighting here. Electricity was installed in the house before we bought it.

Elsie Woolnough (not previously introduced) was a clerical worker at Polikoffs, Goldbarts and other large clothing factories in Hackney and the East End. She paid to have electricity installed in her mother's house where she and her husband lived:

We didn't have electricity until I was married some time. I had three rooms in my mother's house. There was no water upstairs so I had to carry water up and down, and the toilet was right downstairs too. We didn't have a bathroom but what we used to call a wash-house or scullery and a big bungalow bath. We had to light the copper and have a bath that way. There were gas brackets for lighting and my husband decided that we ought to have electric light so my mother had seven points put in and we had six. It worked out at £1 a point and you could pay for it weekly. This must have been about 1936.

Although Eileen and Barry Jones's house on the new estate in Hayes had electricity it was not wired up on the national grid and this proved to be quite a problem:

The estate more or less had its own private electricity supply. They had their own generators and power supply and we paid for it in with the rent. It got overloaded and the whole thing just blew up so then there was no supply and we had gas laid on and I fitted gas mantles up in the rooms. In the end we joined an association on the estate and I think everybody contributed £3 and that paid for the electricity board to come round and rewire the whole house.

The experience of Doris Hanslow, Wynne Cleverley and the others whose new houses were wired for electricity was probably fairly typical of working-class women of the period living in the more prosperous areas of the country. However, since many of the women I interviewed had moved from inner London to new suburban housing estates in the then 'green belt' near the factories where they worked, where virtually all the houses were provided with infrastructural facilities, they were more likely to benefit from such facilities than those (including their own mothers) who lived in much older housing in the run-down inner city areas of London or Birmingham. By the end of the inter-war period the vast majority of the population as a whole lived in houses that were either wired for electricity (8.5

million houses) or piped for gas (10 million houses). Nevertheless this still left one third of households (4 million) without electricity and three-quarters of a million without either source of power, situated mainly in the depressed and rural areas (PEP *Planning* 231, 2 March 1945: 4).

The availability of infrastructural facilities for the modern home in both working- and middle-class homes in the areas of the new industries, and the declining fertility rate which also characterized women of both classes, had an enormous impact in reducing the amount of the domestic labour they had to undertake in comparison with their mothers' generation. However, there still remained vast class differences in the purchase of commodities to aid or replace domestic labour and this meant that the reproduction of labour power in the middle-class household was achieved with the help of more commodity purchases than was the case for the working class. In terms of consumption then it was the middle-class domestic economy that was much more effectively penetrated by the commodity sector of production. Similarly middle-class rather than working-class women represented the essential market for the more costly consumer products of the new industries, particularly electrical appliances.

'Ideal' home and 'ideal' housewife

It should be emphasized that the middle class of the inter-war period was not the same middle class that had existed in the Victorian or Edwardian eras. It now included a much higher proportion of salaried professional employees such as civil servants, accountants, managers, teachers or lawyers and far fewer individual capitalists who owned their own businesses. Both the growth of the salaried classes and the demise of the small capitalist were connected with the changes in the structure of the economy and industry discussed in Chapter 3, and notably with the growth of large corporations, the rationalization of business administration, and the administrative back-up for all this that was provided by the state. All the new government departments, such as the Ministry of Health and the Ministry of Pensions, were located in London and most of the new business corporations had their headquarters in the City. It was London therefore that witnessed the greatest proliferation of the new white-collar occupations and where the growth of the salaried professional middle class was centred.

This new salaried class of people were typically those who bought a semi-detached house in one of the many new private suburban estates that were rapidly springing up on the outskirts of the capital. Nearly 4 million new houses were built during the massive house-

Figure 11 The housewife takes over. Reproduced by permission of the Electricity Council.

building programme of inter-war years, including municipal and private, and suburban estates and garden cities were much favoured by town planners as well as speculative builders (Burnett 1978: 246; Swenarton 1981; H.W. Richardson and Aldcroft 1968: 301–4). These houses had all modern facilities laid on and were designed to be run by the housewife on her own or with a minimum of help. The houses were much smaller than Victorian middle-class homes and arranged on a more modest scale. A large proportion of the new salariat would not have been able to afford a domestic servant even if they had been able to find one and the new suburban housewife was encouraged instead to 'let electricity be your servant'. Since she was going to spend so much time in it, the kitchen was often designed as the pride of the house, spacious, light and airy, overlooking the garden and with ample space for all the appliances she would acquire. This was in sharp contrast to the traditional kitchen which had been a dark and dingy room, hidden away in the basement 'below stairs' where the servants worked. Now that the kitchen was the ideal housewife's prime domain it was fully integrated into the rest of the house. As an electricity industry publication put it:

> It was clear that housewives were not going to use the dirty troublesome coal range they had inflicted on their servants.
>
> (Byers 1981: 24)

The commercial interests of property development companies responsible for building many of the suburban estates, in combination with those of the electricity industry attempting to persuade women to buy more labour saving appliances, were instrumental in creating the view of the ideal home. Married women's place was firmly in the home during this period, at least according to popular ideology. The spread of the 'ideal' easy-to-run home served not only to boost the profits of the construction, electrical and other industries that manufactured products for domestic use but also at the same time to reinforce the cult of domesticity by presenting housework as an activity that was meaningful and pleasurable in itself as well as being newly recognized as socially worthwhile.[2] The 'discovery' of the intrinsic value and virtue of domestic labour must have appeared very ironic to working-class women for whom it had always been a full-time and arduous occupation, and one that was disdained and badly paid when done as a form of paid employment.

The ideal of the 'non-working' housewife had been created earlier in the United States than in Britain, and was drawn in greater detail, but the trends here were in the same direction. After the First World War housework in the United States was no longer portrayed as a chore but rather as an expression of the housewife's personality and devotion to her family. It was imbued with emotional significance:

> Laundering had once been just laundering; now it was an expression of love ... Feeding the family had once been just feeding the family; now it was a way to communicate deep-seated emotions.... Diapering was no longer just diapering, but a time to build the baby's sense of security; cleaning the bathroom sink was not just

cleaning, but an exercise for the maternal instincts, protecting the family from disease.

(Cowan 1976a: 151)[3]

Creative urges could be satisfied in cleaning and cooking. The very health and happiness of husband and children depended on the housewife, so it was imperative that she perform her tasks as well as she possibly could. A child that did badly at school or an unhappy husband were sources of guilt since they reflected her inadequacies as a mother and wife. Magazines and the media did much to encourage this emotionalization of domestic labour and the psychological approach to the housewife.

In Britain the inter-war period saw the first appearance of many new magazines for women. They did not go so far as their American counterparts in highlighting the psychological dimension of domestic labour but rather they cultivated the view of the middle-class housewife as a new kind of craft or professional worker, who ran her house scientifically and managed a host of domestic machinery. Whereas a Victorian lady may have administered a household staff of servants and viewed domestic labour as beneath her, the inter-war housewife could be a specialist technician who put the new sources of power to her own use. They would enable her to engage in light and easy domestic tasks which did not tire her out or make her very dirty. *Good Housekeeping, Woman and Home, Wife and Home,* and *Harpers Bazaar* were the new monthlies that appeared for the first time in the 1920s, aimed primarily at a middle-class audience, soon followed in the 1930s by the weeklies *Woman's Own, Woman's Illustrated,* and *Woman* which were geared to the less well off (Weightman and Humphries 1984: 128; Beauman 1983: 109–10). All encouraged a return to femininity and stressed that aspiring to beauty was no longer incompatible, as in the past, with doing your own domestic work. Then as now they gave beauty tips, budgeting hints, and recipes (often using ready-made mixes and tinned fruit or vegetables), had competitions on 'how to run your home without help' and reported time-and-motion studies that had been applied to the kitchen and 'proved' that efficient organization could greatly reduce the time it was necessary to spend on each task.

Many of the companies that manufactured commodities for household consumption found that women's magazines were the best place to advertise their products since the message they were trying to put over was also echoed by the content of the articles. Clearly the modern ideal of the 'housewife', which was created during this period, was not just an ideological construct nor a reaction against the greater independence women had from the home during

Figure 12 'Electrified' breakfast. Reproduced by permission of the Electricity Council.

the First World War and the Roaring Twenties. It was also linked with the shift in industrial production and the restructuring of the economy towards production for domestic consumption. The success of many of the new industries and therefore of the new centres of capital accumulation relied on the housewife being a reality and not simply an ideal.

Variations by class

With her larger disposable income the middle-class housewife necessarily became the chief target for promotional organizations such as the Electrical Development Association and the Electrical Association for Women (EAW). The former made films extolling the wonders of the new electric home and the latter established local branches to campaign for the wider use of electricity. A survey conducted by the EAW in 1934 found that women spent much less time on housework after their homes were electrified. In an unwired home the housewife spent twenty-six and a half hours a week attending to cooking stoves, lamps, fires, washing, ironing and cleaning but this was reduced by 73 per cent in an electric house to just over seven hours. The chores of making fires (which took nearly ten hours) disappeared completely and the time spent on others dropped dramatically: laundry from 4.3 to 1.6 hours, cleaning from 8.26 to 4.12 and ironing from 2.95 to 1.55 (Edwards 1935; Davidson 1982: 42–3).

Although this report was about working-class homes it was undoubtedly the case that the vast majority of electric appliances were bought and owned by middle-class women. Gas cookers were owned by 68 per cent of all families in 1938 and increasing numbers of electric cookers were installed from the mid-1930s so that nearly 2 million were in use by the outbreak of war. Most working-class households rented their electric cooker from the local electricity showroom (PEP 1945: 67–9). Electric irons were very widely owned by those wired up for electricity and radios almost universally, but the latter were run off accumulators and so did not require a socket. However, the purchase of all other electric appliances – from the smaller and less costly hair dryers, pop toasters, and coffee percolators through the middle-range vacuum cleaners, immersion heaters and electric fires to the very expensive and cumbersome refrigerators and washing machines – was restricted to higher income earners (over £300 a year) and so effectively to middle-class households.[4]

In general working-class women were able to buy only the smaller and cheaper commodity products. Most bought factory produced clothes while a large proportion of their middle-class counterparts were probably still having their costumes and dresses made by dress-makers or were buying individual model clothes available in the large department stores.

The women I interviewed had bought margarine, biscuits, pack-aged food, bread made in bakeries, tinned fruit and some tinned vegetables during the 1930s. Instead of going into the corner shop virtually every day as Nell Williams's mother had done for

> a pen'worth of milk, a penny packet of tea, ha'pence of sugar and ha'pence of jam

they were increasingly buying food that was already weighed and packaged. It was sold in chain stores like the Co-op or Home and Co-lonial and in sizes that meant they did not need to buy staple items every day. However, as they had no fridges they still had to shop for perishables on a more or less daily basis. Tinned salmon and peaches were the Sunday tea treat in Kath Parish's home as in countless others. Doris Sharland (who lived quite near the large Heinz factory in Harlesden) remembered:

> Baked beans was just coming in and spaghetti and we used to think that was lovely. You could get a tin of salmon at Woolworths for 3d.

All had radios by the early 1930s. The experience of Doris Han-slow's family was typical:

> The first radio I remember was the Cat's Whisker with an accumu-lator. You'd take it round to be charged every week. My brother worked in delivery and he brought one home and we were thrilled to bits with it. We all sat round the table and he kept wiggling this little bit of wire to get something. It had earphones so it was turns each because of course there were eight of us. We thought it was so clever.

Jessie Evans's brother bought a gramophone as well as a radio:

> The first record that he bought was When the Red, Red Robin Comes Bob Bob Bobbing Along. That was the first record we ever had and the gramophone was one of those wind-up ones.

By the outbreak of war most had replaced the old flat irons that needed to be heated on the kitchen range or stove with electric irons. But Doris Hanslow was the only one to have a Hoover before the war: she shared it with her mother, taking turns in having it one week at a time each. Most of the others did not need Hoovers as they had no carpets. Lino and a few rugs were the norm but they were by now more likely to clean the rugs with a carpet sweeper than by the tea-leaf method of their mothers:

> Save the tea leaves out of the pot until they were dry, sprinkle them on the rug and leave them for a while, and then brush them off with a hand brush.
>
> (Eileen Jones)

None of the women I interviewed had fridges, washing machines, or spin dryers until the 1950s when they bought them on hire purchase. No one owned a car before the war and they continued to rely on public transport.

Thus laid-on facilities and having fewer children probably had a greater impact in changing the nature and quantity of domestic labour undertaken by working-class women during the inter-war years than did consumer commodities or domestic appliances. The 1945 PEP surveys of household appliances drew attention to piped hot water as the one service that would have the greatest single effect in saving time and labour. Of all those with an annual income of less than £160 in 1945 over 20 per cent were still heating water in pans or kettles, 35 per cent used a solid fuel copper, 25 per cent had a gas boiler but only 2 per cent an electric boiler (PEP 1945: 33). They concluded that

> it cannot be too strongly emphasized that lack of hot water greatly adds to the labour and time involved in washing clothes and dishes and cleaning and scrubbing the house, besides acting as a deterrent to personal hygiene
>
> (PEP 1945: 39)

and foresaw an enormous post-war market for electric immersion heaters or gas geysers comprising large sections of the working class. Writing at a time of impending labour shortage the authors of the survey were not slow to point out that the less time married women had to spend on housework the more they would be available for part-time employment outside of the home.

Until the 1950s then the circuit of production and consumption of consumer goods was differentiated on a class basis. Although more commodities were used in domestic labour overall and the domestic economy as such became much more closely integrated with the sector of commodity production through ties of mutual dependence, it was primarily middle-class women, of the type that might previously have employed servants, who constituted the main consumer market for consumer durables and labour-saving devices. As a consequence, certain aspects of the reproduction of labour power in the middle-class home were achieved on the basis of a much greater integration with the commodity sector than ever existed before.

Domestic service

But commoditization represented only one facet of the change undergone by the middle-class domestic economy during the inter-war years. The other, and closely related, dimension was the decline in domestic service. Dramatic changes occurred in domestic service employment during the period and these too were linked with the changing circuit of production and consumption affecting the domestic economy. On the one hand the shortage of domestic servants was one of the factors which led to the partial commoditization of domestic labour in the middle-class home. On the other, the entry of so many women into factory employment, where they were paid a wage rather than board and lodging plus a small monetary supplement, represented an expansion of the wage economy which in the long run permitted working-class women also to purchase more goods and services for use in the home.

Domestic service employment had begun to decline from the turn of the century and as early as 1896 Charles Booth's survey pointed out that women avoided domestic service wherever possible. The 'servant problem' was therefore a phenomenon which predated the First World War although it came to a head at that time, and so much so that when Vera Brittain went home on leave from the war she commented that

> the universal topic of maids and ration cards now completely dominated the conversation.
>
> (Quoted in Beauman 1983: 107)

Several surveys were conducted in the immediate pre- and post-war period by the government and Labour Party to discover reasons for the shortage and suggest remedies. The general consensus was that low social status, low pay, and lack of leisure time and regular hours of work lay at the root of the problem. Standardizing the conditions of work so as to make them more contractual and raising the social standing of the domestic servant were proposed accordingly as solutions.

'Neutral' social commentators, social scientists and even middle-class suffragettes and feminists saw nothing undesirable in domestic service as a form of employment in itself (no doubt they employed servants themselves and also suffered from the 'problem'). Apart from those forced by circumstances into service, the only real criticisms came from writers on the left such as Joan Beauchamp (1937: 73–6) and John Gollan (1937: 114–18), both members of the Communist Party. Industrial psychologists echoed the demands for raising its status, as did contemporary liberal experts on women's employment. Although Vera Brittain and Pearl Jephcott pressed for the increased entry of women to the professions and an end to the marriage bar they saw no contradiction in arguing at the same time for an expansion of domestic service work on the condition that it was acknowledged by both potential employees and employers as a skilled, worthwhile and valuable occupation. After emphasizing that domestic service offered poor opportunities to the 'enterprising' worker, Vera Brittain went on (1928: 31) to define the 'problem' of domestic service exclusively in terms of the 'great difficulty in obtaining the upper grade of worker'. In similar vein, Pearl Jephcott wrote that:

> The happiness of a great many people could be much increased if we could raise a generation of women who realize that domestic work is a career which demands intelligence, skill, and careful training.
>
> (Jephcott 1942: 82–3)

While a few progressive women writers such as Virginia Woolf or Naomi Mitchison recognized that it was possible for them to give full flight to their good causes or creative urges only because of the attentions of the domestic servants who ran their large upper-class households,[5] the 'servant problem' was a constant theme for many women novelists of the inter-war period. Their heroines seemed to feel their social status necessitated having servants but they had great difficulty in finding or retaining any. Yet once this problem was overcome the heroines frequently complained, in slightly self-deprecating tones, that they were no longer in charge of their own domestic situation. They were taken over by their cooks, housekeepers or nannies who intimidated them and ran the household when really it should have been the mistress who exercised authority over the staff.[6] Women who came from backgrounds where maids had been taken for granted were portrayed as oblivious to the servile social relations of domestic servants.

At the height of the slump in the late 1920s and early 1930s large numbers of women in the depressed areas were unable to find any other work than domestic service. At the same time domestic training was the only kind of training offered to women in 'dole' schools. It was official government policy to encourage unemployed women into domestic service. In addition the transference schemes, established by the Ministry of Labour to transfer the unemployed, and especially the young unemployed, out of the areas of highest unemployment, also concentrated on fixing them up with domestic employment. In the case of south Wales boys as well as girls were trained for such employment and sent to London and the South East of England. A Ministry official even observed that in mid-Rhondda they had more success with boys because the girls showed much less enthusiasm for taking up domestic work. This transference was carried out under the Special Areas Development and Improvement Act but as John Gollan wryly commented (1937: 117–18) the Ministry failed to demonstrate

> in what way the diversion of our youth from industry into flunkeydom assists in 'developing' or 'improving'.

Since domestic service was not an insured occupation those employed in this way would not qualify for unemployment benefit. Therefore the more people classified as domestic servants, the smaller the number eligible to claim dole if they became unemployed.

High unemployment rates and state sponsorship of domestic service employment go a long way to explain the large increase in the numbers of domestic servants recorded in the 1931 Census. Between 1901 and 1921 the numbers had been steadily dropping but between 1921 and 1931 there was a 15 per cent increase in the number of female indoor domestic servants (and of 36 per cent amongst men) to 1.1 million (Cen.Pop. 1931 Gen.Rep.: 151). By the time of the next enumeration, twenty years later, this number had been decimated by more than three-quarters of a million to 343,000. As I argued in Chapter 2, it is legitimate to assume that much of the change in the occupational distribution of women, including the shift away from domestic service, took place during the 1930s and was not simply a phenomenon of the Second World War and the immediate post-war years. Because of this the increase in 1931 can be interpreted as a temporary exception to the long term trend, directly linked with the economic recession, which began to be reversed from the early to mid-1930s as conditions started to improve.

As a gross statistic the Census figure also masked the vast regional differences that in fact characterized domestic service employment. Between 1901 and 1921 the number of indoor domestic servants in the County of London had fallen by a third from 242,000 to 157,000 (NSOL 1930–5 Vol. II: 428). Even though a very large proportion of the national total of domestic servants in 1931 were employed in the Greater London area and the South East, over three-quarters of these had not been born there but had migrated themselves or been actively recruited or 'transferred' from rural and distressed areas.

Over 65 per cent of the total (750,883 out of 1,142,655) worked within these two areas but Health Insurance Society records analysed in the *New Survey of London* at approximately the same time as the Census indicated that less than a quarter overall came from London and the proportion was even less in the younger age groups (NSOL 1930–5 Vol. II: 449). The rural origins of domestic servants are reflected in many of their autobiographies. These often contrast a happy but impoverished childhood in the country or a small town with their rude awakening to employment and city life at the age of 14.[7]

Other significant changes were also occurring in the pattern and composition of domestic service employment which were not reflected in the official statistics. The *New Survey of London* noted the ever growing importance of non-residential work and a large decline in the proportion of residential domestic servants. The new pattern was for women to work on a daily basis rather than to live in, either working part-time as a 'char' or office cleaner or for a full 48-hour week, but fewer and fewer were doing the average 66-hour week of the residential domestic servant (NSOL 1930–5 Vol. II: 450).

In addition, the age composition altered: young women aged between 15 and 25 accounted for almost all of the large decline between 1901 and 1921 (80,000 out of 85,000). This was accompanied by an increasing tendency for women over 45 to enter or re-enter domestic service. Consequently the servant population became concentrated in the older age groups. The lure of factory employment was singled out as the main cause of the scarcity of young servants in London (NSOL 1930–5 Vol. II: 429).

A similar trend was noted in the 1934 social survey of Merseyside: the number of domestic servants there had also dropped by a third between 1901 and 1921, and the number of young domestic servants by even more. Chain stores in Liverpool, Bootle and other towns provided the main competition rather than factories. 'Dailies' had also replaced residents in many one-servant households and accounted for a third of all domestic servants. It was in this group that the juveniles were concentrated (C. Jones 1934 Vol. II: 299–302).

Even at the height of the depression then it was the case that young women did not on the whole enter domestic service whenever alternative employment was available, if their parental home was in the local area. A study of Lewisham and Deptford in south London confirmed this generalization by revealing a large shift away from domestic service to other occupations even during the period covered by the 1931 Census and using Census figures. In Lewisham there was a 50 per cent drop in the proportion of women employed as domestic servants between 1911 and 1931 (from 39.4 to 20.8 per cent) and this was offset by a similar increase (from 22.4 to 44.7 per cent) in the proportion of clerks, typists and shopworkers. In Deptford the drop was not so great, from 20.4 to 12.6 per cent, but there the shift was much more towards industrial employment which more than doubled its share of total employment (from 14.4 to 31.6 per cent of all women employed). Factory work in Deptford was therefore attracting women away from other occupations as well as from domestic service (J. Ryan 1981: 22–30).[8]

It would be fair to say that in the geographical areas of the new industries women whose mothers had worked as domestic servants around the turn of the century were unlikely to do so themselves. Virtually all the mothers of the women I interviewed had engaged in some kind of domestic service work before they married (and many continued afterwards), but they were insistent that their daughters should not follow in their footsteps. Several daughters recalled being threatened as children with being put into service by their mothers as punishment for some misdemeanour. Stella Apsey, born in 1910, who eventually trained as a skilled bookbinder and printer remembered that

> my mother always swore that she'd put me into service because I was such a dunce at school. She said the only thing you're fit for is service. I was no good at spelling you see, such a no-good at school so I couldn't go into an office. My sisters wouldn't take me to work with them because I was a proper tom-boy and showed them up too much. When I left school the headmistress said to Mother: 'Don't worry about her. She'll always earn a living by her hands.' And I more or less always have.

Doris Hanslow's experience was more typical:

> It was very hard going into service in them days. My mother would never have let us even though it was so hard for her and every penny we brought in helped a bit.

Most said that they did not need to go into service because they could get other jobs. As Ann Leadbitter put it, it was bad enough doing her own cleaning without doing somebody else's as well, and Nell Williams's experience of washing out the napkins after helping her mother as a midwife put her off such work. The notion of going into service had been so alien to some of the London women that they misunderstood my question as being about being called up for military service!

Those women I interviewed who had worked as domestic servants typified the changes of the time. Either they had been born in an earlier period when fewer factory jobs were available, or they came from extremely poor families where not having to feed them made a substantial difference to the standard of living of the rest of the family, or they came from one of the depressed areas and moving away into service was the only option open to them. Edith Boyd fell into this category. There was no work in South Shields so she was sent into service and once there it was impossible to get out until she could find her own place to live. Since the custom was for domestic servants to send home all their earnings, getting another job but having to pay for alternative accommodation could have been counterproductive. Barry Jones's four sisters all migrated from Wales to London and worked in domestic service for several years before they all, like Edith Boyd, switched to factory work. Elsie Woolnough's parents were also Welsh and her father was an unemployed miner. But her mother had seen enough of the conditions suffered by Welsh girls who went into service and was adamant that none of her daughters should do so:

> There was no work for girls in Wales at the time and so they used to have to leave home and go into service and the boys had to go down the mines. The girls used to come up to London and come back pregnant. I don't say it happened all the time but it happened quite a lot, and not necessarily only in the big houses. My mother was determined that none of her three girls were going to go into service and her five boys weren't going down the mines.

The whole family moved to London because her father could not find any work at home and when the children grew up they all found other jobs, so that none did in fact have to go into service or down the mines.

Edie Harding was born earlier than most of the other women, in 1896, and went as a scullery maid to work in 1909 for an aristocratic family in a large mansion on the Sussex coast. There were thirteen other servants. Edie was paid £4 10s every three months and rushed to the post office straight away to send it home to her mother in Woolwich. She had no time off except when the family was away and did not go home at all for the first four years. But in 1920 she left service for good, returned to London and got a job in the Western Electric telephone factory assembling telephone receivers:

Q. And did you prefer the factory work to being in service?
A. Oh yes. Well I was able to be free and easy then, wasn't I? It was much more money too.

Wynne Cleverley's first few jobs as scullery maid contrasted starkly with her eventual wage level and responsible position as fore-woman at Philips. Her family was very poor but she won a scholarship to trade school in Hammersmith where she learned cookery. Needless to say this training fitted her only for service:

> I learned all this fancy cooking and didn't use it. I thought going into service was glamorous and I was looking for the uniform and cap but it wasn't glamorous to be a scullery maid! Washing up, scrubbing, it was very hard work. You started at 6 in the morning and worked right through. The wages were £30 a year. Mind you I shared a lovely room with four others. There was a lovely bed, but you weren't in it long enough! The housemaids used to keep their dustpan and brush under their bed so as to save their energy in the morning. When they got up they swept the stairs as they went down. I had every other night off and every other Sunday which was good for those days.

Wynne stayed in service until the General Strike in 1926. In her last job she earned 'board wages' of £1 1s out of which she had to buy her own food and pay towards her lodging. This meant there was little left over to give her mother. When she started at Mullards her wages rose immediately to about £1 10s a week and her hours of work went down considerably:

> I liked the factory much better than service. You had freedom you see. Don't forget you worked certain hours – it may have been long hours – but you still had your evening. When I was in service, amongst other things I still had to dust and clean the house-keeper's room after I had finished in the kitchen and she used to come along and inspect what I'd done. So there was more freedom in the factory. Plus you had your own mates. You were very alone in your own little sphere in service because you did whatever you were told to do and then you went to your room. There was no sitting room for the kitchen staff.

Clearly many other factors were involved in the long term national decline of domestic service apart from the availability of alternative factory employment.[9] Although continuous reference to the 'servant problem' indicated that demand exceeded supply throughout the inter-war period as a whole, the changes in the structure of the middle class, outlined earlier, probably meant that there was also a decline, albeit a proportionately smaller one, in demand as well as in supply. The decline in middle-class family size would have the effect of reducing the numbers of servants required by those who would previously have engaged several and who could still afford them.

But the altered composition of the class was probably of greater overall significance: although more households fell into the category of the middle class than at the turn of the century, the new professional salariat was not as affluent as the business class of the earlier era and did not have the means to employ domestic servants on the same scale, especially since servants now cost more. The *New Survey of London* distinguishes between the 'very rich', on the one hand, who employed a number of servants and were affected last and least by the shortage in supply and 'wealthy middle-class' households, on the other, who in the past had employed one residential servant. These were now forced to adapt to the new situation, resorting in the first instance to two women working on a daily basis but in shifts (from 7 am to 2 pm and from 2 pm to 10 pm) so as to cover the whole day, but later making do with one 'daily'. The 'lower middle class' could not now afford one at all, and this group would have included most of the new suburbanites in their semi-detached ideal homes. This variation within what was broadly conceived as 'the middle class' was confirmed by a comparison of the number of domestic servants per family in more and less wealthy London boroughs. In six West End boroughs there were still 41 women servants for every 100 families in 1921 (a decline of 25 per cent since 1901) while in the four next well-off there were only 12 per 100, representing a dramatic fall of 60 per cent over the same period (NSOL 1930–5 Vol. II: 444, Table II: 465).

Undoubtedly, conditions of domestic service employment changed considerably during the inter-war years as a response to excess demand. Money wages rose, but even so an experienced cook in 1929–30 still earned on average less than £60 a year, and a housemaid less than £50, and this was in London where wages were highest. Nevertheless, this was double the rate noted in the Booth survey for 1894–6 (NSOL 193–5 Vol. II: 436).

On the non-monetary side, employers had to provide better accommodation if they wanted to retain living-in servants. Younger servants were still expected to share attic bedrooms but these were usually better decorated and furnished than in the past. Often there was a sittingroom for common use with easy chairs and a wireless or gramophone. Where houses had piped hot water or a bathroom, servants were now permitted to use the facilities. The fairly widespread custom of having two standards of food, one for the employers and the other for the servants, also began to die out. Time-off increased from the customary half-day every other week reported in so many autobiographies of domestic servants at the time of the First World War to one full day a week and usually a couple of evenings in addition.

In the earlier period servants had been at their employers' beck and call at any time of the day and were expected to work for as many hours as the tasks demanded. Their wages took the form of an annual sum and so did not reflect directly the actual amount of work done nor the length of time spent on it. However, by 1930 servants were in a better position to demand set hours of work when they were first engaged and to stipulate definite times when they they were not to be called upon. The increasing employment of servants on a non-residential basis greatly hastened this transition since they were taken on for a certain number of hours. They were paid an hourly rate and so the trend was towards a much more exact correlation between time worked and wages received than had been the case for their living-in predecessors. Domestic service employment was thus becoming more contractual, and less open-ended and traditionally servile in nature, and money wages were gaining precedence over payment in kind.

Changes like these, which standardized domestic service work and brought it more into line with other work, can be interpreted as a clear response to the competition for women workers between alternative forms of employment. The vast expansion of other kinds of work for women meant that private households now had to compete against factories, shops and offices for their labour and would have little chance of success unless they offered improved pay and conditions. From the point of view of the employee, factory work had certain obvious advantages: set-hours of work and time off, higher wages, a standard contract of employment, and an impersonal relationship with the employer. Employers in domestic service often interfered in what their employees did during their free time and took it upon themselves to impose standards of proper behaviour and morals, to be adhered to at all times while the servant was in their employ; such concerns however were of much less interest to factory owners whose formal rights over their employees extended only as far as the factory gates and for the 48 hours a week while she was there.

Class relations of domestic service

Viewed in broader class terms, domestic service represented a specific form of wage relation involving work inside of the domestic economy but outside of a woman's own home. Although servants were paid wages, domestic service employment was quite different from capitalist wage labour and involved relations of production distinctive both from those of the unpaid family member in the domestic economy and from the wage worker in the commodity sphere. The money wages in any case represented only part of the remuneration since a large proportion of the total was paid in kind, in the form of board and lodging. The labour was bought in order to perform a service and to produce goods for immediate use and direct consumption, rather than to produce commodities to be sold for exchange. The products of domestic labour were privately consumed within the domestic economy and did not enter the circuit of commodity production and consumption. Thus unlike capitalist wage labour, domestic labour was neither bought as a commodity nor in order to produce commodities. Being 'in service' constituted a servile relation of direct personal dependence of the domestic servant on the employer.

The class who employed domestic servants paid for them out of their own pockets, from profit and rent in the era of the individual businessman or landed gentry in the nineteenth century, or out of their own earned income in the later period of the professional salariat. The altered structure of the employing class involved a change in the source of the income out of which domestic employment was funded and a concomitant change in the total circuit of input and output of income for the middle class. However, in contrast with both of these cases, payment of wage labour in the commodity sector was financed out of already accumulated exchange value rather than out of the personal income of the employer.

By comparison with domestic service employment, working in a factory under the class relations of wage labour to capital represented a more progressive form of employment. It gave both a higher money wage based directly on actual time spent at work, and a greater degree of independence from the employer. Whereas domestic servants were only marginally integrated into the circuit of commodity production and consumption, primarily through their small money wages which could be spent on purchasing commodities, factory employees had a direct relation to capital. Their total remuneration came out of exchange value and when it was in turn exchanged for further commodities the circuits of commodity production and exchange were enlarged and deepened, and the cycle of capital accumulation was thereby strengthened. Factory workers were thus much more fully integrated into both sides of the circuit, not only as workers on the production side but also because their larger money wages enabled them to purchase more commodities. The movement of large numbers of women out of employment in the domestic economy and into commodity production during the interwar years therefore had the effect of integrating working-class women much more fully into the production and consumption circuits of capital and at the same time it extended the wage economy further and deeper into the working class.

The new form taken by the middle-class domestic economy and

the decline of domestic service brought about a change in the relationship that had existed between the middle and working class: whereas domestic production had been conducted on a totally different basis by the two classes, now it became much more similar, and this development had a number of important implications for class analysis.

Among the middle class a fundamental change occurred in the reproduction of labour power: where previously they had employed members of another class to perform their domestic labour, they tended now to do it themselves with the aid of domestic commodities and appliances. While the wives of small businessmen in the nineteenth century had not done any domestic work themselves but had instead paid for it to be done by others, their inter-war counterparts of the salaried middle class were much more likely to perform their own domestic labour, albeit on the basis of extensive commodity purchases. Moreover, the change in the composition of the middle class also meant that while domestic labour had been bought out of profit or rent, domestic appliances were now financed out of salaries, that is, earned income.

Since the working class had never employed anybody but always performed its own domestic labour, the changes in the middle-class domestic economy brought their domestic production more into line with the conditions that had always obtained for the working class. The difference between the two classes became more one of the relative size of their income and the greater relative purchasing power of the middle class, rather than of one class employing the other. Both middle and working classes became integrated into the circuit of capitalist consumption in the same way. These trajectories of the two classes were linked through the shift of women out of domestic into capitalist employment which reduced the pool of potentially available domestic servants, and in turn stimulated commodity purchase on the part of the middle class.

Thus the decline of domestic service also resulted in a fundamental alteration in the relation between the middle and working classes. The class of domestic servants progressively disappeared, and so too did the specific class relations of domestic service employment. The fact that the middle class no longer employed the working class as domestic servants meant that the two classes were no longer in the same relation to each other as employer and employee. In the heyday of domestic service in the nineteenth century, a sizeable proportion of the working class as a whole had been directly employed by the middle class. One of the most basic effects of the decline of domestic service therefore was to reduce the proportion of the working class working under the relations of production of domestic service and at the same time to increase greatly the proportion that worked under the classic class relations of industrial wage labour. The entry of large sections of the working class into factory employment put many more of them into a direct relation with capital as industrial wage labourers. The division between capital and labour now became the predominant class division and the class relations of industrial wage labour to capital took precedence over any other form of class relations including those of domestic service.

The comparison was stark: in the earlier period hundreds of thousands of working-class women had worked in the domestic economy of another class in relations of personal dependence on their employer; they were remunerated partly in kind and were paid a retainer rather than a wage directly based on the work they did; they worked on their own or in small groups but always in isolated conditions and they were divided from each other. Now factory employment replaced these relations by those of wage labour, where people worked in collective, if not mass, situations, with no personal relationship to or dependence on the employer, and where they formed a distinct group, subject to the same common conditions, that was ranged against the employers as a group. The different circumstances made it much more possible for industrial workers than for domestic servants to become aware of their common situation and also more feasible for them to unite in collective action.

While the new form of middle-class domestic economy also involved an alteration in the relation between the middle and working class, changes in the working-class domestic economy had complementary but different effects. A greater number of working-class women were able to engage in paid work as such, and of those in paid employment, more were now employed in commodity rather than domestic production. The result of such developments was therefore to unify the class relations under which the majority of working-class women worked in so far as a much higher proportion of the total now became subject to the class relations of wage labour.

Factories competed in a fairly direct way with the employers of domestic servants for female labour, but the middle-class domestic economy represented only one potential source of women factory workers. Changes in the working-class domestic economy too, and particularly the decline in family size and provision of infrastructural facilities, meant that working-class women did not need to spend so long on domestic production or on the reproduction of labour power in their own homes. So they were also drawn out of domestic production in their own home into factory employment. Although changes in the middle-class and working-class domestic economy were very different, they had a similar effect in increasing both the absolute

number and proportion of working-class women who were potentially available for work in the wage economy.

Where the women had already been working outside of their own
home, the movement into factories represented a shift between two
very different forms of employment. Although the demand for domestic servants continued to exceed supply throughout the inter-war
years, I have suggested that the numbers of those in a position to employ servants was also diminishing, and to that extent the contraction
of domestic service reflected the fundamental change in composition
of the middle class, and the demise of the individual small businessman. Women who would in the past have been subject to the
semi-feudal class relations of domestic service and its associated
wage form were now drawn out of domestic production and into the
commodity sector as wage labourers.

However, women who comprised the second source of factory labour were entering paid employment for the first time and
represented a new pool of labour which emerged as a direct consequence of developments in the working-class domestic economy.
This involved a much more basic shift out of unpaid work and into
the wage economy and a large absolute increase in the number of
women available for paid employment as such. In the earlier period
such women would have been fully occupied in domestic production,
directly engaged in the reproduction of labour power of their own
family, producing by their own labour the bulk of the goods and services needed for domestic consumption. But now earning a wage
brought about an enormous change in how they were able to undertake their own domestic labour since it enabled them to buy more
commodities. Once they had entered the wage economy they were in
a position to reproduce their household's labour power on a more
commoditized basis, an ability which was partly due to their being
employed in the production of commodities.

From the broader perspective of the class as a whole, this amounts
to saying that in the past the working class, unlike the middle class,
had directly reproduced its own labour power on its own without employing others or buying much in the way of commodities. Now the
situation was significantly changed: the working-class domestic economy was much more directly tied into the commodity sector and the
wage economy in terms of both production and consumption.

Chapter eight

Women and the total social organization of labour

This book has had two central concerns: first, the distinctive nature of the class relations of women assemblers in the new mass-production industries of inter-war Britain, and second, the connected series of changes within and between the domestic and market economies which formed the necessary background for the emergence of those class relations.

In order to demonstrate the general point that women have class relations in their own right my primary focus has been on the first of these. Far from being a marginal section of the industrial labour force, or peripheral to the main areas of capitalist commodity production, women assembly-line workers constituted a central section of the workforce in the new consumer goods industries. The process of capital accumulation rested to a very significant extent on the use of female labour, and women were assigned a more central class position in capitalist production than had existed before. The class relations of women assemblers were distinctive to them and arose from the specific way in which their labour power was used.

The approach adopted towards the analysis of class relations consists of what might be called a 'combinatory', the overall class relations of any particular group of workers resulting from the combination of two series of relations of production: those under which they work as wage labourers, which are operative in the sphere of paid employment in the public or market economy, and those which operate in the sphere of reproduction, or the domestic economy, and on whose basis labour power is reproduced. It is essential to include both of these series as necessary components in the overall determination of class relations.

The two institutional spheres – market and domestic economies – have been conceptualized as two 'poles' bound in relation to each other. At any given historical period, each has an internal structure and distinctive relations of production which can be analysed in its own terms. At the same time a particular form of structural division and connection exists between the two poles so that they are linked together, loosely or tightly, through a determinate system of relations. So there is also a structure to the polarity – the relation between the two poles – as well as to the internal organization of each. Historically, neither the boundaries between the two poles nor the extent of structural differentiation and degree of interdependence between them have been static. Nor has the proportion of total social labour expended in each been fixed: which particular aspects of production and reproduction have been performed in which pole, and whether men's or women's labour has been located primarily in one rather than the other have also changed over time. This form of polarity – the structure of the connection between the two poles – can be understood only in terms of a meta-level or higher level of explanation.

So, two distinct but complementary levels of analysis are involved in a full explanation of class relations, the first referring to the internal structural principles of each pole and the second to the relations between them. The necessity for analysing each pole in its own right does not detract from the fact that the distinctiveness of each can be fully understood only in its relation to the overall structure which comprises both. For example, the connection between the sexual and technical divisions of labour and the specific relations of production of commodity mass production which lay at the root of women assemblers' class relations are to be analysed in their own terms. But, without also analysing the conditions which made it possible for women to be available to form the central labour force in the first place and to become the prime consumers of mass produced goods, the explanation would remain one sided and incomplete. The location of the two sexes in the polarity at any given historical period, as workers in one or both poles, can be understood only by reference to this second level of analysis which alone is capable of theorizing historical changes and shifts in the polarity. At this higher level, the object of analysis becomes the totality itself, the organization of total social labour, and the shift from one form of organization of total social labour or 'polarity' to another.

If the book had been symmetrical, parallel attention would have been devoted to analysis of the relations of production in the domestic economy as to those in commodity production, to give the underpinning for this more general argument. Nevertheless, Chapters 7 and 6 contain several elements of such an analysis. When brought together they do provide the basis for a more elaborated analytical framework which can theorize both the particular form of polarity characteristic of production and reproduction in the interwar period, and also the necessary changes in the overall structure of relations between the two poles that had to occur in order for this form of polarity to emerge.

Class relations of women assembly workers

But before proceeding to this broader level of explanation, the different strands of analysis of the relations of production of paid employment should be pulled together. These relations of production themselves also comprise three dimensions: first, the type of labour power which different groups of people have to sell and the conditions under which they sell it; second, the form of the wage received in exchange, and third, the way in which that labour power is used once it has been sold.

Certain outstanding features of the women recruited to assembly work in the inter-war period can be seen as effects of the specific conditions under which women sold their labour power at that time. First, the age structure of the assembly labour force was an effect of the discontinuous availability of the women throughout the life cycle. But the pattern of their discontinuity was itself changing during this period. Many employers showed a marked preference for the very young – those aged between 14 and 18 as opposed to those in their 20s – and an aversion to married women, which they enforced by use of the marriage bar. But equally, in several of the new industries, women were employed for longer periods of their adult life.

Second, much of the supply of women for assembly work was drawn from sources that had become newly available for wage labour. In previous generations the young women who now went into factories would have been engaged in domestic labour, either unpaid in their own homes or as domestic servants in other peoples' homes. Changes in domestic production and in family size lay behind this growth in the supply of female wage labour.

Third, the regional location of certain of the new industries in the Midlands and South East, especially in areas where there had previously been little industrial employment for women meant that women entered factory work with no tradition of industrial experience or of trade union organization. Consequently they suffered all the attendant weakness that this involved, including the inability to bargain over wages and conditions.

Fourth, women from Wales, Scotland, the North East and other 'distressed' regions who could not find work in their home area migrated towards the new centres of industrial employment. This 'forced' mobility indicated the absence of equality of opportunity to sell labour power on a national scale. Even after migrating, migrant women sold their labour power on less favourable terms than local women and operated to a considerable extent as a form of replacement labour, entering the types of work which local women no longer wanted. Thus migrant women entered domestic service employment in the London area just as London women were leaving it. Eventually though, many also joined the industrial labour market and migrant women came to comprise an important minority of women recruited to assembly work. For them, however, it had involved a two-stage process, usually following a period of domestic employment.[1]

The recruitment of particular kinds of women – young, single, industrially inexperienced, migrant, and with no formal skills or training – to semi-skilled work in the new industries was thus an effect of the conditions under which women were able to sell their labour power. These four points taken together, the change in the pattern of discontinuity, the shift out of domestic service and the familial economy, the integration of women into factory production for the first time in some towns, and the construction of a new hierarchy of employment *amongst* women with migrants filling the vacuum left at the bottom rung, point to the emergence of a new type of women's labour in the market place. They indicate the preconditions for sale, preconditions that for women were historically shifting. Even within a continuing dual role, women were now more available for waged labour, and conversely, proportionately less available for doing the work typical of a domestic economy in an earlier period.

In return for that sale of their labour, women assemblers received a wage. The wage itself has two sides: its purchasing power or how it fits into consumption, on the one hand; and on the other, how it relates to the use of labour once purchased. That wage was relatively cheap for employers especially in comparison with a skilled male wage, and no doubt this was the reason why women were recruited as the prime source of labour for assembly-line work. But there is also a hierarchy of women's wages, and assembly-line workers were at the top end of the scale of working-class women's wages at this time of restructuring during the inter-war period.[2] Finally, the input of women's wages to family income meant that the structure of the family wage was being fundamentally altered, taken over the working life-cycle. The recruitment of women into mass production for consumption necessitated that in the long term the family wage would be able to purchase a portion of those goods produced now for the first time outside the domestic economy. So the 'family wage' was changing both in its total purchasing power (which is not to say in terms of absolute wealth, but just the range of commodities that it could command) and in the relative input of men's and women's wages.

Turning now to the other face of the assembly-line wage, the way that it was made up with an element of collective bonus, meant that for the first time the level of wages was strictly linked to a predetermined level of output. No other form of payment had such a tight equation between wage costs and output. The rate of exploitation was pre-fixed, at the touch of a button. And this leads directly on to the third dimension of the relations of production of assembly-line work, the actual use of labour power on the assembly line, detailed in Chapters 5 and 6.

As an effect of the rigid sexual division of labour and sex-typing of work operative in the new industries, all women did direct production work on the assembly line and only women did it. Women workers' single and exclusive location in the technical division of labour meant that they alone were subject to machine pacing. Only they were treated as a collective work unit and their payment system, which reflected the particular form of wage exchange they worked under, was also a specific one. These three features characterized the particular use of female labour power and together constituted the distinctive relations of production of assembly-line work.

The gender allocation of work – women to direct assembly work and men to everything else – which directly gave rise to the subjection of women to these class relations had other crucial effects as well. One was to reproduce the division between direct and indirect work, basic to mass-production processes, as a division between women and men. Another was to assemble women together as a homogeneous group, all working under the same conditions and with no internal divisions between them. Men and women consequently confronted each other as groupings with a very different place in the workforce and internal composition: while women were united as a gender by the same conditions under which they worked and divided as a gender from men, men were divided both from women but also from each other by virtue of the different conditions under which different groups of men worked. For women the sexual division of labour was also the most immediate class division. Gender and class relations were coterminous for them but not for men. The sexual division of labour thus supplied the key to the connection between gender relations and class relations.

Such considerations lead to the conclusion that women had a different relation to production and to capital than men. Their point of insertion in the process of capital accumulation was a specific one. The sexual division of labour enmeshed with the technical division of labour in such a way that women's labour power was used in a quite distinct manner from men's. Their relation to capital was unique and so too were their conflicts with it. Since some male workers acted as functionaries of capital, were in charge of the production process and had authority over its workers, their immediate interests and conflicts with capital were quite likely to be very different from those of women.

If class has to do with relations between labour and capital, it follows that differences such as these in the relations of men and women workers to capital constituted class differences. Men and women formed distinct groupings within the working class since the differences between them were of a class nature. The material basis for unity – shared by all who sold their labour power for a wage – was undermined by the different conditions under which they sold their labour power and the different ways in which capital used it. Although men and women workers in the new industries were all 'working class' in the sense of being wage labourers, their class relations with capital were different. However, saying that they had different class relations does not imply that they constituted different classes as such. Nor does talking about the development of new class relations imply the emergence of a 'new' class. Since in any case the relation between capital and labour is continuously restructured, there can be no transhistorical 'working class'.

A major point that does arise from this formulation is that women were the first to pilot a new form of class relations. If the new industries were at the outermost frontier of capitalist development in the inter-war years, then it was women rather than men who were the pioneers of the new form of exchange between labour and capital that accompanied those developments. As the central direct labour force occupying a strategic position in the production process, women assemblers were placed directly at the frontline of the new structures of capital and at the frontline of new forms of control over the work process. Their labour power was more intensely exploited and they were more thoroughly subject to managerial control through mechanical means than any other group of workers in these industries. Women assemblers thus experienced capitalist domination and the unequal exchange between labour and capital in the most acute and purest form that it took at that time, unmitigated either by high wage levels, authority, or fringe benefits. After the Second World War, accelerated expansion of consumer goods industries meant that hundreds of thousands more women entered assembly-line work and so became subject to the same relations of production as their pre-war sisters. It was in this sense that women assemblers in the 1920s and 1930s could justifiably be described as having pioneered or piloted the new class relations that were later to become much more widespread and to affect a larger proportion of the industrial labour force.

In so doing women came to the forefront of the working class as a group occupying an extremely strategic position within the working class, as well as from the point of view of capital accumulation. It was also one of the most obviously exploited. If these developments had been properly recognized for what they were, the whole course of inter-war and subsequent labour organization might well have been different. Yet the significance of women as a key section of the working class, and the opportunities for recruitment and political organization that this offered, were completely lost on the labour movement of the time. Despite all evidence to the contrary, it persisted with its image of the male manual worker as the quintessential proletarian and of male 'breadwinners' as the only truly dependable members of the trade union movement. But if men had been in the same position as women assemblers, labour history would certainly have told us about them. Ironically, it was not until men were employed on the moving track in car plants that assembly-line work was recognized as a particularly exploitative form of work. Male car workers were then accorded a place alongside miners as central to the working class, but women assemblers were never included.[3]

Although women were the first to pioneer the class relations of assembly-line work in Britain, this was not the case in the USA where use of assembly lines in the motor industry preceded their widespread adoption in the light consumer goods industries. Here men had worked on the moving track at Ford since 1914. In Britain, however, fewer industries employed men in mechanized assembly operations during the inter-war period, and where they did, the technology was less developed than in consumer goods industries. Men assembled cars and vacuum cleaners but not usually on a moving track or conveyor belt. It was only after the war that male workers in the British motor industry were subjected to the class relations of assembly-line work on a large scale. During the inter-war years, there was considerable variation between different motor manufacturers: some were still organized on the basis of craft manufacture, while others had assembly lines. But even in this case it was unlikely to be a fully integrated moving track on which all the operations involved in final assembly were combined.

Important structural differences existed, however, between the relations of production of male car assemblers and those of women assemblers. Whereas in the industries that I have examined, women worked under a single wage form and were defined by a single relation to the production process which divided them from men, the same never held for male car assemblers. Car assembly was not defined as a male job as against all others since men did all the different kinds of work. So although they were subject to a similar use of labour power as women assemblers, men were not confined by the sexual division of labour to this single use. They were divided from each other only by differences in class relations. For women the sexual division of labour was implicated in the class relations in a way that it was not for men.

Having said this, it is important that a large proportion of car assemblers both in Britain, Europe and the USA have always been migrant or black men – a group who also sell their labour power under far less favourable conditions than indigenous white men. In situations where black and migrant workers have been disproportionately concentrated on the moving track, in contrast to indigenous and white workers who occupy the higher grades of work, it is clear that racist and imperialist divisions enter into the allocation of work. The operation of racist principles of job allocation subject black and migrant workers to distinctive forms of class relations. Racial divisions thus constitute at the same time class divisions, much in the same way that the sexual division of labour in other assembly industries meant that the gender division was also a class division.

In general however, car plants aside, assembly has been a predominantly female occupation. Among consumer goods assembly-line industries, the motor industry represents an exception rather than the rule, as the only one to have relied so exclusively on male labour. In most others women have been the prime labour force for assembly work, actively recruited by employers.[4]

That there was a structural connection between capital and female labour in assembly industries is indisputable. Suggestions that women who are only temporarily employed cannot have a 'proper' class position fail to realize that the pattern of employment is basic to class relations. Far from undermining that structural relationship, the discontinuous pattern of such women's employment, which meant that the majority worked as assemblers for an average of ten years, was an integral component of it. The structural connection between capital and female labour remained constant despite constantly changing personnel. It could be described in terms analogous to those used by Castles and Kosack (1973: 463) to characterize European migrant labour in the post-war period as 'a permanent group with a rotating membership'.[5] Because of short-term work contracts, migrant workers in Germany, Switzerland, the Netherlands, and other European countries were always temporary and changing. But to be a permanent institution, migrant labour did not require the continuous presence of the same individual migrant workers. On the contrary, rotation of personnel was an essential and distinguishing feature of the class relations of the system. The overall class relations of migrant workers were a product of their dual location in two very different economies, often a subsistence one at home and a much more highly developed capitalist one in Northern Europe.

Similarly, to posit the existence of a systematic connection between capital and female labour and of objective class relations does not require that the individual workers were permanent and unchanging. Indeed being temporary, or more precisely, being perceived by employers as temporary, was absolutely central to the sexual division of labour and to the way that female labour power was used in assembly-line industries. Women's dual location as workers in the domestic and market economies was also a determining factor not only in their location in paid employment but also in their overall class relations.

Organization of total social labour

I turn now to the second or higher level of analysis which deals with the organization of total social labour itself – or the form of polarity – and with the shift from one total organization to another.

Over the last three centuries production in Western capitalist countries has been undertaken under two basic types of institutional arrangement, in the public market economy where goods are produced as commodities to be sold and in the domestic economy for direct consumption. The type and quantity of goods produced in each has changed over time and so has the engagement of men and women in each. The domestic and market economies are to be viewed as two poles connected in a qualitative manner, more or less tightly, by a number of different links as outlined in Chapter 7. These included, on the one hand, the employment and wages of men, and more recently also of women and, on the other, the purchase of commodities for use in the domestic economy.

Although these two spheres operate on the basis of different internal principles and relations of production they should not be conceived as constituting different 'modes of production' in themselves. During the 1970s there was a tendency in some socialist and feminist writing to do this and to treat the domestic economy not as a real capitalist institution but rather as a leftover from feudalism or the early pre-industrial period of capitalism, in contrast to commodity production which alone was interpreted as constituting 'the' capitalist mode of production proper.[6] Because the emphasis was on two modes of production, or on the different internal principles characterizing each sphere, the actual way in which the two were connected with each other at any particular historical conjuncture was not usually a major focus of analysis.

But this formulation does not do justice to the fact that the two spheres have always been linked with each other and that what went on in one was affected by what went on in the other. The two were both integral parts of a single overall system, a societal division of total social labour. The labour available to be employed in the market economy was affected by what went on in the domestic economy. Similarly whether or not the domestic economy could constitute a market for commodity goods depended on its receiving a large enough cash wage to enable purchases on the scale necessary to make mass production viable. Because in any real social formation these two poles do in fact stand in a structured web of links with each other, it is not very helpful to view them as belonging to separate phases of development or modes of production.

The duality between the two spheres was historically and culturally constructed and the form of opposition that now exists between them is peculiar to late twentieth century British society. In peasant economies both men and women were engaged in production for subsistence and immediate consumption.[7] During the course of industrialization men's work as wage labourers was taken up in the production of goods which had nothing directly to do with their own reproduction. Until the beginning of the inter-war period they were employed primarily in capital goods industries producing traditional staples, that is, goods which they did not themselves buy and consume. They produced wealth for their employing class and received a wage sufficient to pay for rent and fuel, and to purchase a minimal number of commodities and raw materials for consumption in the household. But these still required further work to be done on them before they could be consumed. For instance, wages were used to buy clothing material which women made into shirts or to buy flour which women made into bread. The bulk of the labour necessary to turn the raw materials into finished goods was done by women in the domestic economy, either on an unpaid basis as wives or as domestic servants employed by middle- or upper-class households, but in both cases working under relations of production quite different from those of commodity production. In these circumstances the 'family wage' was of a particular kind, had a limited function within the domestic economy, and consisted primarily of men's earnings. Accumulation and expansion of capital in the market economy depended at this time on other capitalist firms, large scale organizations, or railway companies at home or abroad, purchasing the capital goods, rather than on workers' wages being recirculated into the market economy as a result of what they purchased.

When all of this changed with the switch to the mass production of goods for domestic consumption, so too did the overall function of the wage. It assumed much greater importance in the whole circuit of capital accumulation, because the enlargement of capitalist activity in the market economy now depended in a much more central way than before on the domestic economy as a market. At the same time, the function of the wage within the domestic economy also altered. It was used to buy finished goods as opposed to raw materials. This meant that wage workers now purchased the same goods that they had produced so they consumed in the domestic economy what they produced in the market economy. Changes in structure of the family wage (married women now contributing a greater proportion and over a longer time span) and in its size (relatively larger) were also an effect of the interconnected changes between the two spheres. The increasing number of goods for household consumption that became available for purchase as commodities from the inter-war period onwards led to a reduction in the amount of domestic production done on a non-commodity basis within the household. The form and function of the wage altered historically as an effect of the qualitative change in the relationship between the two poles or structure of polarity.

But underlying this change in the function of the wage, there was a more fundamental change, at the level of the total social division of labour. Women could not be in two places at the same time. If they were now in the factory producing the goods once produced in the domestic economy, obviously they were not so 'available for work' in the home itself. Conversely, if they had still to bake bread, make clothes, boil up hot water, and produce eleven children, they would not have been available for work in the factory. A change in the total social division of labour necessitated a change in the wage input for the family. This example demonstrates that changes within one pole were inextricably linked with modifications in the internal structure of the other. Although relations of production were specific to each pole, these changed also as a consequence of changes in the overall structure of the polarity itself.

The different conditions under which the two genders sold their labour power in the market economy was another clear cut instance of how what occurs in one pole is related to the structure of relations between the two. This is of vital significance since differences in the way in which men and women were located in the two poles had a profound effect on the class relations of the two genders. The dominant pattern of women's employment in the market economy has been one of discontinuity but the form of that discontinuity has changed historically. During the period when women were primarily engaged in the labour necessary to transform purchased raw materials into finished goods for household consumption, they were not in a position to sell their labour power in the market economy in the same way as men. For that to become feasible, changes had to occur enabling the production of the goods and services necessary for the reproduction of labour power to be achieved in a different way. Conversely, the release of women into employment in the market economy was an essential condition for successful capitalist production on a mass scale. This release depended amongst other things, on the decline in family size and the amount of time women spent in childbearing and rearing. Chapter 7 demonstrated how closely these two changes, the reduction in the amount of domestic production undertaken on a non-commodity basis and the entry of more women to the labour market, were linked. As a consequence of the changed polarity, women's pattern of paid employment became much more similar to that of men and so there was less differentiation between the way the two genders were inserted in the two poles. Women's wider earning power also undermined a particular form of male domination in the domestic economy, so altering the relations of production within this pole.

In a mode of production where the social production of commodities is separated from the private reproduction of labour power, and men's work is located primarily in one sphere and women's in the other, there are bound to be endemic structural differences in labour market position on the basis of gender. It was only because women took responsibility for the domestic economy that men were able to be continuously available for employment in the first place. They would not have been able to go out to work for 48 hours a week unless someone else, in most cases their wives, did all the work required for their labour power to be reproduced.[8] Women's discontinuous pattern of employment in the wage economy was therefore the precondition of men's very different pattern. There was an integral relation between the two. Men's place in the world of work was predicated on women's place in the home. In other words, the position of each gender in the domestic economy affected its relation to the wage economy, and this applied just as much to men as to women. This is what I have called the 'combinatory', each gender's class relations resulting from the combination of their relations of production in both spheres.

The culminating point of this argument brings us back full circle to the principal subject of the book. Analysis of women's assembly-line work in the inter-war period has located the fulcrum or central pivot around which a historical transformation of the total social division of labour was developing. Women assemblers represented a new social being to which every structural aspect of the new organization of labour was articulated: the new role and structure of the household wage; the new duality and differentiation of commodity production and domestic economy; the changed form of patriarchy within the family; new kinds of gender subordination within work in the public sphere. Mass production relied on changes in the domestic economy which depended on the emergence of new forms of employment for women which in turn rested on mass production. Women assemblers occupied a central place in a changing total structural configuration. This analysis rests on the concept of the total social organization of labour as a structural complex, where changes in one sphere require changes in others. Here I have used the concept to analyse one particular historical complex, but the method could also be employed to examine other historical configurations of total social labour.

Theoretical resonances

It now remains to draw out of the analytical framework developed here some more general implications for socialist feminist theory, particularly as regards questions of class determination, the connection between gender relations and class relations, and gender and the labour process.

What happens to theories of class determination if women's dual insertion in the domestic and market economies is taken fully on board? Why, if men's class position in the wage economy depended so directly on the way they were inserted in the domestic economy, should the domestic economy be totally absent from the theory of class determination? As I see it, something must be very wrong with a conceptual framework capable of according a proper class position only to those people who worked when paid and which cannot credit women whose paid employment was discontinuous with a definitive class position, or women who were never engaged in waged work with any class relations at all on their own account.

The basic problem arises because sociological theories, taking their lead from Marxist ones, look only to paid employment or the market economy for their explanations, and treat class relations at the 'point of production' as if they were self-contained and capable of explanation entirely in their own terms. The world of commodity production is analysed as if it was completely insulated from that of the reproduction of labour power although in reality the two form an integrated structure. Without denying that what is normally thought of as class arises out of the internal dynamics of the wage economy, there is a meta-level without which this would not be able to exist, the organization of total social labour.

Because both conventional academic and Marxist frameworks encompass only one aspect of the overall structure, their theory is necessarily one-sided and partial and this lies at the root of the problem. They have been guilty of privileging the public world of production to the virtual exclusion of the domestic economy. They uncritically reflect the apparent separation between two spheres and in so doing reproduce at a theoretical and conceptual level a socially created division. The inevitable result is a thoroughly sexist theory since the sphere excluded is the one where exclusively women's labour is expended.

But if the relations within one sphere are not determined only from within that sphere alone, as I am arguing, then no theory will be able to do justice to the class relations of either women or men unless it incorporates the labour involved in reproduction as an integral part of the explanation of how and why labour is available for work in the market or wage economy. Class relations in the world of production can be properly understood only in relation to the overall structure of production and reproduction. The definition of class from within one sphere alone is inadequate since the relations within one sphere are not only determined from within that one sphere. Class relations overall combine the relations of production of the two spheres, not just those of commodity production. Conventional analyses, and that includes Marxist ones, which see class as determined only from within this one sphere end up with the untenable position that only men have a proper class position and that of women is dependent on men. When class relations are examined only as they occur in public production, it is impossible to explain what it is that assigns men to them.

It is difficult to explain how this one-sided conceptual framework arose other than as a fairly direct consequence of (male) theorists remaining so much inside the experience of the lived social relations that they were attempting to theorize that they were unable to see them from the outside. Their concepts were formulated from within the dominant problematic which acknowledges only paid work as real work. That male peasants were engaged directly in producing the means of subsistence to reproduce their own labour power has never prevented medieval historians from ascribing class relations to them or from analysing the class relations between the peasantry and feudal lords. Nor have economic anthropologists restricted their investigations of economic relations or of 'work' to the exchange of shells or other tangible forms of payment. On the contrary, highly sophisticated theories have been developed to demonstrate that economic relations may be deeply embedded in and expressed through kinship relations. Without wanting to overdo the point, it is significant that the questions of women's class position and domestic labour were recognized as relevant only after the emergence of the women's movement and of a feminist consciousness.

That women reproduce men's labour power is something that feminists have been writing about for twenty years now. But because the dynamics of the two spheres of production and reproduction have been examined in isolation from each other this recognition has still not been properly integrated into feminist analyses of class. The most common tendency has been to view each sphere in terms of the operation of different internal principles which are separate from each other, capitalism in production, and patriarchy in reproduction. The theoretical problems arising from this have remained at the abstract level of determining the relation between the internal principles, rather than of examining the actual implications of women's work in the home for men's paid employment. Feminist theory has not pushed nearly far enough, in terms of what it means for the analysis of the paid employment of *men*, the recognition that women have undertaken the work involved in reproducing male labour power as well as their own.

On the question of the relations of production under which women labour within the domestic economy, Christine Delphy (1977) and Sylvia Walby (1986b), amongst others, have developed a materialist analysis based on an analogy with the dynamics of class in the wage economy. Both suggest that the relation between women and men in the home can be viewed as analogous to that of worker and capitalist. Men expropriate women's unpaid labour in the domestic economy much in the same way that capitalists exploit workers in commodity production. On this basis it is proposed either that women and men as such (Delphy), or housewives and husbands (Walby), be viewed as distinct and opposing classes in the same way as workers and capitalists in commodity production. Sylvia Walby goes on to suggest that women who are also engaged in paid employment as well as domestic labour have two class positions because of their dual class in two sets of relations of production.

While I agree that women work under two different sets of relations of production and that domestic labour is undertaken under specific relations of production, it does not follow that men and women form two opposing classes in the domestic economy in the accepted sense. It would involve a very long jump from recognizing that men as a gender systematically exploit women's labour in the domestic economy to conceptualizing them as classes, normally understood as an organized social aggregate, quite different from the private and socially insulated relations characteristic of the family. The historical dynamics of a class of men versus a class of women remain obscure. What, in such a class relation, could account for the massive reduction in domestic service; the decline in time spent rearing large numbers of children; the nucleation of the family; or the transfer of reproduction from the domestic economy (for men?) to public production (for capital?)? Furthermore positing the existence of two independent class positions raises a number of problems, the principal one being how these coexist and the form of connection between them. Is one primary and if so which? Is the other then superimposed on top of it? The notion that two completely independent sites exist for the formation of class concedes too much to the analytical separation between 'home and work' which has been a feature of much more conventional theories.

On the other hand, a framework which views class relations in the two spheres as part of a combinatory in the way I have suggested could provide a way forward. If men's place in the sphere of paid work is tied to their place in the domestic economy, then their class relations in the first are linked with the relations of production of the second. The same holds for women. Only an appreciation of the overall relations of production of each gender in both areas can explain why they are able or not able to have a class position in the sphere of paid employment. This does not mean conflating the relations of production of the two spheres: the point rather becomes that of clarifying the connection between them and determining whether they reinforce each other or are in contradiction.

A related set of theoretical questions that has occupied socialist feminists concerns the connection between class relations and gender relations in the world of work. If we believe that both class and gender enter into the organization of the labour process and the workforce, how is the interplay between them to be conceptualized and in a way that avoids reducing one to the other?

The notion that both series of relations, gender and class, were integral components of the labour process has been central to this study. Gender constituted a basic principle of division both of the organization of work and of the workforce in the new assembly-line industries of inter-war Britain. Women's location as assemblers, due to the particular form of occupational segregation by gender prevailing in these industries, carried distinctive class relations. Thus the gender division was also simultaneously a class division. For women the two forms of opposition were inseparable: class and gender relations and divisions were coterminous. Since their class relations were at the same time gender relations and their gender relations were at the same time class relations it would be incorrect to posit the connection either as class with gender superimposed on it or as gender with class superimposed on it.

The sexual division of labour furnished the lynchpin connecting the two series of relations, as the principle whereby men and women were allocated to different niches within the technical division, and hence to different class relations. The particular position occupied by women assemblers carried its own distinctive relations of production. So the sexual division of labour meant that the class relations of assembly-line work were specific to women. In other work processes, characterized by different occupational divisions of labour, there were other particular intersections between gender and class divisions.

I have argued that any particular combination and antagonism between gender and class relations is an effect of a particular historical organization of total social labour. If, however, the question is posed at the abstract level of which determines which, gender as an organizing principle versus class as an organizing principle, as if each were entirely independent of the other, then a whole set of false problems, and solutions, necessarily arises. Two main alternative formulations have been developed (see Chapter 1) by socialist feminists to overcome this false dilemma. In the unitary approach, the sex-gender system, or system of patriarchal relations, is seen as so tightly and inextricably enmeshed with principles emanating from the capitalist organization of production that the two series can be disentangled from each other neither empirically nor even for purposes of analysis. Class domination is necessarily patriarchal and vice versa. This gives rise to the danger that the two series become conflated with each other. The dual systems approach, on the other hand, views the world of paid work as embodying both patriarchy and capitalism as two separate and independent principles of organization each with their own effect. The problem then in this framework is to demonstrate what the connection is between them.

Because the framework of analysis developed here addresses as its central question the specific class relations of women workers, such dichotomies can be avoided. The problems of connecting the sex-gender system with capitalist principles of organization are posed in terms of the intersection of the technical and sexual divisions of labour. When they are in paid employment, women are inserted in a particular location in the technical division of labour: they always have class relations and these can always be analysed. Similarly the sexual division of labour is a fairly universal principle whose effects can also be empirically determined. In the case that I have examined, women assemblers' class relations arose from the operation of both gender and class principles, linked in a determinate manner. The sexual division of labour constituted women as a single category in class terms: class was gendered and gender was classed but in a specific manner. But this particular case should not be taken as a universal one. Under other circumstances gender and class relations may well intersect differently. However, only when we know more about the actual forms of intersection that have existed and the circumstances that give rise to the differences, will we be in a position to develop a more adequate general theory.

What I have proposed is a method of analysis which could also be used to examine the interaction of the sexual with the technical division of labour in other historical cases. Although in real terms the two divisions of labour were always to be found enmeshed with each other on the shopfloor or in the office, the two remain analytically separable and the relation between them empirically demonstrable. From this perspective, the abstract question of the relation between gender and class division can be answered in terms of particular cases. And an accumulation of these will aid in the formulation of a more general theory.

What of the conflict between male and female workers in the new industries? What was the role of men in the establishment of the particular form of occupational segregation by sex? Did their response to it reflect the pursuit of class or gender interests or both? Recent studies have come up with different kinds of answers to these questions. Sylvia Walby's (1986a) survey of the history of women's employment in Britain places the onus for women's inferior position at work firmly on patriarchal forces in general, and on male workers and their organizations in particular. In her work on the adoption of new technologies and gender segregation, Cynthia Cockburn (1983; 1985) also interprets men as actively pursuing their own gender interest in continually excluding women from work involving technological skills.

On the other hand, Ruth Milkman (1987) takes a quite different position. Management, she argues, was the predominant influence in establishing the pattern of gender segregation in the American automobile and electrical goods industries. Two different managerial strategies for controlling labour were adopted in the early development of the industries and these were fundamental in shaping the form of occupational segregation. Once established, ideological constructions played a central role in reproducing the particular gender division and structural inertia set in. The attitude of male workers towards women, and whether they initiated or supported struggles over equal pay or parity, varied according to the prevailing circumstances. Whether their class or gender interests predominated depended on the particular industrial situation confronting them in the years of the Depression, the Second World War and the post-war period.

In the new industries in Britain too the pattern of occupational segregation soon gained the weight of tradition and became quite inflexible. But these theories are not in themselves adequate to explain it. Attributing the increased employment of women to the weakness of the trade unions in the expanding sectors of engineering, as Sylvia Walby does, cannot explain why women were restricted to assembly-line work. On the other hand, British assembly-line industries were characterized by the very mode of managerial control (Fordism) operative in the American automobile industry, which Ruth Milkman puts forward as explaining the absence of women in that industry.[9]

Certainly organized male labour in Britain did not challenge either the employment of women in the new industries or the sexual division of labour. Although the trade unions raised general objections during the 1920s and 1930s to the increased industrial employment of women on the grounds that women were taking their members' jobs, paradoxically none was voiced against the actual recruitment of women as assemblers in the new industries. This could be explained as a consequence of the weakness of the organized labour movement in this area. They were unable to exclude women from the new industries as they had in the older traditional industries, by means of control over entry through craft apprenticeships. Alternatively it could be argued that the form of occupational segregation by gender established in the new industries actually benefited men by assigning all the superior positions to them. Male workers' interests would thus lie in supporting and institutionalizing the inferior position of women.

Even if male workers acquired an entrenched interest in preserving the particular gender segregation of work, it would be facile to view 'men', conceived as a homogeneous collective group, or even the organizations which represented skilled craftworkers, either as having been the driving force behind it or as its main beneficiaries. Within the restructuring of capitalism, the initiative lay squarely with employers, who deliberately recruited a female workforce to direct assembly work. Similarly the financial benefit of using female labour as the largest and most strategic section of their manual labour force was gained by capital and not by male workers. The advantages of dealing with a workforce that was rigidly divided by class and gender accrued also to them. But, as stressed earlier in Chapter 5, the reconstruction of capitalism in the inter-war years by means of the development of mass consumer production was no 'boardroom plot', with capitalists consciously planning where women could best be fitted into the new total social division of labour.

Why if profit maximizing firms reaped such gains from employing women (whose pay rates were so much lower than men's) did they then not deploy women on a much wider scale than in fact occurred or why did they not replace men by women? No doubt there would have been a vociferous outcry from the trade unions if this had occurred, especially if employers attempted to employ women on 'men's' work at women's rates of pay. Part of the reason why this did not happen was because of the inertia and ideological force of sex-typing once it had been fixed. In Chapter 6 I outlined the structural reasons that would also have made crossing the boundaries an impossibility.

But quite apart from these, employers did not have the room for manoeuvre required for such an option. Given the circumstances of the division of total social labour between production and reproduction discussed earlier, substituting women for men on a grand scale was just not feasible. Although the supply of potential women workers was growing during the inter-war years, the increase was a gradual process and depended on changes in their responsibilities in the domestic economy. So long as the majority of married women were fully occupied in activities necessary to reproduce labour power, they could not represent a reserve army ready to be called on to the labour market at a moment's notice.

From their superior position, men on the shopfloor had no reason to be in conflict with women, but for women to have pursued either their class or gender interests would automatically have involved challenging the privileges of men. Although transforming the sexual division of labour was 'objectively' in women's interests, the question of men holding all the better paid jobs, positions of authority and technical know-how never actually became a separate focus of organization for women nor even for much hostility. Women accepted the ideology both of sex-typed occupations and of men's right to better jobs. Despite the fact that men had certain interests – both class and gender based – in maintaining the sexual division of labour, just as women did in removing it, the contradictions that found active expression were those crystallizing around relations with employers rather than with each other.

The basic conflict women assemblers experienced was with capital and it centred on their subjection to machine pacing. All the actions women initiated to resist their conditions of work, from minor acts of sabotage to extended strikes, focused on the speed and control of the line. That the system was overseen and kept in smooth running order by men and that certain groups of male workers gained material benefits from women being machine paced certainly made women's resistance much more difficult and militated against men ever supporting women in their actions. But from the women's perspective, employers were the main enemy. Rate-fixers were clearly understood as being 'on the other side' but the majority of men were caught somewhere in between.

Because class and gender interests were the same for women assemblers, the circumstances under which one might prevail over the other did not arise. Men's actions too arose from their own position in the division of labour. This would involve class interests specific to that position and therefore not common to all men, so that they were divided from each other by class. On the other hand, although all men could theoretically be said to have shared a common gender interest in maintaining the sexual division of labour, they were rarely called upon to unite in its defence during the inter-war period. The pattern of gender segregation was so entrenched that the question never arose. For practical purposes then, men's class interests prevailed, in relation to women and to other men. Thus the issue of which was dominant for men was purely theoretical, a non-problem under the circumstances.

If gender was basic to the organization of the work process so too was work fundamental to the construction of gender relations. Veronica Beechey has argued (1987: 16) for more serious recognition of this fact and for greater attention to be devoted to the construction of men's and women's jobs within the work process. Cynthia Cockburn (1983; 1985) has demonstrated across a variety of industries and workplace situations the importance of the workplace in the construction of femininity and masculinity. And such arguments are fully borne out in the new industries. For women assemblers the workplace represented an important site for the formation of gender, gender identity, gender inequality and gender subordination, as shown in Chapter 6. For example assembly-line work was perceived as light, clean, monotonous and unskilled because women did it and conversely women were perceived as the appropriate gender for the job because it was light, clean, monotonous and unskilled. Either explanation would do and both were used. Femininity was thus used to reinforce the distinction between assembly and all other kinds of work. Although the association between women and repetitive manual work was not unique to assembly industries, the lines of division between male and female workers and the forms of subordination of women to technology, managerial control and men were new and characteristic of this type of work process alone. The sexual division of labour thus not only served as a basic structural principle for organizing the production process and dividing the workforce but also had a formative role in the construction and reconstruction of gender relations. This reverberated back in turn on other social institutions and on other dimensions of the women's lives.

The pattern of gender inequality at work had an important impact, for example, on the formation of women as a distinctive labour market. If the idea of women as having nimble fingers and a high turnover was used as a reason for not equipping them with the training required for jobs other than assembly, then the fact that no women were ever going to receive training in the first instance also determined the place they could occupy in the labour market. Employers used the pattern of gender division that they had established for jobs in the construction of their female labour market. The gender relations of work thus rebounded on the conditions under which women could sell their labour power in the first place. Consequently the unfavourable labour market position of women, which I have presented as a fundamental aspect of their class relations, was also reproduced as an effect of the sexual division of labour already established in the workplace.

Considerations of a similar order also apply to the use of machinery and the detailed division of labour. Assembly lines were not invented with women in mind and the overall technical division of labour of mass production was not developed on the assumption of a particular occupational segregation by gender. Nevertheless, once women were established in their role as assemblers, the design of machinery and the minute subdivision between jobs were no doubt premissed on that assumption.

Feminist theory might benefit from a somewhat more integrated approach to the relations between gender and work, but labour process theory could do with a massive injection of feminism in the first place. There is nothing inherent in this perspective which prevents it from treating women or the industries that employ them as suitable subjects of study, but ever since Braverman's *Labour and Monopoly Capital* was published in 1974, the central preoccupations of his followers have been firmly fixed on men. Not only have women workers been made no more visible than they were in traditional labour history, but the one-sided portrayal of the labour process distorts history by obscuring some of its most significant developments. I have mentioned a number of times that the decline of the traditional craft industries and the deskilling of the craftworker represented only one side of a historical process which also included the rise of new industries. By focusing on what was lost rather than on what replaced it, there could be no recognition of the changing gender structure that accompanied historical developments in the labour process. The case of women assemblers is crucial in this connection. That semi-skilled women, rather than time-served craftsmen, occupied the central strategic position in many mass-production industries has fundamental implications for labour process theory. Any attempt at an adequate understanding of historical developments in the labour process would have to include them.

But when assembly-line labour processes have been examined, a further distortion arises. Because the motor industry has been treated as *the* assembly-line industry par excellence, virtually no attention has been given to any others. Thus assembly-line workers are equated with men in car plants, and Fordism as a mode of managerial control with the motor industry. Yet women assemblers in the electrical engineering, clothing manufacture and food processing industries were equally subjected to collective machine pacing as any car workers, probably in greater numbers and in Britain, at any rate, at an earlier date. In the classic situation at Fords in Michigan, high wages were paid to workers in exchange for their abdication of control over work. But in the mass-production consumer industries that I have looked at, employers managed to get the advantage both of machine pacing and of low labour costs at the same time. They employed women as the main manual labour force and so saved on labour costs. Women assemblers did not receive the equivalent of the $5 day, but assembly-line wage rates were above the norm for women, and this is what drew women into assembly work. The predominant view of the labour process that Fordism never took a firm grip in Britain in the same way as in the United States may well be true of the motor industry. But this certainly does not represent a valid basis for generalization. Recognition that Fordist methods were adopted in a wide range of assembly industries other than the motor industry, and that women rather than men were subjected to them, would have a profound effect on histories of labour as well as of employer strategy.

Future directions

My hope is that the method of analysis developed here admits of wider application than the class relations of women assemblers at a particular conjuncture in British industrial history. Its intention is to open up questions and suggest new ways of exploring them.

First, determining the exact nature of the relations of production under which different occupational groups work opens up a new approach to the analysis of class. Categorizing all wage workers as one homogeneous working class cannot do justice to the complexity of the class structure and the changes it has undergone over the last century, nor is it politically illuminating. On the other hand, squeezing different work situations into predetermined categories and allocating class positions on that basis, following the tradition inaugurated by Poulantzas, raises the question of the adequacy of the categories. Similarly, introducing new and heterogeneous principles of class positioning such as power, authority and control (cf. Carchedi, Olin Wright) can lead to theoretical confusion rather than overcoming the problem. Because there may well be a different dynamic between capital and labour in different industries and for different types of worker, relations are more important than slots or positions. A classificatory approach which fits people into pre-established categories is largely an academic exercise. Naming people as such and such a class, or class 'fraction', or as occupying such and such a 'class location', in itself has nothing to say about the dynamics of class relations and how these change historically.

However, a more fruitful direction may lie in exploring the relations of production of groups of workers occupying different positions in the division of labour, and specifying what is distinctive about them. Although my analysis was restricted to workers employed by private capitalist profit maximizing firms, there is no reason in principle why the same method could not be used for those in state employment and in the service sector. Theories of class could be developed on this basis which articulate the many dimensions of class relations, including the structural divisions of race, gender and region, which acknowledge the historical variety of class relations from the beginning of industrial capitalism up to the present day, and which elaborate a more detailed picture of the contemporary class structure. In this way it would be possible to do justice to the complexity of class and to the material bases of unity and difference between and within the genders and the different national and ethnic groups.

Second, looking at the total organization of labour in society and the way it is allocated between production and reproduction throws new light on what is understood to constitute work, on the connections between public and domestic economies, and the role of men and women in each. What I have outlined represents only the tentative beginning of what could be a much more highly articulated analysis of the relations of production within the domestic economy. Appreciating the nature of the shifts that occurred between the late nineteenth century and the period after the Second World War opens the way for such a development.

For example, it is evident that the form in which women serviced the domestic economy changed quite dramatically between the era of capital goods production and that of mass production. In the nineteenth century women worked in the home on finished raw materials bought in from outside and undertook all the rest of domestic production (whether or not they also worked for a wage). But in the inter-war period, the amount of production undertaken within the household began to diminish.

As part of a separate but related process, domestic servants first emerged and then later disappeared as a distinctive form of labour exclusively employed in domestic production and under specific relations of production. By the time of the inter-war period, other kinds of jobs were available and working-class families no longer sought to save on the costs of reproduction by off-loading their daughters as domestic servants in situations that provided for their board and lodging.

Third, the study of women's employment in the mass-production consumer goods industries needs to be extended to the post Second World War period. I have documented only the early stages of an important new form of employment for women which was subsequently to acquire even greater importance. The analytical framework used here could be broadened to deal also with later developments.

The period after 1945 witnessed a massive expansion of mass-production consumer goods industries in Britain which carried on to a peak in the 1960s and then began to decline from the mid-1970s. The work processes continued to be based on the same sexual division of labour as in the pre-war period with assembly work being done exclusively by women and women being excluded from all other types of work. But the rigidity of gender segregation, despite increasing automation and integration of the production process, gradually came to be explained in terms of new rationalizations (Cockburn 1985; Game and Pringle 1984). The emphasis was no longer so much on the monotonous or 'light and clean' character of assembly work that made it eminently suitable for women, but more on the fact that it was not technological. The dichotomies of clean versus dirty and light versus heavy were transformed into those of technological and non-technological.

However, the kinds of women who went into assembly-line work began to change from the early 1950s. Instead of the school leavers and very young women who had formed the majority of the workforce before the war, this type of work was increasingly done by married women, especially in the years of full employment when a greater number of job opportunities were open to school leavers. During the labour shortage of the 1950s employers were under pressure to find assemblers. The problem was solved in part by altering the structure of the working day and making it more 'flexible'. Part-time and shift working were introduced and became the most common pattern for married women, who could choose which time of the day to work so that paid employment did not threaten their continuing domestic responsibilities.

At the same time, migrant women from Ireland and the New Commonwealth were also actively recruited to assembly work and in many areas of the country largely replaced indigenous and white women in this form of work. Again, as in the case of women from the distressed areas and domestic work in the South East during the inter-war period, migrants were used as a replacement labour force, moving into jobs that indigenous women were at the same time vacating. Women from the Asian subcontinent, the Caribbean and Ireland were concentrated in the lowest positions of manual work while white women gravitated towards various forms of clerical and non-manual work.

Since the late 1970s, consumer goods assembly-line industries in Britain have been in serious decline with resultant widespread factory closures and large scale redundancies. Because of their over-representation in manufacturing industry and as assemblers, ethnic minority women have been particularly badly affected. Food processing was increasingly automated, and the pattern adopted by many large multinational companies, particularly in the field of electrical components and electronics, was to relocate assembly operations in economically less developed countries where labour was yet cheaper. The imperialist and racist aspect of the division of labour became more transparent, while the sexual division of labour remained intransigent. Fifty years on, colonized Third World women were doing similar work to the women described in this book, under even worse conditions.

List of main people interviewed

Name	Date of birth	Occupation
Stella Apsey	1910	bookbinder and paper folder
Ivy Barber	1904	1. apprenticed saleslady
		2. telephone assembler at Siemens factory
Ray Blackman	1901	tailoress in East London clothing factories
Edith Boyd	1911	1. domestic servant
		2. machine operator at Hoover factory
Wynne Cleverley	1909	1. domestic servant
		2. coil winder, later 'inspectoress', at Mullard
Ray Dickens		production manager at Lyons
Fred Douglas		personnel manager at Morphy Richards
Doris Edwards	1922	radio assembler at EMI (information supplied by her husband)
Reg Edwards	1922	manual production worker at EMI
Jessie Evans	1914	radio assembler, later chargehand, at Philips
Doris Hanslow	1910	sewing machinist at Rogers shirt and collar factory
Edie Harding	1896	1. domestic servant
		2. telephone assembler at Western Electric factory
Phil Hardy		production worker at EMI
Eliza Hawkins	1910	packer, machine operator, forelady at Pearce Duff
Barry Jones		1. blacksmith
		2. bicycle assembler, instrument maker, at EMI

Eileen Jones	1922	bicycle and radio assembler at EMI
Ann Leadbitter	1909	various factory jobs including box, toy and telephone cord assembly
Chrissie Minett	1913	biscuit creamer at Peek Frean
Kath Parish	1916	car seat 'trim' worker at Rover
Lil Price	c. 1912	printer of bank notes, stamps etc
Doris Scott	1909	1. jam packer
		2. skilled cake decorator
Doris Sharland	1913	1. manual work at various factories
		2. shop assistant
		3. waitress
		4. bus conductress
Bessie Taylor	1898	1. munitions factory worker
		2. domestic servant
		3. laundry worker
David Taylor		production manager at Lyons
Les White	1914	assembler at Hoover
Nell Williams	c. 1906	biscuit packer at Peek Frean
Doug Witt	1921	office worker at EMI
Elsie Woolnough	1906	clerical and manual work in clothing factories
Winnie Young	1911	biscuit packer at Peek Frean

In addition four group interviews were conducted: two in sheltered housing in Hackney and in Deptford (groups of 7 and 8 women); at Age Concern's Lewisham Skill Centre (14 women and 1 man); at Philips Pensioners' Club (4 women and 3 men). Occupations included assemblers in food, electrical and umbrella factories, shop assistants, clerical workers, domestic servants and tailoresses.

Notes

1 Introduction

1. The term semi-skilled is used following Jefferys (1945) who referred in this way to engineering workers proficient in operating one or two machines. However, it is unclear where women assemblers fitted in official classifications. From the perspective of skilled men in the Amalgamated Engineering Union and other craft unions women were unskilled, but employers described them variously as semi-skilled or unskilled operators. What actual term is used does not really matter very much, since it does not refer to objectively established criteria. It is now widely accepted that skill is to some extent socially constructed and that work traditionally done by women has frequently been classified as unskilled whatever its actual skill component. Thus I call assemblers semi-skilled to acknowledge the considerable expertise and dexterity necessary for high speed assembly work. These were skills which some women learned on the job and others brought to it. Although it was in employers' interests to downgrade the skill component of women's work and to deny that it required any training, I shall show that this was not the case, and that on some occasions when men were assigned to work normally done by women they were unable to do it without training. See, for example, the section on Lyons in Chapter 4.

2. Although it underwent enormous expansion and change during the interwar period, the motor industry was already established by then, and was not a totally new industry. Originally it was organized on the basis of craft manufacture, and this together with the strength of the craft unions were major factors underlying the absence of women from final assembly. The unions exercised considerable control over entry and would have opposed the recruitment of women at lower rates of pay. But an additional factor is that in Birmingham and Coventry, where the industry was concentrated, sufficient alternative factory work was available for women in other manufacturing industries. So a traditional division existed in these towns between the industries in which men and women worked. However, even though women were not engaged in the final assembly of cars, they were in fact very widely employed in the manufacture of motor components. Thus women still constituted a significant portion of the motor

industry taken as a whole, and the association between women and assembly-line work also applies in this case. This point will be elaborated in Chapter 3.

3. 'Relations of production' will be defined below, pp. 19–23.

4. There is a large general literature on inter-war social and economic conditions. For the contemporary view see Brockway (1932), Cole and Cole (1937), Compton and Bott (1940), Graves and Hodge (1940), Greenwood (n.d.), Hutt (1933), Orwell (1937), Priestley (1934), and for more recent accounts Blythe (1963), Branson (1975), Branson and Heinemann (1973), Glynn and Oxborrow (1976), Mowat (1955), and Stevenson (1977).

5. Many of these surveys were conducted by university researchers in the late 1920s and early 1930s. Although primarily concerned with poverty, they also indicated the social effects of changing industrial structure in each area. By far the most comprehensive was that of London (Llewelyn Smith 1930–5), followed by that of Merseyside (Caradog Jones 1934). Other areas surveyed include south Wales (Marquand 1932), Lancashire (Daniels and Jewkes 1932), Bristol (Tout 1938), Southampton (Ford 1934), York (Seebohm Rowntree 1941), Tyneside (Mess 1928), Brynmawr (Jennings 1934), and Cumberland and Furness (Jewkes and Winterbottom 1933a).

6. Beatrice Webb detracted from the Majority Report of the 1919 War Cabinet Committee on Women In Industry advocating a single rate for the job, while the Majority Report recommended that women doing similar work to men should receive equal pay in proportion to output, i.e. equal piece-rates but not equal time-rates (PP Cmd 135 1919; Cmd 167 1919). Discussion of the various principles on which the remuneration of women's work could be based was widespread (Barton 1919a; 1919b; 1921; Drake 1920; Edgeworth 1923; Florence 1931; Hutchins 1915; Fawcett 1918; Rathbone 1917). For useful summaries of the debate see Lewis (1984: 200–5) and Harold Smith (1978).

7. PP., Ministry of Reconstruction Cmd 67 (1919), *Report to the Minister of Labour of the Committee appointed to enquire into the present conditions as to the supply of female domestic servants* (1923), Ministry of Labour and National Service Cmd 6650 1944–5, Labour Party (1931), ILO (1924) and Brittain (1928), Magnus (1934), Myers (1939), and Jephcott (1942). For more detailed discussion of changes in domestic service employment during the inter-war years see Chapters 2 and 7.

8. On women and trade unions see Cole (1939), Drake (1920), Boston (1980), Hinton (1983), Lewenhak (1977), Soldon (1978), Thom (1987) and Chapter 5, pp. 193–4.

9. For example Vera Brittain (1928) and Ray Strachey (1935a).

10. Marx elaborated the concept of the reserve army of labour in *Capital* (1970: 640–4), distinguishing between its latent, floating and stagnant forms. The concept has been applied to migrant labour in post-war Europe by Castles and Kosack (1973) and to women's employment by Beechey (1977), Anthias (1980), and Brueghel (1979) amongst others.

11. Kozak (1976), Braybon (1981) and Marwick (1977) on the First World

War and Summerfield (1984) on the Second World War in Britain, and Milkman (1987) on the Second World War in the United States.

12. See Chapters 7 and 8, especially pp. 267–8, where I argue that if women were fully occupied in necessary domestic labour, then it is incorrect to think of them as constituting a reserve army. Only if the reproduction of labour power was organized on a different basis, or in exceptional circumstances such as war (when women did not have to do nearly so much of the work involved in the daily reproduction of male labour power), could they be considered as a potential reserve army.

13. There is no need to rehearse the arguments. The position of Goldthorpe (1983) has been amply criticized (Garnsey 1978; Heath and Britten 1984; Murgatroyd 1982; Stanworth 1984). Studies using the individual woman or man rather than the family, as the basic unit for class analysis come up with a significant proportion of 'cross class' families (Leiulfsrud and Woodward 1987), so indicating a further range of problems in the approach which bases class on the occupation of the (male) head of household. Allen (1982) sketches an alternative method for analysing women's class position in their own right.

14. Kaluzynska (1980) and Malos (1980) provide comprehensive surveys of the different theoretical positions advanced in what has come to be known as the 'domestic labour debate'.

15. The theory of dual or segmented labour markets has been formulated in general terms (Doeringer and Piore 1971; Edwards *et al.* 1979; Gordon *et al.* 1982; Rubery 1978), and in relation to migrant or black workers (Baron 1979; Bosanquet and Doeringer 1973; Piore 1979), and women (Barron and Norris 1976; Blau 1979; M. Davies 1979; Kenrick 1981; Kessler-Harris 1979).

16. Other proponents of the single system approach to patriarchy/capitalism include McDonagh and Harrison (1978) and I. Young (1981), and of the dual systems approach Beneria (1979), Kuhn (1978), and O'Brien (1981). Dualist writings tend to be based on the distinction between the spheres of production (the economy or capitalism) and reproduction (biology, the family, ideology), a distinction usefully discussed by anthropologists (Meillassoux 1972; O'Laughlin 1977; Edholm *et al.* 1977).

17. Hartmann (1979b) and O'Brien (1981) view capitalism as operative in production and patriarchy in reproduction, while Kuhn (1978) and Mitchell (1974) confine patriarchy to ideology, culture and sexuality.

18. The inadequacy of seeking an explanation of women's oppression solely within familial relations is particularly apparent in relation to black women, for example in post-war Britain. The sexual division of labour in waged work to which black and migrant women are subject could in no way be attributed to the dynamics of the Afro-Caribbean, Asian or any other family. This is not the place to discuss the very fundamental theoretical issues raised for feminism by ethnic divisions between women, resulting from imperialism and racism, but clearly extreme care must be taken to specify the groups of women, as well as the historical period, to which the argument is supposed to apply.

19. Other substantive historical studies exploring the connection between class and gender relations include Lown (1983), M. Ryan (1981), Scott (1986), and Taylor (1983).
20. I shall also not examine in any detail laws, state policies and provisions affecting women's position, or women's education. But all played an important role in forming women for work and would need to be taken into account in any comprehensive theory of the determinants of women's class relations.
21. 'Relations of production' is a Marxist concept embracing the relation of wage exchange between labour and capital, and the production and circulation of commodities for further exchange value. In Marx's definition the relations of production of any given mode of production, such as slavery, feudalism, or capitalism, comprised the relations under which production was organized, and depended on who owned land, labour, tools, machinery, raw materials and other means of production. Different relations of production gave rise to different class relations. 'Relations of production' should not to be confused with the relation 'to' production, a descriptive term referring to the various relationships between workers and the productive process.
22. I am well aware of criticisms of Marx's economic categories, especially of the logical inconsistencies of the concepts of value and surplus value. However I am in no position to develop an alternative and am using surplus value in a general way as the best term available to indicate that different forms of exploitation exist and to provide a means of distinguishing between the relations of production of different groups of workers. The detailed technical criticisms (e.g. of Steedman 1977) do not undermine this kind of application.
23. Beauchamp (1937) and Llewelyn Smith (1930–5) provided the most useful material on women's industrial employment but did not examine assembly-line work in detail. More recent overviews of women's employment during the period are to be found in Davidoff (1956), Rowbotham (1974), Lewis (1984), Roberts (1988), and Beddoe (1989), and case studies of particular industries or towns in J. Castle (1984), Norris (1985), Mikoleit (1986), J. Ryan (1981), and Sarsby (1988).
24. For example the Transport and General Workers Union journal *The Record* had only three articles on women workers during the whole of the inter-war period.

2   The changing pattern of women's employment

1. For details of Doris Sharland, and all other interviewees quoted subsequently see the Appendix.
2. Chrissie Minett started work at the Peek Frean biscuit factory in south London in 1928:

> I went to school one day and to work the next, with my gymslip on and my blouse over the top because we didn't have any other clothes to send me to work in.

We shall meet her again in Chapter 4.

3. Economic activity and participation rates refer to those in a particular category (all women, all women in a particular age group, married or single women) in paid employment. They were seen as being active or participating in the labour force. 'Occupied' women also included those who were unemployed but normally in paid employment. Thus women who performed unpaid domestic labour were not recognized as participating, being economically active or even occupied, and were not conceived as being 'in' the labour force.

    Statistics on 'occupation' are the most biased, conceptually and linguistically. During the inter-war years unemployed women who were encouraged to give up the search for paid work and devote themselves to full-time domestic labour became officially 'unoccupied' and disappeared from labour force figures.

4. Ministry of Labour figures were based on those working in jobs insured against unemployment, and until 1934 excluded all young people under the age of 16. Other important groups also excluded were those engaged in agriculture, practically all civil servants, teachers and nurses, and non-manual workers earning more than £250 a year. Not surprisingly, when Census and Ministry of Labour figures are compared, the latter are consistently lower (as discussed by Buxton and MacKay 1977: 157–8), and this leads to problems in pinpointing the shifting distribution of women between different occupations.

5. The exact figures are as follows:

    Women: total population aged over 14 and total occupied

	1921	1931	1951*
Total population over 14	14,959,282	16,410,894	17,999,293
Total occupied over 14	5,036,727	5,606,043	6,272,876

    Source: Cen. Pop. 1931 Occ. Tab.: 673; Cen. Pop. 1951 Gen. Rep.: 130.
    * 1951 figures refer to those aged 15 and over.

    Hakim's figures show how stable women have been as a percentage of the total labour force throughout the first half of the twentieth century:

    Women as % of total labour force

1911	29.7
1921	29.5
1931	29.7
1951	30.8

    Source: Hakim 1979: 25.

6. It must be assumed that some of this growth was artificial, due to the inclusion of 14- to 16-year-olds in the figures after 1934, and to the shift

of women from uninsured to insured jobs, for example from domestic to factory work. In this way the growth reflected an increase in women in insured occupations as well as an actual increase in employment, but it is impossible to disentangle the two.

7. 26 per cent were aged between 35 and 59, and 5 per cent over 60 in both 1921 and 1931. By 1951 this had changed significantly: 52 per cent of working women were aged under 35, 43 per cent between 35–59, and 5 per cent over 60 (Hakim 1979: 12).

8. Note that widows' pensions were introduced in 1925 and probably account for the declining numbers of older widows who remained in paid employment (Cen. Pop. 1931 Gen. Tab.: 164).

9. Peek Frean adopted this practice from 1933 and relied heavily on experienced married ex-workers during their rush periods at Easter, summer and Christmas. Interestingly, this firm was also one of the first to introduce part-time work after the Second World War.

10. This issue is discussed at length in Chapter 7. It is significant that even when married women did enter the labour market in large numbers after the war, their primary responsibility for the domestic economy was not challenged in any way. On the contrary, the flexible conditions of part-time work were deliberately designed to be compatible with, rather than to undermine, what was considered to be women's prior commitment (Liff 1985; Beechey and Perkins 1987).

11. The participation rate of married women aged 25–35 increased from 9.9 per cent in 1921 to 13.8 per cent in 1931 and 25.2 per cent in 1951, and of those aged 21–24 from 13.2 per cent to 19.3 per cent and 37.7 per cent (Lewis 1984: 150; Cen. Pop.1931 Gen. Rep.: 163; Davidoff 1956: 299–300).

12. The very high figure for the North West is slightly misleading since it includes the 15.4 per cent of women who were out of work in the area. On the other hand, unemployment was considerably lower than average in the South East, and especially in Greater London. If those out of work are subtracted from those occupied it can be seen that the proportion of those employed in London and the South East actually exceeded that in the North West in 1931 (33.9 per cent, 30.4 per cent, and 26.5 per cent respectively).

13. This figure includes both men and women (since the Ministry of Labour did not break down its regional statistics by sex) and probably included some jobs that already existed but had previously been uninsured. On the other hand, as employment in the 14 to 16 age group was rising particularly rapidly in the South East their exclusion means that these figures undoubtedly represent an underestimate, a point emphasized many times in NSOL.

14. The two periods, 1921–31 and 1931–51, are presented separately because the Census categories were reclassified in 1931 and in 1951 and so no direct comparison can be made, except in an extremely general way, to show the overall change between 1921 and 1951. The two figures for 1931 differ according to whether the 1931 or 1951 classification is used, so that the two sets of figures in the Table are not exactly comparable, since certain

of the codes were included, excluded, subdivided or collapsed together.
15. The figures in Table 6 refer to the United Kingdom as a whole, and so include Scotland in addition to England and Wales. They are also subject to the caveats made earlier about categories of workers excluded from Ministry statistics. The year 1938 has been taken as the last pre-war year, so as to avoid including changes in employment that were due to the build-up for the war (e.g. increases in the metal industries) rather than just a continuation of already existing trends.
16. After the end of the war the growth accelerated again so that by 1947 636,000 women were employed in these three industries compared with 220,000 in 1923 and 362,000 in 1938 (*British Labour Statistics* 1971: 214–15).
17. This trend can be seen clearly in studies of local employment change (e.g. J. Ryan 1981; NSOL 1930–5; D.C. Jones 1934). For further discussion of changes in conditions of domestic service employment see Chapter 7.
18. As the proportion of textile and domestic service workers dropped again by 1951, so their concentration in the older age groups was reinforced even though these occupations were of declining significance within these age groups as a whole. For example textile workers dropped from 104 per 1,000 in 1931 to 57 per 1,000 in 1951: in 1931 fewer were aged between 45 and 64 than in 1951 (14 per cent as opposed to 30 per cent) but more were under 25 (40 per cent as opposed to 28 per cent). The age distribution of weavers was older than that of other textile workers who were not so badly affected by the decline: 38 per cent of weavers were aged over 45 (Cen. Pop. 1951 Gen. Rep.: 157).
19. East Sussex had the highest and Leicestershire and Staffordshire the lowest proportion of domestic servants relative to their adult female populations (207, 73 and 76 per 1,000 respectively) (Cen. Pop. 1931 Occ. Tab. B: 664–6).
20. The clothing industry was the one exception: here although the industry lost ground as an employer of women, women became an even larger proportion of the total workforce.
21. Textile weaving appears to be a partial exception to this rule. Men and women performed the same tasks in some sections of weaving and for the same wage rates. However, men tended to earn more than women because they were put in charge of more looms and were also paid for tuning and adjusting the machines (Lewis 1984: 164). Since technical control over the machinery effectively differentiated the actual work and skill status of male weavers from that of women, this example strengthens, rather than undermines, the argument that sex segregation was pretty absolute.
22. The following section is confined to providing quantitative evidence of the pattern of women's employment. More qualitative data appear in Chapter 4, and changes in the organization of the two industries, and in their production processes, are dealt with in Chapters 3 and 5 respectively.
23. In 1938 176,370 people were employed under the Electric Cable, Apparatus, Lamp heading (MOLG December 1938: 468).
24. There were 25,627 women out of 36,495 operatives: 9,085 women were

under 18 (Cen. Prod. 1935 Pt. III: 60).

25. 66 per cent of all employment in biscuits was concentrated in big firms and only 2.7 per cent in small ones (Rostas 1948a: 152).

26. However, the result of this measure by Huntley and Palmer was to exacerbate the factory's perennial shortage of female labour; to relieve the problem management then 'had to import girls from the depressed areas' (Corley 1972: 232).

27. For the effects of mechanization on the gender composition of the workforce in different industries see Chapter 6, pp. 200–2, and for effects on the sexual division of labour of changes in the production process at Peek Frean and Lyons see Chapter 4.

28. *Men:*   total   11,986   *Women:*   total   27,371
           under 18   833   under 18   7,589

Figures for operatives in preserved foods (Cen. Prod. 1935 Pt. III: 93).

29. Nor is the point vitiated by evidence of the large number of men employed in new industries in Slough. Savage's (1988) argument concerns the role of state agencies in creating the supply of labour in the town as a whole (by arranging the transfer of migrant male workers from Wales) rather than the sex-typing of work or the sexual division of labour within factories.

3 The restructuring of industrial capitalism

1. Alice Foley, one of the few women full-time officials in the textiles unions and a committed socialist, described (1973) the humbling experience of meeting Ghandi.

2. Hannah (1983: 140) emphasizes the delay experienced in reaping the benefits of the initial merger wave.

3. However, some of the older industries were increasing productivity as a result of measures to reduce labour costs (wage cuts and lay-offs) and belated mechanization (H.W. Richardson 1967: 76).

4. The proportion of patents coming from firms rose from 15 per cent to 58 per cent between 1914 and 1938 (Hannah 1983: 114).

5. Hannah argues that these merger waves represented the biggest shake-up in the structure of British manufacturing industry to have occurred this century (1983: 101) and sees in them the roots of the corporate economy. On average 188 firms disappeared through mergers every year (1983: 94), following a pattern of sequential acquisition of smaller firms rather than instant monopolization. ICI, Reckitts, and Metal Box are good examples and details are given in their company histories. For ICI see Reader (1970; 1975), for Unilever see Wilson (1954), and for Metal Box see Reader (1976).

6. The experience of small firms established during the inter-war years contrasts sharply with these large companies. Many were not successful and did not survive, especially those set up in parts of the country where unemployment was already high. Foreman-Peck (1985) describes them as chaff rather than seedcorn and emphasizes the cycle of depression which

made it more difficult for small or new firms to succeed where the effects of the depression were worse because of lack of purchasing power to aid consumption.

7. Hannah suggests (1983: 78) that such equipment stimulated new thinking about systems of management control among the Management Research Group and more widely.

8. Loft (1986) argues that the proportion of women accountants declined as the profession was formalized, a process paralleled in the development of other professions too.

9. Miller and O'Leary (1987) discuss the emergence of a discourse of the 'governable person', where every person and every action were to be individually accountable and capable of being accounted for. Techniques and methods were developed in order to measure and compare different actions in terms of efficiency. This is interpreted as part of the general discussion and promotion of efficiency in business during the early twentieth century, a process reflected also in other business practices and in the emergence of industrial psychology. All these practices rested on a similar set of ideas about the individual, the desirability of individual accountability and the possibility of constructing 'scientific' and 'rational' techniques of measurement.

10. The main protagonists are Dowie (1968) and Alford (1981) versus H.W. Richardson (1967) and Buxton and Aldcroft(1979).

11. PEP is now the Policy Studies Institute.

12. The Balfour Committee made its final report in five volumes between 1926 and 1929.

13. Minutes of their meetings are to be found in the Ward Papers held by the Business History Unit of the London School of Economics.

14. Electricity generation was concentrated in the larger and more efficient power stations, and the country was divided into seven self-sufficient areas each with their own grid control centre. Interconnection via the grid reduced the number of new plants that needed to be built.

15. The rate of increase in productivity was not, however, so spectacular in the early years, partly because of the absence of mass-production methods in heavy machinery sections of the industry and also because of the proliferation, alongside the large and dominant producers, of many small firms that used labour intensive methods (Glynn and Oxborrow 1976: 107; Catterall 1979: 255).

16. Associated Electrical Industries was formed in 1926 by the merger of Metropolitan-Vickers and British Thomson Houston, and Electrical and Musical Industries emerged from the amalgamation in 1931 of The Gramophone Company (marketing under the His Masters Voice label) and Columbia Gramophone Limited.

17. Unilever owned its own outlets (the Maypole, Lipton, and Home and Colonial Stores chains) and the CWS owned its own factories, shops and farms. Other multiples were sufficiently large to exert pressure on suppliers and have their own branded goods. This was the case with Marks and Spencer which increased its stores from 140 in 1927 to 230 in 1938 (Pollard 1983: 111).

18. Co-op membership rose from 4.5 million in 1920 to 8.5 million in 1939, and two-thirds of its sales were still in food (Pollard 1983: 111). The Co-op's share of the total retail food trade increased enormously: by 1939 it distributed 25 per cent of all fresh milk supplies and 40 per cent of all butter (Burnett 1979: 293).
19. In flour milling three firms (Rank, Spiller and the CWS) had gained control of 70 per cent of the industry by 1938 (Pollard 1983: 64). Rank and Spillers had purchased and closed down redundant capacity and organized a quota system for maintaining prices and profits through the Millers' Mutual Aid Association. Tate and Lyle cornered the market in sugar, Marsh and Baxter in bacon, Unilever and the CWS in margarine, Cadbury-Fry in chocolate, Heinz in baked beans, and a handful of firms like Jacobs, Peek Frean and Huntley and Palmer in biscuits.
20. Burnett (1979: 305–16) discusses the surveys of food habits, dietary standards and health undertaken in the early 1930s by John Boyd Orr and Sir William Crawford.
21. Of the 30,300 employed in yarn manufacture in 1936, 11,360 were women and virtually all of the 40,000 weavers and the 30,000 engaged in hosiery manufacture were women (Plummer 1937: 218).

4 Five factories

1. Since 1982 Peek Frean has been owned by the American Nabisco company.
2. Helen Jones (1983) argues that the unprecedented expansion of employer welfare schemes from the mid-1920s was concentrated in the newer industries. The principal motive behind private occupational welfare schemes was the promotion of discipline among the workforce and the deflection of trade union loyalties. She suggests that they should be viewed, along with Taylorism and the Bedaux system, in the context of intensifying management strategies.
3. It was normal practice on most assembly lines to have a few workers who could do all the jobs on the line. These 'spare girls' or 'floaters', as they were known, took over so that the belt would not have to stop during tea breaks or when others went to the toilet.
4. After the war Peek Frean was also one of the first firms to introduce part-time work for married women. This arrangement was the subject of a well-known sociological study by Pearl Jephcott *et al.* (1962).
5. EMI's view of married women as 'bread and butter' workers contrasts with the more prevalent and diametrically opposed view of married women as too independent to accept the discipline of assembly work. However, in both cases the strategy of employers was to recruit women who were financially vulnerable, and therefore unlikely to complain or organize resistance. Whether they were married or not was irrelevant to this strategy, though ideas about the propriety of married women working did have some independent weight. See Chapter 6.
6. This is extremely long as assembly lines go, and the longest I have come across for the inter-war period. Philips radio factory, assembling a similar

product, had forty women to a line.

7. Moving belts appear to have been introduced progressively at EMI as elsewhere, first in one section of the factory and then more widely. Even so, an attempt was clearly made to organize production on a moving line principle. The significance of a *moving* belt as an essential element of the assembly-line labour process will be seen again (pp. 135–6) and in Chapter 5. It was this that really gave management complete control over output by enabling them to dictate the speed of work.

8. Joe Lyons was a stallholder at the Liverpool Exhibition and a distant relation, who later became chairman of the public company but was never directly involved with its development or running (D.J. Richardson 1976: 165).

9. Ray Dickens and David Taylor are pseudonyms for the two retired Lyons managers whom I interviewed.

10. This document dates from 1958 but would have applied even more forcefully in the inter-war years.

11. I stress the difference in control over the work process between static and moving conveyors since some writings on employer strategy (e.g. in Gospel and Littler 1983) focus on the continuous flow principle itself as constituting the central innovation of this labour process, and do not distinguish between manual and mechanical flow. But my evidence suggests that the type of flow did make a significant difference, since it determined the degree of control held by operators as opposed to management, and also had important implications for the role of supervision. It would be more accurate to describe static and moving conveyors as earlier and later stages both of the development of the labour process and of management's control over it. Indeed the fact that moving conveyors were eventually introduced throughout assembly industries indicates its recognized advantages for management.

12. Craig Littler (1982) describes the ensuing dispute, arguing that the Bedaux system undermined the authority of supervisors. That it was used to control indirect (as well as direct) workers was the reason for its unpopularity.

13. A number of reasons could be put forward to explain why Hoover did not introduce assembly lines proper. I have already suggested that a mass market for vacuum cleaners did not develop fully until after the Second World War. In addition Hoover was protected from competition by its effective world-wide monopoly position as one of only two manufacturers (the other being the Swedish firm Electrolux), and the only manufacturer (and presumably patent-holder) of the upright model. Such factors would account for the lack of stimulus to increase productivity and reduce labour costs by adopting more mechanized or Fordist production methods.

A further factor is that the manufacturing process was based on production methods similar to those of traditional mechanical engineering, and in such industries the technology for full-blown assembly lines was still rudimentary at this stage. Hoover must have been aware of the advantages to be gained by assembly lines, especially since it was equipped with the latest machinery, but I suspect that technological development was not sufficiently advanced for complete continuous flow manufacture, which would have involved integrating many large and heavy machines into one line. In the absence of this, regrouping existing processes into a proto line, as they did, was probably the best solution.

A possible alternative explanation might attribute both the absence of automated methods and the associated predominance of men to the strength of male workers or their trade unions, in resisting managerial attempts to mechanize or to employ more women. However, there is no evidence to support such an explanation: Hoover was not attempting to introduce a moving line or more women, and the majority of male workers were not unionized or in a strong bargaining position.

5 Women assembling: work, wages and assembly-line production

1. The list could be extended *ad infinitum*. The manual workforce of other food factories such as Heinz and Crosse and Blackwell in London, Chivers in Cambridge, and Cadbury at Bournville near Birmingham was also overwhelmingly female, as was that of Philips radio in Mitcham, Mullard valve plants in South London and in Blackburn, GEC in Coventry, and Pye in Cambridge.

2. I am not suggesting that this amounted in any sense to a second or third 'industrial revolution'. The point is that production methods developed towards mechanization and automation through a number of fairly distinct stages. Despite this, much twentieth-century Marxist discussion of industrial technology blurs over these changes, giving the impression that there was virtually no change between the stage of machinofacture described by Marx and automation in the present day. Debates about when the real subordination to capital actually occurred tend to jump from the mid-nineteenth or early twentieth centuries to the 1980s without much serious consideration of the intervening period. Even when changes in production methods are acknowledged there is no accepted terminology by which to designate them, other than 'Fordism', but this more correctly refers to a particular form of labour process.

3. For evidence of the importance of moving as opposed to static conveyors see Chapter 4, pp. 120 and 135–6 and notes 7 and 11.

4. I have spelled out this point because of the prevalent tendency – again following Braverman – to examine the labour process independently of the whole system of production in which it is embedded and to treat employers' strategies and workers' reactions as constitutive of the system rather than as modifications to it.

5. This distinction between direct and indirect work and workers is not the same as that in Marxist economics between productive and unproductive workers. The argument to be developed here is that while both direct and indirect workers contributed to the production of goods, and hence to the process of creating value, they differed as regards the way in which surplus value was extracted from them.

6. To this extent the consequence of mechanization was rather

the elaboration of a complex, internally differentiated apparatus of collective labour which contained an uneven variety of narrow skills and specific dexterities.

(Elger 1982: 45)

7. Mikoleit (1986: 110–12) gives the following figures for the proportion of skilled workers in the food processing industry: for men 41.9 per cent, 44.7 per cent, and 38.6 per cent in 1921, 1931 and 1951 respectively. The equivalent proportions for women were 28.2, 30.6, and 30.9 per cent, and for men and women taken together 36.5, 39.2, and 35.6 per cent. Skilled bakers and pastry cooks declined by 11.2 per cent between 1931 and 1951, and sugar confectionery makers, moulders and coverers by a massive 58.5 per cent. The continuous flow machinery introduced at Peek Frean and Lyons would no doubt have contributed to the decreasing number of skilled pastry cooks and the automatic machinery installed at Cadbury to that of chocolate moulders. Because Census occupational statistics are so general they mask what must have been the changed content of skilled work. However, they do show that 'other' skilled workers (unspecified) increased in absolute numbers both between 1921 and 1931 and 1931 and 1951, from nearly 18,000 to 23,645 and then to 38,142 in 1951.

8. The sharp decline in apprenticeship dates from around 1910. By 1925 only 32 per cent of youths in the engineering industry were working under apprenticeship schemes and numbers fell further during the following decade under the impact of unemployment and the growth of specialization and piecework. According to Jefferys (1945: 205–6) skilled men no longer had time to teach apprentices and the earnings of unapprenticed youths on piecework far exceeded the traditionally low wages paid to apprentices.

9. All the quotations that follow in this section are taken from my interview with Doris Hanslow.

10. See NSOL (1930–5 Vol. II: 251–349) for details of the spread of the 'factory' trade in women's clothing and the large size of new establishments.

11. There is no contradiction between Craig Littler's suggestion (1982: 123–4) that supervisors represented the main source of resistance to the Bedaux system and the point made here. Under that system supervisors' tasks were reorganized and rationalized, and their effectiveness became subject to greater scrutiny and tighter control from above. This made their conditions of work more similar to those of line workers and drastically undermined their previous position of authority. Supervisors resented these changes and in some cases vehemently resisted the Bedaux system.

12. In the construction industry for example, a bricklayer or plasterer would be paid according to the amount of work he did, $£x$ for y yards of bricks laid or walls plastered. In certain traditional male-dominated sectors of the engineering system the ganger system operated until after the Second World War. Here the ganger negotiated a price with management for the total amount of work to be done by the men in his gang and it was up to them to decide how to organize the work and divide it up between them, subject usually to a maximum time allowance. Frequently skilled men

acted like subcontractors, taking on less skilled workers or labourers to assist in the work they had contracted to do and paying them out of the price. In this case the labourers were only indirectly paid by the firm and the skilled worker was their direct employer.

13. The only exception was the CWS clothing factory in Manchester described by Joan Beauchamp – and the CWS was probably a more enlightened employer than most. There the change from a piece-rate to time-rate payment system simply followed the change in production process and was not confused by the addition of a bonus scheme.

> In the Manchester factory there is a conveyor belt on which 40 operators turn out raincoats at the rate of one every 4½ minutes. Workers on the conveyors get a guaranteed rate of 10d an hour.
> (Beauchamp 1937: 21)

For a 48-hour week, this would amount to 240 pence or £2 exactly which was considered a reasonable wage.

14. This is not the place for a detailed history of women and trade unions in the inter-war period. The total number of women members declined dramatically from over 1.3 million in 1920 to a low of 728,000 in 1933, before rising again to 802,000 in 1939. But even by the outbreak of the Second World War only 6 per cent of engineering and metal workers were unionized (Drake 1939: 249). In his article on 'Trade union difficulties in new areas', John Parker (1939: 241–8), while recognizing that unions needed to alter their methods, basically put the blame for low membership in the new industries on women, young, and migrant workers. For further discussion of women and trade unions see Boston (1980), Lewenhak (1977), and Thom (1987), and of the problems besetting the labour movement in the inter-war years see Hinton (1983).

15. On my use of the concept of surplus value see Chapter 1, note 22.

6 Women assembled: gender and the division of labour

1. I am not suggesting an absolute segregation such that job X was always and in every instance done by women wherever it was found, and job Y by men. See Chapter 2, pp. 56–7 where the point was made that while a particular job might be performed by women in one factory and by men in the neighbouring factory, it was never done by both sexes in the same place. Gender segregation was thus at its most rigid in particular workplaces.

2. This traditional principle of allocation was breached, but only briefly, during the First World War. Established barriers were temporarily suspended so that women could perform skilled 'men's work' from which they were normally excluded. But in the long run this break with the pattern was little more than an exceptional response to exceptional circumstances. After the end of the war, manufacturing industry returned firmly to the status quo ante and women were again restricted to semi-skilled repetition work.

3. The proportion of women operatives was 8.5 per cent in 1924 and 10 per

cent in 1930 (Jefferys 1945: 206).

4. In 1921 there were 75,945 men and 128,760 women tailors, tailors pressers and machinists. In 1931 this had changed to 68,886 men and 136,907 women (Cen. Pop. 1931 Occ. Tab.: 675).

5. This possibility is suggested by Census figures which show an increase in the employment of both sexes between 1921 and 1951 in those parts of the industry where mechanization was most effective. Sometimes this counterbalanced, in terms of overall employment, the dramatic alteration in the sexual division of labour that had occurred on the shopfloor. This was certainly the case at Cadbury in the mid-1930s when the rise in men's employment was sharper than that of women's (Cadbury Brothers 1945: 60). The likely cause for this was the growing proportion of scientific and technical workers, and the creation of managerial and supervisory posts, both of which favoured men (Mikoleit 1986: 91).

6. This argument refers to the different place of women in mass production as opposed to craft manufacture. Women had of course also formed a central section of the direct workforce in the nineteenth-century textile industry, but this was not a traditional craft industry, and men also worked as direct producers on the shopfloor.

7. However, it should be evident that the concept of patriarchy could not itself account for such changes in the form of patriarchal relations on the shopfloor.

8. This argument can be developed more fully (in Chapter 8) only when the other side of the equation, women's work in the domestic economy, has been analysed (in Chapter 7).

9. For most working-class men, of course, there was no career ladder of the type outlined here. Labourers had no formal skill and remained permanently in the lowest position in the male division of labour. Most other manual workers acquired their skill and position in the division of labour early in their working lives and stayed there without rising in position or pay. The same probably applied to the majority of men employed as progress chasers or quality controllers. However, the fact that such new occupations included conditions of employment which were at odds with women's jobs was sufficient reason for women not to be considered as suitable incumbents for them, regardless of the fact that not all men benefited from them.

10. On the feminization of office work in Britain see Klingender (1935), Lockwood (1958), Barker and Downing (1980), Crompton and Jones (1984), and Silverstone (1976).

11. Feminization of the retail trade in London is discussed in NSOL (1930–5) Vol. V, Ch. IV, Jefferys (1954), and D.J. Smith (1982).

12. The suggestion had even been made during the First World War that technical developments simplifying production methods were undertaken in order to suit the 'inferior' capacities of women. In reality, however, both technical and organizational advances, assembly lines and subdivision of labour, represented an intensification of pre-war developments in engineering, and were by-products of the demand for standardized mass produced goods rather than of the need to accommodate technology to

women (Kozak 1976: 126).

13. The issue of the marriage bar is a large one and worthy of much greater attention than I can give it. The exclusion of married women from waged work was obviously linked with their primary role in the domestic economy and with the attempt to maintain this as primary at a time when this might not occur automatically. But how and why these were so connected remains to be examined.

14. The Transport and General Workers Union journal, *The Record*, carried several cartoons and articles in such a vein during the inter-war years. One article entitled 'My New Full-Time Job' by 'One of the Scrapped' was written in the form of a diary by an unemployed man about a day in the life of a househusband (*Record*, Vol. XVII, no.198, March 1938: 212).

7 Homeward bound: changes in domestic production and consumption

1. While agreeing with the evidence and argument of Vanek (1980), Cowan (1974; 1976b), and Zmroczek (1984) that domestic technology does not necessarily reduce the amount of time spent on domestic labour in the home (since the old tasks tend to be replaced by others that are just as time-consuming, and standards rise so that clothes and bedlinen are laundered more frequently than before), it was nevertheless the case that developments such as those outlined did have a profound impact on the amount of labour and time spent on basic domestic tasks. Being able to buy rather than bake one's own bread and having power, lighting, and heating available at the turn of a switch incontrovertibly removed a significant proportion of the hard work from domestic labour, and so released time that could be put to other uses, domestic or otherwise. For discussion of the general issues involved in this question see also Bereano *et al.* (1985: 162–81) and Hartmann (1975).

2. Catherine Hall's (1977) study of changes in the cult of domesticity in inter-war Birmingham highlights the link between the form of domesticity and changes in family size and structure, new housing, and the shift towards domestic consumption.

3. Class differences in the use of domestic technology in the USA during the inter-war years are outlined in Cowan 1983: 172–90.

4. Figures on the ownership of various domestic appliances were given in Chapter 3, p. 83. Further details are supplied in Corley (1966) and PEP (1945).

5. See for instance Virginia Woolf's diary for 13 April 1929 and Naomi Mitchison's autobiography (1979), both quoted by Beauman (1983: 102, 108).

6. E.M. Delafield's *Diary of a Provincial Lady* (1930) and Jan Struther's *Mrs Miniver* (1939) are good examples of such novels.

7. Winifred Foley (*A Child in the Forest* 1974) came from the Forest of Dean, Jean Rennie (*Every Other Sunday* 1955) from Scotland, and Margaret Powell (*Below Stairs* 1968) from Hove. Other autobiographies describing what it was like to be a domestic servant include Elizabeth Flint

(1963) and Molly Weir (1970).

8. A comparison between three groups of employment (service, including dressmaking and laundry work, commercial, including professional and clerical, and industrial) indicated a definite trend over the period towards each of the last two sectors at the expense of the first in both boroughs. Although a higher proportion of women in Deptford worked in factories than in Lewisham, where twice as many were employed in commercial occupations, industrial work was in fact the largest growth sector in both areas. The percentages for the three groups respectively in Lewisham were 61.9, 22.4, and 2.5 in 1911 and this had changed by 1931 to 36.9, 44.7, and 18.3. The corresponding percentages for Deptford were 49.9, 18.3, and 14.4 in 1911 and 32.8, 35.6, and 31.6 in 1931 (J. Ryan 1981 Table X: 30).

9. Teresa McBride (1976) drew attention to the raising of the school leaving age which meant not only that fewer very young girls were available, but also that those who were, were more highly educated and in a position to apply for more qualified jobs demanding higher levels of literacy. At the same time the continuing trend to urbanization removed part of the pool of rural labour from which a high proportion of domestic servants had traditionally been drawn. On the demand side too, the decline in the size of middle-class families meant that fewer nursemaids and other servants were required to service them. Modernization of the home (with running water, gas and electricity) reduced housework and therefore the amount of help required, and the use of external services such as laundries and bakeries had a similar effect. Edward Higgs (1986) also warns against single or simple causal theories of the decline and calls for much more detailed analysis of trends in local areas.

8 Women and the total social organization of labour

1. The very different employment circumstances confronting women in different parts of the country demonstrate the significance during the inter-war period of what Doreen Massey (1984) has called a 'spatial division of labour'. Expansion in one area of the country was connected with decline elsewhere and those impoverished by the contraction were pulled into the expanding areas in their search for work. Uneven regional development and the economic domination of London lay behind a spatial division of labour whereby workers from less developed parts were in a weaker position in the labour market. That the employment situation of migrant women was considerably worse than that of their indigenous counterparts is evidence of material differences between women which resulted in different class relations. As a replacement labour force, migrant women filled the jobs, mainly in domestic service, left behind as local women entered better paid factory or office work.

   There were imperialist dimensions and racist overtones to these processes. The same epithets and criticisms already used against Irish migrants to Britain in the nineteenth century, and later to be endured by Asian and Caribbean settlers from the 1950s, were also applied to those from the 'distressed' areas in the 1930s, and particularly those from Wales. They were described as dirty, breeding like rabbits, overcrowded, taking local people's jobs and houses, undercutting pay rates and so on. During the inter-war years the ethnic and geographical differences were all contained within Britain, with the South East and Midlands as the metropolis, and the North and Celtic fringe as the periphery. In the post-war period, similar factors encouraged migrants from the British colonies, impoverished as a result of imperialism to leave their own countries in search of work, and they too entered the bottom rungs of a segmented labour market. Thus there were important parallels in the situation of migrant workers in the inter-war and post-war periods. These parallels and the circumstances of female migrant labour in the inter-war period merit much more detailed attention than I have been able to give them.

2. Only later was there a further restructuring of the hierarchy, when migrant women, particularly Afro-Caribbean and Asian, became the main female assembly workforce, and by then the wage for this work had dropped right down the ladder of women's wages.

3. In the 1960s a number of sociological studies were devoted to 'the alienation of the assembly-line worker', for example Blauner (1964) and Chinoy (1965). But such workers were assumed to be men in car plants.

4. An important implication of this is that Fordist methods of managerial control including scientific management, machine pacing and speed-ups, were applied disproportionately to women. As a consequence, and contrary to the widely held view, women were more subject to Fordist work processes than men. See p. 279 and note 9.

5. However, Castles and Kosack (1973) do not view the divergent circumstances of migrant and indigenous workers as having any bearing on class. They adhere rigidly to the argument that all workers share the same relation to the process of production and that this defines their common class position. The opposite conclusion is drawn by Gorz (1970) (and to a lesser extent also by Buroway 1976, and Castells 1975) who emphasizes the significance of differences in political and civil rights between the two groups, as well as conditions of employment. Gorz points to the material benefits gained by indigenous workers as a by-product of the racist division of labour as evidence of class differences between the two.

6. The tendency to treat the family and household economy as a non-capitalist institution is implicit for example in Braverman's discussion of the 'universal market' (1974: Chapter 13). Similarly early 'second wave' socialist feminists were concerned primarily to show that gender inequality could not be explained simply as a product of capitalism. Juliet Mitchell (1971) argued for a relatively autonomous sphere of reproduction, organized on principles of operation independent of commodity production. Many other theorists of women's oppression have taken this distinction between reproduction and production as a basic premiss, and concentrate on the former as the prime site for the oppression of women and the rule of men. Because the focus is on the independence of the family and household economy, and on the patriarchal basis of domination within this sphere of reproduction, the question of its mode of connection

with the sphere of production tends to get lost. My point is that despite being characterized by different relations of production, the two spheres do not belong to different modes of production or phases of development. Although capitalism did not 'require' or presuppose a particular family or household form, in practice the structure of the sphere of reproduction, and its integral connection with the market economy, have been basic to the actual history of capitalism as a social formation. See also the discussion in Chapter 1, p. 13 and notes 16 and 17.

7. This is still the case today in European countries, including France, which still have a large peasant-based agricultural sector.

8. *A fortiori*, men could go to war only if women took over the whole of production while they were away fighting. Hence the large scale and exceptional employment of women during the two world wars.

9. Milkman attributes the different patterns of gender segregation in the American auto and electrical industries to opposing managerial strategies adopted as a means of controlling labour and reducing labour costs. Women were widely employed in electrical goods manufacture. It was a relatively unmechanized industry and wages accounted for a high proportion of total production costs. Hence the recruitment of women, who could be paid less than men, and the use of piecework and incentive payment systems to control labour and intensify work. By contrast the auto industry employed few women. It was a more highly mechanized and capital intensive industry where the development of Fordist methods reduced labour costs as a component of total production costs. Here high wages were paid to men in exchange for subordination to the moving track. In this situation management had little incentive to substitute cheaper female labour.

But although the same pattern of gender segregation also obtained in the two industries in Britain, managerial strategies were different. Most of the women-employing mass consumer goods industries were mechanized from the start, and Fordist-type methods were much more in evidence there in the inter-war period than they were in the motor industry. Women were subordinated to mechanized managerial control and at the same time received low wages in the British electrical goods industries. Male car workers on the other hand were not so subject to Fordist methods (cf Lewchuk 1983) but their relatively high wages were based on a system of payment by results.

Milkman's theory cannot therefore account for the British situation. Other factors than the presence or absence of Fordism would be required for an adequate explanation. Moreover the absence of a systematic one-to-one correspondence between the pattern of gender segregation and mode of managerial control must also throw doubt on the validity of her general argument.

References

British Government publications

UK Board of Trade

Census of Production 1924, 1930, 1935
Committee on Industry and Trade (Balfour Committee)
(1926) Survey of Industrial Relations
(1927) Part I Factors in Industrial and Commercial Efficiency
(1928) Part III Survey of Textile Industries
(1928) Part IV Survey of Metal Industries
Census of Population 1921, 1931, 1951

Department of Employment

(1971) *British Labour Statistics. Historical Abstract 1886–1968.*

Home Office

(1930) *A Study of the Factors which have operated in the past and those which are operating now to determine the distribution of women in industry,* Cmd 3508, PP 1929, XVII.

Ministry of Labour

(1923) *Report to the Minister of Labour of the Committee appointed to enquire into the present conditions as to the supply of female domestic servants.*
(1937) *Twenty-Second Abstract of Labour Statistics of the UK, 1922–36,* Cmd 5556, XXVI.
Annual Reports
Gazette (MOLG)

Ministry of Labour and National Service

Report on Post-War Organization of Private Domestic Employment, Cmd 6650, PP 1944–5, V.
(1945) Women in Industry.

Ministry of Reconstruction

Report of the Women's Advisory Committee on the Domestic Service Problem, Cmd 67, PP 1919, XXIX.
Reports from the War Cabinet Committee on Women in Industry, Cmd 135 and 167, 1919, XXXI.
Report of the Women's Employment Committee, Cmd 9239, 1919.

Royal Commission on the Distribution of the Industrial Population
Report, Cmd 6153, PP 1939–40, IV.

Royal Commission on Equal Pay
Report, Cmd 6937, PP 1945–46, XI.

Archive and company material

Bedaux Archive
Microfilms 1–27 transcript.

BBC
(1983) *All Our Working Lives*, Programme on Electronics: transcripts of interviews.

Cadbury Brothers Ltd
(1945) *Industrial Record 1919–39. A review of the interwar years*.

EMI Music Archives (Thorn EMI)
(1920) Management Minutes.
Playback.
A Voice to Remember. The sounds of 75 years on EMI records, 1898–1973.
(1941) Summary of employees being trained in various sections of the factory.

H.J. Heinz Co. Ltd
Heinz News.
(1986) *100 Years of Progress 1886–1986.*
The Works Manager.

Hoover plc
(1963) The Hoover factory at Perivale, Middlesex.
Hoover News.
(1963) Merthyr Tydfil, Glamorgan, The Story of the Enterprise.

References

J. Lyons and Co. Ltd

(1962) Bakery Memorandum.
(1965) The Baking Industry, A Profile.
(1944) Fifty Years. Presentation to George William Booth Esquire.
The Gateway.
Lyons Mail.

Management Research Group

The Ward Papers.

Metal Box

Reader, W.J. (1976) *Metal Box.*

Morphy Richards

McRobert, R. *A Guide to Better Ironing.*
Hollowood, B. (1957) *Morphy Richards Comes of Age 1936–1957.*

Mullard Mitcham

(1924) *The Book of the Wireless Valve.*
Griffiths, C. (1977) *Our Factory. Its history and development.*

Peek Frean

The Biscuit Box.
(1963) Chronological List of Developments in Peek Frean History 1857–1955.
(1951) *The Condensed History of Peek Frean and Co. Ltd.*
'From Little Acorns...' The Story of Peek, Frean and Co., Ltd. A saga of
    biscuit-making.
(1906) Film of Peek Frean.
Historical Survey of Peek Frean. Part Four 1924–41.
1857–1957 A Hundred Years of Biscuit Making by Peek Frean.

Transport and General Workers Union

The Record.

Unpublished theses

Burian, S. (1983) 'Benevolent capitalists? A study of paternalist authority in
    an industrial firm', PhD, University of Cambridge.
Carr, F. (1979) 'Engineering workers and the rise of labour in Coventry',
    PhD, Warwick University.
Castle, J. (1984) 'Factory work for women in inter-war Britain: the
    experience of women workers at GEC and Courtaulds in Coventry,
    1919–39', MA, Warwick University.
Davidoff, L. (1956) 'The employment of married women in England', MA,
    University of London.

Harrop, J. (1966) 'New growth industries in an era of stagnation and depression, 1919–39', MA, University of Liverpool.

Hartmann, H. (1975) 'Capitalism and women's work in the home, 1900–1930', PhD, Yale University.

Kozak, M. (1976) 'Women munition workers in World War I with special reference to engineering', PhD, University of Hull.

Liff, S. (1985) 'Occupational sex-typing: sexual and technical divisions of labour', PhD, University of Manchester.

Mikoleit, G. (1986) 'Industrial restructuring and women's employment: the case of the food industry in inter-war Britain', CNAA MPhil, South Bank Polytechnic.

Norris, J. (1985) 'Gender and class in industry and the home: women silk workers in Macclesfield 1919–39', MA, University of Keele.

Pitfield, D. (1973) 'Labour migration and the regional problem in Britain 1920–39', PhD, University of Stirling.

Richardson, D.J. (1970–1) 'The history of the catering industry, with special reference to the development of J.L. Lyons and Co. Ltd. to 1939', PhD, University of Kent.

Ryan, J. (1981) 'Developments in the employment of women in Lewisham and Deptford in the interwar years', MA, University of Kent.

Whiting, R.C. (1978) 'The working class in the "new industry" towns between the wars: the case of Oxford', DPhil, University of Oxford.

Books and articles

Aldcroft, D.H. (1970) *The Interwar Economy 1918–39*, London: B.T. Batsford.

—— (1983) *The British Economy between the Wars*, Oxford: Philip Allan.

Aldcroft, D.H. and Richardson, H.W. (1969) *The British Economy 1870–1939*, London: Macmillan.

Alford, W.B.E. (1981) 'New industries for old? British industries between the wars', in R. Floud and D. McCloskey (eds) *The Economic History of Britain since 1700*, Volume 2, Cambridge: Cambridge University Press.

Allen, G.C. (1951) *British Industries and their Organization*, London: Longman.

Allen, S. (1982) 'Gender inequality and class formation', in A. Giddens and G. Mackenzie (eds) *Social Class and the Division of Labour*, Cambridge: Cambridge University Press.

Anthias, F. (1980) 'Women and the reserve army of labour: a critique of Veronica Beechey', *Capital and Class* 10, spring: 50–63.

Anthony, S. (1932) *Women's Place in Industry and Home*, London: Routledge.

Barker, J. and Downing, H. (1980) 'Word processing and the transformation of the patriarchal relations of control in the office', *Capital and Class* 10, spring: 64–99.

Baron, H. (1979) 'Racial domination in advanced capitalism: a theory of nationalism and divisions in the labor market', in R.C. Edwards, M. Reich, and D. Gordon (eds) *Labor Market Segmentation*, Lexington,

Mass: D.C. Heath.

Barrett, M. (1980) *Women's Oppression Today*, London: Verso.

Barron, R.D. and Norris, G.M. (1976) 'Sexual divisions and the dual labour market', in S. Allen and D. Leonard Barker (eds) *Dependence and Exploitation in Work and Marriage*, London: Longman/BSA.

Barton, D. (1919a) *Equal Pay for Equal Work*, London: National Union of Societies for Equal Citizenship.

—— (1919b) 'The course of women's wages', *Journal of the Royal Statistical Society* 82, IV: 508–44.

—— (1921) 'Women's minimum wages', *Journal of the Royal Statistical Society* 84, IV: 538–67.

Beauchamp, J. (1937) *Women who Work*, London: Lawrence & Wishart.

Beauman, N. (1983) *A Very Great Profession*, London: Virago.

Beddoe, D. (1989) *Back to Home and Duty. Women between the Wars*, London: Pandora.

Beechey, V. (1977) 'Some notes on female wage labour in capitalist production', *Capital and Class* 3, Autumn: 45–66.

—— (1987) *Unequal Work*, London: Verso.

Beechey, V. and Perkins, T. (1987) *A Matter of Hours*, Cambridge: Polity Press.

Beneria, L. (1979) 'Reproduction, production and the sexual division of labour', *Cambridge Journal of Economics* 3: 203–25.

Bereano, P., Bose, C., and Arnold, E. (1985) 'Kitchen technology and the liberation of women from housework', in W. Faulkner and E. Arnold (eds) *Smothered by Invention*, London: Pluto Press.

Blau, F.D. (1979) 'Sex segregation of workers by enterprise in clerical occupations', in R.C. Edwards, M. Reich and D. Gordon (eds) *Labor Market Segmentation*, Lexington, Mass: D.C. Heath.

Blauner, R. (1964) *Alienation and Freedom*, Chicago, Ill: University of Chicago Press.

Blythe, R. (1963) *The Age of Illusion: England in the Twenties and Thirties 1919–1940*, Harmondsworth: Penguin.

Bosanquet, N. and Doeringer, P.B. (1973) 'Is there a dual labour market in Great Britain?', *Economic Journal* LXXXIII: 421–35.

Boston, S. (1980) *Women Workers and the Trade Union Movement*, London: Davis Poynter.

Branson, N. (1975) *Britain in the 1920s*, London: Weidenfeld & Nicolson.

Branson, N. and Heinemann, M. (1973) *Britain in the 1930s*, London: Panther.

Braverman, H. (1974) *Labor and Monopoly Capital*, New York: Monthly Review Press.

Braybon, G. (1981) *Women Workers in the First World War: The British Experience*, London: Croom Helm.

British Association for the Advancement of Science (1935) *Britain in Depression*, London.

—— (1938) *Britain in Recovery*, London.

Brittain, V. (1928) *Women's Work in Modern England*, London: Noel Douglas.

Brockway, F. (1932) *Hungry England*, London: Victor Gollancz.

Brown, G. (1977) *Sabotage: A Study in Industrial Conflict*, Nottingham: Spokesman Books.

Brueghel, I. (1979) 'Women as a reserve army of labour: a note on recent British experience', *Feminist Review* 3: 12–23.

Burnett, J. (1978) *A Social History of Housing 1815–1970*, Newton Abbott: David & Charles.

—— (1979) *Plenty and Want*, London: Scolar Press.

Buroway, M. (1976) 'The functions and reproduction of migrant labour', *American Journal of Sociology* 81, 5: 1,051–87.

Buxton, N.K. (1980) 'Economic growth in Scotland between the wars', *Economic History Review* 2nd series, XXXIII, 4: 538–55.

Buxton, N.K. and Aldcroft, D.H. (eds) (1979) *British Industry between the Wars. Instability and Industrial Development 1919–39*, London: Scolar Press.

Buxton, N.K. and MacKay, D.I. (1977) *British Employment Statistics*, Oxford: Blackwell/SSRC.

Byers, A. (1981) *Centenary of Service: A History of Electricity in the Home*, London: Electricity Council.

Carchedi, G. (1977) *On the Economic Identification of Social Classes*, London: Routledge & Kegan Paul.

Carr-Saunders, A.M., Jones, D.C., and Moser, C. (1958) *Social Conditions in England and Wales*, Oxford: Oxford University Press.

Castells, M. (1975) 'Immigrant workers and the class struggle in advanced capitalism: the Western European experience', *Politics and Society* 5, 1: 33–66.

Castles, S. and Kosack, G. (1973) *Immigrant Workers and Class Structure in Western Europe*, Oxford: Oxford University Press/Institute of Race Relations.

Catterall, R.E. (1979) 'Electrical engineering', in N.K. Buxton and D.H. Aldcroft (eds) (1979) *British Industry between the Wars. Instability and Industrial Development 1919–39*, London: Scolar Press.

Cavendish, R. (1982) *Women on the Line*, London: Routledge & Kegan Paul.

Chandler, A. (1980) 'The growth of the transnational industrial firm in the US and the UK: a comparative analysis', *Economic History Review* 2nd series, XXXIII, 3: 396–410.

Chandler, A. and Herman, D. (eds) (1980) *Managerial Hierarchies. Comparative Perspectives on the Rise of the Modern Industrial Enterprise*, London: Harvard University Press.

Chinoy, E. (1965) *Automobile Workers and the American Dream*, Boston, Mass: Beacon Press.

Church, R.A. (1978) 'Innovation, monopoly, and the supply of vehicle components in Britain, 1880–1930: the growth of Joseph Lucas Ltd.', *Business History Review* LII, 2: 226–49.

Church, R.A. and Miller, M. (1977) 'The big three: competition, management, and marketing in the British motor industry, 1922–1939', in B. Supple (ed.) *Essays in British Business History*, Oxford: Clarendon Press.

References

Cockburn, C. (1981) 'The material of male power', *Feminist Review* 9: 41–58.

—— (1983) *Brothers. Male Dominance and Technological Change*, London: Pluto Press.

—— (1985) *Machinery of Dominance. Women, Men and Technical Know-how*, London: Pluto Press.

—— (1986) 'The relations of technology. What Implications for theories of sex and class?', in R. Crompton and M. Mann (eds) *Gender and Stratification*, Cambridge: Polity Press.

Cole, G.D.H. (ed.) (1939) *British Trade Unionism Today*, London: Gollancz.

Cole, G.D.H. and Cole, M. (1937) *The Condition of Britain*, London: Gollancz.

Coleman, D.C. (1969) *Courtaulds: An Economic and Social History* 2 volumes, Oxford: Clarendon Press.

—— (1977) 'Courtaulds and the beginning of rayon', in B. Supple (ed.) *Essays in British Business History*, Oxford: Clarendon Press.

Coleman, D.C. and Mathias, P. (eds) (1984) *Enterprise and History. Essays in Honour of Charles Wilson*, Cambridge: Cambridge University Press.

Collins, E.J.T. (1976) 'The "consumer revolution" and the growth of factory foods: changing patterns of bread and cereal eating in Britain in the twentieth century', in D. Oddy and D. Miller (eds) *The Making of the Modern British Diet*, London: Croom Helm.

Compton, M. and Bott, E.H. (1940) *British Industry: Its Changing Structure in Peace and War*, London: Lindsay Drummond.

Corley, T.A.B. (1966) *Domestic Electrical Appliances*, London: Jonathan Cape.

—— (1972) *Quaker Enterprise in Biscuits: Huntley and Palmer of Reading*, London: Hutchinson.

Cowan, R. Schwartz (1974) 'A case study of technological and social change: the washing machine and the working wife', in M. Hartman and L. Banner (eds) *Clio's Consciousness Raised*, New York: Harper & Row.

—— (1976a) 'Two washes in the morning and a bridge party at night. The American housewife between the wars', *Women's Studies* 3, 2: 141–71.

—— (1976b) 'The "industrial revolution" in the home: household technology and social change in the 20th century', *Technology and Culture* 17, 1: 1–23.

—— (1983) *More Work for Mother*, New York: Basic Books.

Crompton, R. and Jones, G. (1984) *White Collar Proletariat: Deskilling and Gender in Clerical Work*, London: Macmillan.

Daniels, C.W. and Jewkes, J. (1932) *Industrial Survey of the Lancashire Area excluding Merseyside*, London: HMSO.

Davidoff, L. and Hall, C. (1987) *Family Fortunes. Men and Women of the English Middle Class, 1780–1850*, London: Hutchinson.

Davidson, C. (1982) *A Woman's Work is Never Done*, London: Chatto & Windus.

Davies, M. (1979) 'Woman's place is at the typewriter: the feminization of the clerical labour force', in R. Edwards, M. Reich, and D. Gordon (eds) *Labor Market Segmentation*, Lexington, Mass: D.C. Heath.

Delafield, E.M. (1930) *Diary of a Provincial Lady*, London: Macmillan.

Delphy, C. (1977) *The Main Enemy*, London: Women's Research and Resources Centre.

—— (1984) *Close to Home: A Materialist Analysis of Women's Oppression*, London: Hutchinson.

Doeringer, P.B. and Piore, M.J. (1971) *Internal Labor Markets and Manpower Adjustments*, Lexington, Mass: D.C. Heath.

Dowie, J.A. (1968) 'Growth in the inter-war economy: some more arithmetic', *Economic History Review* 2nd series, 21: 93–112.

Drake, B. (1919) *Women in the Engineering Trades*, London: Labour Research Department.

—— (1920) *Women in Trade Unions*, London: Labour Research Department.

—— (1939) 'Women in trade unions', in G.D.H. Cole (ed.) *British Trade Unionism Today*, London: Gollancz.

Edgeworth, F.Y. (1922) 'Equal pay to men and women for equal work', *Economic Journal* XXXII: 431–57.

—— (1923) 'Women's wages in relation to economic welfare', *Economic Journal* XXXIII: 487–95.

Edholm, F., Harris, O., and Young, K. (1977) 'Conceptualizing women', *Critique of Anthropology* 3: 101–30.

Edwards, E. (1935) *Report on Electricity in Working Class Homes*, London: Electrical Association for Women.

Edwards, R., Reich, M., and Gordon, D. (eds) (1979) *Labor Market Segmentation*, Lexington, Mass: D.C. Heath.

Eisenstein, Z. (1979) 'Developing a theory of capitalist patriarchy and socialist feminism', in Z. Eisenstein (ed.) *Capitalist Patriarchy and the Case for Socialist Feminism*, New York: Monthly Review Press.

Elger, T. (1982) 'Braverman, capital accumulation and deskilling', in S. Wood (ed.) *The Degradation of Work?*, London: Hutchinson.

Fawcett, M. (1918) 'Equal pay for equal work', *Economic Journal* XXVII, 109: 1–6.

Feminist Review (ed.) (1986) *Waged Work. A Reader*, London: Virago.

Firestone, S. (1974) *The Dialectic of Sex*, New York: Morrow.

Flint, E. (1963) *Hot Bread and Chips*, London: Museum Press.

Florence, P.S. (1931) 'A statistical contribution to the theory of women's wages', *Economic Journal* XLI, March: 19–37.

Foley, A. (1973) *A Bolton Childhood*, Manchester: University of Manchester Extra Mural Department.

Foley, W. (1974) *A Child in the Forest*, London: BBC, Ariel Books.

Ford, P. (1934) *Work and Wealth in a Modern Port*, London: Allen & Unwin.

Foreman-Peck, J.S. (1985) 'Seedcorn or chaff? New firm formation and the performance of the interwar economy', *Economic History Review* XXXVIII, 3: 402–22.

Gales, K. and Marks, P. (1974) 'Twentieth century trends in the work of women in England and Wales', *Journal of the Royal Statistical Society* 137, Part 1: 60–74.

References

Gamarnikow, E., Morgan, D., Purvis, J., and Taylorson, D. (eds) (1983) *Gender, Class and Work*, London: Heinemann/BSA.

Game, A. and Pringle, R. (1984) *Gender at Work*, London: Pluto Press.

Garnsey, E. (1978) 'Women's work and theories of class stratification', *Sociology* 12, 2: 223–43.

Gittins, D. (1982) *Fair Sex: Family Size and Structure, 1900–1939*, London: Hutchinson.

Glynn, S. and Oxborrow, J. (1976) *Inter-war Britain. A Social and Economic History*, London: Allen & Unwin.

Goldthorpe, J.H. (1983) 'Women and class analysis: in defence of the conventional view', *Sociology* 17, 4: 465–88.

Gollan, J. (1937) *Youth in British Industry*, London: Lawrence & Wishart.

Gordon, D., Edwards, R., and Reich, M. (1982) *Segmented Work, Divided Workers*, Cambridge: Cambridge University Press.

Gorz, A. (1970) 'The role of immigrant labour', *New Left Review* 61: 28–31.

Gospel, H.F. and Littler, C.R. (eds) (1983) *Managerial Strategies and Industrial Relations*, London: Heinemann.

Graves, R. and Hodge, A. (1940) *The Long Week-End: A Social History of Great Britain*, 1985 edn, London: Hutchinson.

Greenwood, N. (n.d.) *How the Other Man Lives*, London: Labour Book Service.

Hakim, C. (1979) *Occupational Segregation*, London: HMSO, Department of Employment, Research Paper 9.

Hall, C. (1977) 'Married women at home in Birmingham in the 1920's and 1930's', *Oral History* 5, 2: 62–83.

—— (1980) 'The history of the housewife', in E. Malos (ed.) *The Politics of Housework*, London: Allison & Busby.

Hannah, L. (1977) 'A pioneer of public enterprise: the CEB and the national grid, 1927–40', in B. Supple (ed.) *Essays in British Business History*, Oxford: Clarendon Press.

—— (1979) *Electricity Before Nationalisation*, London: Macmillan.

—— (1983) *The Rise of the Corporate Economy*, London: Methuen.

Harrop, J. (1979) 'Rayon', in N.K. Buxton and D.H. Aldcroft (eds) *British Industry between the Wars. Instability and Industrial Development 1919–39*, London: Scolar Press.

Hartmann, H. (1979a) 'Capitalism, patriarchy and job segregation', in Z. Eisenstein (ed.) *Capitalist Patriarchy and the Case for Socialist Feminism*, New York: Monthly Review Press.

—— (1979b) 'The unhappy marriage of marxism and feminism: towards a more progressive union', *Capital and Class* 8, summer: 1–33.

Heath, A. and Britten, N. (1984) 'Women's jobs do make a difference: a reply to Goldthorpe', *Sociology* 18, 4: 475–90.

Higgs, E. (1986) 'Domestic service and household production', in A. John (ed.) *Unequal Opportunities: Women's Employment in England 1800–1918*, Oxford: Blackwell.

Hinton, J. (1983) *Labour and Socialism: A History of the British Labour Movement 1867–1974*, Brighton: Wheatsheaf.

Hunt, F. (1983) 'The London trade in the printing and binding of books: an

experience in exclusion, dilution and deskilling for women workers',
Women's Studies International Forum 6, 5: 517–24.

Hutchins, B.L. (1915) *Women in Modern Industry*, London: G. Bell & Sons.

—— (1921) 'The present position of women industrial workers', *Economic Journal* XXXI: 462–71.

Hutt, A. (1933) *The Condition of the Working Class in Britain*, London: Martin Lawrence.

ILO (International Labour Organization) (1924) 'Domestic servants in Great Britain: supply and training of servants', *Industrial and Labour Information* 9, 4: 70–3.

James, E. (1960) 'Women at work in twentieth century Britain', *Manchester School of Economic and Social Studies* XXX: 283–99.

Jefferys, J.B. (1945) *The Story of the Engineers*, London: Lawrence & Wishart.

—— (1954) *Retail Trading in Britain 1850–1950*, Cambridge: Cambridge University Press.

Jennings, H. (1934) *Brynmawr: A Study of a Distressed Area*, London: Allenson.

Jephcott, A.P. (1942) *Girls Growing Up*, London: Faber & Faber.

Jephcott, A.P., Seear, N., and Smith, T. (1962) *Married Women Working*, London: Allen & Unwin.

Jewkes, J. and Jewkes, S. (1938) *The Juvenile Labour Market*, London: Gollancz.

Jewkes, J. and Winterbottom, A. (1933a) *An Industrial Survey of Cumberland and Furness*, Manchester: Manchester University Press.

—— (1933b) *Juvenile Unemployment*, London: Allen & Unwin.

Johnman, L. (1986) 'The largest companies of 1935', *Business History* 28, 2: 226–45.

Johnston, J.P. (1976) 'The development of the food canning industry in Britain during the inter-war period', in D. Oddy and D. Miller (eds) *The Making of the Modern British Diet*, London: Croom Helm.

Jones, D. Caradog (ed.) (1934) *The Social Survey of Merseyside* 3 volumes, Liverpool: University Press of Liverpool.

Jones, G. (1985) 'The Gramophone Company: an Anglo-American multinational, 1898–1931', *Business History Review* 59, spring: 76–100.

Jones, H. (1983) 'Employers' welfare schemes and industrial relations in inter-war Britain', *Business History* XXV, 1: 61–75.

Joseph, G. (1983) *Women at Work*, Oxford: Philip Allan.

Kaluzynska, E. (1980) 'Wiping the floor with theory – a survey of writings on housework', *Feminist Review* 6: 27–54.

Kenrick, J. (1981) 'Politics and the construction of women as second class workers', in F. Wilkinson (ed.) *The Dynamics of Labour Market Segmentation*, London: Academic Press.

Kessler-Harris, A. (1979) 'Stratifying by sex: understanding the history of working women', in R. Edwards, M. Reich, and D. Gordon (eds) *Labor Market Segmentation*, Lexington, Mass: D.C. Heath.

Klingender, F.D. (1935) *The Condition of Clerical Labour in Britain*, London: Martin Lawrence.

References

Knowles, K. (1952) *Strikes*, Oxford: Blackwell.

Kuhn, A. (1978) 'Structures of patriarchy and capital', in A. Kuhn and A.M. Wolpe (eds) *Feminism and Materialism*, London: Routledge & Kegan Paul.

Labour Party (1931) *The Domestic Workers' Charter*, London.

Labour Research (1932) Volume XXI.

—— (1933) Volume XXII.

Lee, C.H. (1980) *British Regional Employment Statistics*, Cambridge: Cambridge University Press.

Leeson, R.A. (1973) *Strike, a Live History*, London: Allen & Unwin.

Leiulfsrud, H. and Woodward, A. (1987) 'Women at class crossroads: repudiating conventional theories of family class', *Sociology* 21, 3: 393–412.

Leser, C. (1952) 'Men and women in industry', *Economic Journal* 62, June: 326–44.

—— (1955) 'The supply of women for gainful work in Britain', *Population Studies* IX, 2: 142–7.

Lewchuk, W. (1983) 'Fordism and the British motor car employers', in H. Gospel and C.R. Littler (eds) *Managerial Strategies and Industrial Relations*, London: Heinemann.

Lewenhak, S. (1977) *Women and Trade Unions*, London: Ernest Benn.

Lewis, J. (1980a) *The Politics of Motherhood*, London: Croom Helm.

—— (1980b) 'Search for a real equality: women between the wars', in F. Glover-Smith (ed.) *Class, Culture and Social Change*, Brighton: Harvester Press.

—— (1984) *Women in England 1870–1950*, Brighton: Wheatsheaf.

Littler, C.R. (1982) *The Development of the Labour Process in Capitalist Societies*, London: Heinemann.

Lockwood, D. (1958) *The Blackcoated Worker*, London: Allen & Unwin.

Loft, A. (1986) 'Towards a critical understanding of accounting: the case of cost accounting in the UK, 1914–65', *Accounting, Organizations, and Society* 11, 2: 137–69.

Lown, J. (1983) 'Not so much a factory, more a form of patriarchy: gender and class during industrialization', in E. Gamarnikow, D. Morgan, J. Purvis, and D. Taylorson (eds) *Gender, Class and Work*, London: Heinemann/BSA.

McBride, T. (1976) *The Domestic Revolution*, London: Croom Helm.

McDonagh, R. and Harrison, R. (1978) 'Patriarchy and relations of production', in A. Kuhn and A.M. Wolpe (eds) *Feminism and Materialism*, London: Routledge & Kegan Paul.

Magnus, E. (1934) 'The social, economic and legal conditions of domestic servants I and II', *International Labour Review* XXIX, 2: 190–207 and 3: 336–64.

Malos, E. (ed.) (1980) *The Politics of Housework*, London: Allison and Busby.

Marquand, H.A. (1932) *Industrial Survey of South Wales*, London: HMSO.

Marwick, A. (1977) *Women at War*, London: Croom Helm.

Marx, K. (1886) *Capital Volume I* 1970 edn, London: Lawrence & Wishart.

314

Massey, D. (1984) *Spatial Divisions of Labour*, London: Macmillan.

Mathias, P. (1977) 'Manufacturers and retailing in the food trades: the struggle over margarine', in B. Supple (ed.) *Essays in British Business History*, Oxford: Clarendon Press.

Meillassoux, C. (1972) 'From reproduction to production: a Marxist approach to economic anthropology', *Economy and Society* 1, 1: 93–105.

Mess, H.A. (1928) *Industrial Tyneside*, London: Ernest Benn Ltd.

Milkman, R. (1987) *Gender at Work. The Dynamics of Job Segregation by Sex during World War II*, Urbana, Ill.: University of Illinois Press.

Miller, P. and O'Leary, T. (1987) 'Accounting and the construction of the governable person', *Accounting, Organizations, and Society* 12, 3: 235–65.

Millett, K. (1971) *Sexual Politics*, London: Rupert Hart-Davis.

Mitchell, B.R. and Deane, P. (1962) *Abstract of British Historical Statistics*, Cambridge: Cambridge University Press.

Mitchell, J. (1966) 'Women: the longest revolution', *New Left Review* 40: 11–37.

—— (1971) *Woman's Estate*, Harmondsworth: Penguin.

—— (1974) *Psychoanalysis and Feminism*, London: Allen Lane.

Mitchison, N. (1979) *You May Well Ask*, London: Gollancz.

Mowat, C. (1955) *Britain Between the Wars* 1984 edn, London: Methuen.

Murgatroyd, L. (1982) 'Gender and occupational segregation', *Sociological Review* 30, 4: 574–602.

Myers, C. (1939) 'The servant problem', *Occupational Psychology* XIII, 2: 77–88.

Newsom, J. (1948) *The Education of Girls*, London: Faber.

Nockolds, H. (1976–8) *Lucas: The First Hundred Years* 2 volumes, Newton Abbott: David & Charles.

O'Brien, M. (1981) *The Politics of Reproduction*, London: Routledge & Kegan Paul.

O'Laughlin, B. (1977) 'Production and reproduction: Meillassoux's Femmes, Greniers, et Capitaux', *Critique of Anthropology* 8: 3–32.

Orwell, G. (1937) *The Road to Wigan Pier*, London: Gollancz.

Owen, A.D.K. (1933) *A Survey of the Standard of Living in Sheffield*, in Sheffield Social Survey Committee, Pamphlet 9.

Pagnamenta, P. and Overy, R. (1984) *All Our Working Lives*, London: BBC.

Parker, J. (1939) 'Trade union difficulties in the new areas', in G.D.H. Cole (ed.) *British Trade Unionism Today*, London: Gollancz.

PEP (Political and Economic Planning) (1950) *Engineering Reports* ii, Motor Vehicles.

—— (1945) *The Market for Household Appliances*, Oxford: Oxford University Press.

—— *Planning* (1938) 'Trading estates and industry' VI, 129.

(1945) 'More power to her elbow' XI, 231.

(1948) 'The employment of women' XV, 285.

Phillips, A. and Taylor, B. (1980) 'Sex and skill: notes towards a feminist economics', *Feminist Review* 6: 79–88.

Piore, M. (1979) *Birds of Passage*, Cambridge: Cambridge University Press.

Pitfield, D.E. (1978) 'The quest for an effective regional policy 1934–7',

Regional Studies 12: 429–43.

Plummer, A. (1937) *New British Industries in the Twentieth Century*, London: Pitman.

Pollard, S. (1969) *The Development of the British Economy*, 3rd edn 1983, London: Edward Arnold.

Poulantzas, N. (1978) *Classes in Contemporary Capitalism*, London: Verso.

Powell, M. (1968) *Below Stairs*, London: Peter Davies.

Priestley, J.B. (1934) *English Journey*, 1981 edn, Harmondsworth: Penguin.

Rathbone, E. (1917) 'The remuneration of women's services', *Economic Journal* XXVII: 65–88.

Reader, W.J. (1970; 1975) *Imperial Chemical Industries: A History* 2 volumes, Oxford: Oxford University Press.

Redfern, P. (1938) *The New History of the C.W.S.*, London: Dent.

Rennie, J. (1955) *Every Other Sunday*, London: Arthur Baker.

Richardson, D.J. (1976) 'J. Lyons and Co. Ltd.: caterers and food manufacturers, 1894–1939', in D. Oddy and D. Miller (eds) *The Making of the Modern British Diet*, London: Croom Helm.

Richardson, H.W. (1967) *Economic Recovery in Britain 1932–9*, London: Weidenfeld & Nicolson.

Richardson, H.W. and Aldcroft, D.H. (1968) *Building in the British Economy between the Wars*, London: Allen & Unwin.

Roberts, E. (1988) *Women's Work 1840–1940*, London: Macmillan.

Rostas, L. (1948a) *Productivity, Prices and Distribution in Selected British Industries*, NIESR Occasional Paper 11, Cambridge: Cambridge University Press.

—— (1948b) *Comparative Productivity in British and American Industry*, NIESR Occasional Paper 13, Cambridge: Cambridge University Press.

Rowbotham, S. (1974) *Hidden from History*, London: Pluto Press.

Rowntree, B. Seebohm (1941) *Poverty and Progress. A Second Social Survey of York*, London: Longman.

Rubery, J. (1978) 'Structured labour markets, worker organization and low pay', *Cambridge Journal of Economics* 2: 17–36.

Ryan, M. (1981) *Cradle of the Middle Class. The Family in Oneida County, New York 1790–1865*, Cambridge: Cambridge University Press.

Samuel, R. (1986) 'The cult of planning', *New Socialist* January: 25–9.

Sarsby, J. (1988) *Missuses and Mouldrunners. An Oral History of Women Pottery Workers at Home and at Work*, Milton Keynes: Open University Press.

Saul, S.B. (1960) 'The American impact on British industry, 1895–1914', *Business History* III, 1: 19–38.

Savage, M. (1988) 'Trade unionism, sex segregation, and the state: women's employment in "new industries" in inter-war Britain', *Social History* 13, 2: 209–29.

Sayers, R. (1950) 'Springs of technical progress in Britain 1919–39', *Economic Journal* 60: 275–91.

Scott, A. MacEwan (1986) 'Industrialization, gender segregation and stratification theory', in R. Crompton and M. Mann (eds) *Gender and Stratification*, Cambridge: Polity Press.

Silverstone, R. (1976) 'Office work for women: an historical review', *Business History* 18, 1: 98–110.

Smith, D.J. (1982) 'Women in the local labour market: a case study with particular reference to the retail trades in Britain 1900–1930' in G. Day, L. Caldwell, K. Jones, D. Robbins, and H. Rose (eds) *Diversity and Decomposition in the Labour Market*, London: Gower/BSA.

Smith, H. (1978) 'The issue of "equal pay for equal work" in Great Britain, 1914–19', *Societas* VIII, 1.

Smith, Sir H. Llewelyn (1930–5) *The New Survey of London Life and Labour* 9 volumes, London: King & Son.

Soldon, N. (1978) *Women in British Trade Unions 1874–1976*, London: Gill & Macmillan.

Stanworth, M. (1984) 'Women and class analysis: a reply to John Goldthorpe', *Sociology* 18, 2: 159–69.

Steedman, I. (1977) *Marx after Sraffa*, London: New Left Books.

Stevenson, J. (1977) *Social Conditions in Britain between the Wars*, Harmondsworth: Penguin.

Strachey, R. (1935a) *Careers and Openings for Women*, London: Faber.

—— (1935b) 'Current social statistics: the Census occupations of women', *Opportunity* January Supplement.

—— (ed.) (1936) *Our Freedom and its Results by Five Women*, London: Hogarth Press.

Struther, J. (1939) *Mrs Miniver*, London: Chatto & Windus.

Summerfield, P. (1984) *Women Workers in the Second World War*, London: Croom Helm.

Swenarton, M. (1981) *Homes Fit for Heroes*, London: Heinemann.

Taylor, B. (1983) *Eve and the New Jerusalem*, London: Virago.

Taylor, P. (1976) *Women Domestic Servants 1919–39*, Birmingham University: Centre for Contemporary Cultural Studies.

Taylor, S. (1977) 'The effect of marriage on job possibilities for women and the ideology of the home, Nottingham 1890–1930', *Oral History* 5, 2: 46–61.

Thom, D. (1987) *Feminism and the Labour Movement in Britain 1850–1975*, Brighton: Wheatsheaf.

Thompson, E.P. (1968) *The Making of the English Working Class*, Harmondsworth: Penguin.

Tolliday, S. (1982) *The Development of Industrial Relations in the Rover Motor Company 1900–1960*, mimeo Kings College Cambridge Research Centre.

—— (1983) 'Militancy and organization: women workers and trade unions in the motor trades in the 1930's', *Oral History* 11, 2: 42–55.

Tout, H. (1938) *The Standard of Living in Bristol*, Bristol: Arrowsmith.

Trades Union Congress (1927) *Protective Legislation and Women Workers*, London.

—— (1933) *The TUC examines the Bedaux System of Payment by Results*, London.

Vanek, J. (1980) 'Time spent in housework', in A. Amsden (ed.) *The Economics of Women and Work*, Harmondsworth: Penguin.

Walby, S. (1986a) *Patriarchy at Work*, Cambridge: Polity Press.

—— (1986b) 'Gender, class and stratification. Towards a new approach', in R. Crompton and M. Mann (eds) *Gender and Stratification*, Cambridge: Polity Press.

Weightman, G. and Humphries, S. (1984) *The Making of Modern London*, London: Sidgwick & Jackson.

Weir, M. (1970) *Shoes were for Sunday*, London: Pan Books.

Williams, G. (1945) *Women and Work*, London: Nicholson & Watson.

Wilson, C. (1954) *A History of Unilever* 2 volumes, London: Cassell.

—— (1977) 'Management and policy in large-scale enterprise: Lever Brothers and Unilever, 1918–38', in B. Supple (ed.) *Essays in British Business History*, Oxford: Clarendon Press.

Wood, S. (ed.) (1982) *The Degradation of Work?*, London: Hutchinson.

Wright, E.O. (1978) *Class, Crisis and the State*, London: New Left Books.

Young, I. (1981) 'Beyond the unhappy marriage: a critique of dual systems theory', in L. Sargent (ed.) *The Unhappy Marriage of Marxism and Feminism*, London: Pluto Press.

Zmroczek, C. (1984) *Women's Work: Laundry in the Last Fifty Years*, paper given at British Sociological Association Conference, April.

Index

ABC 127
accountancy 76
advertising campaigns 72, 227
Aldcroft, Derek H. 70, 83, 90–1, 237
Amalgamated Engineering Union
  (AEU) 140, 191, 193
Apsey, Stella 248
assembly lines: car 3, 147, 263–4,
  278–9; clothing industry 51, 161;
  collectivity imposed by 170–5; design of 278; distinctive form of
  production 145–6; EMI 120–2,
  148, figure 7; historical development 149–51; Hoover 142;
  inter-war growth industries 65–6;
  introduction of 94; Lyons 148;
  machine pacing 166–70; male
  exclusion 212–13; Morphy
  Richards 148; new jobs 156–7;
  Peek Frean 105–7, 148; Philips
  175–83; production process
  147–9, 221–2; purpose-built factories 66; sexual composition of
  workforce 4, 200, 203–5, 215;
  work process control 151–4
Associated Electrical Industries
  (AEI) 61, 81, 82
Austin 73, 74, 90

baking trade 127, *see also* Lyons
Balfour Committee 78
Barrett, Michèle 15
Barron, R.D. 12
BBC 79
Beauchamp, Joan 9, 62, 69, 245

Beauman, Nicola 239, 244
Bedaux system: industrial conflict
  191–4, 206; introduction of 76,
  94, 190; Lucas 191–2; Lyons
  128; Morphy Richards 136; Peek
  Frean 96, 97, 102, 105–7, 111;
  Philips 175, 179; Wolsey 140
Bedding, Edie 220–1
Beechey, Veronica 15, 277
Belling 83
bonus systems 173, 186, 187–8,
  260–1
Booth, Charles 244, 251
Boots 81
Boston, Sarah 194
Bott, E.H. 70, 72, 73, 75
Boyd, Edith 29, 33–5, 36–7, 53,
  138–9, 141, 249, Figure 1
Branson, Noreen 70, 74, 91
Braverman, Harry 7, 153, 278
British Celanese 73, 89
British Electrical and Allied Manu-
  facturers Association (BEAMA)
  75, 78
British Iron and Steel Federation 70
British Thomson Houston 61
Brittain, Vera 244, 245
Brockway, Fenner 5
Burnett, John 85, 87, 237
Buxton, N.K. 70, 71
Byers, Anthony 238

Cadbury/Fry 81, 86, 201
C & A 166
capital: accumulation of 65–6, 72,

319